bar code on next page
D0576017
114°10′
114°20′E
Lin Ma Hang
SHA TAU KOK
STARLING INLET
Yung Shue Au
CROOKED HARBOUR
Crooked Island
Ping Chau
Ma Tseuk Leng
Crescent Island
MIRS BAY
Lai Chi Wo
LUK KENG
Sam A Tsuen
DOUBLE HAVEN
Double Island
•486
KWAI TAU LENG
WU KAU TANG
Sam A Chung
Port Island
WONG LENG
640
PAT SIN LENG
CLOUDY HILL
Ting Kok
Tai Mei Tuk
Plover Cove Reservoir
TOLO CHANNEL
Grass Island
SHUEN WAN
LONG HARBOUR
MOUNT HALLOWES
Hoi Ha
YIM TIN TSAI
Ma Shi Chau
TAI PO
Lai Chi Chong
Tan Ka Wan
Sham Chung
TOLO HARBOUR
Tai Tan
SHEK UK SHAN
TAI PO KAU
WU KAI SHA
Sai O
THREE FATHOMS COVE
Yung Shue O
•468
SHARP PEAK
MA ON SHAN
Chek Keng
Tai Long
MA LIU SHUI
Kei Ling Ha Lo Wai
GRASSY HILL
•702
MA ON SHAN
Tai Shui Hang
TAI LONG WAN
FO TAN
Tai Wan
Tai Mong Tsai
Pak Tam Chung
Sai Wan
SHA TIN
Siu Lek Yuen
Tai Wai
SAI KUNG
Yim Tin Tsai
High Island Reservoir
BUFFALO HILL
Shan Ha Wai
HEBE HAVEN
Sharp Island
Kau Sai Chau
High Island
AMAH ROCK
TATE'S CAIRN
Ho Chung
LION ROCK
KOWLOON PEAK
602
ROCKY HARBOUR
SAN PO KONG
Tai Po Tsai
PORT SHELTER
KOWLOON TONG
Tseng Lan Shue
Tiu Chung Chau
Fu Tau Fan Chau
Wang Chau
NGAU TAU KOK
International Airport
Shelter Island
TSEUNG KWAN O
HANG HAU
TO KWA WAN
Bluff Island
Basalt Island
KWUN TONG
Mang Kung Uk
HUNG HOM
TIU KENG LENG
HARBOUR
YAU TONG
JUNK BAY
HIGH JUNK PEAK
Tai Au Mun
LEI YUE MUN
CAUSEWAY BAY
NORTH POINT
CLEAR WATER BAY
SHAU KEI WAN
Junk Island
MOUNT PARKER
KONG ISLAND
CHAI WAN
Ninepin Group
MOUNT COLLINSON
VIOLET HILL
TATHONG CHANNEL
Tung Lung Chau
BIG WAVE BAY
DEEP WATER BAY
REPULSE BAY
THE TWINS
SHEK O
TAI TAM WAN
CHUNG HOM WAN
D'AGUILAR PEAK
STANLEY
STANLEY BAY
Beaufort Island
Po Toi Islands
Sung Kong
Waglan Island
Po Toi
:200 000
8
10
12
14 km
22°20′
22°10′N
LEGEND
Built-up Area
Cultivation
Country Park Boundary
Main Road
Secondary Roads
Light Rail Transit
Mass Transit Railway (over/underground)
Kowloon Canton Railway
Contour (vertical interval 100 metres with supplementary contour at 50 metres)
Sea depth tint values in metres
0
10
20
30
m
CHINA
Beijing
Huang He
KOREA
JAPAN
Nanjing
Shanghai
Chongqing
Chang Jiang
EAST CHINA SEA
INDIA
Fuzhou
Canton
BURMA
MACAU
HONG KONG
TAIWAN
LAOS
VIETNAM
PACIFIC OCEAN
THAILAND
SOUTH CHINA SEA
KAMPUCHEA
PHILIPPINES
Guam
km
1000
km 2000
BRUNEI
MALAYSIA
Sumatra
SINGAPORE
Kalimantan
Sulawesi
Irian Jaya
PAPUA NEW GUINEA
Java
INDONESIA
Cartography by Survey & Mapping Office
Buildings & Lands Department
©Hong Kong Government

AN ILLUSTRATED HISTORY OF HONG KONG

NIGEL CAMERON

Hong Kong
OXFORD UNIVERSITY PRESS
Oxford New York
1991

Oxford University Press

Oxford New York Toronto
Petaling Jaya Singapore Hong Kong Tokyo
Delhi Bombay Calcutta Madras Karachi
Nairobi Dar es Salaam Cape Town
Melbourne Auckland

and associated companies in
Berlin Ibadan

First published 1991
Published in the United States
by Oxford University Press, Inc., New York

British Library Cataloguing in Publication Data

Cameron, Nigel
An illustrated history of Hong Kong.
1. Hong Kong, history
I. Title
951.25
ISBN 0-19-584997-3

Library of Congress Cataloging-in-Publication Data

Cameron, Nigel.
An illustrated history of Hong Kong / Nigel Cameron.
p. cm.
Includes bibliographical references and index.
ISBN 0-19-584997-3 : $45.00 (est.)
1. Hong Kong—History. I. Title.
DS796.H757C36 1991
951.25—dc20 90-48787
CIP

Printed in Hong Kong by Elite Printing Co., Ltd.
Published by Oxford University Press, Warwick House, Hong Kong

IN AFFECTIONATE MEMORY OF
IRENE JOYCE (JO) BOSTON (1909–1989)

CONTENTS

LIST OF COLOUR PLATES

LIST OF MAPS AND FIGURES

Introduction

In the year 1997 when Hong Kong reverts to Chinese sovereignty, a mere one hundred and fifty-six years will have elapsed since it became a British possession. What was then an insignificant mountainous scattering of larger and smaller coastal islands in the South China Sea, the haunt of pirates, the refuge of occasional storm-blown fishermen, peopled by several hundred resident fishers and farmers, changed in a few years into a small, bustling, striving, and strident Victorian seaport of the Orient.

A war with China gave it birth, its other parent being the Western passion for trade. Further wars between the British and the Chinese, basically over that unruly and headlong passion, were to shape Hong Kong's society, while the flux of trade itself conditioned its thinking as well as the physical form of Victoria, its main settlement.

As other ports opened to Western trade up and down the China coast, the fledgling colony faltered but persevered, attaining its apparently final form by the first decade of the twentieth century. The First World War did not deeply affect its fortunes, or greatly alter its outlook or position in the world. By the outbreak of World War II, Hong Kong was little different from the colony of 1910. But this second world conflict ended the colony's life under a brutal Japanese occupation that lasted three years until the tide turned and the British returned, uncertain colonists in a now anti-colonial Orient.

Within a decade of the war's end the Hong Kong of the past was embarked on a curious process of change and development. This process was so unusual in an apparently adult city that it took most Hong Kong people by surprise. The 1949 revolution in China served as the catalyst initiating this unexpected development; the post-war economic climate and the revolution in industrial processes encouraged and continued it. An entirely different colonial entity emerged — modern Hong Kong, a city haphazardly grown into one of the commercial, industrial, and financial giants of the world.

The last part of Hong Kong's colonial history constitutes the period of its real significance in the world. In this, Hong Kong is unlike most places where growth usually follows a more predictable pattern. Gradual decline from greatness is a more usual picture than that of dramatic rebirth.

Historically, Hong Kong is a distinctly odd place. Lacking a background of normal, logical progression to eventual maturity, it turned from a sort of fixed colonial adolescence to an adult state of a genetically improbable kind. The huge success of this new entity imbues it with a quality as unique as it is elusive of description.

The story and significance of Hong Kong, more than that of most cities (or city-states as in some ways it may be seen), is to be sought primarily in early nineteenth-century economic thrust and later in the effects of economic and political upheavals in China. Hong Kong's belated economic success is due in essence to post-World War II capitalist drive and a massive influx of Chinese refugees who became its manpower. In successful combination those factors forged the Hong Kong of today. Equally, they are contributing factors in the coming demise of the territory as a separate political entity in 1997.

In his history of Hong Kong, first published in 1958, the late G. B. Endacott opens the first chapter with the following sentence: 'Hong Kong is a British colony situated on the South-east coast of China.' It is a measure of the profound change in status of the place that today, thirty years on, virtually no one in the world who can read a newspaper any longer needs to be offered that piece of information. Many of them may in fact be wearing clothes or listening to a radio made in Hong Kong. From the barely emerging industrial entity described by Endacott, an astonishingly different Hong Kong has bloomed. Its future, cloudy and disregarded in those early days of the communist revolution in China, is now approaching something like clarity. As its term draws near and the treaty with China terminates Britain's lease in 1997, we shall see the final close of a colourful period.

In the light of those facts, one of the periodic updatings which the passage of time and the press of events requires in considering the history of any place would seem due for Hong Kong. It was still possible in 1958 to regard colonial possessions — those which had not by then been surrendered to their indigenous peoples — with a certain glow of nostalgic pride as Britain relinquished them and their (in colonial terms) insurmountable problems. That opinion is largely unacceptable now. Thirty years on, whatever our personal view may be of colonialism, it can scarcely be identical with that current in the climate of political opinion of 1958. The intervening years have, among myriad other transformations, cast Hong Kong in a role of some significance in the world context, a position it did not then hold. In those three decades major shifts in political thought have taken place, and the perspective we now apply to the scene has sharply altered. Reason enough for a retelling of the story.

However tempting a pastime it may be, gazing into a crystal ball has little relevance in a history, and it requires no clairvoyant faculty to see, and no great courage to admit, that whatever the state of affairs after the colony's return to China in 1997 — a state of affairs promised by the Chinese to remain unchanged for 50 years — a great city which will have passed from the hands of a Western democracy to those of Chinese socialism will be rather unlikely to continue as the same sort of organism for very long. What Hong Kong will become after 1997 must be envisaged as its third state.

It is with the first two historical states of the colony, the pre-industrial and the industrial, that this volume attempts to deal.[1]

1. *The Origins of Confrontation*

HONG KONG was from the very beginning a unique colony. Unlike other lands when the British took them, it was sparsely populated, an island (in the guess of the government *Gazette* of May 1841) of some 7,450 villagers and fishermen. It had not a semblance of mineral wealth, its terrain was mostly mountainous with little flat land, and there was scarcely a tree, far less anything that might be called a forest. As the British Foreign Secretary Lord Palmerston put the matter, in high disgust at the choice, Hong Kong was a 'barren island with hardly a house upon it'. No teeming populace awaited the chance of British employment on plantations or other enterprises, no great river flooded down from some rich hinterland. The local Chinese eked out a paltry living from tiny rice paddies squeezed into valleys, by keeping chickens and a few pigs, and by fishing the local waters. Pirates, indigenous to the China coasts, perched now and then between raids like predators in this or that secluded cove. It was an altogether insignificant place.

The reason for the taking of Hong Kong — that understood by British merchants of the time and only partially comprehended by Lord Palmerston in England — was the need to secure a land base from which they could conduct their business of purveying to China the illegal import opium. For this trade they required only a sheltered deep-water harbour for their ships and a strip of shore for their 'factories',[1] as trading stations were then named. They took Hong Kong as they had taken other places, by force of arms. A small force, admittedly, but deployed without the consent of the rightful owners, the Chinese imperial government. There is some slight room for doubt, indeed, whether the choice of Hong Kong island was entirely a British one. E. J. Eitel, a civil servant in Hong Kong whose book *Europe in China* is a history of the colony's first half century, hints at this. It is conceivable at least that the cunning Qishan, Viceroy of Chili, with whom Captain Elliot negotiated for a base, made the suggestion. Guangzhou, seat of the provincial governor of Guangdong Province, was a mere day's sailing west and up the Zhu Jiang (the Pearl River), and from there it would be simple, in theory at least, to keep an eye on the barbarian colonists and their activities — which, after all, were principally the importation of opium up that same river to

Guangzhou, the sole port at which the Chinese countenanced trade with foreigners. Eitel, who knew personally many of those who participated in the founding of Hong Kong, allows the possibility of Qishan's influence.

One of the fundamentals of Chinese policy towards commercial contacts with non-Chinese peoples, applying equally to tribes from Central Asia and to foreigners who came in ships to its coasts — a policy initiated as long ago as the Ming dynasty — laid down the principle that trade was a privilege granted by a beneficent emperor to the inhabitants of the less desirable regions of the world. To trade with the Chinese could in no sense be considered a right. Conversely, one of the fundamentals of Western thought was, and is, that to trade with those, no matter where, who are willing to purchase and to sell is the natural right of all men.

It was the inevitable contradiction enshrined in those opinions which lay at the root of the history of relationships between the West and China, from the very first time a Western merchant, a Portuguese, arrived at Guangzhou in September 1517 with the serious intent to trade. In fact, the Portuguese ships managed to trade peacefully and returned to Malacca from where they had come, their captain 'loaded with riches and renown'. And Macau, established by the Portuguese on a tiny peninsula at the mouth of the Zhu Jiang, was ceded to Portugual in 1557 — one result of the banning of direct trade between China and Japan, after which the Portuguese fleet of merchantmen became the prime carriers of that commerce in place of the Chinese.

Trade restrictions imposed in the Ming dynasty, and in the early Qing (which succeeded it in 1644), were eased by the late seventeenth century, and foreign vessels called at Xiamen, Fuzhou, and Ningbo. Later, restrictions were reintroduced and British attempts to claim old trading privileges in 1755 met with resistance. Under the Qianlong emperor (1736–95) trade was virtually confined to Guangzhou. It was this restriction, imposed by the Chinese in an attempt to ward off the aggressive attentions of stubborn foreign merchants, and to stem the outflow of silver from the treasury to pay for opium imports, which proved to be one of the principal precipitating causes of what came later to be termed the century of Western aggression and dominance in China.

Guangzhou was to remain the sole legal port where trading was permitted from 1757 until the forcible opening of Nanjing by the British under the terms of what the Chinese justifiably call the First Unequal Treaty of 1842.

British trade with China has a much shorter history than that of the Portuguese. It was not until the mid-eighteenth century that the major part of Western trade with China came to be in British hands, and this was very largely because of the proximity of India. The sub-continent acted as a staging post on lengthy voyages to and from China and was, more importantly, a source of some of the goods which were carried in ever larger quantities to China in British ships.

The monopoly of British trade with China was held by the British East India Company whose principal cargo was the tea to which the British public was so deeply addicted. Other goods from China — porcelain among them — were carried, but tea was the mainstay, the company gradually permitting other merchants to handle other goods. The Chinese, in an effort to regulate trade and to profit by it, had long ago designated a group of merchants in Guangzhou through whom foreign trade was exclusively channelled. This group, called by the British the Co-hong, was required by the authorities in Beijing to pay large sums of money for this privilege. They in turn extracted it from foreign traders in the form of taxes levied by the Guangzhou Maritime Customs with a severity and stringency which varied from time to time in an arbitrary manner.

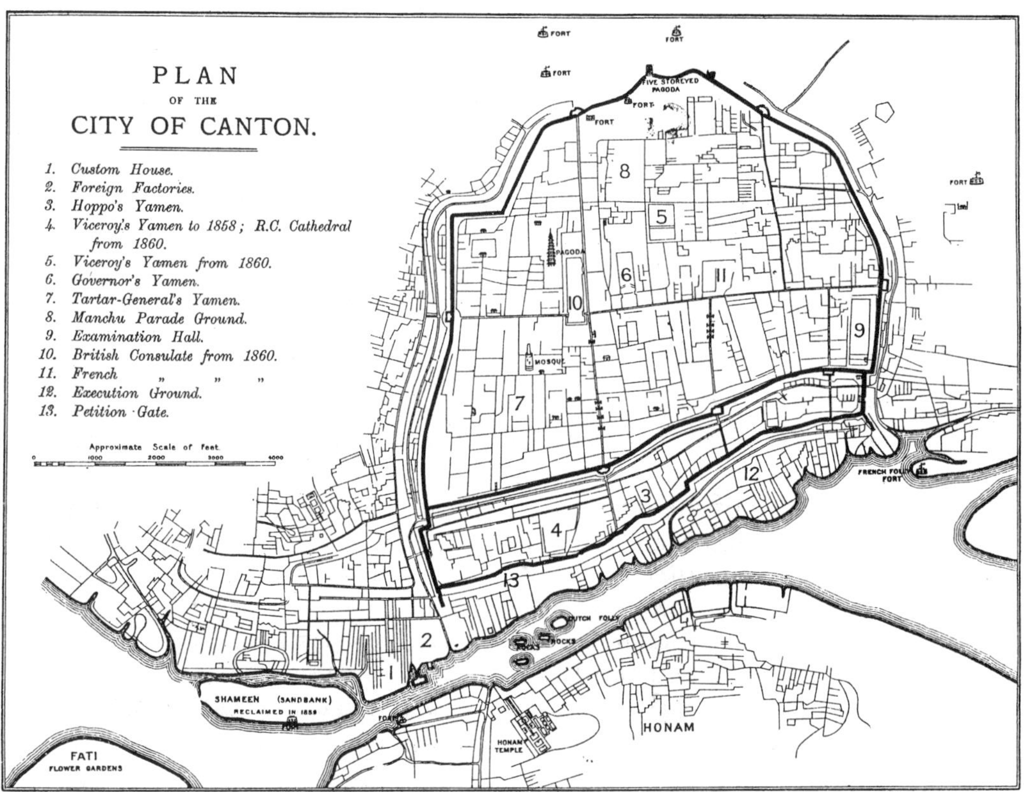

1. A plan of Guangzhou showing the locations of the foreign factories and other principal sites. (*Source*: Morse, *The International Relations of the Chinese Empire*.)

The Co-hong owned what were termed 'factories' — warehouses and residential buildings — situated outside Guangzhou's city limits to the south-east and fronting the river. There foreigners were permitted to live and trade for the 'season' (from October to May each year), after which they were obliged to leave for Macau. These conditions had been accepted with more or less good grace as inevitable, but other constraints on trading became increasingly irksome and were seen by the merchants as approaching the intolerable. The Eight Regulations laid down by the Chinese, while not always applied, included not only the ban on residence and trading during the four summer months but also a ban on movement outside the factories and on entry into Guangzhou itself. Foreigners were forbidden to learn Chinese, although this rule was not always enforced, and all communications with the Co-hong had to be made in Chinese via the officially appointed linguists. Even more vexatious, those communications were required to be couched in the form of petitions and forwarded through the Co-hong to the civil authorities. This, of course, was in line with the Chinese opinion that foreign trade and even the presence of foreigners on Chinese soil was a privilege and in no way a right. Merchants were forbidden to bring their womenfolk with them, and, in theory at least, Chinese servants were not permitted to work in the factories. On a wider horizon, foreign warships were forbidden to enter the mouth of the Zhu Jiang (called by the British, with that combination of romanticism and bravado characteristic of the times, the Bocca Tigris, the Tiger's Mouth).

The effect of those restrictions on the merchants was cumulative and more profound than their content would on the face of it appear to merit. In addition there was the climate of opposing convictions which aroused fury in the merchant breast. And it must also be remembered that in those times there existed an assumption, at least among the less educated members of the foreign community, of their own innate superiority over the Chinese at large; and this was paralleled and mirrored by a strongly held Chinese conviction of similar content.

Behind the details of the regulations, enforced only periodically in time of tension, lay the fact that their strict implementation when the Chinese wished could, and did, bring the unruly traders to heel. To the proud British merchants this was abhorrent.

Both sides erred, both were guilty of misjudgement. The Westerners had no conception of the quality, far less the greatness, of Chinese civilization: the Chinese, having known mostly the rough and ready manners of merchants and seamen, equally had no idea of the attainments of Europeans, classing them as they designated all non-Chinese as *yi*, a word usually rendered in English as 'barbarian' but meaning 'uncultured'. Even the august Lord Macartney, arriving in Beijing in 1793, found that the barges carrying him to Beijing had been labelled 'tributary' by Chinese officials following the normal procedure.

China was in a strong position. The Chinese had little need of any of the merchandise brought by the foreigners, while they appeared to be in great need of China's tea and to a lesser degree its silks, porcelains, and even exotica such as rhubarb (which was regarded in Chinese circles as the loosener of Western bowels without which it appeared they functioned only sporadically and uncertainly). From the inception, the trading profits were very much China's. All that the merchants bought had to be paid for in silver, the sole currency of the country. The Chinese were a virtually self-sufficient people. They had little need of English broadcloth. Small quantities of lead, tin, and copper from Cornish mines were acceptable. But the balance of trade rested with the Chinese. In 1761 the East India Company shipped 2,626,000 pounds of tea from Guangzhou worth £831,000. Forty years later the amount had risen to 23,300,000 pounds at a cost of £3,665,000. Nine-tenths of the stock on board any British ship bound for Guangzhou consisted of silver bullion.

To some extent this unpromising situation (from the British point of view) was offset by what was called the 'country trade', that which was carried on by private merchants trading between India and China, from which the East India Company derived a profit from shipping the goods.

Attempts to redress the conspicuous imbalance of trade were in the end a crucial factor in determining the future course of relations between Britain and China, and were to result in the birth of Hong Kong.

British determination to trade with China was given a further powerful impetus by the Industrial Revolution. By the beginning of the nineteenth century the pioneering East India Company had become an arthritic, deeply conservative organization. In 1833 private traders in cities such as Glasgow and Manchester persuaded the government to end the Company's stranglehold on all British trade. This was received in the Guangzhou factories with glee, the English-language periodical *The Canton Register* of March 1834 declaring roundly that 'British trade to China will be entirely free and unrestricted'.

The realities of the situation were more complex. In the eighteenth century what were called 'agency houses' had been set up, private traders at Guangzhou working for companies in London and India on commission. Gradually such firms began trading on their own account in rice and opium. The best known was Jardine, Matheson and Company which, in the 1830s, acted in both capacities — agency and private trader. The original partners were William Jardine (1785–1843), a ship's surgeon who joined Magniac and Company as their agent at Guangzhou; and James Matheson (1796–1878), who came to South China as Danish Consul at Guangzhou and went into the agency business. He joined Magniac, then controlled by Jardine, and in 1832 the name became Jardine, Matheson and Company. This event was to cast its shadow over the relationship between Britain and China for many a decade to come.

The economic clout of the agency houses proved to be an irresistible force. Before the end of the East India Company's monopoly of British trade there

Dr William Jardine (1785–1843). The portrait by George Chinnery (1774–1852), the most accomplished Western artist to work in the East during the nineteenth century, spending the last 27 years of his life in and around Macau, is one of the artist's most accomplished. Jardine and James Matheson were co-founders of the 'Princely Hong', as Jardine, Matheson and Company came to be known.

were 88 of them in Guangzhou, and by 1837 they numbered 158, and handled more than half of the total British trade there. The Co-hong merchants, charged by the Chinese government to deal with all foreign trade, lacked sufficient capital and were indebted to the foreign traders, by the 1830s owing about $3 million to them at 1.5 per cent interest per month. The Co-hong merchants were further squeezed by their government which arbitrarily extracted from them huge sums — in 1834 almost 500,000 taels of silver, earmarked for the emperor, repairs to the banks of the Huang He (the Yellow River), and presents to the *hoppo*, the head of Chinese Maritime Customs. The situation for the Chinese merchants gradually became intolerable.

The other factor, besides the difficulties encountered at Guangzhou, leading to the seizure of Hong Kong was opium. The subject has been chronicled as the dirtiest scandal of British trade and foreign relations, and set aside by other writers as an inevitable product of the trade imbalance between Britain and a self-sufficient China. Yet, during much of the nineteenth century, opium (called laudanum in Britain) could be bought freely in any chemist's shop and was in regular use before the discovery of aspirin for the alleviation of pain.

The zeal with which merchants traded in opium is well documented, not least in their own letters and other papers, by the Chinese involved, and by those on both sides who wished to suppress the trade. But when the stakes are high, zeal is common enough among the punters. Yet in any balanced summing up it has to be conceded that the whole history of the importation of opium into China by unscrupulous merchants forms one of the most unsavoury and ignoble episodes in British mercantile ventures, surpassed only by the horrors of the slave trade.

A mere outline of the figures involved in the sale of opium shows the scale of the financial exchange that took place. At the time of the first Chinese prohibition edict in 1729 (there were another 47 to follow, 22 of them imperial) about two hundred chests of opium were imported by China in a year. A chest generally weighed 140 pounds, the weight varying with the season and the type, thus the annual total consumption was 28,000 pounds of the drug. In 1767 the total had jumped to around the thousand mark (140,000 pounds). And this comparatively slow increase rocketed from about the turn of the century until the beginning of the Opium War four decades later. Despite what one of the principal merchants called 'the hottest persecution we remember', suppression of the trade by the Chinese was almost always ineffectual, even when the opium ships were driven from Guangzhou to the mouth of the Zhu Jiang in 1820, whereupon the island of Lingding was quickly pressed into service as the new depot. The trade, hitherto fluctuating under attempts at suppression, then increased to 18,670 chests per annum and a price war began between Jardine, Matheson and Company and others selling opium from Western India. This was resolved by the formation of a syndicate of all the opium dealers, and by 1834 the total opium import for the year stood at 16,516 (over 3.3 million pounds) valued at silver $9,654,970. In the following year (1835–6) the total import rose to 27,111 chests (almost 4 million pounds) valued at $17,904,248.

The British were not alone in the trade. Their supplies were grown in India (in some places under duress). There was a sizeable American contribution of opium from Turkey — to the extent that many Chinese thought that country was a part of the United States. The traffic was so profitable that in 1839 *The Chinese Recorder*, published in Guangzhou, summed up the situation in these words:

> The most eminent merchants engaged freely in the traffic... Throughout India and China, many of the most distinguished merchants — men who would be slow to partake in any other than what they regarded as ... honourable pursuits — have been foremost in this traffic.

Opportunities for profit on a massive scale were taken up by both Chinese and foreigners. Chinese law was openly flouted by both sides and, when temporarily enforced, subverted by stealth. In such a climate of opinion the effects of opium on the users was not considered. What was more apparent, at least to the Chinese, was the economic havoc caused by the colossal drain of China's silver into Western pockets.

Even the torpid Beijing authorities at last informed the emperor in 1838 of the plight of Fujian and Guangdong Provinces where nine persons out of 10 were opium addicts. Western travellers remarked that in Chinese towns opium shops were as common as gin shops in England. The causes of opium addiction among the Chinese have been more often investigated than has the parallel English addiction to cheap Dutch gin, without much in the way of solid conclusions — perhaps the squalid and miserable conditions of life for the poor in both places may offer some clues. But there is no doubt of the extent of the addiction to opium. Lin Zexu (1785–1850), a provincial governor soon to occupy centre stage in the opium conflict, affirmed that 1 per cent of the population of China (estimated at about four hundred million) was addicted, and official alarm was considerable. In a letter to the British monarch by Lin and others, drafted but not sent, the ravages are eloquently expressed:

> There is a class of evil foreigner that makes opium and brings it for sale, tempting fools to destroy themselves, merely in order to reap profit... Now the vice [opium smoking] has spread far and wide... But our great Manzhu Empire regards itself as responsible for the habits and morals of its subjects and cannot rest content to see any of them become victims to a deadly poison...[2]

The following year another version of the letter was actually sent, but it seems that it was never received.

The plain fact of the matter was that the Beijing government, having failed in the early stages of opium importation to stop or control it, was now quite incapable of doing so. The problem had become a nation-wide phenomenon involving the very officers of the government who would have to suppress the trade. Corruption was near total.

On the British side was the fact of the enormous sum of money paid out annually for China tea, now more or less balanced by the sum earned from the sale of opium from India — especially from Bengal. The total value of the trade in 1832 was 10 million rupees, in 1837 over 20 million, and in the following year over 30 million. A select committee of the House of Commons in London reported in 1830, and again in 1832, that 'it does not seem advisable to abandon so important a source of revenue as the East India Company's monopoly of opium in Bengal'.[3] Captain Elliot, soon to play his part in the birth of Hong Kong, wrote from Macau in February 1837 to the Foreign Secretary, Lord Palmerston, that the value of opium imported into

China in 1836 was larger than that of all the tea and silk bought from China by Britain. But he deplored the dependence on a 'vast prohibited traffic in an article of vicious luxury ... liable to frequent and prodigious fluctuation'. In the following year, however, the Duke of Wellington remarked that Parliament did not look down on the opium trade but had in fact looked for ways of promoting it. Not surprisingly Jardine, leading importer of opium, in reply to accusations that the trade was mere smuggling, stated with specious reasoning: 'We are not smugglers, gentlemen! It is the Chinese Government, the Chinese officers who smuggle, and who connive at ... smuggling; not we!'[4]

Such, then, were some of the mercantile, financial, political, and human aspects of the opium trade. The results when the Chinese government at last made up its mind to extirpate the trade were predictable. They included the annexation of the island of Hong Kong.

The train of events that led up to that act began to speed up, and the conflict of interests to intensify, with the appointment of Lord Napier as the British government's Superintendent of Trade at Guangzhou following the cessation of the East India Company's monopoly in 1833. Formerly communication with the Chinese authorities had been via the Co-hong. Lord Napier, however, sent officially as Superintendent of Trade, was a government official and not, as the Chinese had requested, a *taipan* or manager. His instructions were, however, to refrain from 'all such conduct, language and demeanour as might needlessly excite jealousy and distrust', and to impress on the British community at Guangzhou 'the duty of conforming to the laws and usages of the Chinese Empire'.

Lord Napier, unfortunately, was a man hopelessly unsuited to such diplomatic address. As the Chinese began to strengthen their defences on the Zhu Jiang, he sent British frigates to cruise off the mouth of the river and 300 soldiers to the Portuguese enclave of Macau. Astutely, the Chinese responded by bottling him up at Guangzhou by means of laying barriers across the river, with fire-ships placed ready to be drifted down-river should the need arise. The Chinese demanded Napier's speedy removal, promising that normal trading would then resume. The British community was at first unsure whether its interests required it to support Napier, but he soon lost their allegiance and was forced to retreat to Macau under Chinese guard — severely harassed by their incessant beating of gongs and firing of crackers. An ill man, once there he shortly died.

Napier's contribution to a tense situation had been to ignore both his instructions and the accepted manner of dealing with the Chinese authorities in almost every particular. The Chinese, in contrast, behaved at all times with strict propriety. The net result of the episode was the worsening of relations and new regulations reinforcing Chinese control of the mercantile community.

Napier was succeeded by another figure later to play his part in the story of

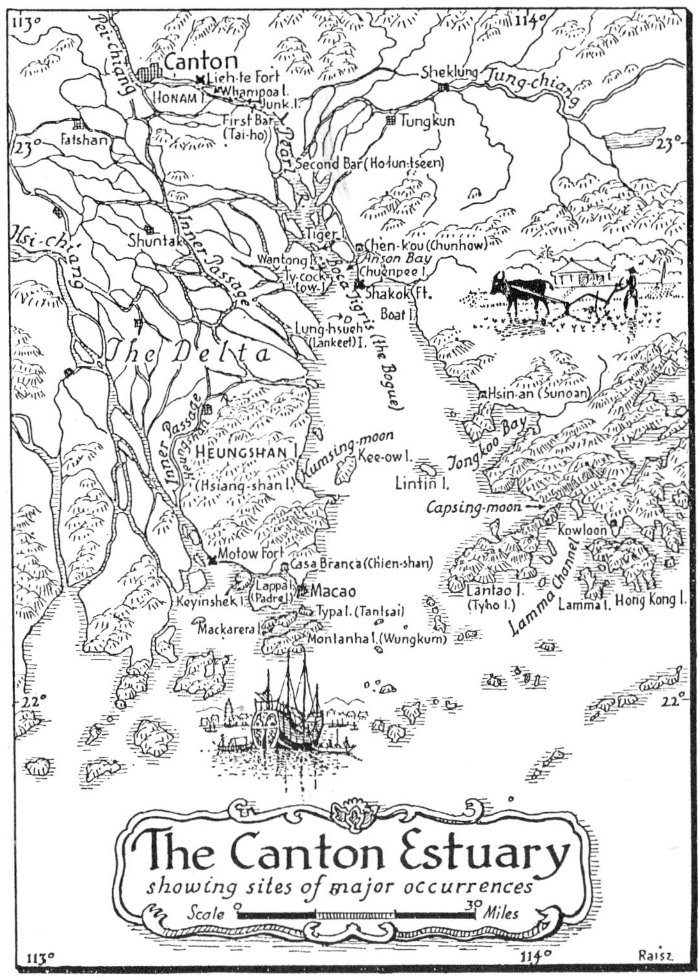

2. The geographical setting of the opium trade and the area in which hostilities took place during the First China War. (*Source*: Chang, *Commissioner Lin and the Opium War*, p. 59. Copyright © 1964 by the President and Fellows of Harvard College.)

Hong Kong, John Francis Davis, a conservative, a Chinese scholar, a man predictably unpopular with the merchants. On his arrival, 85 of the British community dispatched a petition to London demanding a plenipotentiary in his place. Davis resigned.

His successor, Sir George Robinson, appointed in 1835, conceived it best to conduct affairs from a ship moored in the Bocca Tigris. H. B. Morse, in his *International Relations of the Chinese Empire*, characterizes him as 'a bad case of swelled head', and the Chinese ignored his existence. The two years during which he was in office were marked by ever more frequent and potentially dangerous incidents between the two sides. Captain Charles Elliot was appointed in place of Robinson in June 1836.

Charles Elliot, who was to play a large part in the coming events, was born

Captain Charles Elliot (1801–75). This photograph appears to be the sole likeness of the man who decided on Hong Kong as a British base on the China coast.

in 1801, son of the Honourable Hugh Elliot, at one time governor of Madras. At 14 he joined the navy as a volunteer, serving in the Mediterranean. Later he was in India, round the coast of Africa, and in the West Indies, attaining Lieutenant's rank in 1822 and being promoted Captain in August 1828. Still only 27, Elliot retired from the navy, accepted a job in the Colonial and Foreign Office, and later served in Guiana (now Guyana) until 1834. With reluctance he took the post of Master Attendant offered in Napier's mission, which he felt was too humble a job for a man of his experience. In a letter to the Foreign Office written before Elliot's departure for China, Davis had put his seal of approval of Elliot's abilities in somewhat fulsome words: 'The talents, information, and temper of that gentleman would render him eminently suited to the chief station in this country.'

Elliot enters the story of Hong Kong on 1 February 1835 at the gates of Guangzhou, roughed up by the guards as he tried to present a report on an incident on the Zhu Jiang. His principal duties as he saw them were to oil the wheels of trade, to conciliate the Chinese authorities, to act in accordance with the regulations, and to respect Chinese sovereignty. To the Chinese he was something of an anomaly. For all his even-handed dealings with them he appeared as the protector of the opium smugglers. Elliot himself invented a new Chinese term, calling himself *yuan chi* — an employee from afar. Lord Palmerston in London had laid on his shoulders the impossible task of addressing the Chinese authorities directly, not through the Hong merchants, and of refraining from superscribing his communications with the offending word *pin* — petition — both instructions contrary to established Chinese regulations. Elliot continued his courteous diplomatic attempts to communicate directly, but in the end he realized he could not win and retired to Macau. He asked for vessels from India to come to his assistance.

On 3 December 1838 a consignment of about three hundred and fifty pounds of opium was seized by the Chinese as it was being landed at Guangzhou in front of the factories. The event brought Elliot swiftly up-river bearing a document inscribed with the character *pin*. Elliot claimed that he had attempted to put a stop to British opium smuggling but that his lack of authority had prevented him from succeeding. The upshot of the affair was that the Chinese emerged from the exchange with only the slightest dent in their armour of rules and regulations, and the *pin* stayed. Elliot informed them that he had sent away all 11 opium ships from the Huangpu (Whampoa) anchorage, an island 10 miles down-river from Guangzhou. Normal trade was resumed.

The vehemence of the British merchants' feelings, echoed by Elliot and all the other officials, on the subject of equality between the Chinese and themselves must seem — a century and a half later — a somewhat inconsequential, even frivolous matter on which to insist when the stakes were not only opium but the continuation of the whole highly lucrative China trade. Such sentiments were founded on an inbuilt sense of British superiority, a belief which had an almost precise mirror image in the Chinese conviction of *their* own superlative greatness. Unfortunately for the Chinese, although they had every right to exclude opium imports, and while they assuredly possessed greatness as a civilization, power to control the foreigners had long slipped from their hands. This was soon to be resoundingly demonstrated.

A policy of strict enforcement against Chinese participants in opium smuggling and against opium users had been in operation for some time, and at the end of January 1839 Elliot reported that 'the stagnation of the opium traffic at all points . . . [has] been nearly complete for the last four months'. And, a week later: 'The stagnation of the opium traffic . . . and the consequent locking up of the circulating medium is already producing great and general embarrassment.' The Chinese anti-opium drive seemed to be working. 'There seems', wrote Elliot to Palmerston, 'no longer any room to doubt that the Court has firmly determined to suppress, or, more probably, most extensively check the opium trade.'

Gradually, it became obvious to the merchants that a new wind was blowing. Russell and Company, large traders, actually issued a circular in February 1839 to their clients informing them that the firm 'had resolved to discontinue all connection with the opium trade in China'. And they wrote to their London agent: 'If the export of teas is to be kept up, new sources must be opened to produce the means of paying for them.' They hoped 'that the

British government, seeing the danger likely to occur to their revenue from tea will discourage the culture of opium, and in this way only can the trade be cut off'. But most opium traders saw it as the most cost-effective item in the China trade. They waited for the wind to change.

The Chinese government had for some time realized that, its edicts having failed to stem the narcotic tide, new measures were necessary. Added to the economic and social ill-effects of opium, unusually severe droughts, floods, and famine, with consequent civil unrest, had raised the cost of living and sapped army morale. But within the Western community at Guangzhou the new Chinese enforcement measures were regarded with derision. Matheson, a leading dealer in opium, remarked cynically that edicts against opium were so much 'waste paper'. And the *Canton Register* told its readers what they wanted to believe — that China was 'infinitely inferior to Europe in the art of man-killing'. Even if armed conflict occurred, at most it would make only a temporary break in trade. Jardine, now in London, through parliamentary activities, and Matheson, through his influence with Palmerston, were vociferous spokesmen for freedom of trade and equality of address between British and Chinese authorities: and for what amounted to legalization of the opium trade.

But Chinese opinion was hardening. A wide-ranging debate, touched off by an imperial request to provincial authorities to offer views on opium suppression, narrowed the matter down to a policy of drastic action. Details of the massive scale of the Chinese debate, involving large numbers of officials all over the country, make interesting reading, revealing an official China on the whole unaware of the country's vulnerability, still confident of its immemorial sovereignty and the efficacy of its remedies against the barbarians. On the conclusions reached by the Chinese in the great debate, and on the British reaction to the measures instituted as a result, hung in large part the future of China. Not for several centuries had the Chinese known a serious threat to their sovereignty. The climacteric looming in the 1840s was apparent neither to the Chinese nor, in any precise understanding of its portents, to any other nation involved at that time.

The immediate outcome of the Chinese debate was to thrust Lin Zexu under the eye of history, and to lead to the enactment of a new statute under which beheading was decreed for the principals, and strangulation for the accessories dealing with foreigners in opium, while those surrendering illicit stocks before 18 months elapsed would merit pardon. Lin was recalled to Beijing from his post as Governor of Hubei and Hunan, and appointed Imperial Commissioner charged with the suppression of the opium trade. He arrived to take up duty in Guangzhou in 1839. The stage was set for the coming drama.

2. *First Clashes*

LIN ZEXU was born in 1785 to a family whose Ming ancestors had included many a prominent statesman. At the age of 36 he reached the highest ranks of the mandarinate and thereafter was entrusted with a succession of important positions, culminating in his appointment to the governorship of the provinces of Hubei and Hunan.

Lin had taken a leading role in the debate on the opium question during his governorship and was a natural choice for Imperial Commissioner at Guangzhou. Both before he arrived there and after, he attempted to gain as much knowledge as possible of those concerned with the opium trade and of the events connected with it. He reached Guangzhou at eight in the morning of 10 March 1839, was greeted by high officials and observed by, among others, an American, who wrote that Lin had 'a dignified air, rather a harsh or firm expression, was a large corpulent man, with heavy black moustache and long beard, and appeared to be about 60 years of age'.[1] He was in fact 54, stout but of average Chinese height.

The core of his plans lay in an aggressive policy towards Chinese addicts and 'pushers', combined with a firm line in dealing with foreign merchants. He at once reinforced measures which had already had some effect in preventing the landing of opium, demonstrating his considerable abilities. Where he was less capable was in his inaccurate knowledge of Westerners. He had no personal experience of them, relying on Chinese opinion. He supposed that tea and rhubarb were essentials of their diet and that to stop supplying them would result in the foreigners' submission. Bizarre as that may seem, it could be matched by many a Western misconception about China. Lin also thought that foreign merchants were under orders from their governments, and he failed to comprehend that profits from opium financed purchases of tea. But quite correctly he upheld the principle that foreigners on Chinese soil must obey its laws. 'Having come into the territory of the Celestial Court, you should pay obedience to its laws and statutes, equally with the natives of the land.' He informed the emperor that it would only be as a last resort that he would employ force. But, secretly, prudently, he had drawn up plans for an emergency.

After taking stock of the situation in his first week, he upbraided the Hong merchants for involvement in the illegal trade and issued a decree to all foreigners: 'How can you bring hither opium which you do not use in your own country to defraud others of their wealth and to undermine others' lives.' He required them to remit to him their stocks of opium, calling on all foreign merchants to sign a bond that they would refrain from importing it in the future.

He was unsure that with the naval force at his disposal he could remove the opium fleet at Lingding — 'amidst the gigantic waves and billows'. Nevertheless, on 24 March he ordered all trade with Westerners to cease and withdrew the Chinese working in the factories, confining the merchants to their premises on the banks of the Zhu Jiang until they delivered the opium. The 800 Chinese servants left 'as if they were running from a plague'. It was to be 47 days before the blockade was lifted.

Captain Elliot, now bent on force rather than negotiation, had no option and capitulated, agreeing to surrender the stocks. 'There can be neither safety nor honour for either government until Her Majesty's flag flies on these coasts in a secure position.' On the morning of 27 March he notified Lin that 20,283 cases of British-owned opium would be delivered. In fact this was less meaningful than it seemed, for — as Matheson had pointed out before Lin had demanded it — 'not a chest of opium had been sold in Guangzhou for the last five months'. Chinese action to prevent smuggling had taken effect. The situation was now a direct confrontation between the Chinese and British governments in the persons of Lin and Elliot.

Meaningful or not, Lin at this point must have felt that he was winning the day. He publicly destroyed the opium by mixing it with lime and salt and flushing it from specially dug trenches into the sea, a not inconsiderable task since the quantity involved amounted to over four million pounds. Being a literary man, he composed an *Address to the Spirit of the Sea* — 'you who wash away all stains and cleanse all impurities'. He explained: 'If it [the opium] had been cast into the flames, the charred remains might have been collected. Far better to hurl it into the depths, to mingle with the giant floods.' And he added that he was telling the 'Spirit of the Sea' all this so that his watery subjects might be warned and keep away.

The opium stocks were no more; but this was only half of the task with which the emperor had charged Lin. The more difficult part was to prevent more from being imported. None of the merchants would sign his bond, and in this Elliot supported them, meanwhile making overtures to the Portuguese in Macau to allow the British to reside and trade from there. Before a reply could be received from the Portuguese to this rather importunate request (which would, had it been acceded to, have meant their virtually surrendering sovereignty over the peninsula), Elliot issued an order on 11 May to all the British in Guangzhou to leave. Then, on 24 May, he notified the Chinese authorities that he was leaving the scene because of ill health. And in the afternoon he set out for Macau with all the British subjects who had been detained in their factories. Between the determined acts of Lin and the unruly merchants he was a sorely tried man.

A month before, Elliot had put in a request for warships from India, predicting that the upshot of the confinement of the British at Guangzhou would prove the downfall of the Commissioner at the hands of 'Her Majesty's prompt, powerful, and measured intervention'. To Palmerston he wrote that to miss such an opportunity for intervention would be to sacrifice the trade with China. The merchants themselves, a matter of a day after their release from the siege of the factories, sent a deputation to London to press for compensation for their lost opium, which Elliot had rashly promised them would be forthcoming from the British government.

In London, in times when political issues were still debated in powerfully slanted pamphlets published by interested parties, there was much agitation on the subject of the insult to the British flag at Guangzhou and the 'unjustified' imprisonment of merchants in 'appalling conditions', deprived of food and water, and threatened with death. The fact that the merchants were not so deprived, were supplied with food, water, and even, secretly, Chinese servants, and that they suffered little or no hardship during the seige went

Henry Temple Palmerston, 3rd Viscount (1784–1865), Foreign Secretary in 1830, and Prime Minister, 1855–8 and 1859–65. The portrait is by John Partridge, Court Painter to Queen Victoria.

unheeded. Three hundred concerned companies in the British cotton trade applied pressure on Palmerston, complaining bitterly that the interruption in the opium trade had rendered their Indian customers — growers and shippers of the drug — unable to pay for cotton goods from England. Palmerston himself appeared to be dependent on Jardine and his London agent for information on the Guangzhou situation, and in late September 1839 Jardine offered the Foreign Secretary his own views. China's principal ports should be blockaded, he advised, and an apology sought for insults to the British; payment should be demanded for the surrendered opium; an equitable trade treaty should be negotiated as should the opening of other Chinese ports to foreign trade; and various islands on the China coast should be temporarily occupied so as to achieve these ends. He further suggested that it might be necessary to take permanent possession of some island with a safe anchorage. And he put forward Hong Kong as one such island.

Not long after receiving Jardine's suggestions, in October 1839, Palmerston wrote a top secret dispatch to Elliot informing him that he had ordered a naval force to sail, its object the blockade of Guangzhou and the Hai He (the Pei Ho River) leading to Beijing. It was scheduled to arrive in Chinese waters in March 1840.

The decision to go to war with China was taken by Palmerston alone under the heavy influence of Jardine and the suggestions of Elliot and others. Parliament and the British people had no knowledge of his intentions or action until the fleet was on its way to China. There was then no way by which it could be recalled. Palmerston appears to have been wholly convinced that his was the sole method of securing agreement with China on all the relevant issues. Long after, when Palmerston's Chinese war was over, he was to write: 'There is no doubt that this event, which will form an epoch [sic] in the progress of the civilization of the human races, must be attended with the most important advantages to the commercial interests of England.' It was; but as to the progress of civilization, he was mistaken.

Elliot now forbade the British merchants to trade. Commissioner Lin, surprised at his own misjudgement of the situation, urged them to trade. He was also discomfited by the murder of a Chinese by drunken British sailors in a brawl on a visit ashore in Tsim Sha Tsui. Lin demanded, justifiably, the surrender of the culprit. But Elliot could find no clearly guilty man. He explained this and refused to make a scapegoat of any one man. Equally, it was firm Chinese custom that a murder should be expiated by a death sentence — the assumption of collective responsibility being paramount, it need not be carried out on the actual murderer. For Elliot, the issue was one of extraterritoriality, the principle that in litigation between foreigners and Chinese, the law administered shall be that of the defendant's own country. His only possible course was to punish the members of the group for brawling, which he did.

Commissioner Lin now ordered the Portuguese in Macau to expel the British. The Portuguese did not ask them to stay, and on 26 August 1839 they left in their ships and anchored in Hong Kong harbour, in hot, cramped conditions in midsummer. Lin then forbade the Chinese to supply them with food and water. At the end of the month, HMS *Volage* appeared over the horizon from India with news that the frigate *Hyacinth* was on her way. That same day, ironically, Lin was writing to the emperor: 'the mere fact that they [the British in their ships] will be prevented from going ashore and getting fresh water is enough by itself to give power of life and death over them'.

Some fifty vessels sheltered the British civilians and several thousand men in Hong Kong's August and September heat and high humidity. Elliot's continued refusal to hand over a culprit in the affair of the murder effectively stopped the flow of food and water. Lin ordered all springs near the sea to be poisoned, and threatened dire penalties to villagers tempted to make a little money out of the British. By 4 September the food and water situation was serious. Elliot and Captain Smith of the *Volage* took the cutter *Louisa* with the schooner *Pearl* and a pinnace and sailed over to Kowloon. They arrived off the town at midday, confronted by a strong battery and three war junks. With Elliot was the missionary Charles Gutzlaff — sometime spy and paid employee of opium merchants — as interpreter. Two letters were offered to the Chinese officials. One threatened dire consequences should the British be further deprived of food and water. The other urged the local Chinese not to poison the springs. The letters were refused.

Then, in this apparently run-of-the-mill encounter, there were fired the first shots in what proved to be a century of British gunboat diplomacy. The scene is captured brilliantly if with idiosyncratic use of the language by the brother of Elliot's secretary, A. W. Elmslie, in a letter he wrote to London.

After a long interview with the mandarins [we] anchored a short distance from the Junks. At 2 p.m. Capt. Elliot sent a message . . . and told them that if they did not get provisions in half an hour, they would sink the Junks, — The half hour expired, and no provisions arrived. — Captain Smith ordered his Pinnace to fire. . . The Junks then triced up their Boarding nettings, and came into action with us at half pistol shot; our guns were well served with grape and round shot; the first shot we gave them they opened a tremendous and well directed fire upon us, from all their Guns (each Junk had 10 guns, and they brought all these over on the side which we engaged them on). . . The Junk's fire, Thank God! was not enough depressed, or . . . none of us would have lived to tell the Story. — 19 of their Guns we received in mainsail, — the first Broadside I can assure you was not pleasant. . . The Battery opened fire . . . at 3.45 p.m. and their fire was steady and well directed. . . At 4.30, having fired 104 rounds, the cutter had to haul off as she was out of cartridges. The junks immediately made sail after the *Louisa* and at 4.45 they came up with the English vessels. We hove the vessel in stays on their starboard Beam, and the '*Pearl*' on the larboard Bow of the van Junk, and gave them three such Broadsides that it made every Rope in the vessel grin again. — We loaded with Grape the fourth time, and gave them gun for gun. — The shrieking on board was dreadful, but it did not frighten me; this is the very first day I ever shed human blood, and I hope it will be the last.[2]

Commissioner Lin reported two Chinese soldiers killed, two seriously wounded, and four slightly wounded. On the British side, Captain Douglas suffered a flesh wound, and two seamen were seriously wounded. Lin, however, reported to his emperor that at least 17 British were killed and one of their ships sunk. In fact it is doubtful whether Lin ever knew what actually happened for the commander on the spot had the habit, almost universal among Chinese officers, of inflating the glory of his actions to curry favour and gain promotion. Chinese reports of action in this and the following year were mostly fallacious, and the emperor was deceived.

After the shooting, after the Chinese-reported victory, the provisioning of British ships speedily returned to normal, even if the prices were higher than before. On 27 October Elliot moved the ships to Tongkoo Bay (Deep Bay) on the east side of the estuary leading to the Bocca Tigris, a safer anchorage. He had been informed that the fleet of Admiral Guan Tianpei had been reinforced and might attempt to take a captive as token culprit for the murder in Tsim Sha Tsui.

Meanwhile two British merchant ships had signed Lin's bond, and when one of them started off up the Bocca Tigris against Elliot's prohibition the *Volage* tried to intercept. Since the ship was being escorted by Chinese vessels, the warning shot that was fired across her bows was naturally misinterpreted by the Chinese. The engagement that resulted was 'the most serious collision that has ever taken place between Her Majesty's forces and those of this Empire', in the words of Elliot. From the *Volage* the barrage directed at the squadron of 29 Chinese junks holed one and sank another.

Once more, Lin's version of the engagement differed from Elliot's. Both were mendacious in varying degrees. The brief Battle of Chuanbi, as it came to be known, demolished any hope that may have remained in Commissioner Lin's mind of conducting affairs in his own way and of bringing the opium problem to a conclusion. British trade now passed into American hands for almost a year, and in the nine months until mid-June 1840 almost twenty-five million pounds of tea were shipped to England by the Americans, and a further one-half of that weight to Singapore for trans-shipment there.

There things rested, static, deadlocked, until the arrival in June 1840 of the first vessels of the British expeditionary force dispatched surreptitiously by Palmerston. Among the ships, Lin noted in his diary on 13 July, were 'three cart-wheel ships that put the axles in motion by means of fire, and can move rather fast'.[3] He was reminded of the first example he heard of, which had been up at Guangzhou five years previously — the steamer *Jardine*. What he failed to comprehend was that with these paddle steamers lay the means of victory for the British over any junk fleet that he could send against them. Instead he assured the emperor that the defences of Guangzhou were excellent.

Meanwhile the ships of the expeditionary force had not been idle, four of them having sailed up the coast to Zhoushan island whose surrender they demanded. When it was refused the flotilla bombarded the place and troops landed without further opposition. The next day they advanced on Tinghai. 'All the houses were shut up,' a British interpreter reported, 'and the silence of death reigned through all the streets!' In London, *The Times* surrendered to what might be termed an outburst of patriotic glee. 'The British flag waves over a portion of the Chinese empire for the first time!'

Most of the expeditionary force sailed on north to the Hai He, arriving with Elliot aboard on 9 August. Palmerston's letter to the emperor, carried by the fleet, dealt with his complaints about Commissioner Lin's actions at Guangzhou, and this was understood by the Chinese to be the principal British grievance. Mistranslation of the phrase 'to demand from the emperor satisfaction and redress' as 'to beg the emperor to settle and redress a grievance' distorted British intentions. In fact the emperor had given imperial approval to all Lin's actions, but just before the arrival of the fleet changed his mind, ordering the Viceroy of Guangdong-Guangxi, Qishan, to accept all communications from the foreigners, no matter how they might be addressed or in what language. And on 21 August 1840 he angrily addressed Commissioner Lin: 'You speak of having stopped foreign trade, yet a moment after admit that it is still going on. You say you have dealt with offenders against the opium laws, yet admit they are still at large... So far from doing any good, you have merely produced a number of fresh complications...'. The unfortunate Lin was referred to the Board of Punishments on 28 September, and Qishan appointed as his successor, arriving in Guangzhou on 29 November 1840. Lin was kept in Guangzhou after his dismissal, ostensibly as a consultant although he was never consulted.

Commissioner Lin has earned an honourable place in history. He was burdened with an impossible task, that of trying to force foreigners to accept Chinese laws, of suppressing opium smuggling, and of treating all non-Chinese as tributaries. He did not realize that Britain was by far the most powerful country in the world. And he was faced by Elliot whose intent was to secure a new trading relationship with China and to have his country treated on terms of equality — quite apart from the thorny question of opium. The two men, each sincere enough in his own way, both saddled with unrealizable goals, could never have come to terms. Lin Zexu was exiled to Ili in Xinjiang on 28 June 1841. After many a tribulation he was eventually restored to his rank and served with great credit until his death in 1850 at the age of 67, while on the way to attempt the suppression of the Taiping rebels.

His replacement, Qishan, had had an equally distinguished career and was armed before his arrival in Guangzhou with the elements of a very different Chinese policy. He and Elliot entered into negotiations without advancing much towards an agreement. And in the end Elliot tired of what seemed a fruitless process. On 6 January 1841 he sent Qishan an ultimatum to the effect that unless some basis for negotiation was reached by the following morning he would take possession of the twin forts at the Bocca Tigris.

No reply was received. The forts were attacked from the sea while about 1,500 troops were landed and took them from the rear by assault. Chinese resistance was brave and they fought doggedly with the loss of 500 men. On 20 January the Convention of Chuanbi was signed by Qishan, its terms humiliating in the extreme. An indemnity of six million dollars was to be paid by China; Hong Kong island was to be ceded to Britain; British merchants were to be re-established at Guangzhou; there was to be direct official contact between Britain and China on terms of equality. In return, the British promised to evacuate Zhoushan.

Not surprisingly, the Convention was at once repudiated by the emperor. Qishan was summarily dismissed and deported. He failed to appear for the formal signing of the Convention in February, and the forts were retaken. The Guangzhou factories were reoccupied, and by 21 May 1841 all the tea had been shipped out. Qishan's successor unwisely mounted an attack on British shipping at Guangzhou, but Elliot spared the city the shame of occupation. The British sailed away to Hong Kong. Elliot had the dispiriting experience of learning, from the pages of a Macau newspaper, that he had been dismissed from his post. Palmerston had received news of the Convention of Chuanbi and found its terms too soft. Elliot had used 'too much refinement in submitting to their [the Chinese] pretensions'. He continued, in terms hauntingly reminiscent of those used by the emperor in his castigation of Lin:

> You have disobeyed and neglected your instructions; you have deliberately abstained from employing . . . the force placed at your disposal . . . Throughout the whole course of your proceedings you seem to have considered that my instructions were mere waste paper which you might treat with entire disregard.

Palmerston's fury was perhaps a reaction to the failure of his expeditionary force sent without the consent of Parliament to extract a satisfactory treaty from the Chinese.

The facts of the matter were somewhat at variance with the accusations. Palmerston had never succeeded in reaching any clear understanding of the situation which he was attempting to control from afar. His instructions looked good enough on paper, but his penetration into the impasse of opposing convictions held by the two sides was slight. He also seemed to think that he could scare the Chinese more easily than was the case. The rooted 'pretensions', as Palmerston saw them, of the Chinese to their superiority, their dismissal of the idea of equality with foreigners, together with the nature and processes of decision-making in the government of China — all these were but hazily perceived notions which the Foreign Secretary discounted. Unfortunately it was precisely these factors that animated the Chinese resolve, and which formed the everyday constraints of Elliot's dealings with the Chinese. He was also saddled with the grievances and indignation of a pack of tough traders, few of whom had any interest other than making money, and none of whom had a lesser opinion of their British compatriots than the Chinese had of themselves.

3. The Treaty of Nanjing

THE most significant result of those skirmishes over the illegal import of opium was the demonstration to the British authorities, and to the governments of other Western nations, that China — huge, monolithic, mysterious, with its vast population and sprawling pre-industrial way of life — now lay virtually defenceless against the deployment of a comparatively small naval force, one which, moreover, operated from no permanent base and many thousands of miles from home. It was suddenly obvious to all that the ancient realm of China could without great effort be made to dance to a Western tune.

The Convention of Chuanbi, despite its official repudiation by both Britain and China, was considered valid by Captain Elliot who quickly announced its terms, the most immediate of which was the demand for the cession of Hong Kong. This article, however, was encumbered by the unworkable provision that, while holding sovereignty, the British would permit the Chinese customs to levy their dues as if trade were still being conducted on Chinese soil at Huangpu island downstream from Guangzhou. And there were other arrangements to be worked out — trading relations, exchange of criminals, compensation for the seizure of the opium, and — trickiest of all — the equality of British and Chinese officials, and the elimination of the humiliating word 'petition'.

Airily setting aside these problems, and disregarding the absence of agreement to the Convention from London, Commodore J. J. Bremer (a relation through Prince Albert of Queen Victoria) sent a detachment of sailors under Captain Edward Belcher to claim Hong Kong island. Belcher raised the flag at Possession Point. Hong Kong was declared a British possession. Captain Belcher of HMS *Sulphur*, one of the British squadron sent by Palmerston, recounts the event in his two-volume *Voyage Around the World* which appeared two years later in 1843.

> The only important point to which we became officially partners was the cession of the island of Hong Kong, situated off the peninsula of Cow Loon [Kowloon] within the island of Lama... We landed on Monday the 26th January [actually 25 January] at

fifteen minutes past eight, and being 'bona fide' possessors, her majesty's health was drank [sic] with three cheers on Possession Mount.

More formal possession was taken on the following day, 26 January 1841, by Commodore Bremer at the same site to the accompaniment of the first Royal Salute to be fired from all the ships in Hong Kong harbour.

The exact location was a minor eminence on the scrub-covered slopes rising to what was to be called Victoria Peak, from which much of the northern shore of the island could be seen. Here the flag was raised some two and a half years before the new colony was recognized by the British government. The notion of Hong Kong island as a suitable site for a British possession had perhaps first been mooted in the pages of *The Canton Register* of 25 April 1836 — the newspaper founded by Matheson with a circulation among the foreign community of Guangzhou and Macau.

> If the lion's paw is to be put down on any part of the south side of China, let it be Hong Kong: let the lion declare it to be under his guarantee a free port, and in ten years it will be the most considerable mart east of the Cape. The Portuguese made a mistake; they adopted shallow water and exclusive rules. Hong Kong, deep water, and a free port forever![1]

Eitel avers that the seizure of Hong Kong took the merchants by surprise, 'unexpected as the birth of a child into a family generally is to the rest of the children'. And he quotes a memorial written by them some years later: 'Such a settlement as Hong Kong was never actually required by the British merchants.' Endacott is of the opinion that Elliot chose the island because he envisaged trade continuing to be concentrated in the Guangzhou area, and he points out that for just this reason Elliot did not press for the opening of other treaty ports. The sole difference between Guangzhou and Hong Kong was that at the latter the traders would be on their own soil. It would seem at least likely that if Qishan suggested Hong Kong as a British base, it was to get rid of the foreign merchants from Guangzhou while at the same time keeping them in almost visible distance, and thus more susceptible of surveillance.

At first sight the island was scarcely an ideal place on which to establish a trading post and a community. A narrow strip of sloping land on the northern shore lay at the hem of the steep skirts of hills, an improbable site for a settlement of any size. At few other places round the coasts where deep water could be found were there any more hospitable areas on which to build. Most of the island consisted of scrub-covered hills enclosing sharp valleys.

In London, Palmerston had repudiated both the Convention of Chuanbi and the annexation of the island. He was in any case sceptical about Hong Kong as a possible 'mart of trade' and disinclined to believe the merchants would desert Guangzhou for it. To Elliot, dismissing him from his post, he wrote in scathing terms of Hong Kong as 'a barren island with hardly a house upon it'. This was essentially true, but also irrelevant to those traders who wanted to found a trading port on the shores of a deep-water harbour offering a certain amount of shelter from the elements as well as propinquity to the Zhu Jiang and Guangzhou, still the sole port of access to China. Some merchants preferred to wait and see how the settlement might develop.

Unlike Chishan who was sent to Beijing in chains, Elliot was merely recalled and Sir Henry Pottinger appointed in his place. Pottinger arrived with Admiral Sir William Parker in Macau on 10 August 1841, and less than ten days later departed up the coast in HMS *Nemesis* for Xiamen and Ningbo which he captured — an action that affords an immediate clue to his character. There was no absolute need for speed. But even his journey outward from England had been accomplished in record time via what was termed the 'overland route' — by sea to Alexandria, then overland to the Red Sea to connect with a ship sailing eastward. He had arrived in Macau in only 67 days.

Sir Henry Pottinger, Bt. (1789–1856) by Sir Francis Grant, PRA. The fashionable portraitist alludes to Pottinger's activities in the Far East by including beyond the window a scene with a pagoda. Pottinger's strong Irish accent greatly amused the Foreign Secretary, Lord Aberdeen.

Parker came out as the new Commander-in-Chief Far East, while Pottinger held the position of British Plenipotentiary and Superintendent of Trade. Palmerston, having sacked Elliot, had chosen as replacement a man of quick decisions to pursue the war against China. The British and other foreigners were delighted to welcome him.

Pottinger was born in Ireland in 1789, and had left school in Belfast at the age of 12, and gone to sea. His education was therefore sketchy. He served in several demanding positions in India with the East India Company, learned languages rather easily, went on a derring-do spying expedition from Sind to Persia, played a prominent role in the first Afghan War, and returned to England in 1840 after 27 years continuous service abroad. He was then rewarded with a baronetcy.

His first official act at Macau was to refuse to receive any Chinese who was not empowered by the emperor to negotiate. Finding none, he sailed away north to best the Chinese on their home ground. In six days he reached Xiamen. Ningbo fell to his forces and was lucky not to be razed. Returning to Hong Kong in December 1841, he was off again in June 1842, accomplishing the fall of Shanghai and arriving in Nanjing in early August where the Imperial Commissioners Qiying and Yilibu doggedly attempted to open negotiations. Pottinger, intractable, simply stated his terms for settlement, willing only to deal with those who held absolute power to agree. A letter from one of the Commissioners describes the attitude: 'The barbarian Pottinger just knits his brows and says no.' Pottinger himself wrote: 'The basis on which peace between the two countries can be negotiated, has been

The signing of the Treaty of Nanjing aboard HMS *Cornwallis* on 29 August 1842. It seems likely that Pottinger is the figure seated immediately behind the table and to the left, with Qiying (wearing a mandarin hat) on his left.

too frequently notified . . . to be misunderstood, and it remains unchanged.' Entirely at variance with his latest instructions from London, Pottinger held out for the opening of several ports to British trade besides Hong Kong. Against this stone wall of demands, backed by what the Chinese by now knew to be a military and naval force not lightly to be ignored (and threatening Nanjing), the Commissioners gave in. The signing of the Treaty of Nanjing took place on 29 August 1842 aboard one of the expedition's ships, HMS *Cornwallis*.

Pottinger had gained for his Queen and country a resounding victory — the second round in what was to be a succession of victories by gunboat diplomacy. The provisions of the Treaty were harsh:

(a) The ports of Xiamen, Guangzhou, Fuzhou, Ningbo, and Shanghai to be opened to foreign trade and residence.
(b) Consuls to be appointed to these ports and to be able to communicate freely and in conditions of respect with the Chinese authorities.
(c) Hong Kong island to be ceded to Britain.
(d) China to pay six million dollars in compensation for opium 'surrendered as ransom for the lives of British subjects' (despite the fact that everyone knew this was not the reason for its surrender).
(e) The Co-hong monopoly to be abolished and foreigners to be permitted to trade freely. Three million dollars to be paid by Chinese merchants in settlement of debts to British merchants.
(f) $12 million to be paid to offset the costs of the war (which had not been of Chinese making).

Treaties imposed by victors in settlement of their wars are seldom free from a retributive or punitive element, but the Treaty of Nanjing remains one of the most harsh and unfair. It was to be followed by others of a like kind, later to be collectively termed by the Chinese the Unequal Treaties.

The home government was delighted to have achieved its objectives in China. Pottinger received a decoration — Knight Commander of the Order of the Bath. On arrival in the East, Pottinger had not made up his mind about the desirability of Hong Kong as a colony. But by the time the Treaty was signed he was enthusiastic. After all, it was he who had won it for the Crown. In a letter to London he wrote:

> The retention of Hong Kong, is the only single point in which I intentionally exceeded my . . . instructions, but every single hour I passed in this superb country convinced me of the necessity and desirability of possessing such a settlement as an emporium for our trade, and a place from which our subjects in China may be alike protected and controlled.

A Supplementary Treaty of the Bogue, signed in 1843, heaped further humiliations on the Chinese. A 5 per cent tariff was to be charged on all goods, British subjects committing offences in China were to be tried under British law, and the 'most favoured nation' provision was introduced whereby any privileges subsequently granted to other nations by China would be automatically enjoyed by Britain.

What Pottinger, the conquering hero, did not understand, and what a trained diplomat would have realized, was that such conditions virtually ensured that the Chinese would soon disregard them. And this was precisely what occurred. Easy victory had tended to father precipitate decisions. The treaty was ratified by both governments, the instruments exchanged in Hong Kong on 26 June 1843. A new British colony came into being.

After the signing of the Treaty Pottinger entertained the Imperial Commissioner Qiying, who had been described with marked disdain by *The Friend of China* as resembling a 'boiled turnip ... considerably obese ... dressed just like one of the nodding figures in teashop windows at home'. No Government House existed, and Pottinger used accommodation in the Record Office standing a little way uphill from the bay. Two bungalows had been added to it, and it was here on the evening of the signing that Qiying was received. The dinner, described by *The Friend of China* as having been attended by the 'Chinese Commissioner, who with his suite enjoyed themselves merrily', seems to have been a success. It was said that Qiying went so far (it was very far indeed for a Chinese plenipotentiary) as to sing Manzhu songs, to which Pottinger responded with some of his own.

If Pottinger's reactions on signing the Treaty were hearty, those of Queen Victoria were jocular. She wrote to her uncle Leopold, King of the Belgians, 'Albert is so much amused at my having got the island of Hong Kong, and we think Victoria [their eldest daughter] should be called Princess of Hong Kong in addition to Princess Royal.'

The Treaty of Nanjing contained one notable omission — there is no mention of the illicit opium trade, the fundamental issue over which the two signatories had come into collision. In Britain, vacillating public and parliamentary sentiment inclined on the whole to turn a blind eye to the trade. The sophistical government view that it was up to the Chinese to eradicate it by controlling the acts of their own nationals adroitly side-stepped the whole question. The British flag had been raised, as Gladstone later remarked, 'to protect an infamous contraband traffic'. When Pottinger warned the merchants against trading in opium in the new Treaty Ports before the Treaty was ratified, Matheson, of Jardine, Matheson and Company, wrote that 'the plenipotentiary has published a most fiery proclamation against smuggling, but I believe it is like the Chinese edicts ... only intended for the gratification of the Saints in England'. He promptly bought three American vessels in case Pottinger tried to force his will on British ones. In a climate of overt buccaneering the merchants generally got their own way, governors notwithstanding.

4. *Early Hong Kong*

JUST three days after Elliot annexed Hong Kong in January 1841, he issued a proclamation vesting the government of the island in the Chief Superintendent of Trade. All Chinese who lived there were to be governed by the laws of China, and this applied equally to Chinese from other places who might resort to the island. There was only one proviso, that 'every description of torture' be excepted. British and other non-Chinese were to be under the protection of British law. The Chinese were promised 'free exercise of their religious rites, ceremonies, and social customs', to be governed according to the laws, customs, and usages of China, subject to British control. In the same month foreign merchants began to arrive in Hong Kong and size up its possibilities, keeping their bases at Guangzhou and Macau for the moment. And by June when Elliot declared Hong Kong a free port, a rash of uncontrolled construction had already begun to spatter the northern shore of the island with buildings.

One month after the annexation Matheson put up a matshed godown right in the middle of the shoreline below present-day Flagstaff House (now the Museum of Tea Ware), and quite soon after converted that to the first stone structure on the island. There were existing stone quarries to the east at what was to be called Quarry Bay, the source of the foundations laid to support the matshed or wooden buildings that sprang up to form the beginnings of a little township. Construction followed the existing bridle-path which ran along the north shore a few yards from the water's edge, all the way from East Point (in today's Causeway Bay) to West Point (where Western Street now runs). The first Chinese settlements were at Wong Nai Chung (now Happy Valley), and to the west of the central district, later to develop into Taipingshan, an area of dense occupation below Possession Point in today's Possession Street. Soon, Elliot had to consider the validity of this mushroom development. Before matters got more out of hand he decided to demarcate plots of land and define their boundaries.

Captain Belcher, who had raised the flag, had made a quick survey of the coasts and principal hills, and soon after the annexation a start had been made on a road along the line of the bridle-path, which was to be named

In 1839, just before Hong Kong was annexed, the French painter Auguste Borget briefly visited the area, and later made this engraving of a pastoral scene with a bamboo aqueduct.

A view by an unknown Western painter in the early 1840s looking north from Wong Nai Chung Gap over Happy Valley and across the harbour.

Queen's Road. But plots were taken over in what was virtually a free-for-all and land was being sold by Chinese who had no apparent title. A chaotic situation was aggravated by all parties attempting to seize the main chance, and by the more shrewd who wanted to stake claims to land which, in the event of the island's becoming legally British, would dramatically increase in value.

Elliot had the best intentions when he conducted the first sales of land on 14 June 1841. He intended to offer 200 lots of measured land, half of them on the harbour side of the new road — the marine lots — and half on the inland side — the suburban lots. Because of difficulties in completing the surveys only 50 lots were offered, each with a 100-foot frontage to the water and a varying amount of land between it and the road due to the irregularity of the coastline. Some were not worth bidding for and remained unsold, while others went for between £20 and £265. The provisions of sale were that a structure costing at least $1,000 must be built on the land within a limited time (the rate being 4s. 4d. to the dollar). The title to the land was to go to the purchaser outright after a couple of years, a proposal later countermanded by the home government and to be the cause of future problems.

The action took place against a background of uncertainty due to the unresolved situation in regard to China. But Elliot pressed ahead with measures to form the skeleton of an administration, appointing first Captain William Caine, 26th Regiment of Infantry, as Magistrate with wide judicial powers but narrow powers of punishment, the aim being largely to preserve the peace. Serious crime was to be reported to Elliot who would decide the penalty according to British law, while Caine could only levy fines of up to $400, and mete out terms of three months' imprisonment, or 100 lashes. Also appointed at this time were Lieutenant W. Pedder, RN, as Harbourmaster and Marine Magistrate, and J. R. Bird as Clerk of Works responsible for public works. His burdens included the problems posed by the army having established itself at three places — Sai Ying Pun, West Point, and on the east side of a nullah by what is now Garden Road — all sites at which no intelligent planner would have permitted them. There were to be similar problems with both the army and navy retaining sites in the urban area, thus making nonsense of rational city planning throughout the history of Victoria town.

In a settlement of flimsy shelters — a shanty town — weather was an important factor. Being in the subtropical belt, between a vast land mass and the Pacific Ocean, Hong Kong's summer months bring the hazards of nature's more violent whims (see Appendix 2). In the 1840s there was little means of predicting the weather other than Chinese nostrums about cloud colour and clarity or the lack of it. Those indicators and the rapid fall of the barometer were in fact to prove poor predictors of approaching typhoons. On 21 July 1841 a typhoon struck and the seedy lines of matshed and wooden structures that constituted the town were for the most part flattened, some of them even vanishing, never to be seen again. Elliot's deputy A. R. Johnston's own house suffered with the rest, and shipping in the harbour was seriously damaged. A second typhoon four days later completed the destruction, upon which the second of Hong Kong's perennial scourges struck, as fire consumed the huts of the settlement inhabited by the community of Chinese artisans and labourers. Elliot himself, together with Commodore Bremer, was lucky to escape alive when the typhoon struck the cutter in which they were travelling from Macau to Hong Kong. It was time for the settlers to start again.

Pottinger, when he arrived on 10 August 1841 to take over from the disgraced Elliot, at once made it known that nothing should be altered until the decisions of the home government were known. In the brief time he spent in Hong Kong (24 hours) he forbade any further allotment of land, agreed to the building of a barracks and a road to Tai Tam on the eastern tip of the island, and ordered the evacuation of the Kowloon shore where artillery had been placed — the weapons to be resited on Kellett island for harbour defence. He then set out for Xiamen and Ningbo, leaving Johnston in sole charge.

In one respect this proved to be a mistake. An element of self-importance is discernible in Johnston's character and this perhaps prompted him to initiate a correspondence with the Governor-General of India in Pottinger's absence. Almost incredibly, against Pottinger's express order, he recommenced the sale of land. In October he announced: 'It is now found desirable that persons applying for lots of land for the purpose of building upon, should be at once accommodated.' This presumed the sovereignty of Britain despite the repudiation of the Convention of Chuanbi, and defied Pottinger's order which can hardly have been so vague (as Johnston afterwards pleaded) as to mean the reverse of what was intended. It has been suggested that Johnston capitulated at the urgent demands of the importunate merchants. But in fact both Johnston and Caine were speculating in land and the strong suspicion remains that the former used his temporary position to further his own ends.

The October announcement set out a new method of classification for lots into marine, town, and suburban. Marine lots were defined as those not further than 200 feet from the high-water mark, and town lots those in specified other sites on the island — Wong Nai Chung (Happy Valley), Chek Chu (Stanley), and Shek Pai Wan (Aberdeen). All the rest were suburban lots. Specified areas were to be reserved for Chinese habitation.

Pottinger's reactions were predictably disapproving when he heard of all this in November 1841, and he accused Johnston of entirely exceeding his brief. Undeterred, having apparently got the bit between his administrative teeth, Johnston played the great man. In November, Pottinger still away, he sent an account of his actions. A goodly section of Queen's Road had been completed, as had the prison; the Magistracy was being built and so was the Record Office for the use of the Land Officer. A wooden barracks was rising at Stanley and a bridle-path was being cut towards Shek Pai Wan up the steep hills. The Chinese were frenziedly building houses for themselves and it had become essential to lay down building regulations — streets were to be at least 20 feet broad, houses to be set back five feet from the road and to have verandahs. Each Chinese occupant of the area was to have a vote in order to elect three headmen who would make rules for discipline in the bazaar — as Westerners were accustomed to call any native area.

Such had been the fever of construction that Pottinger, returning in December 1841, must have found a very different place from the ragged line of structures he had left a mere five months previously. The population had risen to about 12,000 Chinese residents. 'This settlement', Pottinger gave it as his opinion, 'has already advanced too far to admit of its ever being restored to the authority of the Emperor.'

It was indeed growing fast. The snide *Canton Register*, reacting to Matheson's construction of a house for himself, took the opportunity of remarking that 'on entering the harbour, you perceive the most commanding site, disfigured by a hybrid erection, half New South Wales, half native production'. Matheson did not keep the structure for long. The army, already occupying the surrounding terrain, offered cash for the house, and other sites in exchange. Jardine, Matheson and Company selected two sites at West Point but their principal depot remained at East Point where it was to remain well into the twentieth century. Pottinger relates how on a spot where in mid-1842 he had seen only a 'chaos of immense masses of granite . . . [so] that it was hardly accessible' either on the land or the water side, Jardine's 'by the application of science and extraordinary labour and by an expenditure of about £100,000, have not only made it available for their vast mercantile concerns, but have rendered it a credit and an ornament to the Colony'.[1] By 1843 the godowns were accompanied by two large houses about which one of the Jardine family was later to write with all the smugness of colonial social status:

> As you are aware the Governor and the General have generally the finest [houses], here it is not so, 'who then?' — Jardine's — their house . . . is situated on a Point which overlooks the greater part of the Town, the rooms here are much larger than most houses.[2]

There are few descriptions of Hong Kong at this early stage of its growth. Lord Saltoun, Commander of British Forces in China, who took over the Jardine bungalow, gives an English gentleman's account of his life there, formed as it was in the best imitation of life at home.

> I am to pay 1000 dollars for furniture and pictures and forty dollars a month for rent. The plan . . . is to engage a comprador, a major domo in fact. He finds cook

and helper, wine coolies, table decker... We breakfast at eight, lunch at one and dine at half past six, and ... we generally sit down eight or ten to dinner... Among other things we have a sheep club ... a certain number of us subscribed and sheep are bought from Bengal and also from Sydney... We graze them here on the hill and feed them with grain ... and at one killing you get a hindquarter, and the next a forequarter...[3]

The rapidity with which an urban milieu — if a small one — had been created may be inferred in part from a sentence in Eitel:

The spirits of the community [which had flagged under the onslaught of recent outbreaks of fever and other tropical diseases] were considerably cheered by the appearance, on the new Queen's Road, of the first carriage and pair imported from Manila, as a sign of the coming comforts of civilization.

Further signs can be gleaned from newspaper advertisements of the time. By the middle of 1845, the colony a mere four years old (only two from its official recognition), *The Friend of China* carried the following:

A substantial house consisting of two sitting rooms, each 30 by 20 feet and in height 17 feet, separated by folding doors, five good size bedrooms, with dressing and bathroom to each; a front and back verandah, closed with venetians, each 100 feet long and 12 feet wide, flat roof convenient for exercise and affording a fine view of the harbour... Commodious outbuildings for servants, store room, and offices: a large compound, garden, etc ... surrounded by a good fence...

Yet, appearances and accommodation apart, the colony was only slightly removed from lawlessness. Caine, now Major Caine, Chief Magistrate, assumed the title of Sheriff and Provost Marshal in 1844, and was also Justice of the Peace. Eitel comments on this issue:

As pirates ruled the sea all round Hong Kong, so highway robbers and burglars seem to have things their own way all over the Island. Government House even was entered by robbers (April 26, 1843), three mercantile houses (Dent's, Jardine's, Gillespie's) were attacked in one and the same night (April 28, 1843), The Morrison Institution was plundered by robbers who carried off the Chief Superintendent's Great Seal (May 19, 1843)... No European ventured abroad without a revolver... The principal merchants kept armed constables ... for the protection of their property, having no confidence whatever in the Colonial constables... Every private house inhabited by Europeans had its watchman going the round ... all night and striking a hollow bamboo from time to time in proof of his watchfulness. The scum of the criminal classes of the neighbouring districts looked upon Hong Kong as their Eldorado and upon English law as a mere farce... Imprisonment in the Gaol ... appeared to the half-starved gaol-birds of Canton a coveted boon.[4]

Caine met with severe criticism of his methods of administering justice. One newspaper commented that he and other magistrates 'mete out justice according to the judgement which God has been pleased to grant them; equitably in their own opinion no doubt . . . law, there is none'.

Doubtless, as Endacott says in his brief biography,[5] Caine was 'as ignorant of British law as he was of Chinese laws, customs, and usages'. But in a mushrooming colony for which the British government had refused to recruit a police force (except for three officers) he was forced to rely on untrained troops and his own policies of deterrence. Caine treated the problem with 'ruthless application of flogging with the rattan, with or without imprisonment; indeed flogging was so prevalent that questions were asked in the House of Commons'. He was a hard worker and could be found out on patrol at nights, doing what the home government was too penny-pinching to send officers to perform. 'He remained dignified, and his efficiency was always gentlemanly... The result was that though he was feared he was respected; he was never actively disliked.' Caine himself commented on 'the unpleasantness of my duties' in Hong Kong. 'Nine-tenths of our Chinese subjects and about half of our low European inhabitants have been in the most depraved condition.' Such a sentence from an official, in a report written for Whitehall to read, must constrain the reader to credit it. And in fact Johnston in the previous year had said he 'lacked the means of visiting adequate punishment'. Johnston's prison was full and his powers of sentencing quite inadequate for the nature of the crimes he had to deal with.

The picture of a haphazard, scarcely planned or plannable settlement growing raggedly along a miserably inadequate strip of shelving shore, and administered by a set of amateurs stumbling in the wake of problems they were too few and too inexperienced to solve, is all but inescapable. The dilatory functioning of the home government hampered Pottinger too. In the absence of appointed officials from Britain he was forced to appoint local stopgaps, and in the heated commercial and monetary climate many of the best men for the jobs preferred to make a quick fortune in commerce than a competence in government service. Pottinger's cross was his requirement to serve two masters: the Colonial Office as Governor, and the Foreign Office in his capacity as Plenipotentiary. A further misfortune was that, more than competent in military affairs, he was less than comfortable as an administrator, too impatient for the deliberations and accommodations of bureaucracy with its snail's-pace action.

Pottinger tended to quarrel rather than to coax. Thus he fell out with the navy which had been allowed to unload stores right in the centre of the town during the hostilities, and which now wanted to change its mind about moving to the West Point location. The navy insisted on retaining this central position despite the inconvenience to the community. Pottinger described the depot as a 'perpetual and irreparable detriment to the Colony'.

Not only the navy, but the army too hatched schemes inimical to town planning. The Aldrich plan of 1843, which envisaged a fortified cantonment housing a suggested force of 4,500 men right in the centre of the town, was one. Pottinger rightly felt it certain to arrest all future development. It would, he said, 'turn this face of the island [into] a mere military position . . . in lieu of . . . a vast emporium of commerce and wealth'. He pointed out the absurdity of the plan in the light of the fact that Hong Kong was indefensible against an enemy with a superior naval force.

Pottinger was to fall foul of the army again on the subject of Hong Kong's climate. During the fever epidemic of 1842 the troops were removed to ships in the harbour in an effort to reduce the ravages of the disease, and the commanding officer put all the blame for fatalities on the weather. Pottinger replied with hauteur that he had been 'in some small degree the instrument of [Hong Kong's] becoming a possession of the Crown of England', and 'I am forced to record my total dissent to the insalubrity of the climate'. Sickness among the troops was due in Pottinger's opinion to poor supervision, which permitted them to be out without regard to heat or rain, allowed them to bathe for extended periods, and to drink large quantities of *sam shui* (Chinese spirits). Pottinger was doubtless largely right, but he had omitted to do much about the main culprit in public health matters — sanitation. And in this he set the pattern for many a future administration which cut corners in that fundamental branch of government, with dire consequences, until the very end of the nineteenth century.

Pottinger's troubles were not confined to disputes with the armed forces. He came up against the exacerbated tempers of the merchant community who, under Elliot and abetted later by Johnston's high-handed sale of land, were convinced that purchase conferred perpetual ownership, or at least that it ought to do so under the legal structure in the colony. The home government had other ideas. Pottinger took the brunt of the ensuing wrath, writing ruefully that he had been held up 'not only as the immediate cause of all private dissatisfaction . . . but as the originator . . . of all the public mistakes and oversights'. In a situation in which what Eitel calls 'land-jobbing' was rife, Pottinger was the natural butt when owners discovered their tenure was for 75 years for land to be built on, and for less if not. No grants of land made prior to 26 June 1843, the date of legal cession, were to be recognized as of right. This ignored the fact that grants of land had had to be made in order that administrators (for example) could have sites for houses in place of matsheds. Pottinger, rashly, before the contents of the Colonial Office order were known, had made tampering attempts to clear up anomalies, thereby compounding the confusion. Not surprisingly he was unable to do much other than complain to Lord Stanley in London, while in the meantime the 'land-jobbers' made a killing.

Until this time the little town on the northern shore of the island had been called Queenstown. Pottinger now asked London for approval of the name Victoria, and a proclamation of 29 June 1843 affirmed the name along with the appellation 'the Colony of Hongkong', not 'Hong Kong' as formerly. This style is perpetuated to the present in the names of early institutions such as The Hongkong and Shanghai Banking Corporation and The Hongkong Land Company Limited. The official name has now reverted to 'Hong Kong'.

The nineteenth century witnessed a vast expansion of earnest Christian missionary endeavour and the new colony was not forgotten. Funds had been raised in 1842 to build a colonial church, a union church 'for both Churchmen and Fundamentalists'. A chaplain had been appointed in England but the authorities did not approve of the proposed union church, and services continued to be conducted as before by naval chaplains in the interim matshed church, the first sermon being preached there on Christmas Eve, 1843. The construction of St John's Cathedral was ordered at government expense, actual building being put off for several years as London withheld approval. Meanwhile the Roman Catholic prefect apostolic, Antonio Feliciani, consecrated the Church of the Conception on 18 June 1843, situated at the corner of Wellington and Pottinger Streets, and a seminary for Chinese clergy was opened. Shortly after, the Muslim community set up their mosque on the hill called thereafter Mosque Gardens (now Mosque Street) — Moloshan, Moorish Hill, in Cantonese.

Four existing temples served the Chinese, all already between 75 and 100 years old, at Ap Lei Chau, Stanley, Spring Gardens (at present-day Spring Garden Lane), and Causeway Bay (Tung Lo Wan). And now a fifth was begun on the site of present-day Queen's College. In 1843 the American Baptist Mission started a Chinese church at Sheung Wan market, and the Morrison Education Society school was opened, having been transferred from Macau. Dr Legge of the London Missionary Society transferred the Society's college from Malacca to Hong Kong and opened a seminary and school for training Chinese ministers, naming it the Anglo-Chinese College. The Colonial Chaplain made similar provision for the Church of England at St Paul's College, still in existence. Not the least of all this godly activity was the beginning, in autumn 1843 by the Protestant missionaries of the colony, of the translation of the Bible into Chinese. Known as the Delegates Version, this work was said by Eitel to be 'the best in style though not in literal accuracy' that had appeared until his own day.

Pursuing what must have at times seemed to him an elusive goal — order in the administration — Pottinger attempted to set up councils in mid-1843. The Legislative Council consisted of three members: Caine, J. R. Morrison, formerly a secretary in the Guangzhou Superintendent of Trade's office, and Johnston, with R. Burgass (the Governor's legal adviser) as Clerk of the Council. Pottinger was greatly hampered in the setting up of both Executive and Legislative Councils by the acute scarcity of men willing to serve who were reliable and capable of such civic duties as service implied. The necessity of these bodies had been laid down in a proclamation of 5 April 1843 in the so-called Hong Kong Charter. The Governor was to be allowed, on the advice of the Legislative Council, to make laws for peace, order, and good government subject to these not being disallowed by the home government. Among other matters he was entrusted with the seal of the colony, and empowered to make temporary appointments and suspend public officers pending Her Majesty's pleasure. And his was the prerogative of pardon for convicted criminals as well as power to suspend or remit fines. Also laid down was a rule which in due course brought trouble: in the Governor's absence or incapacity, authority was to be vested in the Lieutenant-Governor or, failing him, in the Colonial Secretary. Guidance also came from Whitehall on the Governor's duties and powers in the working of the administration, and stated that:

> in the very peculiar circumstances of Hong Kong, H. M. Government have thought it right to confer upon you the extra-ordinary power of passing laws independently [of the Legislative Council] should the necessity for such a proceeding arise.

If it did, the Council had the right to dissent and send their reasons to London.

Pottinger was firmly given to understand that Hong Kong was an anomaly of a colony in that its purpose was not to be colonized so much as to be used for diplomatic, military, and commercial purposes. The Governor had three functions: negotiation with the Chinese emperor; superintending the trade of British subjects with China; and regulation of the colony's economy. These functions and other matters made it necessary that 'methods of proceeding unknown in other British colonies must be followed at Hong Kong'.

The powers of the legislature were to include the administration of civil law, police and prisons, lands and their transfer, and the authority to levy taxes. In due time the legislature would have to set up other elements of government such as a Supreme Court. The numbers in the two councils were to be kept small so that the Governor could exert his personal influence, and there was no elective element. Members would be chosen by the Governor although confirmation of appointments lay with the home government.

The thorny topic of legal repugnancy, by which the laws of colonies were required to conform to those of Britain, was not to be strictly applied in Hong Kong where the Chinese were so numerous and had their own traditional ideas and usages. 'It will be necessary that for the government of the Chinese ... the laws and customs of China should supersede those of England', except where Chinese law was in conflict with the 'immutable principles of morality which Christians must regard as binding on themselves at all times and in all places'.

The four-man Legislative Council consisting of Johnston, Morrison, Caine, and Burgass began its duties with gusto in January 1844, 'grappling boldly rather than wisely' (as Eitel has it), before the sudden death of Morrison and the loss of Johnston on sick leave, with problems of Chinese custom. The Council attempted to pass anti-slavery legislation but the ordinance was disallowed by London on the grounds that Britain already had anti-slavery laws which should apply to Hong Kong. The fact that they did so only partially meant that the Chinese custom of bond-servitude was to continue legally for many a decade. Successfully passed ordinances included those dealing with the possession and use of printing presses and the publication of books and papers, which remained on the statute book for over four decades. Legal interest rates were limited to 12 per cent, unlicensed distillation of spirits was prohibited, and rules on the licensing of public houses and for the sale of spirits were laid down.

Whatever regulatory laws were passed to lend a veneer of legality to the opium trade, the fact remained that before Pottinger left the scene Hong Kong had become a much larger version of Lingding island round which the opium ships of the British merchants clustered and from which the drug was stealthily distributed for sale up and down the coast of China. The situation was both fluid and hazardous, potentially inflammable. Legal trade had fallen sharply for a variety of reasons. The Foreign Office had decided that to forbid opium ships the use of the harbour would merely drive the trade elsewhere. But the canny merchants voluntarily removed their ships to neighbouring anchorages and continued with their lucrative trade away from direct sight of the town. Pottinger himself seems to have pinned his hopes on some sort of agreement on legalization of the drug by China, and his popularity with the trading community waned. The root cause of this was a resumé he published of parts of the Supplementary Treaty of the Bogue, signed on 8 October 1843. This partial translation omitted certain important clauses, under which permits to trade in Hong Kong were required by Chinese vessels prior to leaving their home ports; and all Chinese vessels entering Hong Kong waters to trade required a similar permit signed by a British official. The information on these movements was to be conveyed to the authorities at Guangzhou. It was at the time, and is now, unclear why Pottinger omitted translation of those clauses in his version. He did so at his peril, as he rapidly discovered. When the merchant community, through its Chinese compradors, learned the truth it seemed to them either that Pottinger had had the wool pulled over his eyes by Imperial Commissioner Qiying, or that he had deliberately concealed the clauses since they contravened the colony's free port status. In a surge of public obloquy Pottinger's stock hit zero overnight. He was accused of applying a tourniquet to the principal artery of the colony's trade.

No British official was appointed to register Chinese vessels and the offending clauses were simply abandoned. But trade got off to a very poor start, traders beginning to fear that it might turn out to be an 'egregious failure'.

Pottinger was guilty of one other mistake. However unlikeable his subjects may appear to him, no governor can afford to let them see it. Pottinger made it obvious that he regarded the merchant community as little better than a bunch of insalubrious opium purveyors. Such, by and large, they were, but the first Hong Kong Governor succeeded in polarizing society, something which in a still tiny community was unhelpful. The trading community made common social cause with the army and navy against the government.

This in itself would be unimportant were it not for the fact that it set a pattern of social division and antagonism which was to plague Hong Kong society for much of the nineteenth century with unfortunate results.

Despite these antagonisms life in the colony had its more pleasing aspects. The Military Commander, Major-General Lord Saltoun, was the popular president of the Madrigal Society, and other officers of the army and navy vied among themselves

> in reciprocating the social *entente cordiale* which reigned everywhere in the colony outside of Government House and Government Offices... The annual races and regatta ... were still held in Macao, for which purposes a general pilgrimage [there] occupied the latter half of the month of February...[6]

A public subscription was raised for the victims of the Afghan War, and there was public grief when one of the heroes of Kabul, Pottinger's brother (and his expected successor) died in Hong Kong. 'The birth of the first British subject ushered into the world in Hong Kong (January 20, 1843) was the occasion of much social humour.'[7]

Pottinger became a somewhat isolated figure. To accord him his due, he was grossly overworked. 'I have stood alone', he wrote in complaint to Lord Stanley. He had had to act on his 'unassisted judgement' while being unfairly blamed for everything that went wrong. He resigned in July 1843 but had to stay until the following May when his replacement arrived. He had had some of the worst conditions to deal with, and for staff a motley group of amateurs. 'His secretary', a legal historian wrote, 'was an assistant surgeon in the Bombay army; his financial secretary the mate of a ship; his judge an Indian soldier; his assistant judge the second mate of a country ship.'[8]

But Eitel's harsh judgement of Pottinger is not quite merited in any sober view. He was no administrator: he was a successful soldier. It was he, much more than his vociferous critics among residents, who upheld with tenacity the interests of the colony as a whole among a citizenry whose dedicated self-seeking has left in its own record much that is less than pleasing to contemplate. The verdict of a contemporary, the Revd James Legge, the early nineteenth-century sinologue, is perhaps fairer: 'Sir Henry Pottinger was governor of the colony when I came to it, and I was surprised to find that he was not by any means popular. He was a good man, people said, to conquer China, and a bad man to rule Hong Kong.'

5. *Governor Davis — One against All*

In Anglo-Chinese relations during the period between the signing of the Treaty of Nanjing and the spring of 1848, the principal figures were Qiying, the new Viceroy of Guangdong-Guangxi, who acted as Imperial Commissioner, and Sir John Davis, Governor of Hong Kong, whose term there ended in May of that year. Of the two the more important and influential in the evolving situation was Qiying. The lengthy correspondence carried on between them over the whole period, following on from Qiying's numerous dispatches to Pottinger, makes interesting reading.[1] Innumerable matters large and small are introduced — many potentially explosive in the delicate state of the relationship between the two countries. These are then discussed and opinions exchanged on their resolution — on Qiying's part almost invariably with aplomb and diplomatic finesse. The picture that emerges is of a patient and practised negotiator coping with a somewhat irascible governor possessing much less skill in his task.

Mr John F. Davis, as he was on arrival in Hong Kong on 7 May 1844, was knighted in July the following year for his services in reorganizing its government. The home government evidently thought highly of him, but that was an opinion totally at variance with the estimation of his character and governorship held by the majority of Hong Kong residents.

Taken at face value, Davis's qualifications for appointment as Governor of the colony were compelling. Born in 1795, Davis was the son of an East India Company official, and at the age of 18 he joined that company and was posted to Guangzhou. The youth was of a scholarly disposition and immediately began to learn Chinese there. Within two years he published his first translation from that language and continued throughout his long life to publish further volumes including poetry, a novel, and other Chinese works. He eventually wrote (in 1836) *The Chinese: a general description of China and its inhabitants*, which for long remained the standard work on the subject.

Davis worked his way up to the chairmanship of the Company's Select Committee at Guangzhou, later acting as second Superintendent of Trade under Napier, and succeeding him in October 1834. He resigned after three

A portrait of Sir John Davis by a Chinese painter, 1845.

months, alleging his powers to control 'the ill-conduct of British subjects in China' were too slight and that he left 'in despair'. In fact these words were written 10 years later, just before he became Governor of Hong Kong. They perhaps indicate his feelings on the appointment. Davis was a conservative, regretting the end of the Company's monopoly and the free-for-all which ensued — of which Hong Kong merchants appeared to him a later incarnation. Like Pottinger, he was to serve two masters in London, while living in a community of disaffected merchants who felt cheated over land ownership and also over the missing clauses in the English version of the Supplementary Treaty. Trade was in the doldrums and there was little that any governor could have done about it.

With him Davis brought a team of professionals to replace some of Pottinger's amateurs. Socially, the most distinguished of them was Frederick Bruce, son of the Earl of Elgin. He was appointed Colonial Secretary, but served only 15 months before leaving. His successor was William Caine, formerly the first Magistrate and destined to be a hardy perennial in Hong Kong. The new Colonial Treasurer was Robert Montgomery Martin, given the post as a reward for serving as a doctor in other colonies and for contributing to the 10-volume *History of British Colonies*. In a matter of two months after his arrival he tendered two lengthy reports, one on the colony's finances and another on everything else he thought was wrong — with consequences which will appear later.

Also among Davis's suite was William T. Mercer, his nephew, acting as private secretary. Twenty-two on arrival, Mercer had studied law without taking the Bar examinations and although, as Endacott says, 'nepotism gave him his chance', his subsequent successful career of 20 years in Hong Kong was due entirely to his own brilliance.

R. D. Cay came out as Registrar of the Supreme Court, and J. Pope, the Civil Engineer, who is thought to have been the author of an early design for St John's Cathedral, Government House, and government offices. A month after their arrival, J. W. Hulme arrived to fill the post of Chief Justice — a man of 'excitable temperament [who] may be led on convivial occasions to transgress the limits of . . . decorum'.[2] He was to be constantly at loggerheads with Davis, and their relationship was to lead to one of the colony's most appalling scandals.

A. F. Shelley arrived soon after Hulme and was made Auditor-General, while the post of Attorney-General was given to Paul Ivy Sterling after seven other barristers had refused it because of the colony's evil reputation in matters of health. And he only accepted when the salary of £1,500 was raised to £2,500 with the right to engage in private practice. He stayed for a decade, becoming an Executive Councillor.

With this mixed but generally competent team Davis settled in, his first substantial step being to enlarge both Executive and Legislative Councils in spite of the Colonial Office ruling that they were to have only three members each. On orders from Lord Stanley in London, he had to undo this action. The Commanding Officer, Major-General D'Aguilar, the Chief Justice, and the Attorney-General were appointed to the Legislative Council, while the Commanding Officer, the Colonial Secretary, and the Chief Magistrate, Major Caine, formed the Executive Council — the Governor chairing both.

There was a firm British policy, which Davis was charged to carry out, that no colony should be dependent on the British taxpayer for support. Quite correctly Davis instituted the processes through which this might be achieved. When he arrived, the home government was acting as financial parent to a dubiously legitimate colonial child. Sir James Stephen, Permanent Under-Secretary in the Colonial Office, in London voiced the warning: 'This promises to be a very expensive colony.' Expenditure in the first Davis year in Hong Kong was £72,841 against the sum of £22,242 that he had managed to squeeze out of the reluctant community which until then had never paid a cent in tax while expecting as of right the utmost freedom from official interference and demanding government help as soon as trouble arose. 'It is much easier', Davis was to write to Lord Stanley in November 1844, 'to govern the twenty thousand Chinese inhabitants of this Colony, than the few hundreds of English.' Given the unpopularity of the measures he had to take it was hardly surprising that he came in for heavy criticism; but his disdain of the merchant fraternity did nothing to improve his image.

Raising revenue in those early days posed a problem. Davis could not impose customs duties because Hong Kong was a free port. His answer was to levy land rents as his main source of revenue, and to supplement these by farming out to the highest bidder various monopolies, and by the sale of licences. The monopolies were for the sale of opium, generally called the 'opium farm', quarrying stone, and handling salt. Wine and spirit merchants, pawnbrokers, and billiard-room operators had to pay for their licences. A percentage tax was levied on goods sold at auction. A proposed duty on the consumption of wine and spirits had to be dropped (at the unanimous request of the Legislative Council). A tax on all property was introduced to pay for the police force.

With the imposition of 75-year leases on all land already in force, the demand for rates and taxes on property sparked off a furore. The home government held that residents should assess themselves through some form of municipal organization, the assessment to yield $325,840, but Davis thought it prudent to reduce this by 40 per cent. His ingenuity in fabricating schemes to raise money was considerable. He tried developing the roads so as to open up new sites for building, and allocated land for the Chinese in an attempt to stop them squatting. He even invited Australian colonists to come and settle the south of the island and graze sheep and cattle there, a scheme vetoed by London. He made a valiant effort to end land speculation by finding out what land was held by those who appeared to have no intention of building on it; and by charging a 10 per cent deposit on all land sales. The figures achieved in those ways were quite impressive: the colonial revenue of £22,242 in 1845 rose by 1847 to £31,078 against expenditures of, respectively, £72,841 and £50,599. The deficit made up by Britain fell from £49,000 in 1845 to £36,900 in 1846, £31,000 in 1847, and £25,000 in 1848.

To his credit also, Davis was energetic in his efforts to put the policing of the colony on a sounder basis. As Pottinger's requests for manpower had been refused, Davis turned to the Indians in the army, and in November 1844 one havildar, two sergeants, and 20 rank and file were taken on, and more were to join them later. Urgent requests to London in spring 1845 produced Charles May, a London police officer, as Superintendent of Police, accompanied by two inspectors. May faced a situation in which only 47 of an original force of 90 European recruited seamen and soldiers remained. Selecting 41 of those and adding 30 more from the army, his total force was 71 Europeans, 46 Indians, and 51 local Chinese — 168 in all. For them he asked for more generous pay and pensions, together with better housing for the Indians. He then put together a small unit of marine police to patrol the lawless waters of the harbour.

For years the home government complained about the expense of the police force, urging economy and objecting to the cost of pensions. When the police were offered pensions on half pay after 15 years service or a 20 per cent pay rise, they all elected for the latter. Rapid turnover of personnel meant low efficiency and morale, and drunkenness and corruption were common, so that an announcement in 1848 warned that it was unsafe to wander out of town after dark. It should perhaps be recalled that a police force was still a novelty in Britain at this time and Hong Kong was possibly better off than some places there. In the face of continued immigration of every criminal Tom, Dick, and Harry from Guangzhou, the task of any police force would have been hard. During Davis's temporary absence up the China coast in September 1844, the Lieutenant-Governor, D'Aguilar, cancelled what was termed the 'Bamboo Ordinance' under which householders' watchmen beat bamboo poles at intervals in the night. The ensuing silence permitted all to sleep again, including the watchmen. Government House was burgled once more. Flogging appeared to have little effect and, after questions in the Commons, was stopped. For four months criminals had an easier time, before it was reintroduced.

Piracy round the coasts was rampant and endemic. Charles May's heavily armed police boat did good work until wrecked in late 1848, and then the pirates preyed on every junk they could catch, and were even joined in their exploits by European sailors. One police headache was the difficulty of telling a pirate junk from a peaceful trader, both being heavily armed. Deportation was tried and, irony of ironies, one convict ship conveying prisoners to Penang in January 1848 was taken over by the convicts on board.

Pottinger had suggested that one way to reduce crime might be to register all citizens. Now Davis took this up, displaying his egalitarianism and his equal lack of understanding of those he governed. He proposed to register not only the Chinese but Westerners as well. The Chinese opted for passive resistance: indignant Europeans held the first public meeting to take place in the colony and condemned the idea as 'iniquitous, unconstitutional, and un-English in principle'. Davis responded to their written protest by calling them 'this ill-conducted opposition'. Worse still, the translation of the ordinance into faulty Chinese convinced the rest of the population that the payment levied for registration ($1 for them, $5 for Europeans) was a monthly due and not an annual one. Westerners saw in the proposal the sole difference between them and the Chinese being couched in humiliating monetary terms. The whole idea was a century ahead of popular thinking and the Western community 'rose up ... in wrathful indignation, feeling their personal respect, their national honour, the liberty of the subject trampled under foot ...' according to Eitel who must have known some of them.[3]

Hong Kong came to a standstill as all Chinese clerks and servants walked out. The Chinese population prepared to leave in a body, *The Friend of China* reporting them liable to 'bear squeezing to any ordinary extent' but not to that of extracting from them half their monthly wages, as in the 'blundering translation'. Davis then informed the Europeans that the measure would not be enforced for another two months, and tardily began a process of consultation. The brilliant but entirely scholarly intelligence of the Governor was quite unsuited to the evaluation of public opinion, and therefore of forming judicious policies where it was involved. On 13 November 1844 the Legislative Council passed an amending ordinance requiring registration only for those whom Eitel calls 'the lowest classes'. Eventually, only those earning less than $500 were registered — virtually only Chinese. The Chinese doubtless assessed the dubious quality of the Governor and government responsible for the episode.

Another area of dispute insufficiently clarified by the Colonial Office was the question of whether the Chinese in Hong Kong should be judged (and if guilty punished) under Chinese or British law. Davis thought that since the Chinese came voluntarily to the colony to work they should be subject to British law. But the ordinance of 1844 setting up the Supreme Court gave it powers to punish them under Chinese law, as did that governing the magistrates. Davis pleaded that Chinese punishments such as amputating the queue, wearing the cangue, and flogging, had all been tried without much effect. The Chinese had no money to pay fines and seemed undeterred by imprisonment. The Colonial Office was wary. 'The dilemma is between ruling Chinese people by English law and requiring judges to administer in H. M.'s name the law of China.' Sir James Stephen thought that 'effective restraint . . . and a government not to be trifled with' were fundamentally important and ought to be attained 'even at the expense of adopting a policy the most opposed to our feelings and prepossessions'. A large grey area remained. In practice the Chinese were at liberty to conduct their lives according to their own customs and laws. Only when they came into conflict with law and order and the British criminal code did British legal processes apply. An ordinance of 1 January 1845 prescribed for second-offender triad society members the barbaric punishment of branding on the cheek (unaccountably termed 'painless' by Endacott) and expulsion to China. The Colonial Office rejected this. Qiying, Imperial Commissioner and Viceroy of Guangdong-Guangxi, objected to criminals being sent into his domains, urging that they should be judged by Hong Kong Chinese officials. Davis parried by stating that no one had compelled the Chinese to come to the colony and that if they wanted to live in Hong Kong they must expect the treatment meted out to other citizens — and the same protection. In rejecting cheek branding, the Colonial Office suggested (amendment 12, 1845) branding under the arm instead. Such were the common opinions held by otherwise quite reasonable men, and such the status of those who had the misfortune not to be born British, in early colonial Hong Kong.

The whole question was much too knotty and disputatious to be successfully tackled at the time. An ordinance of 6 May 1846 laid down that all the laws of England when the colony first obtained its legislature (on 5 April 1843) should be deemed in force 'when applicable'. And it was probably wise enough to leave the matter like that for the time being.

The Chinese government, however, continued to claim control over the Chinese living in Hong Kong. All unknown to the British administration (it would appear) a Chinese official regularly sold fishing licences at Stanley.[4] Davis took the matter up with Qiying in several dispatches, and the latter eventually disclaimed such rights.[5]

The old problem, opium, still festered. China had almost given up attempting to stop its importation. Davis had written to the Colonial Secretary before he left England that opium could not be tolerated in the colony. The opinion in British government circles was that China should make up its mind to control, or (possibly) legalize imports, and that the British government had no obligation to assist in the execution of Chinese law. Soon after his arrival in Hong Kong Davis wrote home that 'opium is now tacitly tolerated by the Chinese government', adding that Qiying admitted the Chinese policy on opium could be disregarded. 'Under the circumstances,' wrote Davis, 'any scruples on our part . . . appear to me to be more than superfluous.' He sold the monopoly for sales of opium in the colony on a yearly basis. Lurking behind all the considerations on the British side of the opium question lay the fact that the government of India depended substantially for its revenues on sales of opium which was mostly grown in its territories.

There were isolated protests from the Legislative Council about 'taxing vice for revenue'. But Davis reported to London in 1844 that 'almost every person possessed of capital who is not connected with government . . . is employed in the opium trade'. By 1845, some 80 Hong Kong vessels were carrying opium, 19 of them belonging to Jardine, Matheson and Company. Clearly if Davis wished for legalization in China he could hardly press for abolition in Hong Kong.

The man who made the remark about taxing vice for revenue was Martin, the Colonial Treasurer, who now vigorously opposed government policy on opium. The Governor, supported as he was by the Colonial Office, must have wished he had never brought him to Hong Kong. Davis sold the 1845–6 opium monopoly to a notorious land speculator, George Duddell. But this, like numbers of Davis's actions, proved financially a failure, covering only local sales of the drug. Chinese dealers at once circumvented the regulations by buying opium which they swore to export, and then selling it locally. Davis then amended the ordinance and raised £4,275 by selling the monopoly to a group of Chinese business men. They, more realistic than the Governor, employed their own enforcement squads and an armed vessel to maintain their monopoly intact. Even so, profits declined and Davis replaced the monopoly in 1847 with a system of licensing.

Martin continued to be a thorn in his flesh. His estimate of the colony's financial viability was one of extreme pessimism. Annual expenses in 1844, Martin calculated, were £50,000, excluding defence and public works, and income was below £6,000.[6] He foresaw a permanent deficit budget — trade increasingly favouring other ports. Hong Kong, he said, was a 'small barren unhealthy and valueless island'. The two men quarrelled over China policy, and when Martin announced his intention to go to London to put his point of view Davis refused him leave. Martin went of his own volition, causing Davis to say he had in effect resigned. Martin's crusade in London against Hong Kong had only one effect — it was a factor in the setting up of a Parliamentary Select Committee of Enquiry into the China Trade in 1847.

There had been no way for Davis to dissuade Martin from his headlong rush into criticism and disparagement of the government. But in another incident in which judgement was required, Davis can be squarely faulted. Admittedly his opponent this time had the wholehearted backing of the mercantile community, a fact that should have forewarned the Governor.

J. W. Hulme had come out to Hong Kong to enjoy the benefits of a generous salary which allowed him to provide for his large family, and to indulge his strongly convivial nature. Hulme and Davis were early set on a collision course when the former realized that the Police Magistrates Caine, in his second capacity, and C. B. Hillier, appointed by Davis, considered themselves as executive officers reporting directly to the Governor. Hulme remonstrated with Davis, holding the view that it was unethical for agents of the law to report directly to a political figure. Soon, in Eitel's words, 'the community began to take sides' — in fact to come down on Hulme's side of the dispute. An incident in the summer of 1846 brought matters to a head. An obstreperous Englishman in Guangzhou pushed over a hawker's stall allegedly causing a riot, and was fined by Davis (in his capacity as Superintendent of Trade) $200 for damage estimated at $46,000. The offender, Charles Compton, took his case to the Supreme Court and Hulme, as Chief Justice, gave judgement in favour of the plaintiff, pronouncing Davis's sentence 'unjust, excessive, and illegal ... evincing a total disregard for all forms of law... The whole proceedings were so irregular as to render all that occurred perfect nullity'. The two Magistrates, perhaps with Davis's connivance, then began systematically to refer to the Supreme Court even the most trivial offences.

The ensuing public and unsavoury squabble, one of the more scandalous of that series of atrabilious disputes which were periodically to rock Hong Kong's administration and society, remains perhaps unequalled in its vituperation in colonial records. Davis wrote to the Colonial Office in indignation: 'It will never do to have two plenipotentiaries in China, one doing justice to our ally [China], and the other immediately undoing it.' As long as Hulme was in his post, the English in Guangzhou 'would feel they can shoot the Chinese with impunity'. In his mind there was no turning back. He had to get rid of the Chief Justice. A letter to the Secretary of State for the Colonies in London put his point of view officially; another, to Lord Palmerston, privately alleged that Hulme was a habitual drunkard. Palmerston sent this letter to Lord Grey (the Colonial Secretary), despite its private nature. Grey, although the letter was private and not addressed to him, insisted that the charges were too serious to pass without public notice. He ordered Davis to allow Hulme the chance to refute them. Davis, who had never intended to bring Hulme's bibulous proclivities into the open, merely to use their existence privately to back up his case for getting rid of him, was completely nonplussed. He resigned in August 1847 but had to stay on as Governor.

On Hulme's side of the affair there was a background animosity of an equally personal and petty kind. He and his family had taken passage to Hong Kong in the same ship as Davis, and when the whole party had to change vessels at Bombay, the *Spiteful* which was to take them onward was found to be too small to accommodate the Judge and his family as well as the Governor and his suite. Hulme had to follow in another ship which he said cost him an extra £250. Doubtless that rankled alongside the later encounters with Davis's disdain of a community whose sympathies were all with Hulme.

The public enquiry was held in November 1847 in an atmosphere dangerously charged. Davis had little to do with it and the proceedings were perfunctory and irregular. There were three specific charges against Hulme: that at a public entertainment on 22 November 1845 aboard the flagship HMS *Agincourt* in Hong Kong harbour, he was in such a state of intoxication as to attract public attention; that on 23 July 1846 in the house of Major-General D'Aguilar, the Commander-in-Chief, he was intoxicated and unable to look after himself; and that he was a habitual drunkard. D'Aguilar, believing the Englishman's home to be his castle, sprang to the defence. Two members of the Executive Council, before which the hearing was held, who were called to give evidence against Hulme were therefore both his accusers and his judges; other witnesses were no longer in Hong Kong. Hulme explained his unsteady gait on the precarious grounds of his varicose veins. The outcome was that he was judged guilty of the first but innocent of the second and third charges. He was suspended from office. He left Hong Kong in the following month in a blaze of glory, replete with a gold snuff box and testimonials from the citizenry, firecrackers, and libations of champagne. Davis appointed his secretary, W. T. Mercer, in Hulme's place.

But that was not to be the last of Hulme. The Colonial Office (with some wisdom) declared the charges against him not proven. Hulme returned to the colony, to the great satisfaction of Hong Kong society.

The Compton affair and other 'indignities' suffered by the British at the hands of the Chinese at Guangzhou, and the arrival of a dispatch from London, dated 12 January 1847, urging the punishment of the Chinese guilty of such 'outrages', put Davis on his mettle. The Secretary of State assured him that:

the British government will not tolerate that a Chinese mob shall with impunity maltreat British subjects . . . and that, if the Chinese Authorities will not . . . punish and prevent such outrages, the British government will be obliged to take the matter into their own hands.

Davis seems to have taken this almost as a declaration of war. Eitel opines that he 'lost his head completely'. And certainly the champion of fair dealing for the Chinese now embarked on a strange course. Davis persuaded his Commander-in-Chief, D'Aguilar, secretly to reconnoitre the defences of the forts guarding the mouth of the Zhu Jiang. Finding that they were virtually unmanned, he mobilized a force of 1,000 men and on the morning of 2 April 1847 three naval vessels and a chartered steamer, with the Governor and the Major-General on board, set out for the Bogue. They took the forts and sailed up-river. The following day they landed the troops at Guangzhou.

After an interval, perhaps required to regain some composure at this totally unexpected turn of events, Qiying met Davis. The ensuing exchange of letters between them affirms what was demanded by Davis and what conceded by Qiying. Eitel, unjustly, states that Qiying 'as usual satisfied [Davis] with empty promises'. In fact certain privileges were accorded to the British at Guangzhou, and Qiying did indeed mete out punishment to the various Chinese involved in assaults on British subjects there. His was a strong and subtle hand and he played it well, for he knew that short of all-out war the British could not impose their will in any but minor ways.[7] Qiying's policy was based on this. In one sense, however, Davis had won his private war and gained at least on paper the result that the British government wanted.

Davis, an isolated figure, sincere, often misguided in practical matters, seldom deigning to consult informed or popular opinion, surprised when he found himself in an erudite minority of one, must have found his last months in Hong Kong a disappointing end to a frustrating term of office. The obloquy accorded him was all but unanimous — and was clearly demonstrated when he presented a cup for an event at Happy Valley racecourse, a race for which not a single horse was entered.

To an extent he was unjustly maligned. His was not the fault that trade declined, but the community blamed him for it. His achievements in putting the colony's administrative structure on a firmer basis were overlooked. He was too much the scholar to find acceptance among that raw community in Hong Kong. And at his going the community pointedly ignored him. The comment in *The Friend of China* echoed popular opinion. 'Never, surely, in the Heavens above, or in the earth beneath, or in the waters under the earth, did there ever exist, embodied or disembodied, such a pleasant little gentleman as Sir John Davis.' If the sarcasm is laboured, the message is loud and clear. Another paper preferred a more direct approach, stating that the Governor evidently preferred to walk out rather than to be kicked out.

Sir John, however, went on to an illustrious career in Chinese studies, founding a scholarship at Oxford for the study of the language, and receiving a baronetcy in 1876. He died at the age of 95.

6. *Early Victoria — Fabric and Society*

FEW substantial accounts of what Hong Kong was like as a place at the time of Davis's departure have survived. Perhaps few were written. Murdoch Bruce, Inspector of Buildings since Pottinger's time and a draughtsman of considerable accomplishment, has left among his other work a delightful picture of Spring Gardens in Wanchai (where there is still a lane of that name). The pillared verandahs of the houses face the harbour and boats drawn up at the quay, with Jardine's godowns in the distance. Women and children seem just to have landed and are talking to a bowing Chinese while another lady walks her dog. Not a whiff of opium sullies the air. We are far from the stews of Taipingshan and from the disorderly disputes of antagonistic civil servants. This, on the surface, is a politer world.

The mild and learned missionary, James Legge, who served in Hong Kong for 40 years, losing his wife and four of his six children to its endemic fevers, gave an account of the place as it was during the time of Davis. 'The hillsides now occupied by the graceful terraces of our city then presented a very different appearance...'. From a little to the west of Possession Point 'the streets running down from [Hollywood Road] to the Queen's Road, were ... indicated in rudimentary fashion... Eastward there was little but a naval store and tents and huts peopled by the 55th Regiment'. East of that:

> all was blank to the bluff where the civil hospital rises... On the other side of the road were some godowns... The next European buildings were Gibb, Livingstone & Co's premises, enclosed within a ring fence ... where partners and employees still managed to reside.

Running up the sides of the Peak were

> thread-like paths with a Chinese house here and there, but the ground was mainly boulder and sandy gravel. Turning to the west where Wellington Street turns into Queen's Road you could see a few Chinese houses, and Jervois Street was in the

course of formation, [the houses to the north of it] having the waters of the bay [harbour] washing about among them.

From there eastward, Legge continues,

on to Pottinger Street, Queen's Road was pretty well lined with Chinese houses; the Central Market was formed; and on the other side were some foreign stores and a tavern or two. Looking up Pottinger Street you could see the Magistracy and the Gaol of the day [where later buildings with the same functions stand today] where the dreaded Major Caine presided.

Eastward a little:

a few English merchants had established themselves, and . . . the Commercial Inn was a place of great resort on the west of D'Aguilar Street, not then so named . . . and just opposite it was a small house called the Birdcage out of which was hatched the Hong Kong Dispensary. All the space between Wyndham Street and Wellington Street was garden ground [with a house belonging to Mr Brain of Dent and Company]. That great firm had its headquarters where the Hongkong Hotel now is [where Central Building now stands]. On the Parade Ground [site of the present Hilton Hotel] was a small mat building . . . the Colonial Church: about where the Cathedral and Government Offices now stand [and still do] were the unpretending

Lieut. Walford Thomas Bellairs, RN (*c.*1794–1850), pictured the young settlement of Victoria in June 1846.

An English school artist painted the same scene in the late 1840s.

Government Offices of that early time and the Post Office. Far up might be seen a barracks, out of which have been fashioned the present Albany residences [today's high-rise building still bears that name], and beyond the site of the present Government House was a small bungalow where Sir Henry Pottinger and Sir John Davis after him held court... On the right was the General's House, looking much as it does now [Flagstaff House, as it was later named, remained the residence of Commanding Officers until a century after Legge was speaking, and later became the Museum of Tea Ware].

The missionary goes on: 'Following the bend of the road ... we came to Spring Gardens.' Then eastward there was 'little Morrison Hill' where the Education Society 'was in vigorous action'.

Arrived at the Happy Valley there were to be seen only fields of rice and sweet potatoes ... and on the heights above it were rising two or three houses built by Mr Mercer of Jardine, Matheson & Co. All those proved homes of fever and death, and were soon abandoned. Beyond the valley ... came the offices of the great firm [Jardine's] with workmen still busy about them.[1]

The Revd James Legge, the distinguished Scottish-born missionary and Chinese scholar, shown here with his assistants.

A glance at the maps opposite shows decisively how the pattern of Hong Kong's central area was thus haphazardly formed and how the plan of the late-twentieth-century city has scarcely changed in basic layout.

A radically different view of Hong Kong at this time is to be found in one of the two reports by Martin, the Colonial Treasurer, which Davis treated lightly but was later forced to reconsider. The climate was unhealthy, he wrote, the nature of the terrain would prevent the growth of a sizeable town, the decomposing granite on which the place stood gave out fetid odours productive of disease, the mandarins prevented respectable Chinese from coming to Hong Kong. The conditions for commercial prosperity were absent, and in any case the harbour was filling up with silt. 'I have in vain sought for one valuable quality . . . I can see no justification for the British government spending one shilling on Hong Kong.'

The British government, from time to time, then and later, was half-inclined to agree. The Colonial Office wrote in Davis's time that 'the mercantile body have altogether mistaken the object of Great Britain in the occupation of Hong Kong . . . [a place that] except for the security of commerce is unnecessary'.

The population of this 'unnecessary' place at the annexation had been estimated (in May 1841) at 7,450 villagers and fishermen. By October of that year local papers were suggesting that it had risen to 15,000. In mid-1845 the Clerk to the Magistrate's Court, Samuel Fearon, reported that the first six months of the Registration Ordinance showed a total of 23,817 persons in various categories (see Appendix 3).

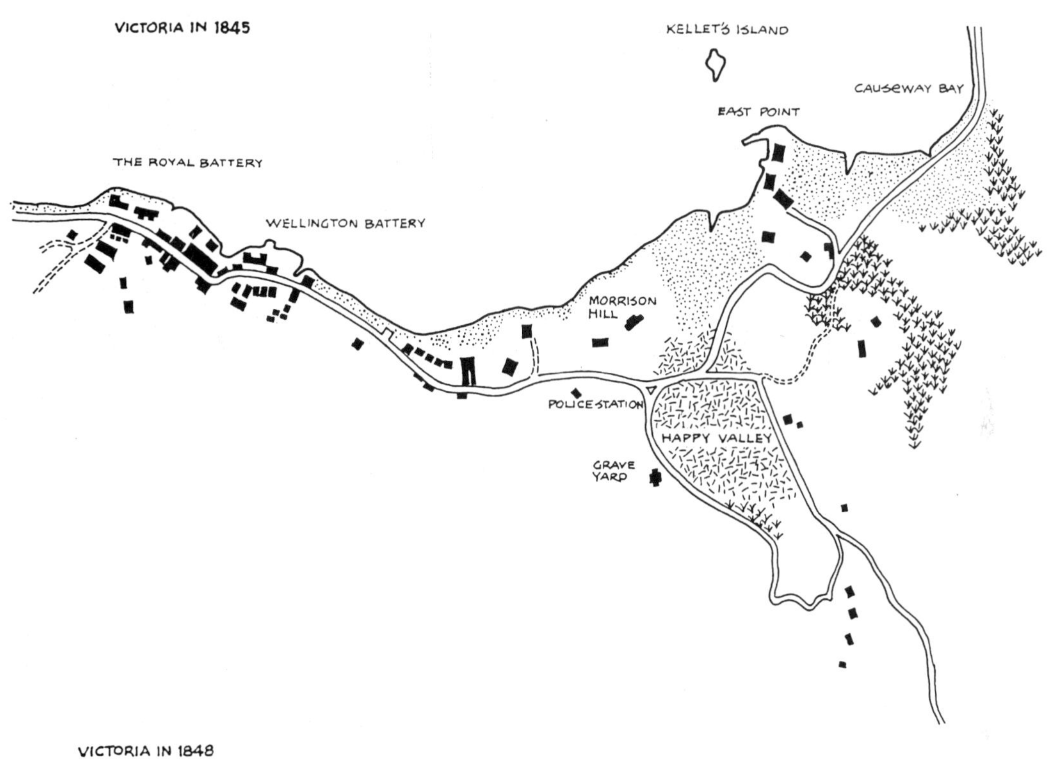

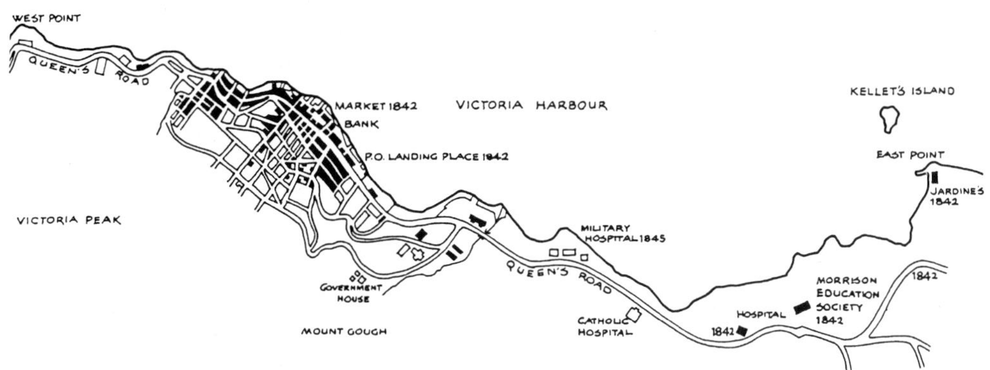

3. Victoria in 1845 and 1848. From the haphazard scatter of buildings in the first few years of the settlement, a pattern of streets has taken shape. Major changes to the pattern took place only as later reclamations were made.

Fearon noted that British occupation had brought thousands of Chinese to Hong Kong, the majority Hakka, whom he describes as 'careless of moral obligations, unscrupulous, unrespected'. Such snap judgements made by Westerners are a constant feature throughout the history of the colony. They were made by men with no knowledge of the Chinese language, only the haziest idea of the structure of Chinese society, and almost no knowledge of the fundamentals of Chinese belief and custom: yet they were all automatic 'China experts' on setting foot in the colony. Their pronouncements were seldom consonant with the facts, and even more rarely in line with the opinions of people who understood the Chinese language and dealt face to face with the people so casually condemned.

One conclusion to be drawn from the population figures is that a great influx of Chinese immigrants occurred soon after the British arrived, but no estimate of turnover of the population is attempted. The population statistics reveal a startling preponderance of males over females in all sections of the community. Other figures spell out the context of life in a settlement under active construction. One report of 1844 mentions 100 houses being built, and in the 1845 Registrar's report the number of stone and brick buildings is put at 264 European and 436 Chinese, which allows more deductions to be made, given the large number of Chinese and the few foreign residents. Shortage of accommodation had prompted Pottinger to build housing for his principal officials (the Albany, mentioned by Legge), to which the Colonial Office objected. Future officials were to fend for themselves like the rest of the community — a source of conflict since they had not the means of earning the sums common among the merchants.

Government House when Davis had arrived was still the suite of three rooms by the Record Office, hastily erected for the reception of Qiying after the Treaty of Nanjing. Noting this, he wrote to Lord Stanley:

> No residence at present exists for the Governor . . . beyond a detached ground floor of two or three rooms . . . Behind this is another . . . in which the Private Secretary sleeps. The inconvenience as well as the unhealthiness of such an abode might tempt me to incur an outlay of more than £10,000 on account of a Government House, according to a plan . . . now preparing: but I feel great reluctance to proceed on this without Your Lordship's approval, and until the lapse of this summer shall have determined whether the sickness and mortality of last year proceeded from . . . the public residence having been fixed on the north side of the ridge of which this island consists.

He toyed with the idea of moving the town to the southern shores which might prove more salubrious, but there was no deep water for a harbour there. Soon he moved up the hill to what had been Johnston's house, at one time rented by Pottinger. This was a two-storey building with large rooms

The formal reception of Qiying, the Chinese Imperial Commissioner, by the British authorities in Hong Kong in November 1845 (left to right, as inscribed on the painting): 'The Honble F. M. Bruce; Major Caine, Chief Magistrate; Lord Cochrane, ADC; M. General D'Aguilar; attendant Mandarin; Keying [Qiying] (quite unworthy of him); Chaou Chongling, Keying's Secretary; Mr Gutzlaff, Interpreter; Sir John Dent; Adml. Sir Thomas Cochrane; Capt. B. Tung, Prefect of Canton; attendant Mandarin'. Inscriptions for two further figures are missing from the right-hand margin.

and a verandah round three sides. In August 1844 he wrote to Stanley: 'My own present residence (lately the Land Office) is quite commodious enough to enable me to dispense with any other one until order shall be received from home for its erection, but the actual condition of the public offices' might necessitate permanent ones being built soon.

The plan for a Government House which Davis received did not please him, and he thought little of its draughtsman, the Surveyor-General Gordon.[2] In May 1845 he submitted to London that 'the principal remaining sources of extraordinary expenditure are the church, the Government offices and court of justice, and the Governor's residence — which last I am quite content to postpone until all others are completed'.

By the autumn of 1846 tenders were finally called for both Government House and government offices. The Commander-in-Chief, who had been building at his own expense, moved into his handsome Head Quarter (later Flagstaff) House. Davis then appears to have given up, as did the Colonial Office. In March 1847 the required buildings had all been finished except a court house and Government House. With those exceptions Government Hill, as it came to be called (flanking what is now Garden Road), was substantially complete from the parade ground at its lower end up through the site of the government offices to the Government House site.

St John's Cathedral, the Parade Ground with troops drilling.

Under Davis a start had been made on roads, even if they were rudimentary and after rain frequently impassable. Little more than paths, they wandered over the hills to Aberdeen and Stanley, and west towards the military camp at Sai Ying Pun. The eventual aim was to construct a ring road around the island. Once roads reached the various villages, police stations were built in the more important ones — Aberdeen and Stanley. A cemetery had been laid out on the western side of Happy Valley in 1845 with a small chapel. The prison that had been put up was quite inadequate for the number of prisoners, with only 15 cells, and from it the chain gang emerged at dawn to work on road-building.

While crime was one continuing bane of the colony, another was disease. The annual summer fever epidemics varied in severity, giving the place an evil name. The year 1843 was particularly bad, one regiment losing 100 men between June and mid-August. A Committee of Public Health was set up but it achieved little. With such a flurry of construction, some essential drainage was installed and after this there were years when fever, malarial and other, was a less serious killer. It was universally believed that its cause was the combination of heat and offensive smells — a thesis which hot, watery Happy Valley's death toll appeared to confirm. Its paddy fields having proved so unfavourable to health, the early houses there were soon empty. The siting there of the cemetery was perhaps an unconscious comment on the insalubrious location. By 1846 the rice farmers were bought out, the valley drained, and the chain gang set to build a road around it for recreational purposes.

One of the first Western institutions the foreigners brought to China was the hospital. An American ophthalmic surgeon, Dr Peter Parker, had established one at Guangzhou in 1835 which proved popular — he even prescribed a truss for Lin Zexu's hernia. In Hong Kong a Parsee merchant named Herjeebhoy Rustomjee offered $12,000 for the construction of a seamen's hospital, but in the fragile state of Hong Kong trade he became bankrupt before he had paid up. Later, in 1844, several commercial companies got together with subscriptions and a hospital was built on high ground near Morrison Hill. Davis had been refused a Colonial Surgeon on the grounds that only if 'private benevolence' proved insufficient could such an appointment be made. But a Dr A. Anderson was employed to treat the police and lower-grade government servants.

The beginnings of Western-style education may be traced to the transfer from Macau to Hong Kong of the Morrison Education Society School whose aim was to gain converts to Christianity by this means. The results were mixed. In part, the requirement of absorbing a Christian ethic in place of the traditional Chinese one tended to create a class of Chinese who, when they grew up, were inclined to despise their fellow men, whom they began to see (as Westerners at the time did) as inferior beings. The School principal, the Reverend Samuel Brown, noted that he had 'overheard students who had noticed an instance of "falsehood and low cunning" among Chinese, say with a look of disgust, "this is Chinese"'.[3] He had begun the process of Westernization that was to produce a group of Chinese whose superficial understanding of the West and of the English language fitted them for the mostly minor jobs in Western businesses which they filled with such acumen. Brown wrote:

> To have a class of young Chinese men on whom we may depend for truth, even though partially educated, living among us in our public and private office, will assuredly be worth to the community all their educational costs. Nor will it be to our comfort and advantage alone, for such a class will influence others that have not enjoyed equal advantages with themselves.[4]

These solemn predictions were fulfilled in the future when just such young Chinese were to succeed (if unintentionally) in the task not of evangelizing China but of introducing revolutionary ideas from the West. What in effect happened was the implantation of the idea in impressionable Chinese minds that China — Chinese civilization — lacked some ingredient of crucial value which only Western philosophy and religion could supply. It was inferred that the duty of those 'enlightened' Chinese was to pass that knowledge on. They did. A century of Western influence, sacred as well as secular, was to mould the Chinese and segments of China in ways that the Reverend Brown could not have envisaged and would have deeply disliked.

Accounts of Hong Kong in the 1840s reveal a community divided into virtually non-communicating groups. The few scores of wealthy traders formed one such exclusive group of Westerners. They had little or nothing in common with other groups save that they all had to exist on a smallish island with few recreational outlets. They had little inclination for mingling with the Chinese although some had Chinese mistresses. There was a small but growing group of poor whites, mostly seamen who had settled in Hong Kong, characterized by Endacott in a resounding phrase as 'the off-scourings of the port', who made a living as best they could and tended to marry or live with Chinese women in Chinese residential areas, all but totally cut off from intercourse with other Westerners. A large Parsee community kept itself to itself and had its own graveyard at West Point. Other Indians formed a tight group. And by Europeans and others the large Chinese community was treated with the thoughtless contempt due to people seen as natural inferiors. Hong Kong resembled some outlandish ant-heap inhabited by several species who closely resembled each other anatomically, but whose customs and habits inclined them to ignore each other most of the time so as to perform their separate functions — one dominant but numerically small species having the means to inflict its will on the others, who had little means of retaliation.

The Chinese were subject to laws which discriminated against them. Forbidden to go out of doors after nine in the evening unless bearing written permission, they were required even then to carry lanterns to signal their presence. The first Bishop of Victoria, the Right Reverend George Smith, on an exploratory visit in 1844–6, expressed his view that the colony was quite unsuited to his intended missionary plans. Westerners, he wrote, were hated for their 'moral improprieties and insolent behaviour', which he saw even in their conduct in the streets. The Chinese, whose behaviour he also castigated, were 'treated as a degraded race of people'.[5]

In the Hong Kong of those years could be seen in microcosm the beginning of what was to become 'the European century in China'. The macrocosm of great China brought, to use a Victorian phrase, to its knees, began with the insistent Western traders at Guangzhou and their demonstration of power in the annexation of Hong Kong and the exacting of treaties whose terms the West dictated at gunpoint. The passivity of the Chinese response was in part a traditional reaction to what could not be avoided, and in part the seizing of the opportunity to co-operate with the foreigners as a means of self-advancement. Thus the Chinese who most successfully understood the needs and ways of the foreigners became the most successful in financial terms, and often the leaders of Chinese society in places such as Hong Kong and the Treaty Ports.

With legitimate trade in the doldrums since it was confined to the Treaty Ports, Hong Kong got off to a shaky start. To offset this, traffic in opium became the mainstay along with the smuggling of salt (an imperial monopoly in China), and of tea. Davis had written in 1845 that Chinese small boats came in numbers loaded with cargoes of tea which had not passed through the Chinese customs.

Since it was a free port there are no reliable figures for trade at this time, no record being kept on a colony-wide basis of imports and exports. While the Harbourmaster kept shipping returns, these are no more than indications of trading volume (see Appendix 4). Ships called at Hong Kong for reasons other than trade — for the latest information on conditions in the area, for water, food, and other stores. All were included in the lists.

British exports to Hong Kong were largely beer, gin, wines, earthenware, cotton goods, coal, meat, and iron bars. From India imports were mostly opium and cotton. The export of British manufactured goods via Hong Kong to China was less by about half a million dollars in 1850 than the 1844 figure. Chinese consumption of opium increased from 28,508 chests in 1842 to 43,075 in 1849. By 1850 a memorandum from the Governor noted that at least three-quarters of the entire Indian opium crop from 1845 to 1849 was off-loaded at Hong Kong and re-shipped from there, most of the foreign vessels proceeding empty up the coast to engage in lawful trading at Shanghai, Tianjin, and Ningbo. On their return journeys they bypassed Hong Kong, one inducement being that at Huangpu island up the Zhu Jiang there were facilities for repair, whereas Hong Kong had none until the construction of the Lamont Dock at Aberdeen in 1857.

On the whole, trade remained sluggish until the end of the decade, when a turn came in the economic tide. One factor was an increase in the river steamer trade with Guangzhou which offered faster transport and insurance for cargoes carried in the safety of large steamers. Another factor was the discovery of gold in California in 1848 and the 'gold rush' which, along with the cataclysm of the Taiping Rebellion (1850–64) in China, sent waves of the homeless and starving to join the immigrants to America. Passage money for the Chinese at $50 a head was paid to the owners of ships and consignees in Hong Kong, materially assisting the economy.

As a result of large numbers of Chinese taking up residence on the other side of the Pacific, demand arose there for Chinese goods of many kinds, and ships began to be loaded with such commodities as rice, ginger, and other foodstuffs, as well as Chinese furniture and other household goods destined for the United States. The first reports of vessels with such cargoes came from the Harbourmaster in 1849, rising from 23 in that year to 34 in 1852.

In the wake of massive upheavals as the Taiping forces swept through wide areas of southern and central China, the Chinese population of the colony grew rapidly. From 1853 to 1855 the numbers rose from 39,017 to 72,607. There was even a transitory period when, to escape the Taiping threat to Guangzhou, the junk trade of that port transferred itself to Hong Kong. Through all this, smuggling became ever more extensive and intensive due to the paralysis of the Chinese Imperial Customs. A downturn in this boom occurred when the Taiping armies cut through the great tea-growing and silk-producing areas of China disrupting production for a time.

A Select Committee of Parliament set up in 1847 'to enquire into the present state of the commercial relations between Great Britain and China' produced a report whose preamble made the point that so far as Hong Kong was concerned no great commercial advantage had been achieved. Rather, the treaty stipulations opening the Treaty Ports, thus encouraging shipping to sail directly to them and bypass Hong Kong, debarred it from performing its function as an entrepôt to the region. Hong Kong also 'appears to have laboured under other [disadvantages], created by a system of monopolies . . . and petty regulations, peculiarly unsuited to its position and prejudicial to its progress'. These had been the result of action taken to maintain security and order 'in the midst of a vagabond and piratical population' and also from an intent to raise revenue for the maintenance of its civil government. The report thought this to be contrary to the true interests of the settlement. 'Nor do we think it right,' the report stated, 'that the burden of maintaining that which is rather a post of general trade . . . than a colony in the ordinary sense, should be thrown in any great degree on the merchants or other persons who may be resident upon it.' A revision of the administrative structure was advised. The report also criticized the predicament of the Governor, responsible to the Colonial Office as Governor, and to the Foreign Office as Plenipotentiary and Superintendent of Trade.

The merchants were mollified by the implied agreement with their anger over the vague nature of the initial land tenure agreements, which seemed to point to there having been a breach of faith. Another important recommendation was that 'a share in the administration of the ordinary and local affairs of the island should be given by some system of municipal government to the British residents'. And they were reminded that the best interests of commerce between Britain and China would be served 'by studying a conciliatory demeanour'. The formerly disgruntled merchants were pleased, viewing the report as heavy censure of Davis's policies.

Most of Hong Kong's inbuilt inadequacies and problems, natural and man-induced, had by this time reared their contentious, implacable, unlovely heads in a society frequently, and singularly, at odds with itself. The colony was more than ready for a new Governor.

7. *Governor Bonham*

It was in the baleful grip of economic stringency that Sir Samuel George Bonham began his six-year governorship of Hong Kong. All who were connected with the colony — whether in the Colonial and Foreign Offices in London, in Parliament where the Hong Kong vote had to be annually approved, in India where the funds of the administration were largely dependent on the sale via Hong Kong of opium, or in the merchants' houses and ruling circles of the colony itself — all knew by the end of Davis's reign and the arrival of Bonham in March 1848 that the economy was in exceedingly poor shape. It was no longer possible to see Hong Kong in that hopeful light mostly thrown on its prospects in years past, and there were few who now felt the colony was a viable entity. One significant point came in December 1848 when 130 persons returned their landholdings. Forty-nine were speculative, but the remaining 76 belonged to genuine buyers despondent at the failure of the bright prospect of former years. The present was uncertain, the future opaque. The revenue from land dropped by one-fifth.

It was said at the time that if Hong Kong were to receive an angel as governor it would still be dissatisfied. Bonham, no angel, managed however by means of a cordial, outgoing nature to be its first popular Governor. A Frenchman of the time described him as a bon vivant who performed his function *tranquillement*. He combined that aspect with the caution, prudence, and disinclination to do anything imaginative which characterize the more conformist British civil servants. Whitehall, for once, seemed to have made the right choice.

Born in 1803, son of a captain in the East India Company's Maritime Service, Bonham was given a legal training before leaving for the East to join the Company's administrative arm. By 1837, barely 34 years old, he was Governor of the Straits Settlements, Singapore, Malacca, and Penang. A decade later he was appointed to Hong Kong and set out, honoured with the Order of the Bath. As his career demonstrated, Bonham was not lacking in talent, but perhaps his meteoric rise reflected more the punctilious carrying out of Whitehall's orders than real brilliance. Eitel calls him 'this model Governor ... of the Colony',[1] but Endacott offers as comment only that he

Sir Samuel George Bonham — a contemporary photograph which catches something of the Governor's character.

had 'a nice sense of what was better left alone'.[2] Palmerston thought Bonham's 'practical common sense'[3] was his chief quality. Taken together, these sentiments sum up not only the man but his work in the colony.

He arrived, in stark contrast to the exit of Davis, to cheers from the community. His first priority, one which was to remain a major preoccupation, was to implement the decisions of the 1847 Select Committee. Inherent in any solution he might discover for the problems it posed was the financial crisis. Without financial stability nothing could be tackled in a realistic manner. The gravity of the situation emerged in the first summer of Bonham's time when revised estimates showed even less revenue and higher expenditure than had been anticipated. This forced a request to London for funds, to which Earl Grey, Secretary of State, responded by pointing out that the Hong Kong vote had already gone through at £25,000 and that was all that could be sent. Expenditure would have to be cut 'at whatever inconvenience'. He insisted on a 'rapid diminution in the parliamentary vote in future years'. The colony, in short, would have to pay its own way.

To make matters worse, the Board of Audit for the colonies now discovered expenditure of £23,000 in Hong Kong's early days which had never been accounted for — Elliot and Pottinger having apparently drawn from military funds for government expenses. The ensuing financial tangle took five years to sort out, with an anxious Colonial Office fearing future Hong Kong votes might be in jeopardy. Earl Grey's attitude stiffened further.

In haste, Bonham cancelled all public works other than those in hand. And in a gesture of magnanimity unparalleled in all colonial history, he balanced the budget by delaying payment of his own salary until the following financial year. Little could he have expected the next blow from London. Earl Grey demanded that a rigorous investigation be made into every aspect of expenditure so as to make permanent rules for the better financial management of Hong Kong.

The outcome of Bonham's investigations was a root-and-branch reorganization of the administration, involving the abolition of several positions and combining of two or more others as a single appointment. Thus, the offices of Treasurer, Colonial Surgeon, Surveyor-General, and Assistant Harbourmaster were abolished. The duties of Surveyor-General and Colonial Surgeon were to be performed by military personnel working part time, and the Chief Magistrate was to take on the work of Registrar-General with an increase in salary. The job of Treasurer was to be done by the Colonial Secretary and his salary reduced. The suggestion was made that the Foreign Office might pay one-third of the Governor's salary (for his work as Plenipotentiary). Police expenditure was to be reduced. Bonham described the Judiciary as 'the most overpaid and underworked department' and suggested stinging cuts in salaries. Not surprisingly, some officers at once resigned on account of their now uncertain future.

In the outcome, the post of Treasurer was not abolished, and the Colonial Secretary's job was combined with that of Auditor. The able Registrar-General succumbed to the lure of the Californian gold rush of 1848 but was soon back in Hong Kong, down on his luck. Many of Bonham's drastic cuts in manpower, which were to take place as the posts fell vacant, proved unnecessary.

Bonham then tackled the military. His basic concept was that 1,200 men forming six companies of British and three companies of Ceylon Rifles would be a sufficient garrison, its senior officer a colonel whose salary would be less than that of the usual major-general. He had intended to reduce numbers in the Artillery, Engineer, and Ordnance Corps, but such cuts would have meant that his own proposals to use military personnel part time in civil offices would be invalidated.

These swingeing cuts had the desired result. The expenditure of £62,658 in 1848 plunged to £36,418 in 1853 and, on Bonham's retirement in 1854, to £31,509. The parliamentary grant tumbled from £25,000 in 1848 to £8,500 in 1853. The cost of the army and navy, a charge on the British taxpayer, fell almost as dramatically from £80,778 to £50,346 in the same period. Yet Britain remained dissatisfied at the cost of maintaining Hong Kong. Bonham was seen to have done well, but the colony was regarded as a dubious asset.

As he took measures to alleviate Hong Kong's financial problems, Bonham began to implement the Select Committee's wish to straighten out the tricky question of land. The mercantile community had pointed out how unjust was the 'questionable policy' of making a small part of the community foot the bill for a colony maintained on behalf of all, and of British trade in general. They complained that rents were too high because at the original land auctions too few lots had been offered, causing unwarranted competition for them, rents thereby being driven up. They wanted lower rents on rented property, and revision of lease agreements.

Bonham's response was to set up a Land Committee in 1850 and he asked aggrieved lot-holders to place their claims before it. In spite of the vehemence with which they had made a case to the Colonial Secretary in London, only 11 of them complied. Of those, five had their claims about excessive rents recognized — half of the land involved belonging to the notorious land speculator George Duddell. Eventually the land question burned itself out. Later a single payment secured ownership and an annual 'rate' was set.

On taxation Bonham took the pulse of the people and said no to any fundamental change. The merchants, however, were not satisfied. In January 1849 they sent a petition to Parliament regretting that apart from the land problem, little had been done to implement the directives of the Select Committee, most importantly on the question of giving citizens a say in the affairs of the colony. They again pointed out that since the island was essential for the conduct and protection of the China trade as a whole, the cost of its administration should not fall on them alone. Some sort of jurisdiction should be theirs. But this produced no tangible result.

Bonham, discovering that there were only 23 persons in the colony fit under the property qualification to serve as jurymen, reduced the sum involved from $1,000 to $500. In January 1849 he published a draft ordinance designed to regulate the flogging of prisoners. At this the residents rose up in protest, insisting that flogging was the only means to punish Chinese criminals. Prudently, faced with this unexpected hitch, Bonham mothballed the measure and turned to weightier matters.

He now made an attempt to remove the friction between the Police Magistrates and the Chief Justice which had so inflamed Hulme and cost Davis his last shred of credibility. He created a bench of magistrates to be independent of government, with powers greater than those generally accorded, by establishing a Court of Petty Sessions. This was a failure. The low level of expertise displayed by the Court was not conducive to the aims for which the Court had been set up, and Hulme, the Chief Justice, apparently still sensitive to possible slights to his authority, was unhappy about it. As ever, the groundswell of bitterness and jealousy that seemed as endemic as Hong Kong's fevers took charge of saner councils.

Lord Grey had asked Bonham to suggest two men who would make worthy additions to the Legislative Council. The Governor asked the unofficial Justices of the Peace to nominate two persons, the decision to be officially his own. They were sworn in. He then asked the Justices if they would take control of the Police provided they could raise additional revenue to make up the deficit in the Police rate. They refused. But Bonham was unjustly accused of establishing the Justices, at the stroke of a pen, as a new 'untitled commercial aristocracy'.[4] Hulme was delighted at this failure and remained wary of Bonham. Hulme retired in 1854, replete with a document testifying to the community's high esteem and to his 'undeviating impartiality and uprightness', a commendation which Eitel quotes without comment.[5]

Yet another administrative conundrum, for which no precise model existed in other colonies, was how to deal with a Chinese population often exploited on account of their ignorance of British law, and subject to abuse by their fellow men who secured Supreme Court affidavits, alleging some civil misdemeanour by newly arrived persons, and then extorted money from them. The Chinese petitioned Bonham for permission to settle in their own way those cases in which the participants were all Chinese. The truth of the matter was that the petition was designed to regularize what had for years been fact — no such cases had come before the Supreme Court in the past six years. The thirty thousand or so Chinese residents of the colony were now a force and a voice to be harkened to — their activities accounted for about one-quarter of all trade — and Bonham complied. He put through an ordinance empowering Chinese headmen to settle civil disputes provided that all parties were willing to abide by their decisions. The headmen were to be salaried, the money coming from special rates collected from the Chinese, who were to set the level of such taxes themselves. The ordinance was a voluntary one, to operate only in those Chinese districts which asked for it.

Whatever the cause, the crime rate did fall during Bonham's term of office. The 674 felonies of 1850 dwindled to 471 in 1853. Yet the colony was far from tranquil. Piracy was still an everyday occurrence. A series of engagements between the navy and pirate fleets resulting in naval victory was greeted with great joy in 'commercial circles', their gratitude taking the form of presentation services of silver plate with £200 each to the two captains involved. The pirate menace was, however, not susceptible to eradication at this time, however effective naval action might now and then be.

The Taiping Rebellion, begun in 1850 and not suppressed until 1864, was led by a deluded Chinese who had elaborated his own version of Christianity. The repercussions of the Rebellion in China, whose ravages eventually cost the lives of an estimated twenty million people and the almost total destruction of livelihood in several provinces, made for pandemic lawlessness which spilled over into Hong Kong as it did into other areas of China itself. Bonham, as he left the colony, remarked that 'to suppress [piracy] is impossible without the co-operation of the Chinese government. This . . . I have repeatedly requested without avail'. And in the current lawless state of China he was correct in supposing that it would not be forthcoming.

As ever when trouble erupted in China, the population of Hong Kong swelled. The 1848 total of 21,514 became 39,107 by 1853. And one interesting detail emerged — the percentage of females among the Chinese population grew from one-fifth to one-third, a clear sign that more families were taking up residence in contrast to the former immigrant gangs of male labourers. The European population showed a much smaller increase — from 642 to 776, excluding the armed services. The murder of J. M. F. Amaral, the Governor of Macau, in late 1849 sent a wave of Portuguese flying to the security of Hong Kong. The housing situation for this swelling number of people improved with the construction of more houses, and by 1853 there were 491 European and 2,416 Chinese houses recorded. In the Chinese residential area of Taipingshan the great fire of 28 December 1851 resulted (apart from the tragic casualties) in the clearance of the area, in reclamation of land from the harbour, and in the construction of Bonham Strand, providing more space to build on — a project under the Governor's liberal influence.

As trade gradually improved, confounding the merchants' pessimism, financial retrenchment became less important, permitting the completion on 1 October 1855, to a design by Charles Cleverly, of Government House at a cost of £14,940. But the delays had been so long that Bonham never lived in it. He spent the remainder of his term in Spring Gardens in a house with a 'fine well of spring water'.

The trend towards financial improvement was not, however, accompanied by sustained diminution in another of the colony's hardships — the epidemics of various fevers. Life cannot have been carefree in a community which, in 1848, had a mortality rate from fever among Chinese civilians of 1.14 per cent, among non-European (Indian) troops of 5.14 per cent, and among European military personnel of 20.43 per cent. The next year was better, but in 1850 the European civilian death toll amounted to 10 per cent, and the rate among European troops was 23.94 per cent. Incredible as it may appear, the Colonial Office stubbornly refused money for a hospital for civilians. Bonham, on his own initiative, took a house for the purpose. Disease, fluctuating in severity from year to year, continued sporadically to threaten the life and serenity of the colony.

The presence of the Taiping rebels at Nanjing, where their headquarters had been established in March 1853, cast doubts over the always fragile relationship between China and Hong Kong. Bonham had no intention of exacerbating relations between Beijing and the Tian Wang or Heavenly King (as the leader of the Taiping rebels styled himself) now enthroned at Nanjing. He tried in fact to maintain strict British neutrality. Yet he was anxious to see for himself the realities of the situation. With the backing of the merchant communities of both Hong Kong and Shanghai, he left on HMS *Hermes* in March 1853 for Nanjing. The home government withheld approval.

The Taiping Rebellion in China presented something of a mystery to Westerners in Hong Kong and elsewhere. It had been set off in 1850 by a Chinese who had absorbed a garbled version of Christianity from missionary activities in Guangdong Province. The army which he gathered together, in order to impose his version of the Christian faith on China, was at first well disciplined, but later turned into a scourge, a marauding rabble, looting and killing, razing whole towns as it swept through the country. There was some hope in foreign minds, at least in the beginning, that the Manzhu government might be unseated by this 'Christian' force 'which would be more likely to bring about that moral regeneration of the nation without which China would never fully enter into the comity of nations'. Eitel, whose pronouncement this was, shared the general opinion that the Chinese were uncivilized and that only Christianity could convert them into one of the right-thinking peoples of the world. It was an opinion that powered almost the whole of nineteenth-century Western thinking not only about China but about the rest of the world, and which was responsible for many a bizarre policy.

Bonham went to Nanjing to explain to the Taiping leaders the concept of British neutrality, just as he and others had tried to impress this on the Imperial government of China. The proposition was viewed rather differently by the Chinese who had discovered that such neutrality was non-existent except when it was to British advantage. Bonham discovered in Nanjing that any hope of a stable (far less truly Christian) regime in China in the event of a major Taiping victory over the Imperial Qing government was mere illusion. The Taiping were as anti-foreign and un-Christian as the Manzhu. He returned a wiser man, unfairly castigated by the home government for having gone at all.

The Bonham years, as all agreed when he retired in 1854 at the age of 50, had proved much better than those of Davis. Trade had picked up with the discovery of gold in California and Australia, Chinese immigrants to both areas passing through Hong Kong, and the depredations of the Taiping rebellion produced a continuing flood of immigrants to the territory. Japan was just beginning to open up to foreign trade at American prompting, and Hong Kong was now regularly visited by flotillas of square-rigged American whalers. An ice-house had been built at the foot of a street in central Victoria, to the gratification of Westerners boiling in their heavy Victorian British clothing in the heat of the colony's summers. Ice came from Alaska packed in straw or sawdust, and was dragged up from the shoreline to the ice-house on Queen's Road where Ice House Street, still so named, met it at the water's edge. Regular steam-ship sailings between Europe and the colony were established, the telegrams they carried from Hong Kong being sent off by wire when the ships reached Trieste or Gibraltar. Yet, oddly enough, this quickening in the pace of communication was not entirely welcomed by the merchants since it also heightened the competition. The formerly leisured life in which fortunes were made in a year or two became marginally more taxing. It now took a decade to make a fortune.

It was during Bonham's time that the Governor's jurisdiction over the consuls in the Treaty Ports, established at the Treaty of Nanjing, was abolished, but the separation of gubernatorial powers from those of Superintendent of Trade was to take several more years.

Bonham was on the whole a reasonable man, and his term of office reflects that. His one curious failing was a firm belief that the study of the Chinese language warped the intellect and undermined the capacity for good judgement. This belief caused him to appoint and promote men who had no knowledge of the language, something hardly conducive to a better understanding of the majority of the colony's inhabitants.

8. Bowring's War with China

THE next Governor of Hong Kong was a man of restless energy, great conceit, and brilliant mind. The complexity of his character was such that he defeated his own cherished ambition — to attain the status of an internationally known and respected figure. An appraisal of his character and career is relevant to the consideration of his work as Governor in early Hong Kong, at a time when governors and their actions exercised a more telling effect on the colony than in later times.

Sir John Bowring was 57 when he first came to the East. He would not have done so but for his ill luck in losing his fortune by injudicious investment in an ironworks which failed in a trade depression, forcing him to seek an income-producing appointment. Bowring had been privately educated and apprenticed to an Exeter merchant, later working in London as a clerk and gaining experience during the course of business journeys to various European countries. He then set up in business for himself and acquired a smattering of various languages,[1] coming to see his role in life in promoting the dominance of 'commerce and Christianity in natural and necessary alliance' — a curiously English nineteenth-century concept.

At 32 he became editor of the *Westminster Review* whose championship of radical views under Jeremy Bentham was much to Bowring's taste. He began making translations from various languages and was awarded a doctorate by Gröningen University in Holland in 1829. Eitel, with some justification, comments: 'to use ... his own epigrammatic critique of Byron ... more could be said of his genius than of his character... His natural abilities were marked by great versatility but appeared to lack in depth'.[2]

Standing for Parliament for Bolton, he was elected in 1841, and took an interest in Hong Kong affairs, perhaps, as Endacott suggests, because his son was with Jardine's. Bowring then took the post of Consul at Guangzhou in 1849, where he seems to have aroused unfavourable comment from the merchants there from the start. His own remarks a little later when he was appointed Governor of Hong Kong bear out the impression of conceit in his character: 'To China I went ... accredited not to Peking alone but to Japan, Siam, China, and Corea, I believe to a greater number of human beings

Sir John Bowring, an engraving by W. Holl from the portrait by Bryan Edward Duppa (*fl.* 1832–53).

(indeed no less than one-third of the human race) than any individual has been accredited before.'[3]

Bowring left Guangzhou on medical grounds and returned to England where he was knighted and secured the governorship of Hong Kong. 'Thus', writes the sarcastic Eitel, 'bearing his blushing honours thick upon him, he sailed to China with the sound of glory ringing in his ears.'

Within a fortnight of his arrival on 13 April 1854, Britain declared war against Russia, and Hong Kong feared that the Siberian fleet might attempt intervention in its waters. Bowring rushed off northward in an effort to intercept the fleet, but this turned out to be a wild-goose chase since the Russians had already departed. Still, fear of sea-borne attack lingered, rising to panic proportions in June 1854 when the Lieutenant-Governor summarized the defenceless state of the colony. Batteries were put up at once. Hong Kong patriots subscribed £2,500, and sent it to London to aid 'the noble struggle against Russian Aggression' in the Crimean War.

The question of separating the governorship from the other functions attached to it arose again at this time, in 1854, a solution being adopted by the Colonial Office in the form of a reprehensible compromise, with Bowring the hapless victim. It was decreed that he was to act as Plenipotentiary and Superintendent of Trade, but to be Governor in name only. William Caine became Lieutenant-Governor with the clear understanding that he and he alone had control over the local colonial administration. To give him his due, Bowring, his salary cut in half, at first tried to make the best of a ludicrous position and, seated as he was in the new Government House, must have felt it keenly. 'I have China, Corea, Siam. I have no time for Hong Kong', he said.

Inevitably it was not long before he began to interfere with Caine's jurisdiction and encountered the latter's justified resentment. When the matter was referred home, Lord Palmerston put an end to the anomalous situation and made Bowring Governor in fact, but with no rise from half pay.

How this came about is worth recording, a typical instance of the way the affairs of the colony turned into acrimonious confrontations between administrators and others. In February 1855 a temporary Colonial Chaplain was appointed in the person of the Revd William Baxter who came out from England. Belatedly it was discovered that he was a fugitive debtor. Bishop Smith refused to countenance him. An army chaplain was then appointed as a stopgap, but Bowring objected, demanding to know who had authorized the appointment. Caine replied that he had first consulted both the Bishop and members of the Executive Council, and presumed Bowring would agree. This precipitated a divergence of opinion about who should preside over the Council — Bowring saying that he should always be chairman, even if what was under discussion related solely to Hong Kong (over which Caine ruled). Palmerston, tardily, saw the position was 'an administrative solecism'. It may perhaps be wondered why he had not seen that in the first instance. Bowring then suggested that Caine should be retired, but Palmerston declined that since Caine had not been the cause of the problem. Caine remained, powerless, in the sinecure post of Lieutenant-Governor until his retirement in 1859.

For a candid look at Bowring's Hong Kong at this time, a certain Albert Smith, an entertainer from London, offers a forthright note. 'To breakfast with Sir John Bowring, walking up pretty winding paths with wild convolvulus and bamboo blooming all the way. Found him in the garden with a native cutting flowers for the table.'[4] Smith had a good eye for his unfamiliar surroundings.

> As we drove along the Happy Valley [we] passed Mr Jardine's at East Point . . . the granite rocks coming nearly down to the sea — water rills falling — Chinese graves and fishing stations all the way. Many people out in carriages, and some Yankees in light iron four-wheeled trotting gigs; and also a string of Mr Jardine's horses led out for airing by black grooms.[5]

Albert Smith continues, remarking that the local 'journals are mostly filled with infinitesimally unimportant local squabbles, in which the names of Mr Anstey, Mr Bridges, Ma-chow-wang, Sir John Bowring, and Mr Caldwell are pitched about here and there'.[6]

Bowring was nothing if not busy. His policy towards China was to result in war, yet in England he had been the vociferous president of the Peace Society, whose aims were the abolition of war and the settlement of international disputes by conciliation. The inherent contradiction between his policies and his philosophy is evident in his attempts to make friends with Hong Kong

Chinese by talking with them in Cantonese, and by attending their parties and theatrical entertainments. At the same time his attitude to problems with the Chinese authorities in China was to approach in summary fashion with the threat of force. Yet he tried to be fair to all, rescuing a wrongfully imprisoned British subject from the Chinese, and being conspicuously even-handed to Chinese involved in Consular Court cases at Guangzhou. The Hong Kong Chinese thought him fair-minded and often tried to enlist his services. But he combined mildness towards them with total inflexibility when it came to the slightest infraction of the treaties between Britain and China.

Bowring's instructions on China were to avoid the use of force: yet he was ready with threats to get his way in a situation which he must have known had existed ever since the treaties were signed. This concerned British nationals in Guangzhou. In theory they had freedom of movement there, but were often molested, sometimes on account of their own high-handed attitude to the Chinese; and their right of residence had now and then been denied. As Governor, Bowring dealt with the Imperial Commissioner Yeh Mingchen, to whom he wrote on 17 April 1854 (four days after his arrival in Hong Kong) requesting a meeting.[7] Yeh replied on 25 April that he would be glad to see Bowring but that military campaigns were taking all his time. On the same day Bowring wrote again to the Commissioner, saying that he had been instructed to revise the Treaty of Nanjing, to gain entry to Guangzhou, to obtain the abolition of the tea commission, to establish regular meetings with Chinese officials, to lease land for merchants in Henan, and to obtain redress for Britons attacked by Chinese. He insisted that meetings be held in Yeh's *yamen* (official residence). Two days later he wrote again, to the effect that such meetings should take precedence over Yeh's military affairs. And on the following day he wrote once more urging payment of the debt of a Chinese to an Indian merchant. On 7 May Yeh replied that he could not force the people of Guangzhou to admit foreigners into the city; that the tea commission was introduced not by his government but by foreign tea merchants; that leasing land should be agreed between the parties concerned; that Chinese officials were not trying to avoid foreign envoys. He promised to write separately on the proposed meeting. In a separate letter on the same day Yeh proposed to meet the Governor on 22 May outside Guangzhou. The furious pace of this correspondence was one set by Bowring.

This situation continued until an incident, in itself trivial, brought war. The makings of the trouble were simple. Chinese owners of ships who were lessees of Crown Land in the colony were allowed, under an ordinance of 1855, the protection of the British flag as if their ships were British-owned. To achieve this all they had to do was to inscribe the names of their vessels on the colonial register. Not surprisingly, with piracy rife, many did so. One of these ships was the lorcha *Arrow*, Chinese-owned and with a British captain. Unfortunately when the incident occurred its registration had expired. When boarded at Guangzhou by the Chinese authorities in the autumn of 1856, the crew were imprisoned, charged with piracy. Typically, the Governor went on the attack at once, on 12 October. He defended the Guangzhou Consul's (Harry Parkes) demand for an apology and the swift return of the crew. He then wrote that, his two-day ultimatum having expired, the navy had taken an imperial junk hostage. On 21 October Yeh replied that no flag was flying when the *Arrow* was boarded, that its crew testified to its Chinese ownership, and that the registration had been bought at Hong Kong. He requested that further sales of registrations should cease, as laid down in the treaty. In a subsequent letter Yeh asked by which section of the treaty was it permissible for the navy to take Chinese ships hostage in the Zhu Jiang.

Sir Harry Parkes, British Consul at Guangzhou, taking his leave of the old Co-hong merchants.

This minor incident was made by Bowring the excuse for hostilities. The real cause was the underlying grievance that the Chinese would not consent to treaty revision. The Treaty of Nanjing in fact contained no clause relating to revision, and the Chinese were entirely within their rights in refusing it. They were, however, foolish not to have learned the lesson taught them by the Royal Navy in previous confrontations.

Bowring saw the affair as his chance to settle once and for all the question of his right to official meetings with Chinese representatives at Guangzhou, and to secure safe entry for British personnel into that city. His advisers, Parkes and Thomas Wade, an interpreter at the Supreme Court trained by Gutzlaff, saw it (and Parkes stated this) as the inevitable conflict between Christian civilization and semi-civilized paganism. Admiral Sir Michael Seymour, Senior Naval Officer, Hong Kong, then bombarded and demolished some Chinese forts and the Commissioner's house in Guangzhou. But Yeh had already moved out. Seymour continued with more bombardments, but Yeh did not give in. He was in a strong position, able to command large reinforcements. Whereupon Bowring's policy was upheld and an expeditionary force was dispatched from England. The force was diverted to deal with the Indian Mutiny, and it was not until the final month of 1857 that Britain, joined by France which had grievances of its own, was ready for war.

In the long interval, a continuous stream of letters passed between Bowring and the properly obstinate Yeh, and between Bowring and the Viceroy of Guangdong-Guangxi. The politeness of the Chinese in their missives is remarkable; they never give an inch and continue stone-walling in diplomatic language, even congratulating Bowring for not assisting the rebels when the Taiping threat to Guangzhou was at its most hazardous.

Palmerston now decided to sever the powers of Plenipotentiary from the governorship of Hong Kong, removing Bowring from the former and sending out Lord Elgin as Plenipotentiary in July 1857. Negotiations with the Chinese were continued by Elgin, totally ignoring Bowring. Guangzhou was taken in early 1858 and the allied forces moved north where a treaty was signed in June at Tianjin. Separate treaties were signed by China with Britain, France, the United States, and Russia. These may, however, be regarded as one settlement because of the operation of the most-favoured-nation clause, by which what China granted to one nation she must grant to others.

The treaties contained provision for the exchange of ministers, granting them right of residence in Beijing, and excusing them from performing the *kowtow*. Foreigners were permitted to travel within China with their passports countersigned by local Chinese authorities; the opening of 10 ports to trade was projected, with foreign ships allowed to trade on the Yangzi (Yangtze River); warships could call at any Chinese port for supplies and repairs; missionaries were to be allowed into China and protected by the Chinese government; British Consuls were to have jurisdiction in disputes between British subjects, while a mixed court of Consul and Chinese Magistrate would settle those between British and Chinese; in criminal cases the accused would be tried under the laws of his own country. Four million taels each were to be paid to Britain and France as reparation (for a war *they* had carried into China). The use of the character *yi* (barbarian) was forbidden.

The signing of the Treaty of Tianjin on 26 June 1858. Lord Elgin is seated centre, and Admiral Seymour is at the table on the right with Gui Liang. He and Hua Shang (left) were Imperial Commissioners.

A supplementary agreement was worked out at Shanghai in October in which, for Hong Kong at least, the most significant change was the imposition of a tariff duty on the importation of opium. In effect this legalized the opium trade, and the hopes of decades of merchants at last became a reality. The duties were to be collected by the newly formed Chinese Maritime Customs Service, established in 1854 and headed by its first Chinese Inspector, the bravely named Horatio Nelson Lay.

The Imperial Commissioner (and stubborn patriot) Yeh met a sad fate. He was captured in the taking of Guangzhou in January 1858 ‘when his apartments were . . . burst into . . . by blue jackets of HMS *Sanspareil* and he was, while climbing over a wall, caught in the strong arms of Sir Astley Cooper Key whilst Commodore Elliot’s coxwain “twisted the august tail of the Imperial Commissioner round his fist”’.[8] The temper of the times implicit in this is evident in the combination of schoolboy glee and the total inability to see the Chinese side of the coin.

Yeh was sent into exile in Calcutta where he died. While in Hong Kong *en route*, Bowring at last had the chance to see him aboard a naval vessel. But Yeh, unbowed in defeat, refused to talk, and the Governor’s little triumph in the meeting rang somewhat hollow. Guangzhou was now governed by a mixed commission consisting of Harry Parkes, the Consul, a Royal Marine officer, a French naval officer, and Governor Pi Chengzhao.

The Chinese refused to ratify the Treaty of Tianjin, an act of foolhardiness as disastrous as it was brave. The treaty made China the plaything of Western political and commercial ambitions. To ratify it was to hand over the country to foreign control. Ratification was only obtained after the Anglo-French occupation of Beijing and the sacking and burning of the Imperial Summer Palace in 1860. The eventual treaty contained yet further provisions favouring the Western powers. Tianjin became a Treaty Port; at Hong Kong, Kowloon Point and Stonecutters island were ceded to Britain in perpetuity, and the recruitment of Chinese labour for work abroad was permitted. The direct gains for Hong Kong were the *de facto* legalization of opium, the acquisition of strategic territory, and the profits which would accrue from the traffic in coolies passing through the colony.

Bowring, lately shorn of his appointment to the millions of whom he had boasted, was now in charge solely of the few thousands in Hong Kong, and the Supreme Court was soon to cease to be the appeal court of British subjects in the Treaty Ports. The post of Superintendent of Trade was given to the British Minister in Beijing.

In the period leading up to the Treaty of Tianjin, Hong Kong was intimately embroiled in the conflict. Bowring, having instituted a policy, found, after the first attack on Guangzhou in November 1856, that he was unable to press it home. Commissioner Yeh perceived Admiral Seymour's withdrawal with his small force as a Chinese victory, and ordered no co-operation with the British. Setting fire to the Guangzhou factories, he also destroyed the port facilities at Huangpu island. And then placards began to blossom in Hong Kong urging the Chinese to struggle against the foreigners.

There can be no doubt of the depth of Chinese resentment. A month or so after this exchange of letters,[9] in January 1857, Westerners eating their fresh breakfast bread, baked by the E Sing Bakery owned by a Chinese named Cheong Ah Lum, became suddenly ill, some of them seriously. It was soon discovered that the cause was a plentiful dosage of arsenic added to the bread. Luckily enough, the quantity was so generous that most people quickly vomited their breakfast and absorbed little of the poison. Prudently, Ah Lum had left with his family for Macau before breakfast. Brought back, he alleged that he too had been poisoned. He was tried and acquitted, but 52 of his employees were thrown into gaol. That facility being temporarily full, their actual destination was a 15-feet-square room in a police station where they were to remain for four days. Ten of them were then tried, but the rest suffered for another 15 days in that Black Hole of Hong Kong before release. It says much for the residents, European and Chinese alike, that their vigorous protests were what secured the prisoners' release, although with the proviso that they leave the colony.

Hundreds more Chinese were deported. The baking of bread was taken over by George Duddell, one of the colony's most devious crooks. Shortly after, his bakery burned down, doubtless on Chinese orders.

The story was not yet ended. William Tarrant, editor of *The Friend of China*, took it upon himself to sue Ah Lum for damages, and was awarded $1,000. Prudence once more prompted the baker to quit Hong Kong before Tarrant could collect his winnings. Not to be cheated, Tarrant then accused Dr T. W. Bridges, the Acting Colonial Secretary, of letting the culprit escape. Bridges then brought a suit for libel against Tarrant who was forced to pay £100 compensation — a sum subscribed by sympathizers. This was the 'infinitesimally unimportant' squabble that Albert Smith read about during his visit.

Before the ratification of the treaty, Hong Kong was a tense place. The poisoning was but one incident heightening the nervousness that people felt and tending to exacerbate the series of public scandals and bouts of outrageous behaviour during the years of Bowring's governorship. One source of dispute was the Attorney-General, T. Chisholm Anstey, a rabid, prejudiced man who seemed incapable of minding his own business and was frequently overcome by the desire to mind others' for them. *The Times*, with commendable restraint, called him 'a man of imperfectly regulated energies'. His first target in Hong Kong was the barrister, Dr T. W. Bridges, whom he indirectly accused of extortion and malpractice. Bridges was a colourful character, a barrister who advertised his services in two brightly coloured signs in English and Chinese outside his office in Queen's Road. He lent money at exorbitant rates of interest, and his chambers were often stacked with goods left as security. Accusations were levelled at him of having had financial dealings, while he was Acting Colonial Secretary, with the man who obtained the opium monopoly at that time. A committee of enquiry found that, while Bridges accepted a 'retaining fee' from the monopolist, this could not be regarded as *cumshaw* — the local term for a bribe.

Escaping once from Anstey's zeal, Bridges was soon implicated in an enquiry into the affairs of Daniel R. Caldwell, Registrar-General and Protector of the Chinese. Caldwell was accused of irregularities in the licensing of brothels, and of consorting with Ma Chow Wong, a notorious informer on pirate activities who in the end turned pirate himself. The scandal of succulent quality which then convulsed colonial society formed another part of the newspaper reports that amused Albert Smith. The commission of enquiry found Caldwell guilty of four of Anstey's 19 charges, yet by some process of chop logic at the same time found that his guilt was not such that he should be dismissed. Nor was guilt sufficient to prevent his continuance as a Justice of the Peace.

The depths to which members of the administration could sink were demonstrated when, during the enquiry, it appeared that documents found at

Ma Chow Wong's house implicated Caldwell, and that these had been burnt by Bridges to whom, conducting an enquiry on Caldwell's behalf, they were taken. Tarrant, irrepressible, offered the opinion in his newspaper that Caldwell had been cleared by deception, by a 'contemptible and dramatic trick on the part of the Government'. For this he was charged with libel. At his trial Bridges admitted having destroyed the papers, and to being a close friend of Caldwell. Tarrant was then acquitted and even managed to extract damages from the government.

Tarrant continued to write of Caine's 'compradoric methods'. Caine, about to leave the colony for good, judged it time to clear his name, instituting proceedings for libel after a 'particularly sharp comment' in *The Friend of China* in August 1859. Shrewdly, Caine retained the services of every barrister in the colony to conduct his defence, forcing Tarrant to conduct his own. Tarrant was found guilty, fined £50, and sent to gaol for a year. But questions about the case were asked in Parliament and his release ordered. He was at once gaoled again for debt to Bridges but once more saved by public subscription. There was no doubt that public sympathy lay with Tarrant. His zeal in upholding the public good, however, was heavily admixed with the desire to sell more copies of his newspaper.

The Times in London summed up the situation in Hong Kong during these days: 'Every official man's hand in Hong Kong was against his neighbour . . . and any attempt to deal in London judicially with these congeries of intrigues, accusations, and animosities must fail.' With a nice turn of wit, the Colonial Secretary, Bulwer Lytton, when asked in the Commons to lay the papers dealing with the accusations on the table, replied that he 'shrank from the responsibility . . .'. He 'would rather lay the table on them'. They revealed, he said, 'hatred, malice, and uncharitableness in every possible variety and aspect' of Hong Kong life.

How much of this profound social disarray was to be traced to the tensions and unease generated by the situation *vis-à-vis* the Chinese, and how much to the inability of Bowring to take firm control of his administration, must remain a matter for argument; but assuredly the Governor was at odds with the majority sentiment in the colony. The legislation he introduced affecting the Chinese conflicted sharply with the liberal sentiments he expressed at other times. The need to cope with a situation which he had basically failed to control caused him to over-react, and this in turn induced popular counter-reaction of some strength.

Bowring had plans to add an elected element to the Legislative Council by giving the vote to holders of Crown Land, irrespective of race, who were paying a minimum of £10 annual rent. In public works his schemes were ambitious and included the reclamation of land and construction of a praya at Happy Valley. He pieced together the ground for the Botanical Gardens up the hill from Government House for public recreation. His schemes for the education of poorer Chinese were far ahead of his time, and he recognized that the needs of 'a large population of children of native mothers by foreigners of all classes' were 'beginning to ripen into a dangerous element out of the dunghill of neglect. They seem to be wholly uncared for.'

Bowring turned to the problem posed by extortion and illicit fees, setting up a commission. But immediately the fact had to be faced that those who paid such fees to obtain access to officials were quite unwilling to come forward and disclose details of any actual case. Bowring had, in this, to admit defeat. 'We rule in ignorance,' he remarked, 'they obey in blindness.' And with that pretty epigram he perforce shelved the question. The cadet training scheme[10] would, he felt sure, in the fullness of time produce a body of incorruptible administrators skilled in the Chinese language, able to act as a sound bridge between populace and rulers. Foreign Office approval for the scheme to supply the Consular Service in China with cadets was eventually forthcoming, but it fell to a future governor to implement it in the colony.

Most of Bowring's other plans, given the state of the colony, were scarcely susceptible of implementation. The Governor was at heart a reformer faced with a situation over which he failed to find the means of control. In London the Colonial Secretary, Lord John Russell, remarked with some rightness but with little sympathy that Bowring 'was rather wild on all subjects'. That is perhaps a characteristic of reformers.

In a further attempt to ameliorate the situation between governed and administration, Bowring revived what Bonham had abolished — the office of Registrar-General, to which he added the title Protector of the Chinese. To this office he appointed Caldwell, who was a good linguist. Given the character of this official, widely held to be in league with the pirate Ma Chow Wong, the Colonial Office was reluctant to concur.

This liberal aspect in the Governor's outlook appeared in many of his actions but was flawed in detail. His idea that Chinese ought to have the chance to fill responsible positions in the administration was frowned on by London, the Secretary of State remarking:

> If you should hereafter be able to select from the Chinese inhabitants persons deserving of confidence whom you may think fit to hold this [Justice of the Peace] or any other administrative office I should be willing to assent... The experiment, however, should be very cautiously made... I should not think it wise to place a Chinese in any position in which he would exercise authority alone without a check on the part of British officials.

So Chinese working as clerks and student interpreters in the Magistracy and other departments, a first step to higher posts, were in fact denied promotion to any important appointment in Bowring's time.

In the wake of a revival in trade and public demand for a voice in the colony's affairs, the question of enlarging the Legislative Council by means of increased unofficial membership, and even of introducing an elective element, came under scrutiny. Public meetings in support were held, and in response Bowring proposed that three unofficial members be included, elected triennially from the ranks of the Justices of the Peace. London vetoed the scheme, saying that simple nomination would do the same job. The Secretary of State had no objection to a small increase in numbers in the Council, but 'I shall . . . rely on your continuing to administer the Government in conformity with the principles on which it has been Established, and not parting with due Authority, which [is] best calculated to secure the general welfare of a Community placed in such exceptional conditions.' The Council was increased by adding one unofficial and one official member. The Legislative Council then consisted of: the Governor, Lieutenant-Governor, Chief Justice, Colonial Secretary, Attorney-General, Surveyor-General, Chief Magistrate, and J. F. Edger, J. Jardine, and G. Lyall.

Unlike many another Governor, Bowring showed some concern about sanitation, appointing an army doctor, J. Caroll Dempster, on the death of Dr William Morrison. Dempster turned out to be a harsh critic, his first report noting regretfully that in 1854 Hong Kong presented 'so much filth . . . Cowsheds, pigsties, stagnant pools' in Taipingshan. He wanted drainage, sewerage, the laying of pavements, efficient scavenging. He noted the crowded, miserable housing. His next report stated that nothing had happened except the construction of a few dustbins, and these were being used by the Chinese as latrines. Having seen as many as 16 men in one cell he condemned the inhuman overcrowding in the gaol, and in his 1856 report he again complained of no action being taken, and of being fobbed off with the statement that things were 'under consideration'. He underlined that phrase. Dempster's justification in his strictures came in the cruel form of a cholera epidemic in the following year, 1857.

The Surveyor-General attempted to defend his position, but the ultimate culprit must be seen in Bowring whose ineptitude permitted the growing menace of the sanitary hazard. He responded with the Buildings and Nuisances Ordinance of 1856. And therein lay another quagmire of disputed authority. The Magistrates found it hard to interpret, and the Justices handed down decisions quite contrary to its spirit. To Bowring's remonstrances they replied with tart comments on interference by the administration with the due process of justice. In law, the Justices were correct, if unhelpful. Bowring referred the matter to the Colonial Office which did not favour his approach. Then, boldly, he created a post of Inspector of Nuisances, the first step towards the later creation of a Sanitary Department. But the Governor failed completely to grasp the implications of the absence of both a sanitation and a public health authority.

Population, health, and water supply are at all times interrelated, acutely in times of rapid population growth, and even more closely in climatic conditions such as those in Hong Kong. The overspill of the Taiping disturbances in China, together with the drift of manpower to service the rising trade of the colony, contributed to population growth in the Bowring years. Between 1853 and 1859 the population more than doubled. It was small wonder that inadequate sanitation was matched by inadequate water supply, compounding the gravity of the situation. Many larger dwellings, such as Bowring's old house in Spring Gardens, had wells, but the average Chinese family was dependent on the erratic flow of water from streams and rivulets coursing down the hills. These were little gushers in the rainy season, but most dwindled to a trickle in the dry months. Bowring was neither the first nor the last Governor who took the curious view that provision of water supplies was not the business of government. In Bowring, with his liberal principles, it was more surprising than in some others. He suggested that a private company be formed which could levy charges for supplying water. Here, once again, he came into collision with the Legislative Council who argued for government funding. The enthusiast for a plan to bring water to the town, via a conduit from an existing pool at Pok Fu Lam round the western slopes of the Peak, was W. T. Mercer, the Colonial Secretary. He pointed out that precisely when the streams lessen in volume or dry up, is the time of greatest fire hazard. The scheme was estimated to cost £25,000, but nothing was done about it until the next administration.

Slightly more success attended Bowring's plan to enlarge the area available for building on the north shore of Hong Kong island. He proposed a reclamation stretching out into the harbour from Happy Valley, achieved by means of draining the swampy ground and filling it in with soil and rubble. This was to continue westward, rationalizing the contour of the shore, to the central district. The praya scheme met with immediate opposition from the majority of those with premises and land fronting the harbour all the way from the central district to Causeway Bay, whose seaward outlets might thereby be blocked. The scheme had commercial potential in the provision of new land for building, and it allowed for public access to the harbour at various points, something that had been restricted by previous haphazard development. The whole problem had been recognized in earlier days by the first Colonial Engineer, Gordon, but not until the time of Bowring were there enough financial resources to contemplate a new praya. And even then the Governor had to accumulate the necessary funds in various ways.

Reclamation as well as construction was involved, finished off by a stout sea wall. The scheme was announced in November 1855. Under it the marine lot holders were to pay rent, additional to that for their original holdings, for the illicit reclamation of land made by them, and were also to contribute to the cost of the new sea wall. Under threat, as might have been expected, they held animated protest meetings and the whole issue was referred to London.

London endorsed it. But only some of the Westerners agreed; and there were Chinese protesters too.

While this series of confrontations was being sorted out a start was made in areas where there was no objection — at Happy Valley where the praya scheme interlocked with the Bowrington Praya scheme extending seaward the area fronting Happy Valley. In central district J. M. Dent, holding land between there and the military cantonment, refused to give way. Bowring drafted an ordinance to apply compulsion, only to be frustrated when the official members of the Legislative Council (contrary to custom) voted against it with the unofficials. The praya was completed long after, and Bowring's name was not applied to it. His name survives only in Bowrington Road in the area of his reclamation north of Happy Valley, and in a canal near by which has nowadays disappeared under Canal Road.

The colony's financial state continued to be healthy, revenue reaching more than £62,000 by 1858, and funds for law and order — the 'police rate' — rose from a little over £3,000 to somewhat over £13,000 in Bowring's time. The new, legal, status of the opium trade allowed the Governor to reintroduce the opium monopoly in 1858, and that brought in another £4,508, all but equal to the revenue from licences for spirits. Yet he failed to balance his budget. Expenditure in 1858 marginally exceeded revenue, largely through increased spending on public works; and had he been able to push through other schemes that his liberal mind suggested for the well-being of the colony, the deficit would have been much bigger.

For a man so well-meaning as Sir John Bowring, his actual achievements were not great. This was in part the result of his character defects. On arrival he inherited a colony in fragile financial condition, but that soon took an upturn beyond expectations, partly because of his efforts but more importantly because of external factors. Bowring inherited, too, a society among which there were numerous self-seeking individuals with no scruples about engaging in social warfare with anyone who crossed their paths or seemed to question their overweening pride or to eye their hypersensitive pockets. To this flammable situation in a house of buccaneers Bowring added the irritant of his high-handed manner, the combustible material of his liberal ideas which were shared by few, a tendency to be far ahead of Hong Kong times, and, anathema to almost all, his treating of the Chinese as equals under the law. A conflagration in society naturally followed. His abilities were striking, but not in the field of administration or personal relations. He cared for the things of the mind — setting up a small museum in a room in the Supreme Court — more than for the frequently squalid trade which it was his duty to encourage. A liberal man, a political radical, a reformer, and a Unitarian, Bowring was all the things the traders of Hong Kong disliked and distrusted. A man of peace, he none the less brought war to China, and sowed confusion in an administration whose workings he had set out to clarify.

Bowring, approaching seventy, had lost what he most wished to have — the honour attached to achieving a settlement with China. His errors of judgement had impelled Palmerston to send Elgin to replace him. It cannot have been easy to remain at the seat of operations as an impotent spectator in the process he wished to control. But he did so with tolerable grace. Bowring left Hong Kong studiously ignored by the Western population and, like Davis before him, the object of spontaneous marks of respect from the Chinese.

In all this there must, it would seem, have been some fundamental lessons to be learned in London.

9. *Consolidation under Robinson*

IN the opinion of *The Times* when Sir Hercules Robinson took up office as Governor of Hong Kong, it was 'the worst period in the colony's history'. The leader-writer assessed its reputation in accurate if arch terms:

> Hong Kong is always connected with some fatal pestilence, some doubtful war, or some discreditable internal squabble, so much so, that . . . the name of this noisy, bustling, quarrelsome, discontented little island may not inaptly be used as a euphonious synonym for a place not mentionable to ears polite.

Sir Hercules, after less than nine months there, appeared to concur, and he was to write to the Duke of Newcastle, Secretary of State for the Colonies: 'Indeed Hong Kong is totally unlike any other British Dependency and its position is in many respects so grotesquely anomalous . . .'.

If Bowring had been a small man with big ideas, Robinson was a big man with generally smallish ideas which he proved capable of having carried out efficiently. For once the Colonial Office had sent the right man at the right time.

In reality, it may be suspected, almost any firm, competent administrator not consumed with his own personal theories, any normally balanced, fairly experienced civil servant endowed with a will to govern, could probably have done as well as Robinson. What the 'discontented little island' needed, for once it received. Aged 35 when he arrived in September 1859, Robinson brought with him some experience in government appointments in England, and a spell as President of Montserrat in the West Indies. It was from the Lieutenant-Governorship of St Christopher that he was hurried out to the disputatious colony, with his young wife and infant daughter.

In several ways Robinson had luck on his side. Many of the assorted rogues in government service had left. That smudgy character (the adjective appears by coincidence for the first time in the year of Robinson's arrival) Caine, friend of Bridges and Caldwell, had just retired. Hulme, Chief Justice, was about to remove his bibulous self and his burgeoning family in April of 1860. Anstey, litigious Attorney-General, had left under a cloud the previous January and was to learn on arrival in England that he was not to return.

W. T. Mercer, a man who had skated fairly gracefully over the thin and sullied ice of Bowring's administration, and who was to administer the government in Robinson's absence, was still in the colony — a perennial from Davis's days who Bonham thought had 'a capacity far above the office he holds'. Still at work, too, was Charles May whose appointments had all been in the Police Department, and whose dogged efforts to clean it up over the 34 years of his stay went hand in hand with his ownership of a well-known group of brothels, in more or less seemly fashion. And there was D. R. Caldwell, Registrar-General, a character as nefarious and pliant as any in the colony's history, with whom the new Governor had at once to deal.

The collusion between Caldwell and Bridges, and the prosecution of Tarrant, which had left one of the indelible stains on the Bowring era, focused suspicion on both when Tarrant was acquitted. No one seriously believed that they were innocent, and in both Hong Kong and London there was pressure to reopen the case. Robinson was ordered to set up a public enquiry. During the course of it Bridges left the colony and was never heard of again, his fortune doubtless sufficient to support him, in the style to which he was accustomed in Hong Kong, in anonymity elsewhere. The Executive Council, before whom the enquiry was held, now included none of the old coterie of civil servants and merchants, with the exception of Mercer. The hearings,

The Executive Council in 1860, Sir Hercules Robinson seated wearing a top hat. W. T. Mercer, Colonial Secretary, is seated on the left, with Mr Leslie of Dent and Company, and Col. Haythorne, Captain Superintendent of Police, on the right.

held sporadically, covered a period of 13 months, the Council faced continually by 'equivocation, proved unreliability of witnesses, problems of interpretation and translation, and failure to produce evidence'. Caldwell was suspended as unfit to continue in his office because of his association with Ma Chow Wong. Yet some years later another administration was to find a use for his services. His Chinese wife, a former brothel girl, continued after his death in possession of the brothels into the 1890s. May, Superintendent of Police, who was implicated in the affair, was exonerated.

Possibly even before he left London and certainly after the first few months of his tenure in Hong Kong, Robinson was convinced that the prime need in the colony was broad-based civil service reform. He complained in his first Annual Report in 1859 about the absence of it, and thereafter aimed at achieving a properly organized administration under his control. He revived the cadet scheme. Recognizing another of the chronic ills of the service — the opportunity for corruption — Robinson raised salaries and instituted a Civil List of offices and their appropriate salaries, obviating the need to re-vote them every year. He also enforced the principle that official members of the Legislative Council might not vote against any action proposed by the Governor, and he forbade communication by any member with the press on official matters. Finally, in this sensitive area, he introduced a pension scheme for civil servants.

It is on the basis of these measures in regard to the structure of the administration and its relations with the public, that the colony's public service has stood ever since. In its establishment may be seen Robinson's prime importance in Hong Kong history. He recognized that to fight against corruption and other endemic abuses in the administration was futile in the absence of trained personnel, financial inducement, and the assurance of a pensioned future.

The new Governor then tackled the press, which had been responsible for stirring the pot of social ill-ease. The hypocrisy of much press activity in Hong Kong to that date consisted of its posing as the guardian of public morals, and then turning to the self-serving dissemination of scandal, and now and then printing outright malicious libel. While adhering to the principle of press freedom, Robinson now required all editors to pay much larger sums of money as surety of their good faith. And he began publication (from 1862) of the Government Gazette in a Chinese as well as the existing English version, for the first time affording the majority race the chance of reading ordinances and other official matters affecting them.

Robinson's attention to the Chinese majority stands in interesting contrast to the attitude of most of his predecessors and successors who usually made the mistake of ignoring them, or regarding them as a criminal class or as irredeemable savages. On his estimate, at most a mere 500 of the 120,000 Chinese in the colony knew anything about British laws or how they were administered. One comical example of that ignorance was the continued payments by the Chinese of salt revenues to extortionist gangs, even though the salt monopoly had been abolished in 1858. Robinson ceased trying to govern the Chinese through their own headmen and made the Registrar-General the channel of communication with the government. But in 1860 he met Chinese opposition when he introduced closer control over pawnbroking. The pawnbrokers shut up shop and went on strike. So, too, did the cargo-coolies, and also the chair-coolies when he wanted to register them in 1861 and 1863. He took a firm line, refusing concessions. Registration took place.

With the Governor no longer responsible to consular officials in China, the island slowly ceased to be regarded as the centre for British trade and influence in the Far East. The Kowloon peninsula came once more to the forefront, as hostilities with China were renewed in 1860 to force the ratification of the Treaty of Tianjin. Anglo-French forces encamped there before embarking for the north. Bruce, British Minister in China, wanted Kowloon retained as part of the indemnity the Chinese would be made to pay at the conclusion of the treaty. Harry Parkes was entrusted with the negotiations. The result was positive. On 26 March 1860 the area south of a line drawn between Kowloon Fort and a point opposite Stonecutters island was leased in perpetuity to Britain and was handed over to Hong Kong. Charles May was made Special Commissioner, to employ Chinese laws and usage as far as he could. The Convention of Beijing in October 1860 cancelled the lease and ceded it outright as a Hong Kong dependency 'with a view to maintaining law and order in and about the harbour of Hong Kong'. It then came to light that there was no official record of ownership and tenancies of the land. What deeds did exist, did not define boundaries. And there had been neither time nor opportunity to carry out the necessary cadastral survey. At once a swarm of claimants appeared waving spurious deeds and clamouring for compensation. The successful ones were to get 999-year leases on the same rental terms as previously. Inevitably justice was rough and ready, and where serious doubts were felt the land was sold, the proceeds being shared among claimants under Chinese official supervision.

The problems were far from solved, however. A dispute boiled up between the Hong Kong government and the military, who claimed the whole area as a cantonment where all the troops in the colony could be housed. Ragged arguments dragged on for four years, pre-empting organization of the land for building or for recreation (as Robinson wished) to relieve what was seen as population pressure on Hong Kong island. The south-west portion of the peninsula, in his view, should be devoted to commerce and wharves since it fronted deep water, and he appointed a commission to sort the matter out. But the members of the commission — naval, military, and civil — failed to agree. Eventually Robinson managed to reserve the land he wanted for commercial purposes, but his scheme for a praya running from the point at Tsim Sha Tsui to the boundary opposite Stonecutters island was never implemented. Compensation for dispossessed Chinese (over $29,000) was delayed until 1864; but those not dispossessed received their 999-year leases; others were granted leases only sufficient to ensure they built durable structures.

During the debate the new Secretary of State for War, Sir George Cornewall Lewis, had taken up the cudgels on behalf of the army, and the Kowloon land use controversy was not to be finally settled, with plots marked out for sale and a sea wall built, until 1864. The absurd demands of both army and navy in Hong Kong's early history were responsible for the postponing or even abandoning of many a good plan, and for malformation of what could have been intelligently designed urban areas.

At this time the Colonial Office woke up to the fact that the annual budget of Hong Kong had never been voted by the Legislative Council, as was standard practice in other colonies. And the Council from that time on did so. The local Post Office, previously run by the postal authorities in England, was now taken over and run locally. At first British 'stamp labels' were to be used, but London decreed that Hong Kong should print its own, and various denominations were designed, the colour being chosen by the Postmaster-General, F. W. Mitchell. Robinson tried to get the Legislative Council to agree to an ordinance under which all vessels would carry Hong Kong mail free of charge, but they 'stoutly resisted its passage as interference with free trade'. As in Britain when first introduced, the use of stamps in Hong Kong was 'hailed by the community with little satisfaction' and 'apprehension of inconvenience'.

A steam-assisted sailing ship in Hong Kong waters in 1860.

The Governor now began to apply his mind to the predicament of the courts, where pressure of work was excessive due to the number of cases admitted from the Treaty Ports, and also resulting from the colony's increasing population. From 1851, when the number of cases heard in the colony was 1,922, the workload had increased fourfold by 1860. Robinson set up a Summary Court and judges to relieve the High Court and Magistrates Courts, at the same time abolishing the offices of Chief and Assistant Magistrate in favour of two Police Magistrates. In this connection a knowledge of Chinese was seen as important — more important even than extensive legal qualifications. Robinson's attitude to competence in Chinese brought the offer of $10 a month to any official who would learn — but there were only three takers.

The total inadequacy of the gaol had been apparent for many a year, one of the grey areas in the colony's administration which tended to darken in hue with the passing of time. Under Robinson the whole topic of police and detention resurfaced. Bowring's gaol was too small even before it opened in 1862. Since then prisoners had greatly increased in numbers. A new gaol was urgently needed but, as usual in Hong Kong, the process of getting one was tortuous. Robinson wanted the gaol on Stonecutters island, out of the urban area. But the cost of building it and the time factor worried him. A stopgap in the shape of a hulk named *Royal Saxon* was bought and moored off Stonecutters, and filled with 280 convicts. Chinese squatters on the island were compensated and cleared. Then a boat with 38 convicts aboard capsized alongside the *Royal Saxon*, and an enquiry gave a verdict of accidental death, but was critical of discipline in the prison hulk and of the unseaworthy nature of the capsized craft. The superintendent of the *Royal Saxon* was dismissed and the vessel brought nearer to the shore so that the inmates could reach land via a gangway. This they promptly did in a mass escape of 100 in 1864. None was recaptured.

Simultaneously, for similar reasons, prisoners were escaping from the old gaol on Hollywood Road, principally by the monsoon drains. A new superintendent named Douglas was appointed and the situation improved — the gaol thereafter being commonly referred to as Douglas Hotel.

Yet the colony's crime problem was far from solved. A battle in Kowloon lasting several days between Punti villagers and Hakka settlers had to be stopped. An opium scandal came to light, in which Indian merchants and an Englishman in charge of opium stocks aboard the receiving ship *Tropic* had defrauded the Chartered Mercantile Bank of two million dollars in 1862. Then the vaults of another bank were entered in 1865 by 'drain gangs' using stormwater drains from which to excavate tunnels under the floors. The bank lost $63,000 in notes and £11,000 in gold ingots, some of the notes being discovered on the following morning floating about the streets.

Perhaps the major failure of the period, partly attributable to Robinson, which fortunately did not result immediately in tragedy, concerned the old trio of interlinked problems — water supply, sanitation, and public health. When the Governor arrived there was a period of acute water shortage after poor summer rains. To this he responded, reviving a project shelved in Bowring's time, by offering a prize of $1,000 for the best scheme for bringing an adequate water supply to Victoria town. A civil employee of the Royal Engineers, R. B. Rawling, won the prize for a scheme envisaging the construction of a reservoir at Pok Fu Lam on the south-west slopes of the Peak, and a conduit to lead the water round the hills to the north slopes at a level which later came to be named Conduit Road. Modified a little, the work was put in hand with Rawling supervising, at an estimated cost of £25,000 plus another £5,000 to provide for a future extension. The scheduled completion date was 1861–2, and provision was made for a water rate to be levied at 2 per cent of the value of properties supplied. But water from Pok Fu Lam failed to flow until 1864, and then in quantities far from the copious supply promised. An extension to the scheme to furnish water to the eastern parts of the town had to be constructed in the first year of operation at an extra cost of $10,000.

This first major attempt to provide adequate water supplies was a partial failure, and as the population continued to increase it became even less satisfactory. The operation may be seen as the archetype of others repeated *ad nauseam* in decades to come, with reluctant administrations grudgingly enlarging, modifying, and tinkering with what in the first place had been insufficient schemes. Robinson, although to his credit he got the first scheme going, was no wiser than others in perceiving the future in terms of population and water. In many ways Hong Kong was still like a small frontier town clapped together in response to the basic needs of gold prospectors. Sanitation was the last priority. But at least the town had a Governor with the relevant facts to hand, even if he did not visit those sections where the problem was at its most gruesome.

Dr L. Murray, a new Colonial Surgeon, arrived in 1859 to take charge of the new civil hospital, and was permitted to take up private practice to eke out his miserable salary. The following year, 1860, his report landed on the Governor's desk with what, when read, must have sounded in retrospect a sickening thud. It was suppressed. In 1861 Murray tried again, making the same charges and recounting the same dire tale. It was returned to him for revision. Perhaps his language was on the outspoken side of tact, but the enormity of the conditions Murray described excused a conscientious medical officer some little intemperance of wording. Drainage and sewerage, he wrote, 'had never received adequate attention, nor been carried out on any comprehensive plan' — hardly surprising since there was only one Inspector of Nuisances, and the police usually did not trouble him with cases that would require his attention. Murray condemned the methods of collection of refuse and 'night soil', and suggested it be done before people went out to work. (In later times, until the mid-twentieth century, in parts of the colony where there was no sewerage, night soil was still being collected in the hours of darkness.)

The hospital, Murray said, was inadequate, with no wards for infectious (as opposed to other) diseases, no provision for Chinese patients, no baths or means of that ordinary cleanliness 'most often useful to medical treatment'. His sarcasm may have been what Robinson disliked. The prison with its stench and overcrowding, its lack of ventilation, he noted as 'beyond description'. Staff continually changed. He complained of the severity of floggings and the permanent deformities left by chaining. Yet in his previous year's report he had stated that 'the Chinese thrive amazingly in confinement and after a few months' incarceration are sent out fat and healthy'. A further year's experience in Hong Kong had apparently altered his first impression of this. If Robinson was irked by the style of the reports, it was hardly the mark of a responsible official to suppress them — for, sarcasm aside, what they described was a public health predicament teetering on the edge of public calamity.

Some reforms were made, nibbling at a monstrously dangerous state of affairs. The civil hospital was enlarged and destitute Chinese were admitted. A medical superintendent was appointed to the hospital (the first one was dismissed for locking his door at night so that he could not be disturbed). The prevalence of cholera in China and Japan, and nearer home on Stonecutters island among the convicts, brought about the appointment of a Sanitary Committee in December 1862. And this committee reported the same appalling state of affairs as had been described by Murray (but in milder language) suggesting radical rethinking about the drainage 'system'. The Surveyor-General stated that the reason for the dismal state of sanitation was the unexpectedly high rate of population growth. He failed to remark on another — the extraordinary negligence of the government. The Colonial Office, informed of the cost of improvements, replied coldly that these might not be undertaken until the colony's revenues could pay for them. In spite of these conditions the general health of the population was passably good. But the makings of disaster lurked all around.

However alarming in terms of public health, the upsurge of the population was a contributory factor in Hong Kong's increasing prosperity. While in 1851 there were only 1,600 foreigners among a Chinese population of 85,330, by 1865 foreigners numbered 2,034, 'coloured' persons (Indians) 1,645, and Chinese 121,825. In the same period the income from land leases expanded just short of a hundredfold to £30,866. The revenue from auctions, largely engendered by Chinese, doubled in 1861 compared to the previous year. So too did levies for police and later water, while government revenues almost trebled to £175,717 in 1865 — as did expenditure. The home government viewing all this with a somewhat acquisitive eye, never keen to spend on the 'anomalous' colony, then exacted £20,000 in annual contribution to the upkeep of the military presence in Hong Kong — over Robinson's and the Legislative Council's strong protests. Payments began in 1865 and continue down to the present day.

As prosperity increased there came a time to reconsider the old and vexed question of the currency — what was legal tender. The problem was a confused and confusing one, product of off-the-cuff decisions in the past, and of making do in the absence of any currency at all other than that of China and the internationally used Maria Theresa and Mexican dollars. Part of the problem was the number and variety of coins allowed as legal tender — various types of silver dollar, British and Indian coins, copper Chinese 'cash'. The difficulties had been recognized in Bowring's time but it was not then considered the opportune moment to make changes. Robinson reported that the currency proclamation of 1844, allowing the use of British and Indian silver and gold coins with silver dollars, was now outdated as all commercial accounts were kept in dollars. Little money was collected in sterling. The dollar was valued at four shillings and two pence. Chinese cash were valued in accordance with the weight of silver in the dollar (usually about 1,200 cash to the dollar). The Governor's proposals to mint a Hong Kong coinage in London proved in part unacceptable, because they involved large numbers of low-value coins of considerable weight, implying heavy transport costs.

Eventually the Colonial Office agreed that the colony's accounts might be kept in dollars, a reform introduced on 1 July 1862. Robinson proposed setting up a Hong Kong mint to coin its own dollars, cash, and one- and 10-cent coins. Until such time as the mint could begin operations, the coins were made at the London Mint. These went into circulation in January 1864. The costly project of the Hong Kong Mint was left for the next governor to bring to fruition.

Along with currency reform came the wider question of banks and banking. Hong Kong's first bank was a branch of the Oriental Bank established in 1845. Twelve years were to pass before its notes were recognized as legal tender; even then the bank was required to provide monthly information on the state of its note circulation. By the time a competing bank had appeared in 1857, notes in circulation amounted to $342,965. The Chartered and Mercantile Bank of India opened in August 1857, followed by the Bank of India, Australia and China, and by the Agra and United Service Bank; and by that time there existed rules for official recognition of banks.

All the existing banks in the colony were primarily involved in exchange operations. The need was felt for what we would nowadays call a merchant bank. The first step was taken by Dent and Company who in the summer of 1864 announced that they and others were contemplating forming a local bank to oil the wheels of trade between China and Japan. The Hongkong and Shanghai Banking Corporation was set up with a capital of $5 million in 20,000 shares. Merchants who formed the original committee included 14 from the largest trading houses in Hong Kong. The first manager, V. Kresser, took up his post on 1 January 1865. The bank was the first to profit under the new limited liability regulations passed on that day, and officially opened for business on 3 March.

The first European staff of the Hongkong and Shanghai Bank.

Among other novelties in Robinson's time were the setting up of a Chamber of Commerce in May 1861, in an effort to protect commercial interests now that the Governor was no longer Superintendent of Trade; and the abolition of imprisonment for debt in the same year, bringing colonial law into line with that of Britain.

Robinson had arrived in Hong Kong somewhat in the way an emergency service answers a call. He was prepared for the worst in a colony which he described as 'publicly and socially ill at ease with itself'.[1] In his second

By 1861 Hong Kong was only 20 years old but the town of Victoria had grown remarkably, as this Chinese school painting shows. Paddle-steamers, three-masted men-of-war with square ports for cannon, clipper ships, and junks fill the harbour. The town, with the Cathedral and Government House above, covers the lower slopes, with Taipingshan in the right third of the picture.

Annual Report he remained sceptical about the idea that it could ever blossom into a considerable settlement, or would ever reach one-quarter of the size of Guangzhou. Nevertheless he developed an affection for the place, and on the whole its residents warmed to him — offering him a laudatory address as he went on leave for his 'indefatigable zeal and efficiency' in promoting public welfare and his 'kindness and urbanity [in] private intercourse'.[2] It is easy to point to his deficiencies. That 'zeal and efficiency' could scarcely be said to have extended to public health. But those were days of more casual attitudes to mortality from infectious disease of unknown cause. Yet a code of prudent practice in public sanitation was well accepted in Britain as some sort of preventative measure. It was this that Robinson neglected to enforce.

In assessing Robinson's effect on Hong Kong, Eitel is less enthusiastic than were its citizens. While giving the Governor his due for keeping the peace and setting the colony back on its feet after the shambles left by his predecessor, he implies that Robinson was fortunate to have W. T. Mercer, without whom he would have been 'infinitely less successful'. Bowring had called him 'one of the most accomplished men in the colony but an unwilling reformer'. That was true. But it was Mercer who had recommended the scoundrel Bridges (a college friend) as Attorney-General under Bowring. He escaped unscathed in the ensuing scandal, writing to the Colonial Secretary: 'I have had a long and friendly but never intimate acquaintance with Dr Bridges.'[3] Perhaps that was the literal truth. During the absences of Robinson and after he left, Mercer administered the government for a total period of almost three years before leaving Hong Kong in May 1867. He had been in the colony since 1844. But he failed to secure what he really wanted, a colonial governorship.

There were, however, welcome signs of change in Hong Kong, both socially and materially, a new sophistication befitting a more settled place. The picture formerly characterized by quarrelsome men in and out of government, of a barbarous place filled with unruly merchants and rough Chinese under venal administrators, had by the end of Robinson's governorship greatly altered. This dawning civic pride was to be symbolized by the erection of a clock tower, that epitome of mid-Victorian values. The tower, 80 feet high, rose at the junction of Pedder Street and Queen's Road, vaguely baroque, quite in keeping with the surrounding architecture, holding a white-

The clock tower at the corner of Pedder Street, seen from Des Voeux Road on the waterfront, with Jardine's on the right and the former premises of Dent and Company opposite. The photograph is by Afong, a Chinese who did a thriving trade in local views in the 1870s.

faced clock, the gift of shipping tycoon Douglas Lapraik. Even at the time of its building, this reminder of the need to watch the fleeting hours constituted a slight obstruction to the traffic, and it stood there apparently immovable through a 29-year newspaper campaign to take it down, waged by a member of the Hong Kong Club, M. J. D. Stephens. The clock tower finally succumbed in 1913 when the congestion of rickshaws (introduced from Japan

The Hong Kong Club on the corner of Queen's Road and Wyndham Street was established in 1846. From it were excluded 'shopkeepers, Chinese, Indians, women, and other undesirables'.

after it was erected), carriages, and sedan chairs round its base became intolerable. The clock itself was preserved and appeared with Lapraik's name attached in the new Post Office built in the early twentieth century.

By March 1865 when Robinson left, shade trees had been planted in several streets of the town and, on the first day of January that year, to general amazement, the new gas street lighting was turned on. It seemed to many that a new era had arrived.

An East India Company officer, rolled chart in hand, points to his ship. Chinese school, *c.*1800.

Tea being packed for sale to Western merchants. Chinese school, late eighteenth century.

Opium ships at Lingding Island. W. J. Huggins, 1824.

A street in Guangzhou. William Prinsep, 1838.

A view of the Guangzhou factories. American, French, British, and Danish flags flank the church. Attributed to the Youqua, *c.*1850.

Admiral Sir William Parker, Commander-in-Chief, who arrived in Macau in August 1841. Unknown artist.

Howqua (Wu Bingjian), the senior Chinese merchant at Guangzhou, painted by Tinqua, *c.*1830–40.

A young Chinese merchant at Guangzhou, painted by the artist whom Westerners called Spoilum (Guan Zuolin), early nineteenth century.

An unflattering portrait of Commissioner Lin by a Chinese artist, *c.*1840.

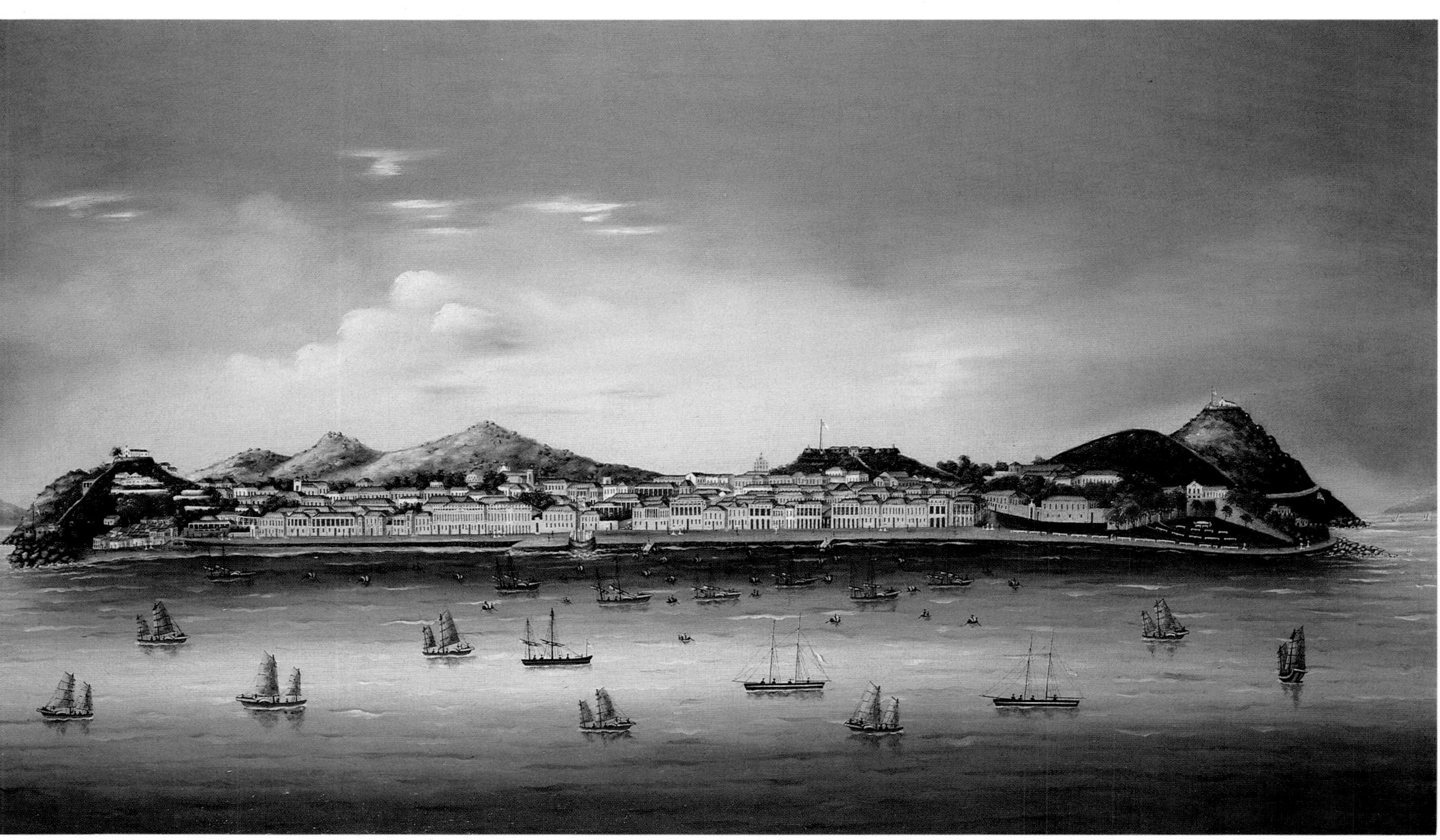

Macau, where the foreign merchants spent the off season, away from the Guangzhou factories. Chinese artist. Datable to before 1844.

Possibly the earliest oil painting of Hong Kong island, showing the path along the north shore (right) as it approaches the early waterfront settlement which became the town of Victoria. The Chinese name, 'Skirt String Island', was derived from the appearance of this path. Chinese artist, undated.

The opium clipper *Red Rover*, built in Calcutta in late 1829, one of the fastest of her kind ever built. She eventually belonged to Jardine, Matheson and Company and could make three round trips a year to and from India, laden with opium. William J. Huggins (1771–1845), undated.

Two medals awarded to Sir Henry Pottinger for service in India and China. Sold at Christie's, London, in 1988.

10. The Growth of Chinese Institutions, and the Problems of Education

STOCKTAKING is such a complex phenomenon even in a small society that it is not easily accomplished at a given moment of its life. The balance of achievement and failure, the appearance of trends, are easier to discern in retrospect, although then they lack the muscle of contemporaneity.

In 1866 when Sir Richard Graves Macdonnell arrived as its Governor, Hong Kong was not threatened by any immediate problem, other than those perennial ones present since the inception. In its 35 years the colony had produced more than its share of antagonisms — between governors and their administrations, between governors and governed, and among the citizens themselves. The existence of a master and menial relationship between Westerners and Chinese of an ancient and proud, if decayed, civilization, could not be expected to result in easy social harmony. Yet the odd thing was that the mix of Western, capitalist, mercantile activity and the Chinese capacity for dedicated, intelligent work, allowed both sides to thrive. Despite insanitary conditions, the Chinese were evidently better off than in China, or they would have returned there; and the cleverer among them were making good money. The two communities went their separate ways in all things save for the common ground of commercial pursuits. Doubtless the Chinese brought with them to Hong Kong many of the detractions of late Qing life in Guangdong Province, and the Westerners the shortcomings of Victorian Britain and nineteenth-century Europe; and these were exaggerated by deracination. These underlay the bitterness of some of the social battles which raged.

The human consequences of the mushrooming of the Chinese population would have alarmed more caring rulers. But the growth of wealth among those who in the nineteenth century might be presumed to have it makes remarkable reading. A.R. Johnston in the *Journal of the Royal Geographical*

Society lists 388 Chinese traders, doubtless mostly with small capital resources, among them two compradors. *The Chinese Directory* for 1872 lists 55 general merchants, 17 charterers, eight contractors, 16 gold dealers, seven money-changers, 18 opium dealers, six prepared opium dealers, two coal merchants, 41 marine compradors and ship chandlers, and 45 foreign-firm compradors. It was from among the last two categories that there emerged a Chinese élite. And from their ranks were drawn the people reflected in an earlier set of figures which showed that, among 1,999 persons liable for police rates of above £10, a remarkable 1,637 were Chinese, and only 186 British — the rest being other foreigners. Among 773 rated at over £40, there were 410 Chinese. The trend is clear.

The number of Chinese compradors working for foreign companies was a fairly reliable guide to colonial commercial growth, and also to the rise of a Chinese élite. In 1876 there were 142 brokers, 215 trading *hong* merchants, and 67 marine compradors. By 1881, the figures were 455, 393, and 113 respectively. At the beginning of the twentieth century a visiting Member of Parliament, Sir Henry Norman, could write: 'The Chinese merchant is crowding out the British middleman . . . it cannot be long before the bulk of the real estate . . . is owned by Chinese.' The Chinese merchants seemed to him 'among the richest men in the community'.[1]

The rising affluence of this section of the Chinese, coupled with the need, especially acute for people living under an alien form of rule, to acquire a communal identity, began in the 1860s and 1870s to give birth to such institutions as the Tung Wah Hospital, established by an ordinance of 1870 and opened by the Governor two years later. The response of the Chinese attempting to fit into a foreign system was twofold. First, they tried to adapt to its strange ways; second, they attempted to form some kind of organization through whose aegis the British authorities could be persuaded that they were responsible members of society. But in nineteenth-century Hong Kong, Chinese society lacked that class of ranking men whose minds had been nurtured and proved in the traditional Chinese Civil Service examinations — men who in China were the leaders. In Hong Kong these men, who would have been able to communicate effectively in terms of trained intelligence with their rulers, were simply not there — so the Chinese had to form new societies.

The first of these were the triads, secret societies which today sound a note of menace, but which in nineteenth-century Hong Kong probably did as much good as harm. 'On balance,' Maurice Freedman writes, 'the secret societies were essentially movements which, while they may have found some of their leaders among members of officialdom and the gentry, expressed an opposition to the state characteristic of the poor and the peasantry.'[2] In the four years 1879–82 the average annual number of Chinese arrested for being out without a pass or a light at night was 1,000. They lived in a society of

Westerners of whose laws they were either ignorant or uncomprehending, and whose hold over them seemed tyrannical, arbitrary, even at times cruel. No European ranking police officer, for example, in this period was a Chinese speaker. The Chinese had no recourse but their temples or religious associations which cut across dialectal, regional, and other divisions.

The Tung Wah rose to fill a communication gap between Chinese who felt a responsibility for the community as a whole, and the government. Its origins went back to a petition of 1851 signed by 14 Chinese. It asked for a grant of land on which to build a temple where, if they died in the colony, they would have a place to deposit their ancestral tablets, so that later 'their fellow villagers or connections visiting Hong Kong could carry them home'. The temple, soon constructed, came to be used as a place where dying Chinese were deposited. In April 1869 the Acting Registrar-General visited this temple and found the 'dead and dying huddled together indiscriminately in small filthy rooms'. It was this situation which prompted the opening of a subscription list by wealthy Chinese for the establishment of a regular Chinese hospital.

The Chinese subscribed $40,000 and the government donated $15,000 and a site, together with $100,000 as capital, described as 'a gift from the Queen

The reception hall of the Tung Wah Hospital.

to the Chinese community', but which actually came from the Gambling Fund. The Tung Wah was what the ordinance described as 'a Chinese Hospital for the care and treatment of the indigent sick to be supported by voluntary contributions'. As such it has continued ever since. The first Chairman was Leung Hok-chau, comprador in Gibb, Livingstone and Company. Among the directors were the comprador of the Hongkong and Shanghai Banking Corporation, Lo Chen-kong, and Wong Shing who was Dr Legge's collaborator in his translation of the Chinese Classics.

Tung Wah activities on behalf of the poor and the sick expanded. The financial and later business management demands on its Chairman, Directors, and committee members increased so greatly that they came to be recruited only from that segment of Chinese society characterized by wealth and a sense of social responsibility. The Tung Wah in time acquired much property and invested its funds with great skill.

Aside from its medical, charitable, and educational activities, the Tung Wah came to represent the interests of the Chinese at large. The composition of its committee — always including the wealthiest Chinese in Hong Kong and later on practically always the Chinese on the Legislative Council — ensured it a voice. And that voice in several ways took over the duties of the Protector of the Chinese when that office was eventually abolished. The person responsible for the Chinese was the Registrar-General. For him the Tung Wah proved to be his ear on the otherwise hermetic Chinese world; and for the Chinese, knowing that members of the Tung Wah directorate had the ear of the Registrar-General was an important political fact. There existed between the authorities and the Chinese, via the Tung Wah, an unacknowledged symbiotic relationship.

By the late 1870s, Lethbridge notes,

> the directorate did begin to act as though it had inherited the magisterial function . . . and the trappings of the imperial Mandarinate. At the formal opening of the Hospital in 1872, the full committee, some 70 or 80 in number, were 'all dressed in Mandarin costume, some even with peacock's feathers attached to their buttons'.[3]

The late nineteenth century had brought the antique rules of the Civil Service examinations in China so far into disrepute that degrees could be purchased. But what was important was that the directorate and committee members saw themselves in the role of mandarins. Each year at the spring and autumn festivals they went in a body to the Man Mo Temple to participate in the sacrifices to Confucius, the rituals being identical with those carried out by the magistrates of imperial China. The cult of Confucius was encouraged by the Tung Wah by the funding of Confucian schools. Other signs of the Tung Wah's regulatory scope within the Chinese community were such activities as the conveying of corpses to China for burial, sending the sick and destitute back to their villages, and collecting money from overseas Chinese for famine relief in China. It became, in Middleton Smith's words, 'probably one of the largest philanthropic institutions in existence'.[4]

In this way, on their own initiative, in response to the needs of a population unrepresented in the government of the community, the Chinese made a start on the regulation of their part of that community.

Except in such publications as the journal of the Royal Asiatic Society and the like, and in some scholarly books, the history of Hong Kong has been documented and expounded largely from a Western point of view. Possibly only a Chinese could successfully do otherwise. Europeans take the stage as principals, the Chinese relegated to the role of virtual extras. Only the most powerful moves made by such organizations as the Tung Wah found acknowledgement until very recently. A detailed history of the interaction of such Chinese bodies with officials and official thinking in the government in the one hundred and fifty or so years of the colony has yet to be attempted, and until it is written there can be no balanced history of Hong Kong. Yet it is at least possible to argue that the gathering stability, as well as the more general evolution of Hong Kong, owed something to such informal exchanges. Government of a majority Chinese population by mostly non-Chinese-speaking officials has certainly been eased by the existence of communicating Chinese bodies, and the interactions have allowed the Chinese some feeling that their way of life has a certain weight in the broadly Western-style management of the colony.

The Tung Wah (that 'eleemosynary corporation' as Eitel calls it) has had counterparts in at least two other influential kindred societies — the Po Leung Kuk and the District Watch Committee.

The beginnings of the Po Leung Kuk lie in an old Chinese custom which tangled with British law and British Victorian views on sexual morality. Gutzlaff's census of Hong Kong in 1844 recorded among the 1,300 Chinese residents only 315 families, and of the 436 permanent houses only 13 were private Chinese dwellings. Chinese houses, that year, were outnumbered by the 32 brothels. In the 1870s this state of affairs was not greatly altered. Charles May, by then Police Magistrate, wrote in 1877 that only one in six Chinese women in Hong Kong lived with one man 'either in marriage or in concubinage, and all the rest come under the denomination of prostitutes to whom money being offered they would consent to sexual intercourse'. A Chinese doctor who owned a chemist's shop in Taipingshan and had worked in the colony for 23 years, stated that the percentage of 'respectable' Chinese women was in the region of about 25 per cent. The census of 1876 showed 24,387 Chinese women in Hong Kong and 81,025 Chinese men. The incidence of prostitution was, not surprisingly, high.

When the Po Leung Kuk was founded in 1878 (its official English name is the Society for the Protection of Women and Girls) it was within this context.

There was extensive trafficking in females, most of whom were brought into the colony from China by Chinese living on immoral earnings — brothel brokers, brothel mesdames, and pimps. Chinese males were reluctant to expose their wives and families to the abnormal conditions in the colony (in comparison to those in the average South China village, social conditions were abnormal, even if the money was good). A contemporary comment in 1860 argues that 'the dearness of house rents may partly account for this as houses with apartments exclusively for the females are very expensive; out of all proportion to what the Chinese are accustomed to pay in China'.[5] There was little repugnance in Chinese thinking to prostitution. The restraints simply operated less firmly in Hong Kong where there were no village elders.

In parallel ran the ancient Chinese custom of buying and selling girls as domestic servants — called *mui tsai* (Mandarin: *mei zu*) meaning 'little sister'. The custom was open to abuses but it answered the need both for domestic help and the relief of poorer families with numerous girls to feed. Nominal adoption of the girl in return for a fee paid to her parents was the usual way this worked. The Attorney-General in 1878 was of the opinion that the practice was not an offence in law; the Governor, Hennessy, thought otherwise. At the same time there was much kidnapping of girls for transport to South-east Asia. Chinese feeling was strong on this subject, and a petition was forwarded to the Governor for permission to set up an Anti-kidnap Association employing detectives. He responded by setting up a committee including Eitel to discuss the matter, and permission was granted. Thus was born the Po Leung Kuk. Its early existence was threatened by the Chief Justice who insisted that domestic servitude was illegal. The matter was eventually referred to England where the Colonial Office, recognizing the deep-seated nature of the Chinese custom, sided with the Governor.

The main function of the new society, the detection of kidnapping of girls for immoral purposes, was energetically pursued by employing detectives who gathered information both openly and clandestinely. But the society, having apprehended kidnappers, then had the job of looking after the kidnapped girls, whom they clothed, housed, and fed until *mui tsai* employment could be arranged or until suitable matches could be made for them. While no doubt an element of self-serving entered into the operation, as it produced a stream of suitable domestic servants for the well-to-do Chinese running the society, it would be unfair and incorrect to see its work as only that. The expenses were subsidized by leading members of the community, and the society was aided by the Tung Wah which provided shelter, and by the Man Mo Temple. In time the Po Leung Kuk became a kind of junior associate of the Tung Wah. But it was not an affluent organization and by 1892 an ordinance was drafted to assist it. This came under heavy criticism in the Legislative Council, T. H. Whitehead of the Chartered Bank calling the Kuk a secret society. The ensuing accusations and counter claims among members

Dr Kai Ho Kai and Sir James Stewart Lockhart at the opening of the Po Leung Kuk in 1896.

of the administration and the Chinese and others dragged on until the Colonial Secretary, J. H. Stewart Lockhart, recommended the society be given legal status and a grant. The ordinance of incorporation became law in 1894, establishing a permanent board. This was Lockhart's personal triumph; a second, since it was he who in 1891 had succeeded in establishing the Chinese District Watch Committee.

Between 1888 and 1892, proving its usefulness, the Po Leung Kuk restored no less than 2,412 males and females to their families, married off 218 women, and arranged the adoption of 46 children. The society was also effective in dealing with the provisions of the Protection of Women and Girls ordinance of 1899.

The Registrar-General had in the Po Leung Kuk one more effective channel of communication with and a source of information about Chinese affairs, and the Chinese had the ear of the administration. During Lockhart's time the office of Registrar-General became one of much greater import in the government, the importance of the Society rising with it. The inference must be, with regard to Lockhart and other officials in these years, that they sought in the regulation, recognition, and funding of such societies, to incorporate the opinions of a rising Chinese class of influential men into the counsels of government. But it was initially Chinese pressure that brought about the formation of the societies, which were later seen by both Chinese and British as useful means of stabilizing aspects of a community in need of mutual understanding.

Both the Tung Wah and the Po Leung Kuk must be seen as powerful forces delaying any too abrupt Westernization in matters affecting the Chinese at large.

The third organization was the District Watch Committee. An American researcher, Lennox A. Mills,[6] after a period spent in the colony, called it 'in reality the Chinese Executive Council in Hong Kong'. Yet 'legally, it is merely a committee of fifteen Chinese who meet under the chairmanship of the Secretary for Chinese Affairs to manage the District Watch Force'. At the time he was writing (1941), this was a body of 120 Chinese constables and detectives recruited and funded by the Committee to patrol the Chinese areas of urban Hong Kong island and Kowloon. The Committee, consisting of wealthy Chinese from all walks of life, included the unofficials of the Legislative and Executive Councils, and so exercised considerable political power within the Chinese community. Hence its opinions were listened to by the government. Its origins lay far back in the nineteenth century.

The few inhabitants of Hong Kong, when the British arrived, lived within the traditional structure of South Chinese rural society, bound by kinship, clan loyalties, and (other than the boat-dwellers) by the wider forms of social integration and controls found in any Chinese country community. The British assumed quite otherwise, lumping these people together with the piratical boat-people and with immigrants who arrived after the colony was annexed. The latter were mostly urban Chinese lacking roots in Hong Kong, and soon outnumbered the local inhabitants. They, and the newly arrived Westerners, were in this sense similar to each other and differed from the indigenous people. Soon both were faced with the problems of maintaining law and order in their own communities, and, as to the Westerners, within all communities. Both parties soon discovered that the answer was at least in part to employ their own guards for their property; and some householders, individually or collectively, employed street watchmen too.

The Chinese were rootedly opposed to being regulated by Western standards. Even in the first decade of the colony they had formed their own associations. The committee of the Man Mo Temple, Eitel relates:

> rose to eminence as a sort of unrecognized and unofficial local government board . . . [They] secretly controlled native affairs, acted as commercial arbiters, arranged for the due reception of mandarins passing through the Colony, negotiated the sale of official titles, and formed the unofficial link between the Chinese residents of Hong Kong and the Canton authorities.

This preceded the recognition of the Tung Wah committee. Naturally such organizations acted somewhat clandestinely — the risk of antagonizing the British authorities being very real.

The District Watch Committee was formed after a meeting of the Chinese community on 1 February 1866. The Registrar-General reported in 1867: 'After much discussion, the community of the Five Districts to the west of the Parade Ground, agreed to elect a certain number of their body to act as Watchmen, whose pay should be disbursed by themselves'. They petitioned the government for permission to organize a force of Chinese watchmen, claiming that rough elements in Guangzhou intended to celebrate the New Year by coming to Hong Kong 'with the object of committing extensive robberies under cover of a conflagration'.[7] The suggested force commended itself to the Governor, and by an ordinance (No. 7, 1866) the District Watch Committee came into being. Doubtless the rumours of 'rough elements' had been used as a good excuse for forming what was in effect their own police force, paid and controlled by the Chinese. They had every reason. The regular police (if such they may be termed) were corrupt, drunken, and venal — and offered little or no protection to the Chinese. The duties of the new force and its usefulness expanded, and its success may be measured by its longevity — it remained intact until 1949. The controlling Committee always included members or ex-members of the Tung Wah and Po Leung Kuk Committees, and the trio of organizations formed a body of considerable power outside the government. It was a force in most aspects benign, solidly advisory, even cautionary, at the elbow of the administration.

The utility, the necessity of such groupings in the Hong Kong context cannot be denied. Where there is no social contact between two sections of a society it is all but impossible for either side fully to understand the other. There was of course, unacknowledged, even unmentionable in that era, the shady world of sexual relationships between Western males and their Chinese mistresses. But that was scarcely a bridge for understanding ordinary Chinese life and opinion. Nearer the mark was another small world — the affectionate relationships that flourished between Western children and their Chinese amahs. Many of those youngsters picked up Cantonese, becoming quite fluent, and were able, in the licence allowed to children, to make lasting bonds of friendship which they would recall in adult life with pleasure and some understanding of the Chinese.

In another aspect of life, Victorian British and the Chinese had something in common — the thirst for education. The fitful, faltering, muddled process by which Hong Kong's children were accorded an education reflected with fair accuracy the condition of a society more dependent than most, indeed outrageously so in this context, on conditions and influences from other lands. Piecemeal, the structure of the educational system in the colony accommodated itself to the complicated social, racial, and trans-cultural facts of life there. The meeting of an evolving British nineteenth-century social, religious, and educational scene, vociferously conveyed to Hong Kong, with its static Chinese counterpart inlaid in a Hong Kong commercial society of Westerners far from home, resulted in an educational dilemma. The story of education in the colony reflected (and to some extent still reflects) these facts.

The movement in Britain which culminated in the passing of the Education Act in 1870 was reflected in Hong Kong in the growing emphasis placed by all religious bodies on teaching, along with the faith, simple literate skills to the Chinese. For their part the Chinese were far from unwilling pupils, accustomed as they were to consider that only through education was it possible to reach high rank in the old system. If this meant, in the new one in Hong Kong, that a certain amount of foreign religion had to be imbibed, it was no great matter.

Seen in perspective, the nineteenth-century expansion of education in Hong Kong has to be set against a background of British evangelical fervour which insisted on the depravity of unregenerate human nature and the necessity of Christian conversion. Applied to the Chinese, this tended to elicit from them the response of selecting from the process only what they wanted. This pragmatism meant in practice that the educational aspect of missionary endeavour was sifted out and utilized, while Christianity was often politely, even usually, set aside.

There were numerous differences between traditional Chinese education and that in the West. Chinese characters and their correct pronunciation have to be laboriously learned, each new word a new character, a process which takes much longer than learning to read in a language composed of a limited alphabet. Chinese teaching was mostly on an individual master and pupil basis, not in classes, and was paid for by the paterfamilias or a patron. The reason for attending a Western school is implied in an account by a Chinese of being sent to Mrs Gutzlaff's school in Macau in 1835. Yung Wing was seven when his family sent him.

> As foreign intercourse with China was just beginning to grow, my parents, anticipating that it might soon assume the proportions of a tidal wave, [took] time by the forelock and put one of their sons to learning English that he might become one of the ... interpreters and ... make his way into the business and diplomatic world.[8]

But other responses more in line with missionary intent were not uncommon. In an essay headed 'Why do you wish to get an education?' set by a teacher in the Morrison Education Society School, a pupil wrote: 'If you convey a heathen boy to a place filled by Christian and delightful boys, he will soon be like one of them; and if you transmit a Christian boy to a heathen village ... he will soon work the same deeds as they.'[9] The Christian message has not been understood, but the English language has been learned.

In early Hong Kong, Christian schools, and also colleges and seminaries for training Chinese youths for the ministry, were a feature. But there was also a genuine interest in all these institutions in education for its own sake. Oddly enough the first government grants were paid to Chinese schools, not to those of the missionary bodies.

After sketching the beginnings of schooling in Hong Kong — the nine Confucian Chinese schools, and others started by missionary societies in the 1840s — Eitel remarks that Sir John Davis

> devised early in 1847, in imitation of the English religious education grants then hotly discussed in Parliament, a government Grant-in-Aid scheme to provide non-compulsory religious education in Chinese schools under the direction of the Educational Committee . . . That . . . Davis was to some extent a religious visionary, may be inferred from a dispatch . . . to the Colonial Office . . . 'If these schools were eventually placed in charge of native Christian teachers, bred up by the Protestant Missionaries, it would afford the most rational prospect of converting the native population of the Island.' *Sancta simplicitas!*[10]

The government-assisted schools were brought under Bishop Smith, chairman of the Educational Committee, and acted as feeders for St Paul's College. The college produced not a single

> native minister or any official interpreter, [but] many of the best educated native residents . . . received their training there. The same may be said for Dr Legge's Anglo-Chinese College which also failed to produce a native preacher or teacher but trained some eminent English-speaking Chinese.

There were detractions, it seems, to this educational process. Scholars of the colleges

> gained . . . an unenviable notoriety in Police Court cases. Hence the public drew the inference that, in the case of Chinese youths, an English education, even when conducted on a religious basis, fails to effect any moral reform, and rather tends to draw out the vicious elements inherent in the Chinese character.[11]

The mercantile community then began to withdraw support from missionary schools.

Several schools closed in the late 1840s, but the Roman Catholic missions opened others which gave Portuguese youth an English education, thus beginning the process which 'eventually filled commercial and government offices with Portuguese clerks', a situation which continued until the third quarter of the twentieth century. 'The paralysis which came over education' disappeared by 1859 when Bishop Smith's wife started the Diocesan Native Training School. St Paul's College took on a new lease of life under Dr J. Fryer and prospered while he was in charge.

Then there was Miss Baxter who, 'besides much Samaritan activity among all classes of the community ... commenced to labour for the education of the Eurasian children of the Colony'.[12] Previously she had set up schools in Mosque Street and in Staunton Street, and these were eventually amalgamated in Bonham Road in Baxter House. Miss Sophia Harriet Baxter's Diocesan Native Female School used English as the medium of instruction and went well until, to her horror, she discovered that most of her Chinese pupils once they left school became the mistresses of the many European bachelors in Hong Kong. Harriet Baxter inspired both directly and indirectly a string of schools which outlasted her death in 1865 as the Baxter Vernacular Schools,

Pupils and masters at Queen's College. Only one boy is dressed in European style (at the right, second row from the front).

some later taken over by the Church Missionary Society. She was not alone in her work of educating girls in Hong Kong. There were the Daughters of Charity, the Misses Legge of the London Missionary Society, and Miss Eaton who arrived in 1862, later to marry E. J. Eitel.

The Morrison Education Society, first granted land by Pottinger, had existed in various guises, supported latterly by funds from mercantile houses. And this was to be its undoing. In 1867, Dent and Company failed, depriving it of its principal source of revenue.

The Chinese were equally early in setting up their schools on traditional lines. Gutzlaff, the Chinese Secretary, stated that in 1845 there were eight such schools, two 'supported by foreigners' and all housed in hovels. He proposed each should have a government grant of $10 per month. He also asked for free schools to be set up for the Chinese. But the Colonial Office wanted more information — curricula, teaching methods, staffing — before it acted; and in the end it came to the conclusion that the 'most effective, almost indispensible auxiliaries' in colonial education were the missionary societies.

At this time the controversy raging in Britain over establishing a national system of education led to great caution being exercised in the granting of public funds for the support of sectarian education there. Grants for Hong Kong were refused for British children's education, but for Chinese schools 'where the contribution required is moderate' and 'no religious differences can arise', and for three schools in Aberdeen, Stanley, and Victoria town, grants of $10 were allowed as requested. Thus, in 1847, the small beginnings of a public education system were put in place.

Further progress towards a rational comprehensive system was marred by

A Chinese artist's painting of the Last Supper. A delightful amalgam of Chinese setting and reminiscences of Western paintings of the event.

the indecision of the authorities in London and in Hong Kong on the relative merits of secular and religious society schools and teaching, and about the weight given to various subjects (Chinese Classics, other secular subjects, and Christian instruction), in schools for Chinese pupils. In detail the story is one of begrudged money, miserable teachers dominating the scene, followed by 'native Christian' teachers and the dominance of the Christian ethic in instruction. Yet another fact leading to conflict was the difference in aims of men such as Legge, Smith, and the Revd Vincent Staunton, all active in the schools question. The Bishop decreed that half the pupils' days should be devoted to the Scriptures and to 'books composed under the superintendence of foreigners', and the other half to the Chinese Classics. He wanted the schools to act as feeders to his own St Paul's College. The College prepared its students for the Anglican ministry, received financial help from the Foreign Office to assist in turning out interpreters for the consular service, and appears to have offered some sort of general education as well. Its popularity with the Chinese lay in the economic advantages accruing from a knowledge of English.

The policy of the Education Committee was to encourage the study of English not only for its own sake, but 'to act as a bond of union between the many thousands of Chinese who have made this place their residence and the handful of Europeans by whom they are governed'. Progress was naturally slow, school buildings 'confined, dirty and altogether unsuitable'. Attendance at all schools was sporadic. Aberdeen and Stanley pupils went off fishing with their parents for days, even weeks, and at a quite tender age left school to work. The 1850 education report remarks on this problem that much as the Chinese wanted education 'this was secondary to his attachment to gain'. The fact that poor fisher-folk had first to make a livelihood, and that their children had to take part from an early age, was ignored.

Under Bowring with his liberal thrust and non-Anglican outlook the attempt 'to wean the natives from their religious opinions and practices' was opposed. He thought that Chinese schools should be run by laymen. He wrote to London in 1854: 'It is quite monstrous to see a charge of £8,260 for police . . . contrasted with an expenditure of £120 for the instruction of the people.'[13] That, of course, depended on one's outlook on state subsidies for education. But in fact the existing schools in 1854 had places for only 150 of the estimated 8,800 Hong Kong Chinese children of school age. This was possibly not out of step with the situation in Britain. The Education Committee, however, offered four proposals: suitable school buildings ought to be provided; a system of apprentice teachers ought to be introduced; all schools capable of enlargement should have assistant masters able to teach English; an Inspector of Schools should be appointed to make weekly inspections of all government schools.

In May 1856 a German missionary, the Revd W. Lobscheid, was made

Inspector. A programme of expansion began, and in Bowring's time the number of schools receiving grants more than trebled to 19, while the number of children attending greatly increased. The annual cost of education rose from 1854 to 1859 from a paltry £120 to £1,200. Now there were three schools for Hakka children, and Victoria had five for others. Most other schools were tiny backward places in villages, difficult to supervise. After 1858 girls had a school of their own in Victoria. Bowring complained that while only the missionaries gave active assistance to his schemes, 'yet they have special objects that unfit them for general and popular education'. Bishop Smith remained at the helm but Bowring's secular ideas had made a dent in the religion-dominated scheme of things. His successor, Robinson, brought back the 1860 Education Committee as the Board of Education, although still under Bishop Smith.

This and similar conflations of Chinese and English educational basics were to remain the model for Chinese education for long enough, although in schools entirely controlled by the Chinese the education followed traditional Chinese lines and pupils for the most part learned individually from a master, classes being the exception.

Legge now suggested that the government schools in Victoria should close and their pupils join a new central school under a European headmaster. In a large and specially designed building, and with a trained master to do the actual teaching, Legge hoped to raise standards. Teaching in English would be given more prominence, the demand for it permitting a fee to be charged, leaving Chinese education free. The headmaster was to take over the inspection of outlying schools.

This scheme virtually sacrificed what education there was in village schools in favour of a (possibly) efficient central academy in town. It may be that this was the sole choice that offered at the time — there is not enough information to tell. Frederick Stewart was appointed headmaster and the Central School opened on 1 January 1862. Legge seems to have edged Lobscheid out in 1860. Within two years the new school had 140 pupils and had to build a new wing for 90 more. The difficulty of supervising village schools remained and some were closed. Headmaster Stewart believed in secular education, and after Bishop Smith retired the Board of Education was abolished (1865), its encouragement of teaching the Scriptures becoming one of his targets. But his hopes that secular government schools would attract more Chinese pupils away from the purely Chinese schools were not fulfilled. The Chinese who could afford to pay for education did not want their children taught alongside those of the poorer classes. They showed their preference for traditional Chinese education free from government supervision and free from Western tendencies. Christian instruction seemed not to be the obstacle since more Chinese attended mission schools than private Chinese ones, and their policies were similar to those of the former Board of Education schools —

A Chinese merchant and his son photographed in 1861. The boy has a pocket watch attached to his belt.

equal doses of Chinese Classics and Christianity. They were also non-fee-paying and could experiment in methodology. Schools of several kinds developed to serve a variety of requirements.

The real fillip to education, at least as regards numbers in the mission schools, came after the Treaty of Tianjin and the Taiping troubles, which sent missionaries to China and floods of refugees to Hong Kong. By the mid-1860s there were fifteen or sixteen schools or groups of schools run by missions, as well as Miss Baxter's establishment which, after its inadvertent training for concubinage, concentrated on boys and Eurasians. By 1865 it was estimated that of the approximately fourteen thousand children of school age, something slightly under two thousand were attending schools of one kind and another. But the whole question of education for the Chinese was far from settled, reflecting to some extent the unsettled state of thought on the subject of education in Britain.

Given the nature of the obstacles in the way of education for the Chinese population — illiteracy among parents, poverty, the need to employ children to augment the family income, Christian teachers whose heart was mainly in evangelism and little in Chinese scholarship, government hesitation on everything from finance to curricula — it was hardly surprising that the chaos of those years continued. Yet, slowly, the Chinese learned how to place their children to best advantage in the institutions most likely to provide them with the required fluency in English and understanding of Western business methods.

11. *Macdonnell and the Lawless 'Depot'*

SIR Richard Graves Macdonnell took over as Governor of Hong Kong in March 1866. Once again it was to prove true that the character of a Governor had a profound effect on the development of the colony during his term. Macdonnell was to require all his administrative skills, all his expertise in argument both within the colony and in the corridors of power in London in order to make his mark.

Successive Colonial Office civil servants and successive Governors of Hong Kong are on monotonous record as having verbally thrown up their hands in despair at the unique situation of the colony. Macdonnell was no exception.

Sir Richard Graves Macdonnell, Governor from 1866 to 1872.

Just a year after his arrival he wrote to the Secretary of State in London: 'There is no parallel between this and any other British settlement. It is a mere depot...'.[1] By this time he ought to have been in a position to judge. The problems he had to face were very different from those he had dealt with as Governor in Gambia, in the West Indies, in South Australia, and in Nova Scotia. The majority of people whom he was to govern in Hong Kong did not belong there and did not on the whole intend to pass the rest of their days in the colony. Trade recession and financial stringency were to limit some of his efforts. Piracy, police corruption and ineffectiveness were matters requiring urgent attention — as was finding means to curb the obsessive gambling of the Chinese. And in these matters he was hampered by the almost hysterical mood of evangelism in England at the time which inspired (if that is the apt word) the counsels of Parliament. Fortunately Macdonnell was not a Bowring or the colony might have come to a dead stop in the late sixties.

The several problem areas with which the Governor had to deal were in their own ways separate entities, but as frequently happened in Hong Kong all were closely tangled in what must have seemed at times an unravellable skein. Macdonnell, unlike Bowring, was dogged in his approach and pragmatic and forceful in his methods. This gained him criticism and abuse from London, but a measure of respect in Hong Kong. The colony itself was the eventual benefactor, and he left it after six difficult years in marginally better shape than that in which he had found it.

The Duke of Edinburgh, the first member of the royal family to visit Hong Kong, arrived on 2 November 1869 aboard HMS *Galatea*.

The 12 months prior to his arrival had seen the colony administered by W. T. Mercer, whose dearest wish had been to be appointed Governor when Robinson left. Unfairly, for he had served Hong Kong well, that wish was not granted. Even when he had attempted to leave Hong Kong he had been thwarted and refused a pension. It was said of him at the time that 'gentlemanly and scholarly person' as he was, 'he seems discontented and used up'.[2]

The dark extent of his disillusionment became apparent when the incoming Governor, Macdonnell, and his family discovered that Government House had been left by Mercer unprovided with even the commonest household necessities. The passion of his bitterness was then abundantly demonstrated. Mercer continued in office for another year but the Governor studiously ignored him. Thus departed the last of the old brigade.

Macdonnell's first reaction to the 'depot' was to institute enquiries into every department of government. He found plenty of material to criticize. 'The police are the most ineffective . . . that I ever came in contact with.' So much so that 'literally nothing is known of the haunts of pirates who frequent Hong Kong'. Piracy at the time was one of the main topics of public concern. He lambasted the state of sanitation, the prison system, the inadequate water supply, and concluded that the colony, consequent on Mercer's administration, was headed straight for bankruptcy.

None of this was mere expostulation. Nor was the Governor's response half-hearted. After only four months in the colony he had mapped out reform measures covering many aspects — increased taxation, control of Chinese vessels, registration of dwellings and servants, methods of controlling piracy and eventually eliminating it, branding and deportation of criminals, moves to improve public order and cleanliness. Such a package added up to a fresh policy intended to be viewed as a whole, as a mosaic rather than as the tesserae of which it was composed.

The Colonial Office, apparently convinced that the Governor intended to usurp its authority, responded by accusing Macdonnell of an 'entire pre-occupation with his own views'. Macdonnell's was certainly a dominant personality, buttressed by 20 years' experience in colonial government. He deserved more understanding than that.

The corner-stone on which all these measures depended was finance. Beginning in 1866 the great recession had set in. Many a company, under-capitalized and vulnerable, failed to weather the slump. The spectacular crash of Dent and Company with debts of over $5 million brought down others in shock waves that spread up the China coast. Among the dozen or so foreign banks only six survived to the end of the year. Surprisingly, despite Dent's crash, the Hongkong and Shanghai Bank stood firm. But a decade of uncertainty in trade and banking followed.

The influx of Chinese virtually ceased. Revenue from land sales dried up. That rather airily conceived scheme, the Hong Kong Mint, proved, even in its construction, a drag on the economy; and when it opened in May 1866 it failed to pay its way — as Macdonnell had foreseen. To cover expenses the Mint had to coin at least $27,000 a day, but output seldom reached $15,000. The Governor estimated it would take the next two and a half years to turn the deposited silver bullion into coin. The banks soon began to withdraw their silver, fearing losses if they held on. Macdonnell's enquiry brought to light a sorry picture: not only had the flow of silver to the Mint ceased, but the very machinery was inadequate; worst of all, it was now impossible to buy silver bullion on terms that would make the minting of coins profitable. With expenses calculated at between $50,000 and $60,000 a year, all work came to a stop. The Mint closed in April 1868, its machinery bringing $60,000 from the buyer — the Japanese government.

Macdonnell appears to have been misinformed by the Colonial Office before he left London on the financial state of Hong Kong. He arrived with the idea that it was good. But during Mercer's housekeeping interregnum the situation had changed. Whereas in January 1863 there was a balance of $475,000, by 1865 it had declined to $55,000. Macdonnell had perforce to seek immediate ways and means to rectify the situation. He began by putting a stop to all but urgently needed public works and delaying payment of the colony's contribution to military expenditure. Then he borrowed $80,000 from the Hongkong and Shanghai Bank to meet unavoidable expenses. Sensibly he sought means of increasing taxation by means of a Stamp Ordinance. From October 1867 all official documents (banknotes included) were to pay stamp duties calculated *in toto* to cover the estimated deficit of $120,000 each year. The result was almost immediate: expenditure for that year remained within revenue, and in 1868, despite paying off arrears in the military contribution, a surplus of $140,000 was posted. The total revenue in that year stood at what Eitel calls 'an astounding sum' of $1,134,105, with expenditure at $991,811. Eitel continues:

> Instead of rejoicing over this result, the mercantile community, engulfed in a slough of despond ... pointed with groans ... to the Stamp Ordinance which had taken $101,000 [out of their pockets in one year.] Sir Richard could boast of having so regulated the finances, that, during a period of unexampled commercial disasters in China, the Colony emerged from a state of insolvency to one of assured financial stability.[3]

It was now said that Macdonnell would never have had to introduce the measure had he been allowed a free hand in dealing with the gambling problem. There was some basis for this opinion.

The suppression of gambling was the Governor's next cross. He bore it with flexibility, verve, and inventiveness in the face of narrow-minded, obdurate civil servants in London. To be fair, the mood in Britain at this time was one of resolute piety, abhorrence of all gambling, and stiffening of national (or at least notional) morality. In Hong Kong Macdonnell hardly breathed the same air. The Chinese passion for all forms of gambling was a fact of life; and it was also part and parcel of the question of law and order and of the police corruption he had noticed on arrival. The problem was how to regulate gambling (or legislate against it altogether?), how to end police corruption, and at the same time restore the force of law.

Having said that nothing was known of the haunts of pirates infesting Hong Kong waters, Macdonnell shrewdly suspected the involvement of local interests — 'the parties that fit them out'. But dealing with them had to fit into the grand strategy of eliminating other evils. An increase in police efficiency, a special piracy court, close supervision of Chinese ashore and afloat, a prohibition on carrying arms and ammunition aboard Chinese junks — these were the mainstays of action, along with an attempt at closer contact with the Chinese élite.

Macdonnell's ordinance calling for the registration of houses and servants also made the Registrar-General responsible for issuing summonses to Chinese. All householders were to be held responsible for the unlawful acts of members and for payment of fines — a system not unlike the traditional doctrine of collective responsibility which had the force of law in China.

More directly aimed at piracy, another ordinance instituted the registration and control of all junks so that, in theory, no vessel could enter or leave harbour without clearance. Anti-piracy measures, directed against Chinese, required the assent of the Colonial Office, given despite their protests. The effect was immediate. Every junk in the harbour hoisted sail and left, together with 2,000 Chinese. But the exodus did not last long. Reassurances brought them back. Soon over two thousand junks had applied for licences and permits. Strengthening of the marine police was to be supplemented by the presence of a steamer which was being built. Until it could be brought into service the Governor fitted out a junk as substitute. Its name, *Preposterous*, sparked off numerous quips among the wits of whom Hong Kong has always had a good supply. But the piracy court came to nothing in a tangle of legal niceties.

The times were such in the waters of the South China Sea that Chinese and other vessels of all kinds armed themselves in self defence. The result was that it was hard to separate what were peaceable junks from those with offensive intent. By July 1868 proclamations went out in both Guangzhou and Hong Kong under which Chinese fishing vessels were to be disarmed. The Viceroy took no action, whereupon Macdonnell cancelled the proclamation in the colony and refused to disarm junks as planned. A Colonial Office reprimand followed.

Thus, by greater and smaller means, in the face of a reluctant home government, piracy was tackled piecemeal and the incidence gradually declined. Involvement of the police in all this brought into focus the corruption in the force centring on illegal gambling houses. This led to Macdonnell's most controversial campaign. Starting from the fact that 'more than half the [police] inspectors were in receipt of monthly allowances' from brothels and gaming houses, the Governor's reasoning told him he must rigidly confine gambling to licensed premises, or give up hope of real police reform.

The public turning point came when a policeman was accused of taking a bribe but was acquitted because there was no ordinance under which he could be charged. Gambling was then seen by those in control of it as an almost legal activity since they could bribe the police with impunity. Macdonnell determined, therefore, to license a small number of places, and in September 1867 the crucial ordinance on Order and Cleanliness appeared. This apparently innocuous document contained in clause 17 words that allowed Macdonnell 'to pass such rules, regulations, and conditions as may be deemed expedient for the total suppression or in the meanwhile for the better limitation and control of gambling in the colony'. This clause covered the decision already taken to license gambling, an action which had been refused to Bowring and Robinson.

Macdonnell had thereby nailed his colours to the mast. He was against the evils of gambling but he knew that his first priority was reform of the police and the eradication of corruption within it. With his usual oratorical skill he defended his actions to the Legislative Council, and in written dispatches to London. In July 1867, 11 gaming houses were opened under the Registrar-General's control. (Prior to this, owners of gaming houses had offered between $200,000 and $365,000 per annum for a licence — an indication of the profits to be made.) The Colonial Office had grudgingly agreed to the licensing but with the fatal proviso that the fees were not to be considered as part of general revenue but to be used strictly for police purposes.

Macdonnell bent his efforts towards getting round this — to him — unreasonable condition; not, as Eitel confirms,

> because revenue was his real object but because the Chinese [holders] of the gaming licence would, if paying a heavy fee [for it], be compelled by their own interests to form a detective police for the suppression of unlicenced gambling, and these detectives would then co-operate with the Police Force for the arrest and detention of dangerous characters who flock to gaming houses as moths to light.

So the Governor informed the Colonial Office in January 1867 that farming out the licences was the sole means to establish permitted gaming houses, and that with an income from this source of approximately $200,000 per annum the colony might be able to resume paying the 'Military Contribution'.

The Order and Cleanliness Ordinance received royal assent. Macdonnell was informed by telegraph and disclosed it to the public on 10 July 1867.

(The Governor was the first to be at the receiving end of the new electric telegraph which connected the colony with London via the submarine cable to Shanghai and thence via the Danish Trans-Siberian line. Both he and some of his successors were somewhat reluctant admirers of this facility, which deprived them of the freer rein they had enjoyed when formerly separated from London by a couple of months.)

At first all seemed to go well with the scheme, its sole opponents the 'moral six' clergymen who took their objections as far as Parliament, accusing the Governor of acting in 'an underhand and unenglish way' and of 'barefaced hypocrisy' in thinking that licensing led to suppression. Macdonnell's enquiries revealed a daily total of 14,630 Chinese and 204 European gamblers (before he forbade the latter to gamble). But by the end of the year abuses had come to light. Some licensees were illegally trading their licences at high prices. And, acting in concert, licensees had taken on an agent in the person of Mr Caldwell, paying him the 'monstrous salary of $20,000 per annum'. Caldwell, trading on former government connections and his long liaison with the more dubious elements in Chinese society, had found a lucrative post. The Colonial Secretary, the Duke of Buckingham, expressed his 'entire disapproval of those proceedings which your dispatch discloses'.

The incoming Liberal government in Britain in December 1868 was strongly Nonconformist. Lord Granville as Colonial Secretary took the view that the whole exercise in Hong Kong in regard to gambling was only to be countenanced as a step to total elimination. Money derived therefrom must be used solely for the suppression of gambling. The Governor counter-claimed that licensing had aided in crime detection, and that no fewer than 50 criminals had been arrested on the information of licensees. He was nothing if not persistent, feeling that he knew more about how to deal with gambling than did the Colonial Secretary. He was probably right; but he underestimated the strength of the Nonconformist lobby in London.

Granville complained of the tone of the Governor's replies to him and detailed the exact objects for which revenues from gambling could properly be spent. A dispute between them followed, only ending when Granville wrote bluntly: 'You will take these instructions for your guidance.' Granville was in something of a quandary. The only tenable stance in the face of Parliamentary criticism was that Hong Kong should not be the recipient of money from licensed vice.

The Governor's numerous reasoned arguments were eventually to no avail against Parliament's new-found godliness, and Macdonnell's final appeal in March 1870 was denied. Granville ordered him to repay $129,701 to the special fund, and to give up the steamer *Victoria* which he had commissioned for police work (it was sold to the Chinese government). But his last impassioned plea is worth recording. Of the money from licensed gaming he wrote: 'let the money be thrown into the sea as soon as it is paid, but do not let the hold which it gives the Government over the licensees be abandoned'. Brave words.

At this point Macdonnell decided to take home leave. Opinion in Hong Kong was slightly turning against the licensing scheme, and in the Governor's absence the Acting Governor, Major-General Whitfield, with the concurrence of the Legislative Council, issued on 1 January 1871 a proclamation closing the gaming houses and withdrawing licences. Granville immediately countermanded it, allowing no change in the Governor's absence. The Chief Justice put out a statement that in the years 1867–8 almost one million dollars had been staked and lost in government gaming houses. The public, he said, had been the losers.

Chinese opinion now turned against licensing. A Chinese-inspired petition wanted to know why foreigners were excluded from gambling while Chinese were allowed to 'engulf themselves'. Returning from leave in December 1871, Macdonnell cancelled licences as from 20 January 1872. But he refused to permit the suppression of gambling to fall into the hands of the police, making the Registrar-General and the Captain Superintendent of Police *personally* responsible. The Governor's basic conflict was with the irrelevance of the Nonconformist British conscience as expressed in Parliament. The problem was neither ameliorated nor solved. It was now simply ignored. A Nonconformist home government had achieved precisely what it aimed to eliminate.

Having failed to root out police corruption in this way, Macdonnell tackled it in another. Finding the Police Captain Superintendent incompetent, he replaced him by a cadet officer, W. M. Deane. He brought in 100 Sikhs as policemen. The Governor thought so highly of these men that he ordered another 100. Sikhs remained for long in the police force and form a significant element in the population even today. Eight British police officers were either dismissed or allowed to resign in a further effort to clean the Augean stables. But the whole matter, fraught with problems and hampered by lack of money, appeared insoluble.

In a slightly improved financial climate before he left, Macdonnell was able to recruit in January 1872 an extra 22 Scottish police, introducing thereby a body of men as yet untainted by the colony's depraved ways. He thought that the rising crime rate was also due to a 'living wave of crime' washed down from China by disturbed conditions there, and frustrating all his efforts to make Hong Kong 'more habitable'. His efforts were virtually in vain.

A policy of deterrence seemed the most efficient way to deal with criminality. But the impeccable logic of flogging and branding (with a small broad arrow on the ear-lobe, inflicted on criminals who opted for deportation, thus making identification easier if they returned) was not approved by the Secretary of State. Yet only six months after Macdonnell arrived the convict population had diminished by 162 and by September 1867 stood at

363 — 351 fewer still. The idea of deterring criminal persons from entering the colony was naturally approved by all, but the home government frowned on the means, which stood in contrast to the more humane treatment in Britain. The error of the Colonial Office, repeated frequently in Hong Kong history, was to take as the basis of its stance on various issues the approved opinion and moral climate of Britain at any given time, and to apply it in Hong Kong. Soon, the deportation of criminals was abolished on orders from London, and banishment could only be enforced on non-British subjects if they were regarded as dangerous to the peace. Thus, after 1870, crime and criminal violence seriously rose, so much so that the Justices of the Peace demanded an enquiry. In their view life and property had never before been at such risk. Eventually, in the face of the extreme reluctance of the home authorities, Macdonnell was permitted to bring back flogging and branding. And he buttressed these measures by building several new police stations and by ordering that all the police stations in the colony should be connected by telegraph.

The Reform Act of 1867 in Britain, extending the franchise, was reflected in Hong Kong in renewed local demand for changes in the constitution of the Legislative Council. A Reform Association belatedly came into being in 1869, said later by Macdonnell to have 'died out through sheer inanition'.[4] Constitutional reform, however, had gone ahead when Macdonnell received instructions on this subject in October 1865. The old balance of six government and three non-government members of the Council was to be retained. The Chief Justice, Colonial Secretary, Attorney-General, Treasurer, and Auditor-General were to be official members ex officio; while four others — one government official and three private individuals — were nominated as unofficial members, with the official members having precedence. The official members' right to vote as they saw fit was ended.

> HM Government have the right to consider opposition by official members of the Legislative Council to its settled policy as incompatible with retention of office... I am equally of opinion that they are, if required to do so, to support by their vote and not to oppose by any public act, a policy which may originate with the Governor.[5]

The Governor had both an ordinary and a casting vote.

The unwillingness of the merchant community to act with a sense of civic responsibility rather than from sheer selfishness resulted in another area of frustration for Macdonnell and the community. One of the more than usually numerous typhoons which hit Hong Kong in this period had almost destroyed the Central Praya in August 1867 (see Appendix 2). Macdonnell notified the lot holders on the affected portions that they would have to contribute a reasonable sum towards the cost of rebuilding. They refused. He called a conference with the Colonial Secretary (C. C. Smith who had been one of the first cadets to have Chinese language training under Dr Legge), who told them the Attorney-General had ruled that each of them had a legal liability under the terms of their leases for maintenance of the sea wall. The lot holders, armed with other legal opinion, claimed that the terms referred to drains, roads, and the like, but not to sea walls. The conference broke up in confusion. In a test case (popularly termed 'the Great Praya case'), the jury gave a verdict for the defendant in February 1868. And the Governor had to be content from then on to agree that the sea wall was a public responsibility.

The need, identified by Eitel six long years back as Sir Richard Macdonnell arrived, had been for 'a Caesar'. At his departure in April 1872, the same writer summed up the Governor's term of office, misquoting Shakespeare's line: 'Here was a Caesar! Whence comes such another?'[6] Macdonnell's struggles with the 'depot' and equally with a Colonial Office which often enough failed to appreciate the problems and their sources in Hong Kong, had been valiant indeed. That he had failed in several attempts cannot be attributed to lack of energy, effort, or forethought. There are some problems confronting governments which, at a given time, seem not susceptible of solution, and have to await a more propitious moment.

12. *Colonial Appeasement*

THERE was no great need for another Caesar. An experienced civil servant was what was required in Hong Kong to continue where Macdonnell left off. Sir Arthur Kennedy was all that. He arrived in April 1872, his background army and then four governorships — two in Africa, one in Canada, a fourth in Australia. It seemed that Whitehall had again made a reasonable choice.

Sensibly, Kennedy's first concern was law and order. The Police Commission set up by Macdonnell reported a few months after he arrived in Hong Kong. Its findings were not unanimously agreed, but it recommended an Anglo-Chinese force with more strength and better pay and conditions. This chimed well with the views of Dr Legge who was all for Chinese police as the best means of gaining the confidence of leading Chinese and of the community at large. But Charles May, resident in the colony since 1844 and closely associated with the police, was strongly against this, dismissing the Chinese police in Hong Kong as 'useless, physically and morally'.

Kennedy sat on the report for a year, withholding comment. Gradually he was coming to the conclusion that a Chinese force was the right answer. He raised the pay scales of constables and set Chinese-speaking cadet officers over them. 'We shall learn to rely on them more than at present', he said. While the Colonial Office protested over the expense, Kennedy stood firm. He kept the Sikhs as gaol guards, but thought the Commander-in-Chief, Major-General Whitfield's idea of recruiting West Indian police 'little short of insanity' since it would be taken as an affront to the whole Chinese community. Improvement in the efficiency of the force could not be an overnight matter. The number of Chinese police was balanced by an equal number of Indian police until well into the twentieth century. The introduction of Chinese officers in the twentieth century, when gradually they became more numerous than British officers, completed the transformation to a predominantly Chinese force.

Kennedy was far from being a violent or harsh man, yet in his attempts to deal with the high crime rate he evidently felt that branding and deportation were essential; and doubtless the Colonial Secretary would have vetoed their removal since it was he who had forced their reintroduction on Macdonnell.

Kennedy explained in 1873, perhaps in an effort to soften the impact of such procedures, that 'the miscalled system of branding which is merely tattooing with Indian ink, is seldom resorted to, but works well'. The gaol population fell in 1873 to 331, and on Stonecutters island only the chapel was now in use, functioning as a hospital for infectious diseases, predominantly smallpox.

The solution or partial solution of one problem in Hong Kong generally led to, or was at least closely followed by, the appearance of another. While gambling had been more or less suppressed within Hong Kong boundaries, it now grew large in the Kowloon peninsula north of the boundary dividing the British area from the Chinese. In reality this gambling was merely *open* gambling; in clubs and unlicensed resorts the practice had not been stamped out in Hong Kong, merely hidden from view. An officially closed eye was trained on it.

An upsurge in crime occurred in 1876 from another source. The lowering of fares in a cut-throat price war between the operators of various river steamers plying between Guangzhou and the colony resulted in an influx of undesirables. In three weeks the gaol population rose from 386 to 519. Kennedy reacted by reinforcing the deportation law and by appointing a commission of enquiry. But he also revised outdated gaol regulations. Extra food for prisoners was to be ordered much more sparingly.

The disastrous consequences of 'the most destructive typhoon in the history of the Colony' of 24 September 1874, focused attention on the whole

The disastrous typhoon of 1874 played havoc with the colonial cemetery at Happy Valley.

question of public works. The civil hospital was virtually destroyed, as were 200 houses and three miles of the praya. The central area was left without a praya, to all intents and purposes, and when the wind and water receded the appalling devastation shocked the colony. It was evident that the praya had been of faulty construction, and now that it had been agreed in the wake of the 1867 typhoon damage that repairs were the job of the government, Kennedy was faced with the extremely tricky task of obtaining agreement on details of reconstruction from all those with lots on the waterfront, of finding the money for rebuilding, and of achieving a greatly improved structure. These factors meshed with another — a decision on the extent of reclamation that might conveniently be carried out at this time. The Chinese lot holders at the western end of the town were keen to reclaim land and increase their holdings; but their expectations were frustrated by the 1875 board of enquiry which decided against reclamation in the Sai Ying Pun and Sheung Wan areas. Kennedy himself thought that in the central area 'no reclamations were likely ever to be made' because of the howl of protest from lot holders that would attend any such proposal. The marine lots were by now very valuable, and any reclamation would distance them from the shore. He determined to rebuild the sea wall so that it would be proof against further typhoon damage.

The crucial section as regards town planning was that part lying in front of the naval and military areas. Obviously, for both, access to the harbour was vital. The two cantonments covered much of the hillside descending to the harbour just east of Central District. Queen's Road, running parallel to the water here, was the sole link with Wan Chai to the east, now a growing suburb. Victoria, viewed as a whole, was, as the Surveyor-General J. M. Price said, effectively 'strangled at its waist'. The only other link between the two parts of the town was to be constructed later some distance up the hill and named Kennedy Road. For the moment Queen's Road had no rival (and, although much widened, in terms of through traffic still has none). One other important aspect was the fact that the sea-bed was silting up in front of the naval base, leaving the pier high and dry at low tide.

The natural, indeed the only intelligent scheme was that advocated by Price — to extend the Praya in front of the naval base and military area so as to link the eastern and central prayas and 'ease the unceasing native and foreign traffic through the Queen's Road Central'. Deep water would adjoin such a new sea wall and the planned curve at that point would, because of the currents, have a scouring action and prevent renewed silting. Through the wall there would be entries for smaller craft, and a mechanical swing bridge would permit the passage of larger vessels for refitting in the dock. The military were against this good plan because of the expense. Kennedy strongly advocated its adoption hoping, as nearly all Governors have had to hope, for financial assistance from home — in this case from both the Admiralty and the War Office. The authorities in London agreed to the plan only on the understanding that the colony would bear the expense. The Executive Council and unofficials of the Legislative Council accepted the proviso, but in the face of the colony's having to foot the total bill, it was agreed to abandon the scheme and merely to reconstruct the central Praya to resist natural hazards. Even this the home government wanted to postpone. Kennedy however, had wisely already gone ahead in order to keep the water out of the town, the record enshrining his opinion that the larger scheme would have to be undertaken some time in the future.

A contributory factor in the failure of the Praya development was the use of the telegraph and the shortened transit time for goods from Europe after the opening of the Suez Canal in November 1869. In combination, these two new facilities meant that merchants no longer had to warehouse large stocks in order to take advantage of price changes, for stocks could now be received much more expeditiously. A whole train of events followed from this: the large godowns in Eastern District became superfluous, and as a result the labour force moved from Eastern to Western District seeking other employment; and this in turn prompted the laying out of Kennedy Town, partly on reclaimed land. Further, rental values in Eastern District fell steeply because of the labour migration — by 40 to 50 per cent — and those who paid Crown rents sought a reduction, which Kennedy refused. This in turn forced the consideration of an alternative east–west route skirting the southern boundary of the military area — uphill from the shore — which was first proposed by Kennedy and taken up by his successor.

In public works Kennedy was fortunate in that the inept L. H. Moorsom, Surveyor-General, happened to retire as he arrived, and was replaced by the admirable Price, to whose attention the Governor recommended the sadly inadequate water supply position. Because of appalling miscalculations, the Pok Fu Lam scheme generated only about one-third of the predicted volume. Price now constructed a conduit along the 500-foot contour (today's Conduit Road) to bring an adequate supply to Central and Western Districts, and this came into operation in 1877. Eastern District was however inadequately provided for, and Price then proposed to bring water from the Tai Tam area via a tunnel through the hills — a scheme that looked both neat and efficient until it was calculated that the cost would be in the region of £350,000. The scheme was referred to a consultant in England who produced a scaled-down version at an estimated cost of £136,000. Government revenues being good but not abundant, this idea was whittled down to one that would cost £50,000, and which could be enlarged in the future.

The destruction of the civil hospital by the 1874 typhoon meant that a replacement had to be set up quickly. Temporary arrangements were made. But even before the typhoon, when the new Colonial Surgeon, Dr Phineas Ayres, first arrived in November 1873 he had attempted to hasten the building of a new one. By now the matter was urgent. Once more the Colonial Office intervened, insisting that the plans for the new building be prepared in London. And when, after considerable delay, these arrived they turned out to be quite unsuited to Hong Kong. Kennedy pressed for leave to start the building at once but was smartly informed by telegraph (how he must have hated the invention!) not to incur avoidable expense. The building of the hospital started in 1874. With the Pok Fu Lam waterworks, a new Harbourmaster's office (1872), and the Central School, it was one of several major public works initiated by Kennedy. The construction of the school was

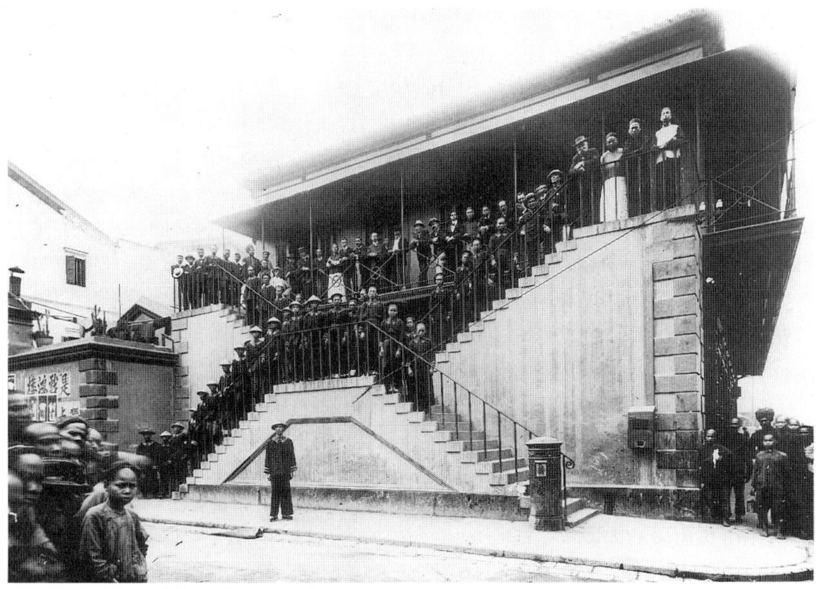

The old Harbour Office seen from Wing Lok Street, *c.*1880.

delayed because of some doubt about the structure, which was to cost $52,000. It was built after Kennedy had left. His major memorial must be the Grant-in-Aid scheme through which voluntary schools were financed.

In constitutional matters some important changes were made in Kennedy's time. From London his instructions relating to Legislative Council proceedings were amended to give it the power to debate any question if duly proposed and seconded — not just on the Governor's initiative, which was now limited to matters of finance. In 1872 a Finance Committee composed of all members of the Council, presided over by the senior member, was set up, to which the Governor was to submit financial business for consideration. This meant that unofficial members had more chance of taking an independent line — something they immediately did. After the typhoon they recorded their displeasure with W. M. Deane, Superintendent of Police, for keeping the police in their barracks during the storm. They wanted to reduce his salary and, dissatisfied with the way it was organized, to cut the vote for the fire brigade — intemperate demands, and short-sighted, given the circumstances.

Membership of the Executive Council was increased to five: the ex-officio members were the Commander-in-Chief, the Colonial Secretary, and the Attorney-General; J. P. Price, the Surveyor-General, and C. C. Smith (one of the first three cadets recruited in England in 1862), who was now Registrar-General, were made members but not by virtue of the offices they held. The office of Acting Governor, whose occupant stood in for the Governor in his absence or incapacity, had been held since the time of Caine in 1854 by the chief military officer of the colony. The exception was Mercer who, after Caine left in 1859, deputized for him as Colonial Secretary until Macdonnell arrived; at which time the Major-General commanding the troops became again Acting Governor. In Kennedy's time the change was made back to the Colonial Secretary administering as Acting Governor. The argument from London was that senior executives should be able to look forward to exercising responsibility in that capacity, and that in any case they were better suited to deal with the administration than was the chief military man. The trigger that activated all this was doubtless the absurd Major-General Whitfield's conduct in Macdonnell's absence. At that time, in the role of Major-General, Whitfield was in the habit of addressing letters to himself in his capacity as Acting Governor — 'a whimsical proceeding', as one Colonial Office official charitably put it. The War Office was informed that the senior army officer in the colony must not act as Acting Governor.

At this point Kennedy, his wife seriously ill in England, was invited to come home for consultations, the Colonial Secretary to administer the government as Acting Governor in his absence. Kennedy commented on this change of policy. The news, he said 'has nearly caused General Colborne [the military incumbent at the time] a fit. He has fairly exploded, and judging from the effect ... he must have had an enormous stock of explosive matter stored up'. Colborne wrote in protest to the War Office, and refused to attend meetings of the Executive Council, something which Kennedy opined, 'was not attended by any ill-effects for the Colony'.[1] Not at least until, because of a shortage of qualified members, and the absence of others on leave, a quorum of the Council could not be mustered.

Price was then appointed to the Council as deputy to the Colonial Secretary, and Colborne resumed his uncooperative posture. It was pointed out to him that when he had been absent from Hong Kong, he had made his own military secretary take his place on the Council, and had therefore no leg to stand on in his refusal to acquiesce in the Governor's appointing a deputy for the Colonial Secretary. Civil and military relations were for a time strained, a fact remarked on in the Colonial Office: 'There is always a row between the

Government and the General in Hong Kong . . . and I conclude that it is one of the local occupations.'[2] While official London was often perspicacious in such pettyfogging disputes, the Colonial Office's grasp of the essentials of more grave situations in the colony was patchy, as many a governor discovered while he wrestled with intractable local problems. In the days of sea transport, even after the opening of the Suez Canal took weeks off the journey, no Colonial Office official in office ever visited Hong Kong.

On his way to England the Governor was informed of his wife's death, and from Singapore he returned to Hong Kong, where he was to remain for several more years.

Two of the obscure but important practical problems that troubled the commercial community in the years 1872–6 had to do with certain substances added to grey shirting exported from England, and to tea leaves both in China and in England. What was known as the 'sizing question' was related to the fact that the addition of size (a substance to stiffen the fabric) to the shirting material appeared to cause mildew during its transport to Hong Kong. During the Crimean War with Russia, tallow for sizing became too expensive, and the cheaper China clay was used as a substitute. This required the use of certain deliquescent salts to decrease the damaging effect of the clay on the fabric. These salts were the culprit, causing mildew in transit. The matter was complicated by several factors, the most dramatic of which was that the badly mildewed cloth arriving in Hong Kong, when condemned and returned to England was, miraculously, found to be in perfect condition and free of mildew. It evidently dried out in the less humid northern climate. Serious losses to Hong Kong merchants occurred, and no feasible solution seemed available.

Likewise with tea. In 1874 import duties on tea in England fell by about 50 per cent. At once complaints were voiced by the tea-drinking public on the adulteration of tea by strange leaves and a greater proportion of tea dust. As in the mildew question, each side accused the other. The mildewed shirting caused Chinese buyers to start buying cloth from India; the adulteration of China tea caused the British consumer to turn to Indian teas. India reaped the benefit in both controversies.

Kennedy was the first Governor to invite Chinese guests to Government House receptions and other social gatherings. Most of these were compradors of the big foreign firms. The practice was said by Westerners to be 'distasteful to most English merchants, but Sir Arthur stoutly adhered to it'. His outlook on the Chinese was even-handed. Soon after he arrived a Chinese delegation called on him, and he informed them that the Chinese could always have access to him when they had things of substance to say. They had only to give him notice and bring an interpreter. The directors, both ingoing and outgoing, of the Tung Wah Hospital came to pay their respects once a year. On their first visit in December 1872 they requested the Governor to pass an ordinance punishing adultery in Chinese women. This was a somewhat odd request considering that every one of the deputation had several wives and was, in English law, a bigamist and liable to punishment as such. The request seems to have been designed to deter one or other concubine from flight, perhaps to the bosom of another member of the deputation. The following year the directors requested some form of municipal government for the Chinese community, and the authorization of elections among them for a Chinese Municipal Board to assist the Registrar-General with advice on all Chinese matters — an apparently worthwhile idea. In 1874 they wanted compulsory registration of all active and sleeping partners in Chinese shops and firms. Later they asked for an improved bankruptcy law, the building of a typhoon shelter for small craft, a town hall, and a lepers' asylum on some small island. These, it would seem, were mostly reasonable requests made by responsible, forward-looking men. The Governor, however, found himself able to accede to only one — granting a site for a public meeting place. It is possible that his wife's death had a more profound influence on Kennedy than is on record, and his mind turned away from the liberality of the early years of his office. Later, he introduced an order 'couched in language of the most extraordinary circumlocution'[3] which in effect gave Chinese with any petition or grievance leave to communicate with the government only through the Registrar-General. Great caution had supervened.

The extent of the administration's lack of understanding of the Chinese, and its faltering control, were demonstrated in August 1872 when a small tax was levied on Chinese coolie rooming-houses in an attempt to control insanitary conditions. A strike of all the carrying coolies broke out at once. Considering the minuscule wages of these men, their solidarity was remarkable, indicating genuine grievance. They ended the strike only on condition that the government would repeal the tax. The government repealed it.

Some reorganization was introduced in the judiciary. Judge Ball of the Summary Court, suffering from epilepsy, retired in 1872, and this court was abolished. J. Paunceforte, Attorney-General since 1866, became Puisne Judge but left the same year to become Chief Justice of the Leeward Islands, and was succeeded by F. Snowdon. The post of Attorney-General was filled for two years by John Bramston, and on his appointment to a Colonial Office position he was followed by G. Phillippo.

Sir Arthur Kennedy was perhaps as good a Governor as any in the colony's history. His approach to his task was determined, generally fair, and unclouded by personal idiosyncrasies. When a situation arose which had no obvious solution, or when no precise mode of action presented itself, he appointed a committee to look at it from more than one man's point of view; and he did this more often than any of his predecessors and than many of his successors in the nineteenth century. It was typical of his administration that the Gardens and Afforestation Department was very active and that the systematic planting of trees in the city moved forward. Kennedy's was a friendly approach, both administratively and personally, and while he withdrew from his initial openness with the Chinese he was still regarded by them as understanding of their attitudes. He fought doggedly against the difficult problem posed by the 'blockade' but failed to master it any more than had Macdonnell (see Chapter 14). His one major failure was his disregard of the appallingly insanitary condition of the colony. From reading the reports of the Surveyor-General and the Colonial Surgeon he could not possibly have been unaware of it. Perhaps, as his retreat from closer contacts with the Chinese may indicate, he was in greater distress at the loss of his wife than history relates. Eitel hints at it when he writes of Lady Kennedy's death that she was 'highly revered by Hong Kong residents as she had always given a tone of gentleness to the sterner rule of even the least severe Governor of Hong Kong'.

The appreciation of residents was seen at Kennedy's departure in March 1877. Later, on the news of his death in the Red Sea in June 1883, on the return voyage to England from his appointment as Governor of Queensland, a public meeting determined to set up a statue to him, appropriately enough in the Botanical Gardens, where it remained until removed by the Japanese during the Second World War. Eitel calls him 'one of those few men who deserve a statue because they do not need one'.

Sir Arthur Kennedy's statue stood in the Botanical Gardens until the Japanese removed it during the occupation in World War II.

13. *Mr Hennessy's Proceedings*

G. R. Sayer introduces the next Governor of Hong Kong, who arrived in April 1877, in a paragraph of gentle irony:

Under the appeasing influence of Kennedy . . . an unusual calm had fallen upon the colony and British and Chinese had settled down side by side to make hay while the sun shone. In these circumstances one might have expected the continuance of so happy a state of affairs would have been assured, at any rate by sending a second Sir Arthur to succeed the first. But, if the Secretary of State frowned on exuberance, he was no less fearful of stagnation and accordingly . . . cast about for one who could be depended upon to keep things moving. There is no doubt that he was entirely successful.

Mr (later Sir) John Pope Hennessy was then near the end of his tour as Governor of the Windward Islands, and on him the choice fell. Having planted the scion of these islands in the soil of Hong Kong, both the Colonial Office and the colony were to reap a predictable — but apparently unforeseen — crop. The driving force behind the actions of the new Governor lay in the nature of the man himself. There were two factors or conditions. The first is best defined by quoting from a brief given to the Secretary of State by a leading civil servant. Commenting on the turmoil in Hong Kong during Hennessy's term there, in which the British community had ceased to accept invitations to Government House, he wrote:

To my mind the history of all this trouble is a simple one. Mr Hennessy observes on arriving that long residence among Chinese, & familiarity with the Chinese character, has led the residents of Hong Kong to believe that a Chinaman is not to be dealt with as an Englishman or even as an Indian or Malay might be. He thinks this inhuman, and determines to set to work vigorously to reform what he believes to be a grave abuse. But, having no political wisdom, he proceeds in such a manner as to alienate from him all public sympathy and support, & ultimately to cause a sort of panic as to his intentions & their probable results.[1]

The second factor lay in precisely what the official defined as the English attitude to the Chinese. His characterization of it was undeniably right, as any reading of the relevant documents demonstrates.

Both forces in the upheaval that took place in the colony may be seen at work in the comparatively trivial matter of the use of the Hong Kong Museum in the City Hall. The Chairman of the Museum Committee was William Keswick of Jardine's. The museum enjoyed a small government grant but was substantially supported by subscription from the leading merchant houses, and from the rates which were paid by all who owned property, Chinese and foreigners alike. Hennessy discovered that Chinese were admitted to the museum and library in the mornings only. At lunch the museum was closed and cleaned, and in the afternoon it was reserved exclusively for foreigners. At a meeting in the museum in 1876, both Keswick and the Governor agreed to sound out prominent Chinese business men for funds for an extension which would make the museum 'a place of amusement and instruction to the Chinese'. The meeting noted that in the previous week 14,000 Chinese had visited it and the library, and only 300 Europeans. Hennessy found it all the more reprehensible, in view of the figures, that the Chinese should be confined to morning visiting. He wanted to open the museum to all during normal hours. Keswick expressed his view that the Chinese use of the museum was already excessive, and their presence unsavoury. Hennessy thereupon cut off the government grant. The Colonial Office upheld him, Lord Kimberley, Secretary of State, commenting dryly that 'garlic-eating ratepayers must be endured by those who use their money'. The attitude of Lord Kimberley was at base the same as that implicit in the colonial attitude which attempted segregation by race, but British principles of imperial policy had to be seen to be practised, and the Secretary of State to be seen to uphold them. Apartheid could not be officially condoned, even if it was a fact.

The dispute might have died away in time had not the Governor's anger at what he correctly saw as the community's racist stance got the better of his sense. He proceeded to stop the sale of liquor at all functions in the City Hall on the legitimate ground that a licence had never been applied for. But, as the Secretary of State wrote testily, 'a little tact might usefully have replaced these impassioned harangues'.

And there in a nutshell lay both the nub and the rub. Hennessy's endowment of liberal and progressive ideas, sincerely held, was hardly balanced by a store of political or even ordinary tactful sense. The visit of the King of Hawaii to Hong Kong in 1881 once more demonstrated the proposition. Keswick, honorary Hawaiian Consul in the colony, went out to the King's ship when it anchored in the harbour to invite him to stay at Jardine House. It was tactless of him too, no doubt. Hennessy, getting word of this, and while Keswick was still on board with the King, sent his official 12-oar barge bearing 'an invitation from the Governor ... in the name of the Queen, to be his guest'. The King, protocol having been thrust under his nose, could scarcely do other than comply, much to the ire of William Keswick. Hennessy, as usual, informed the Secretary of State of events. Lord Kimberley, wisely, dismissed it as a 'miserable squabble'.

One more example of Hennessy's capacity to put his foot in things occurred during a luncheon given a day or two after the barge incident. The host was Paul Catchick Chater, a wealthy business man and later philanthropist. Hennessy made a speech in which, apparently intending jest, he referred to 'trifling incidents ... in past years, such as the killing of Captain Cook by His Majesty's predecessor'. Either the prandial level of inebriation was rather high or the King was a forbearing monarch, for he did not leave the table.

Hennessy, like the two governors before and one after him, was an Irishman. Men of very different temperaments, both Macdonnell and Kennedy were, when it came to major decisions, realists. Hennessy was not. For him the standard concept of the colony as a place where 'an Englishman could not only careen his ship without interference, but also dwell in peace and security ashore', as Kennedy had put it, was not enough. Hennessy was a man of lively human sympathy which, untypically for his time, he extended to all races. Mere toleration was not in his book. The consensus of opinion among Westerners was that the Chinese were a necessary adjunct to commerce, and that when one or other of them transgressed, the effective correctional methods were flogging, branding, expulsion. Apart from the question of humane sentiments, the Chinese, as Hennessy pointed out, were in many cases large taxpayers and as such had claim to a say on the body which dispensed the taxpayers' money. In the debate in Britain at the time on the question of the management of criminals, the swing was towards reform, prisoners' aid societies, and re-education. It is doubtful if anyone regarded this as applicable to Chinese criminals in Hong Kong. Hennessy was in a minority of one in merchant and governing circles. His isolation seemed to fuel the flames of his temperament. Encouraged by the abolition of convict transportation 20 years previously in Britain, he penned a series of dispatches home very soon after arriving, condemning Hong Kong's whole penal system. Pointing out that much crime was of a petty nature, mendicancy, unlicensed hawking, and being out at night without a pass, he mentioned that in the past year only two in five were not first offenders. He criticized the gaol system which made no attempt to separate first from habitual offenders, and failed to apply any moral or other educational procedures. He found the habit of voluntary branding and deportation in return for full or partial remission of a sentence entirely inequitable, since under it good and bad, short- and long-term prisoners received the same treatment. He objected to the sentence of deportation on other grounds — that it was used for criminals but also to remove Chinese women who in many cases had lived in Hong Kong for years but at the age of seventy or eighty were too old to work. Under the existing law, he said, he had 'with pain and reluctance' deported them.

On the subject of the gaol, Hennessy thundered against the foreign turnkeys who were often in trouble for drunkenness, brutalized by administering numberless floggings, and yet were retained in their positions. Hennessy dismissed the worst of them and began the recruitment and training of men brought out from England. He refused to free any prisoner before he had served at least two-thirds of his sentence, and announced his aim was to abolish branding — then, for some reason, carried out on the neck rather than on the ear lobe. There was nothing in all those opinions and suggested alterations in practice which would have caused even the twitch of an eyebrow in Britain at that time. Hennessy's problem was that he was not in Britain but in Hong Kong. Public opinion (from mostly ill-educated, morally self-righteous instant experts) was set in dead opposition to the increasingly liberal climate in Britain — because the subjects were Chinese, not British. It must remain in doubt whether, even by the exercise of that tact which Hennessy lacked, *any* governor at the time could have carried into practice, without antagonizing the foreign community, the kind of reforms Hennessy on the whole justifiably wanted.

The usual nostrum for the easement of social conflict in Hong Kong, a public meeting to express indignation and to formulate a petition to the Colonial Office, was applied by the residents on the cricket ground in October 1878 — prompted by the previous year's rise in crime, said to be the result of the Governor's lenient policies. The meeting demanded the return of public flogging and deportation. The petition also requested an enquiry into the administration of the criminal law, and into relations between the Governor and officials.

The leading light in this was William Keswick, an unofficial member of the Legislative Council. Against this petition the Chinese submitted their own address to the Governor, signed by a large number of leading figures, supporting his policies. The Secretary of State (who must have been a sorely tried official at this time), in response to both documents, upheld the Governor in most aspects but feared the effects of his policies. Hennessy was asked to prepare plans for the reform of penal legislation, the conduct of the gaol, and methods of implementing his policies.

His proposals included the siting of a new gaol on Stonecutters island, its design suited to the segregation of prisoners in various categories. But the Secretary of State in London disagreed, preferring a site on Hong Kong island. Hennessy then constructed 40 cells in the basement of Victoria gaol as a tentative beginning to reform, and abolished flogging except in cases of violent crime. Perhaps the most significant revision of the penal laws was the dropping of legislation specifically directed against the Chinese — measures dating from the panic months of 1857 in the wake of the *Arrow* incident. The Banishment Ordinance of 1882 was altered and banishment retained at the discretion of the Governor, and to be for not more than five years, and not to be applied only to Chinese but to all.

Generally speaking, Hennessy's policies in these matters were effective. Yet most Westerners in Hong Kong persisted in clinging to the short-term view, accusing him of encouraging crime and intending to abolish deportation and flogging altogether — something he had never suggested.

In a society in which numerous female children constituted a threat to the economic security of Chinese families, a society moreover in which concubinage and the *mui tsai* system were approved by most, and which was physically removed from the constraints inherent in village life over the border, the problem of kidnapping was bound to arise. We have seen in Chapter 10 the stance of Hong Kong's Chinese community in relation to kidnapping and *mui tsai* in the formation of the Po Leung Kuk, and also the opinion of the Chief Justice that the system was repugnant to British law. The situation worsened in the wake of rising numbers of cases of kidnapping. Women and girls were lured on false pretences to the colony from where they were sent overseas to satisfy South-east Asian demand; or they were disposed of in Hong Kong itself. The price might be as high as $345 for the former and $45 for Hong Kong. Women were treated exactly as if they were commodities.

To the protests of the Chief Justice, the cautious Attorney-General suggested he confine his remarks to the cases of kidnapping which came to his court, leaving aside the question of *mui tsai* itself which was to be construed as a form of adoption. The Chinese themselves were clear on the difference between it and kidnapping. But the liberal Hennessy found his conscience troubled. On the one hand he was firmly against traffic in human beings: on the other he wished to respect Chinese customs permissible within the framework of British law in its colonial setting. In the end he refused action on the *mui tsai* question, preferring wisely to leave more or less well alone.

There had been a marked increase in the Chinese population between 1872 and 1876, amounting to 15,000 in a total colonial population of about 122,000. But the figure for British males fell in the same period by 86, a figure representing perhaps as much as a quarter of the total in Hong Kong. This would have been an absolute fall but for an influx of Portuguese, consequent on the ravages of the 1874 typhoon. Chinese businesses were increasing in number and prosperity causing, it seemed, a corresponding shrinkage in the foreign business sector. The Chinese by now had gained a certain expertise in marketing Western goods and, being Chinese, were in a better position to deal directly with their compatriots in China. Responding to this changing pattern, Hennessy reported in 1878: 'One sees warehouses that a few years ago were in the midst of a European district ... now in occupation of the

Chinese.' In the business district of the colony at least, the segregation of the races was breaking down a little. Formerly Chinese had clustered together in the east and to the west of Central District, and a clause in the leases of Central District properties restricted construction to Western-style buildings. Hennessy, in 1877, took the Chinese side.

> There being no legal impediment in the way, and it being a matter of principal importance that no obstruction should be put in the way of the natural course of trade . . . permits [may] be freely granted for native structures along any part of the Queen's Road, and business streets immediately adjoining

a line drawn between Upper Wyndham Street, Hollywood Road, and Aberdeen Street.[2]

Hennessy thought this was the minimum area into which the Chinese should be allowed to infiltrate. The Registrar-General, C. C. Smith, however, opposed the whole idea. Lord Carnarvon upheld the Governor, but another serious objection was put forward by the Commander-in-Chief, General Donovan. An irascible figure, chronically at odds with the Governor, he protested, pointing to the insanitary condition of most Chinese housing which might introduce a health hazard. This resulted, benignly for once, even salutarily, in the sending out from London of Osbert Chadwick to report on the sanitary conditions in Hong Kong (see Chapter 14).

The other, less welcome, consequence of granting the Chinese permission to spread out from their former ghettos, led to what is nowadays termed a hiccup in the economy. The new census of 1881 revealed a population of 160,402 — the increase in Chinese amounting to almost 21,000, and of Europeans to 273. The liberalization of the law, together with the pressure of Chinese entrepreneurs indicated by the figures, brought about an unexpected and very considerable speculation in land by the Chinese. Between January 1880 and May 1881 they bought land and property worth $1.7 million from foreign owners and a further $17,705 worth from the government. The frenzy of speculative purchases and opportunist selling drove up the price of land and property during 1881 to an extravagantly unrealistic degree. The bubble burst, as financial bubbles always have done — to the eternal astonishment of the speculators — in the autumn of 1881, the principal sufferers being the leading lights of the Chinese business community. The inevitable bankruptcies reflected a price fall of about 45 per cent, and were followed by vigorous litigation, the property market for the time being 'encumbered by the estates of the embarrassed owners', as Eitel puts it.

The old problem of securing adequate supplies of a suitable silver currency turned up again at this juncture, and various suggestions were advanced. The Chamber of Commerce wanted to introduce the American trade dollar and Hennessy suggested the legalization of Japanese yen in the light of increasing trade with that country. Local business men presented a petition proposing that as there seemed no hope of having a Hong Kong dollar coined in Britain the Mint (of unhappy memory) should be revived. A note of high comedy, in the light of the débâcle over the original Mint, was sounded by the discovery that some enterprising Chinese were manufacturing, 'in the village of Tokwawan' on the Kowloon peninsula, immense quantities of cash for export to Annam and Tongking (now in North Vietnam) where no facilities for minting existed. In court no conviction could be secured since there appeared to be no law forbidding the manufacture of coins. Whereupon the colony was flooded with these cash until the Gazette published a warning in October 1879 that they were not legal tender. The speculation can hardly be resisted that had the operation of the Mint in Hong Kong been put in private Chinese hands, the coinage problem might have been solved to the satisfaction of all. Hennessy, as so often, did nothing at all.

When he did take action it generally caused a flurry in the colony, and often in London too. A member of the Legislative Council, H. B. Gibb, departed from Hong Kong on leave in January 1880. Hennessy at once appointed a Chinese, Ng Choy, in his place. On the face of it, Ng Choy was an eligible appointee — a British subject born in Singapore, educated in England, the first Chinese to be called to the English Bar and the first to practise at the Hong Kong Bar. Giving his reasons, the Governor offered the information that he had consulted the 'wealthy and better Chinese', who had supported Ng Choy. A Chinese memorial sent to London in 1879 had claimed that as they outnumbered the foreigners 10 to one 'it would be fair to allow the Chinese community a share in the management of the affairs of the colony'. And Hennessy had previously, in Labuan (a British island possession off Borneo) when he governed there, made such a Chinese appointment; and Singapore had a Chinese on its Legislative Council. So there was precedent enough.

The Governor's proposal of 1880 was for a reorganization of the Council to contain six official members all holding named offices, and five unofficials, of whom four were to be British and one Chinese. But the Colonial Secretary demurred, deciding that Ng Choy's appointment was temporary, either until Gibb's return or at most for three years. His argument was that in the event of strained relations with China, and the Governor's need to consult the Council, the presence of a Chinese would raise difficulty. He also felt that a Chinese merchant would be better than a barrister. Doubtless he mistrusted the trained wits of a lawyer. At the root of the matter lay suspicion of Hennessy. As a former Secretary of State, Lord Carnarvon, had said: 'I am afraid that a watchful eye is necessary over Mr Hennessy's proceedings.' In this case, however, the suspicion was probably incorrect and also unjust. In July 1880 when Gibb finally resigned from the Council, Hennessy had come out strongly in favour of a permanent Chinese member, bearing in mind that the Chinese were the largest owners of property, contributing 90 per cent of the revenue, as well as being at the root of Hong Kong's prosperity. Later, in August 1881, the Governor appointed the Indian E. R. Belilios, one of the two leading opium merchants and a Director of the Hongkong and Shanghai Bank, to the Council. This was regarded locally as unexceptional.

The story of Eitel, however, another non-British citizen, turned out rather curiously. Ernest Johann Eitel came from Württemberg in Germany and became a missionary with the Lutherans in Guangzhou, and later with the London Missionary Society. He married an English missionary, Mary Eaton, but the Lutherans would not accept her because she was English. Later still, with a family to support, he moved to Hong Kong in 1870. Eitel gained a reputation for his *Chinese Dictionary in the Cantonese Dialect* and other publications. In 1875 he had been appointed honorary Director of Chinese Studies by Kennedy. Hennessy elevated him to the paid position of Inspector of Schools and Chinese Secretary at a salary of £1,000 a year, and later still as Head of the Interpretation Department his salary doubled. He remained Hennessy's Private Secretary and confidant.

E. J. Eitel, the first historian of Hong Kong. This photograph appears to be the only likeness of him.

Hennessy's marriage to Kitty Low, daughter of the Colonial Treasurer in Labuan, was not a particularly happy one. His brooding temperament and his wife's rather child-like outlook (she was only 17 when they married) did not agree well. In Hong Kong the Governor became friendly with the colony's leading Queen's Counsel, Thomas Hayllar, and his wife. Hayllar had a reputation as a womanizer. Hennessy's favoured form of relaxation from the cares of office was to spend weekends on a steam yacht; whereas Kitty disliked the sea. He was often accompanied by Hayllar, but the latter began to cry off — often at the last moment. On one such occasion, as the Governor was about to cast off, a note from Hayllar arrived begging to be excused. Hennessy at once made all haste to Mountain Lodge, his official summer residence on the Peak, and in his wife's boudoir, he said, he found her with Hayllar engrossed in a book which the latter attempted to hide under a cushion. The book — a catalogue of the Museo Boronico in Naples — contained illustrations of classical male and female figures which Hennessy said were indecent. He turned the amorous QC out of the house.

The affair might have ended in stalemate had it not been for an encounter between the Governor and Hayllar on a quiet path near Mountain Lodge. Hennessy claimed Hayllar insulted him and that he struck the reprobate with his umbrella. Hayllar said this was unprovoked and that the Governor had attacked him in a frenzy. He retrieved the weapon and mounted its handle with a silver plaque in his house with the legend 'A memento of the battle of Mountain Lodge.' The story is told amusingly, and more fully, by Hennessy's grandson, James Pope-Hennessy, in his book, *Verandah*.

Two accounts of the affair reached London — Hayllar's and a covering letter from the Governor. The former made no mention of Hennessy's wife. And for once the Governor had been discreet. No action was taken. But, when the Hennessys were leaving for Beijing, the Governor, with infinite indiscretion, instructed Eitel to show his dispatches on the affair to all members of the Legislative Council who might be interested. Hayllar, when he heard of this, set a trap. He sent a friendly member of the Council to see Eitel, who showed him the correspondence and argued the Governor's case. The visitor then made a sworn statement to Hayllar's lawyer and a writ was issued against Eitel for $25,000 damages.

Hennessy's grandson in his book *Verandah* avers that the Governor 'vowed to make the lawsuit his own', but the case never came to court. After a period of intrigue and negotiation by those concerned, Eitel was forced to write two letters of apology to Hayllar, and Hennessy himself was obliged to compose a conciliatory statement. He now looked rather askance at his former confidant, and when Eitel offered to resign, the resignation was accepted.

Eitel was never popular in Hong Kong, perhaps because of his Teutonic outlook (and later because of his confidential relationship with the Governor), but in the Colonial Office there was sympathy for him. When the Governor went on leave and was prevented by London from returning, Eitel continued on as Inspector of Schools until he retired in 1897. In his book *Europe in China*, he gives what is mostly a fair estimate of the quality of Hennessy's administration.

On many an occasion Hennessy discomposed the members of the administration; now and then he crossed swords with one or other of them. When he discovered that a Chinese woman had had to sell her son to pay a fine imposed by C. C. Smith, the Registrar-General, he set up a commission to enquire into the workings of that department. He accused Smith of illegal and immoral practices and put a stop to the system of informers used to incriminate prostitutes. No two men ever differed more essentially over policy towards the Chinese. Smith, who had every reason to think that on the retiral of the Colonial Secretary in Hong Kong (J. Gardiner Austin) in 1878, he would be appointed to that position, discovered that the Governor had secured a new man for the job — W. H. Marsh — and Smith had to look elsewhere for such an appointment.

Hennessy now attempted a wide reorganization of administrative arrangements in relation to the Chinese. His intention was to reduce the powers of the Registrar-General by setting up a new Department of Interpretation under a senior civil servant responsible for translation in the courts, and acting as Chinese Secretary as well. He had in mind for the job none other than Eitel. But here the Colonial Office jibbed. Hennessy was reminded that the purpose of the cadet scheme was to supply men qualified to occupy the highest posts without the need of an interpreter, and that the Registrar-General's job was to act as the official channel of communication between the Chinese and the government. In fact Hennessy's proposed scheme might have worked better than the existing arrangements, but the whole idea was shelved.

Having got rid of one potential Colonial Secretary, C. C. Smith, Hennessy now quarrelled with his own appointee in the position. Marsh found his job no job at all, for Hennessy handled all the business himself. Another casualty was Frederick Stewart, headmaster of the Central School, who had on one occasion refused the post of Registrar-General and accepted that of Police Magistrate where he thought he would be less under the thumb of the Governor. Hennessy also accused the Harbourmaster of laxity in examining shiploads of emigrants. Relations between the Governor and his officials were rapidly turning into the farce which had blemished the reign of Davis. General Donovan had ceased to attend the meetings of the Executive Council or to send his deputy. But worse was to come. There was but one military band in Hong Kong, and it was under the General's command. Whether maliciously or not, he had ordered the band to play at a dinner party organized by him on the Queen's birthday in May 1880. Hennessy had organized his own, official, birthday party, only to discover the essential musicians were otherwise engaged. Local communication being what it was, an appeal was sent to the War Office in London and brought a telegraphed order to the General to abandon his party and send the band to Government House. In terms of protocol the General was clearly in the wrong. Presumably he failed to grace Government House on the occasion.

Given the circumstances, the acrimony and the dumb insolence which was the reaction of the officers of government towards the Governor — it is surprising that the finances of the colony remained good, even advancing into modest prosperity. Part of this was directly attributable to the influx of Chinese and the steady expansion of trade. But to give Hennessy his due, the remainder of the increase in revenues was the result of the stamp-selling agency which he had set up on a commission basis. The revenue from opium also increased, from $132,000 to $205,000, when he broke the opium licence ring. The Governor also wished to reduce the incidence of taxation on the Chinese, especially the junk owners; but the Legislative Council made the counter-suggestion of reducing the municipal rates by 2 per cent. The Secretary of State refused this measure in view of the urgency of the public works to be undertaken. The revenue of the colony, without added taxation, rose from $947,637 in 1878 to almost $1.25 million in 1882.

The state of public works and the successive delays in their implementation, demonstrate Hennessy's inefficiency and the disarray which his governorship induced in the administration. Virtually the sole project which went ahead was the rebuilding of the Praya, begun under Kennedy. The Central School, urgently needed in 1876, was at the end of Hennessy's term not yet in being. The Civil Hospital, wrecked in the 1874 typhoon, its temporary premises gutted by fire, then took over the Lock Hospital and a new school building at Sai Ying Pun. It had been Kennedy's suggestion that the Lock Hospital be converted to a general hospital, and when the Civil Hospital was established in those premises Hennessy appeared to believe that this had been accomplished; and he so reported to London. His assumption of almost all the work of his administrators obviously placed an intolerable load on him, and such confusions were the inevitable result. Having suggested a new gaol, not one stone of it was ever put in place. Muddled thinking on the Tai Tam water supply scheme effectively held it up. The Governor appeared to be under the delusion that to provide water tanks for fire-fighting would do much to solve the water problem, apparently oblivious of the point that people must drink and also wash and cook. Other indefensible ideas of his on sanitation (which fall more appropriately in Chapter 14) were bound up with his unsound opinions on water supply.

More appropriate to Hong Kong was Hennessy's interest in the budding science of meteorology. Weather prediction was obviously something worth pursuing in the context of the Hong Kong climate. The Governor proposed an observatory for Mount Elgin in Kowloon. Later, in 1881, he charged his Aide de Camp, Major Palmer of the Royal Engineers, to draw up a much more elaborate plan of what he proposed to call the Kangxi Observatory after the Chinese emperor whose interest in astronomy was fired by the scholar-Jesuits at his court in the late seventeenth century. Palmer's scheme was to cost an initial $33,000, with an annual maintenance of $10,000. This was put to the Legislative Council in August 1881, with the colonial estimates for 1882 which included $20,000 for the observatory and time-ball. Hennessy reminded the Council:

> The experience of the last few years will be enough to convince us of the importance of meteorological observations for the China Sea. I received within the last few days two telegrams from the government of Manila and the Council are aware that they indicated the full force of the gale we have recently experienced... In the same way we shall be able to make observations that will not only be useful to ourselves, but to all parts of the China Sea.

The expensive project was strongly championed by the *Hong Kong Telegraph*, but the Colonial Office was sceptical. The Governor was told to go no further pending consultations in London. The Surveyor-General, John Price, took another look at the project in May 1882 and suggested a different scheme, the cost of which was about half of the previous one. London considered this 'sufficient for the requirements of the colony'.

Qualified men were sent out from England and the building was begun. A note of restraint was introduced by the Colonial Office when the Secretary of State wrote, commenting on Hennessy's suggestion for naming the observatory: 'As to [this] perhaps "The Hong Kong Observatory" will be enough for the present modest proposal.'[3] And a notation on the correspondence about the scheme adds a laconic touch: 'Pass over in silence Sir J. P. Hennessy's proposal to name it after Kong Hi [Kangxi], and the idea will probably drop into oblivion.'[4] The Observatory was completed after Hennessy left Hong Kong.

Characteristically, having in mind the severe loss of life among the boat people in the 1874 typhoon, Hennessy proposed to construct a breakwater at Causeway Bay as a refuge for junks in future storms. London insisted that the plans be scrutinized by a specialist consulting engineer, Sir John Goode, and allowed the cost of the work to come out of the special gambling fund. But by the end of 1881 nothing had been done and no plans for the breakwater had reached London. On being asked, Hennessy merely complained of the inefficiency of Price. But, as with most of the other lapsed schemes, the reasons lay in the Governor himself, whose energies were consumed by the crime problem, the huge load of work he shouldered, and in altercations with his officials on almost every topic that arose. 'For excellent reasons, convincingly expressed,' writes Endacott, 'the programme of urgently needed public works was held up during the whole of his governorship.'[5] Those 'excellent reasons' in fact covered Hennessy's administrative ineptitude.

Almost the only success of Hennessy's term of office was the reform of the Grant-in-Aid scheme in 1879. By a few alterations in the wording of the official code, which was approved by the Colonial Office, the secular system of education was confined to government schools, and the Grant-in-Aid schools were set free to devote their whole curricula to education, whether secular or religious, in both primary and secondary subjects. This was a giant step forward. On Hennessy's arrival in 1877 there were 41 schools in the colony with 2,922 pupils; when he left in 1882 there were 80 schools with an enrolment of 5,182 pupils — all under government supervision. No credit was ever accorded him by the Europeans in Hong Kong for this considerable achievement.

Governor Hennessy (wearing top hat) with members of the Legislative Council and others, photographed with the King of the Sandwich Islands (today's Hawaii) when the latter visited Hong Kong.

However miserable his overall record, Hennessy's enlightened policies towards the Chinese were far in advance of the times — so far, indeed, that in attempting to put the theory of racial equality into governmental practice, he deeply antagonized the ultra-conservative Westerners, so that by the time of his going they were not on speaking terms with him except on official business. Hennessy was an ineffectual administrator, inefficient, unable to delegate. The Colonial Office viewed him and all his deeds with extreme reserve; the colony with something approaching derision.

There is a brief glimpse of Hennessy in the description of the great fire that raged on Christmas night 1878, which destroyed a large amount of property on Queen's Road. Three hundred and sixty-eight houses were razed before it was extinguished on Boxing Day. Miss Isabella Bird arrived by sea at the height of the blaze.

> Streets choked with household goods and the costly contents of shops, treasured books and nicknacks lying on the ... pavements ... Chinamen dragging their possessions to the hills; Chinawomen ... carrying their children on their backs ... officers black with smoke working at the hose like firemen ... and Mr Pope Hennessy, the Governor, ubiquitous in a chair with four scarlet bearers...[6]

Later he was to quit his sedan and lend a hand with the hoses.

There is a glimpse of another aspect, in a photograph taken of the official party on the visit of the King of Hawaii. A stuffy, lumpish group of men, his officials, sit and stand in untidy rows. Amid them, the King on his right, sits Hennessy, a pale top hat perched forward rakishly over his eyes, elegant, singular as an actor in a football crowd. He did not and could not belong.

A question poses itself: why was Hennessy ever sent out to Hong Kong when, as one civil servant in London noted, 'he has muddled the finances of every colony he has governed'? The Secretary of State once sent Hennessy copies of 39 dispatches which he had left unanswered, and was finally driven to having those on which he most urgently required action printed and published in Hong Kong for the populace to examine.

In March 1882, this dandified, emotional, well-intentioned, and by then hopelessly isolated figure at last left Hong Kong. The Chinese were hyperbolical in their praise, the British equally cutting in their disdain. The praise was genuine enough, recording Chinese recognition that at least one foreign man, and a Governor at that, considered them to be equals in an appallingly unegalitarian place. Perhaps that thought, as he left the colony, formed a small island of comfort in the bitter sea of ostracism.

14. *Public Health, and the Blockade*

AMONG the problems affecting nineteenth-century Hong Kong were several which seemed down the years to be more intractable than others — water supply, sanitation, and public health. One more, affecting the terms of three successive governors, came to be known as 'the blockade'.

There was really no excuse for the continuing saga of Hong Kong's inadequate water supply, given the relative smallness of the population and the state of Western hydraulic engineering expertise. And the history of China's own very ancient water supply facilities in the cities of the mainland point an accusatory finger at nineteenth-century Hong Kong administrators' inertia. The problem lay not with mechanics but in part with a failure to tackle the question seriously; and in part with the chronic stinginess of the Colonial Office. Yet another factor was the fact that the ruling classes in the colony lived in virtually total isolation from the Chinese majority, unaware of conditions. Furthermore, successive administrations were chary of interfering with Chinese custom in this and other matters. There seemed to be no answers to the situation until the Chinese could be co-opted somehow into the workings of the administration. And there was little or no will towards achieving that.

By 1881 the Chinese population had reached almost 200,000 — a rise of 32 per cent in 15 years. Dr I. Murray, the Colonial Surgeon who had arrived in 1859, in his 1870 report complained that it was 'not creditable ... that after the unhealthy condition [of the drains] had been pointed out by myself and the Sanitary Commission, they should remain as they are, a source of disease and death'.[1] He castigated the government for doing nothing when approached by the owners of marine lots complaining of untreated sewage fouling the shores, and pointed out that lack of funds was no excuse in the face of 'the most dangerous nuisance'. He also called for better hospitals, the registration of all deaths, for tree-planting, and the liberal use of that Victorian kill-all, carbolic, in every drain, as palliative measures.

Governor Macdonnell made a stab at that sort of improvement when he started paving Taipingshan and installing surface drainage, but his energies were soon deflected to what appeared to him more urgent tasks in the suppression of gambling and piracy. Still, he was a carbolic enthusiast and made sure a good supply of it was available.

On Murray's retirement in 1872 after 14 years' service, he was succeeded by McCoy who soon died and was in turn replaced by Dr Phineas Ayres who arrived as the new Colonial Surgeon in 1873. The mortality among Colonial Surgeons in itself offers a sharp comment on public health in the colony. The first, appointed in 1845, was dead within a year, the next survived a mere eight months. The third lasted almost seven years. Ayres was the longest serving nineteenth-century incumbent and retired in 1897, after almost a quarter of a century in the post.

He had begun with some gusto, condemning the conditions he discovered. His January 1874 report pin-pointed the cases of typhoid originating in brothels, which were indescribably filthy with rooms constructed within other rooms, and without in many cases any sanitation at all. A few months later he condemned domestic accommodation where houses were occupied by from five to 10 families, dwellings unfit 'to put pigs in'. These houses were owned by rich Europeans and Chinese 'who squeeze those who have no power to make their complaints known'. He wrote in his April 1875 report:

> I have made a series of inspections in company with Mr Price the Surveyor-General. The result of these inspections goes to prove that however much on the surface the town of Victoria may appear cleaner than most Eastern towns, beneath the surface it would be difficult to find a filthier condition of things.
>
> My first series of inspections discovered that pigs were kept in houses all over the town in hundreds, and that pigsties were to be found under the beds and in the kitchens of the first, second, and third floors. I visited many houses in which over a hundred pigs were kept, every bed in these houses had large pigs in a sty constructed underneath it, and . . . the late Inspector of Markets, whose duty it was to see that pigs were kept in proper places, [had given people Government licences to keep their pigs there].
>
> Imagine houses whose upper floors are constructed of thin board, with wide interstices between them, and whose lower floors are inhabited, and the state they would be in under these circumstances, with pigs urine etc. dropping through from floor to floor.[2]

Ayres goes on to detail the unsuitable construction of those houses, their total lack of sanitation or, where there was any, the broken and half-choked pipes that led no further than from the kitchen (also in use as a lavatory) to the gully outside. There were further horrors. 'Cows were only to be found in the basement, but goats and sheep, like pigs, might be found on any floor. Pigs and sheep were kept until they were wanted for slaughter, goats and

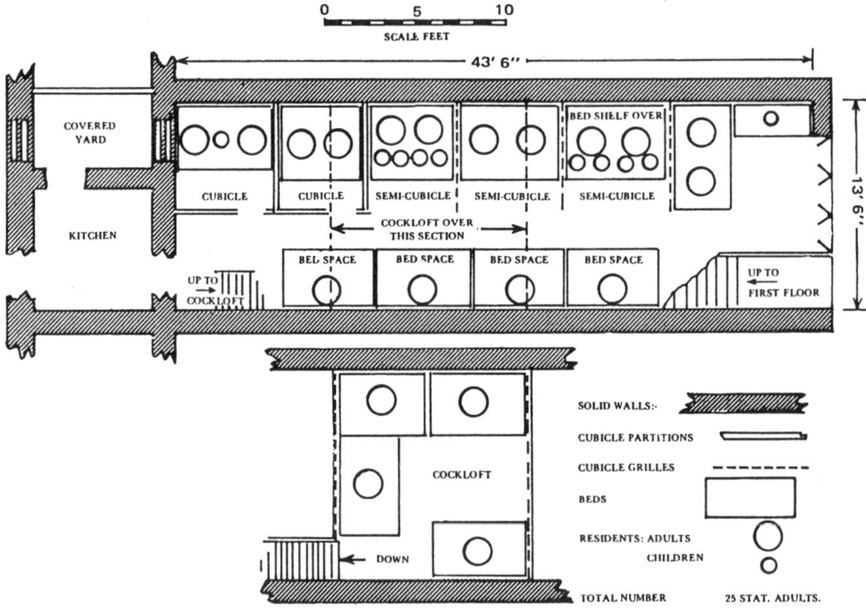

4. Plan of a typical tenement house in a congested district, built before 1903. The conditions described by Dr Ayres were to be found in houses such as this, with grossly overcrowded accommodation. (*Source*: *Report of the Housing Commission 1935*.)

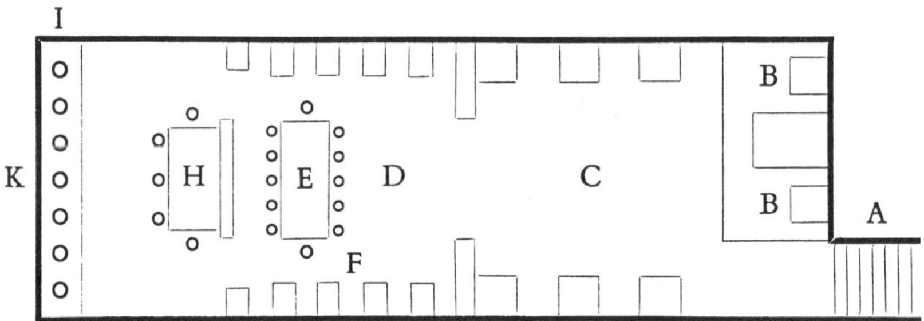

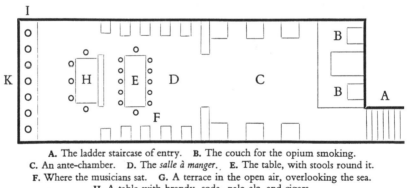

A. The ladder staircase of entry. **B.** The couch for the opium smoking.
C. An ante-chamber. **D.** The *salle à manger*. **E.** The table, with stools round it.
F. Where the musicians sat. **G.** A terrace in the open air, overlooking the sea.
H. A table with brandy, soda, pale ale, and cigars.
I. Flowers in pots on the edge of the terrace. **K.** Hong-Kong harbour.

5. Plan of the first floor public rooms of a wealthy Chinese house, that of the P. &. O. comprador. The dimensions of the house are similar to those of the tenement house. (*Source*: Smith, *To China and Back*.)

cows for dairy purposes.' Goats were led round from house to house and milked, as required by the customer.

It was not only the Chinese whose health was at risk. Ayres discovered, among many others, one 'dairy' which supplied most of the households in Caine Road, then the preserve of European families and situated just up the

Part of Taipingshan about 1868 in a photograph by William Pryor Floyd.

hill from the pullulating slum of Taipingshan. This 'dairy' was in the basement of a house between Shelley Street and Peel Street, the entry via a gully leading from the former. The basement consisted of cellars whose sole light came from doors or windows on to the gully. To milk or tend the cows required the use of a lamp to dispel the gloom. And, as the cows had been quartered there since they were calves, the full-grown animals had to be slaughtered *in situ* and then carved up because there was no other way they could be got out. Of another house, Ayres wrote, 'I found a quarter of beef hanging over the bed of a man who was in the last stages of smallpox.'

The highly charged language of Ayres' reports was instrumental in their suppression; and unfortunately the facts he reported were read as less significant than their implicit condemnation of those in authority who had permitted the public health perils thus revealed. With the suppression of his reports it is perhaps not surprising that Ayres, in frustration at their fate, dealt in later ones with less controversial aspects of the sanitary situation. He had also come to realize that in the absence of drastically changed building ordinances there was little that could be done about the potentially disastrous state of sanitary affairs.

What government impotence and inertia failed to do, the great fire of 1878 largely achieved for them, Ayres calling the destruction of much of Taipingshan in that year 'a sanitary dispensation of Providence'. Hennessy was saved the responsibility for an even greater disaster — rampant epidemic — by those cleansing flames. The Governor's blindness to the dangers was due to his conviction that 'the Chinese inhabitants maintain that the attempts now and then made ... to force what is called "Western sanitary science" upon them were not based on sound principles'. They should be allowed to build houses of the Guangzhou type with earth closets. Hennessy completely opposed the introduction of flushing toilets. What he failed to see — blinded by prejudice — was the dire overcrowding in Hong Kong which negated whatever might be reasonable in Guangzhou. Had he read the reports of Dr Peter Parker working as a medical missionary there (one of whose patients had been Commissioner Lin), Hennessy might have formed a different view.

It took another of Hong Kong's episodes of infighting and backbiting to spring the Ayres reports out of the Secretariat and lodge them on the desks of the Colonial Office. Hennessy's ordinance permitting Chinese housing in what were formerly European preserves so incensed the choleric General Donovan that he complained of the nuisance near the barracks 'giving ocular, auricular, and nasal demonstration' that Chinese were unfitted to live near Westerners. He cited the Ayres reports as proof. As a result, the Surgeon-General of the army was dispatched to Hong Kong, and his report of 1 September 1880 condemned not only the sanitary conditions but also the policy of the Governor. The Colonial Office then demanded to see the Ayres reports and sent out Osbert Chadwick, a former Royal Engineers officer, to make a full-scale enquiry. His report in 1882 turned out to have even further-reaching effects than he could have suspected, in that it formed the basis on which the Sanitary Board, precursor of the Urban Council, came into being.

Chadwick was almost the ideal man for the job. Not confining his investigations to sanitation, he surveyed the social picture of the colony in an attempt to place its problems in their context. He probed the views of the Chinese, who surprised him by their openness in receiving him.

The Chadwick report scotched all Hennessy's sanitary ideas as invalid in Hong Kong. Fortunately it was submitted after the Governor had left. Calling for energetic remedial measures, the report pointed out that even in Chinese systems correct drainage is required. Noting that the water supply in the colony was inadequate, Chadwick made the point that neither 'the proposed works, nor works many times larger, would satisfy the wants of the city', while the water rate charges were unjustly applied. He considered that a new building ordinance was essential, and that apart from rectifying defective or absent house drainage which he called 'radically bad', the whole town should be supplied with effective drainage. He separated the questions of ordinary scavenging and the collection of the euphemistically named 'night soil'. Collections were to be made by a trained sanitary staff under an appointed officer. Chinese involvement and co-operation should be obtained by using the district watchmen to enforce the process, and for this they ought to be paid extra. All those connected with the sanitary process should be closely in touch with the Registrar-General's office. There should be more public toilets, more baths, new markets — and a proper water supply for Kowloon across the harbour.

The report shows Chadwick pointing out the means by which Chinese could be involved, means suggested in his conversations with them when they frequently called his attention to points requiring alteration or improvement. The fear that the town might 'outgrow itself', expressed by an 1845 visitor, had proved all too true, and the barest amenities — water, drainage, and health care — had not kept pace.

The report reached Hong Kong in 1882, before a new Governor was appointed and during the administration of W. H. Marsh, the Colonial Secretary, recently knighted. His tenure was regarded by the Western community as a welcome respite from the ministrations of Hennessy who, arrived in England, began accusing the colony of being the distributor of £1,000,000 worth of opium a month to China. The figure was nearer to £200,000. But it required the appointment of a commission to repudiate his accusation, and it was on Sir William Marsh's shoulders that the brunt of the dispute fell.

As it affected the economic viability of the colony, the so-called Chinese customs 'blockade' of Hong Kong was quite as serious a matter as that hanging sword of Damocles, an outbreak of epidemic disease. The background lay in the confused state of relations with Chinese customs authorities over a clause in the 1858 Treaty of Tianjin. As ever, the root of the problem was opium. The clause in question laid down that opium, now legalized, could only be carried in foreign vessels, and these were confined to trading in the Treaty Ports where the import duty on opium and the *likin* transit tax were enforceable. This provision was largely disregarded by the Chinese in Hong Kong whose junks, under British protection, carried opium to China. The Chinese, however, regarded all Chinese-owned vessels, even if the owners lived in Hong Kong or the craft had (as did the *Arrow*) a British captain, as Chinese and therefore illegally trading. The Chinese government was, in consequence, losing revenues which it would have collected had the opium been carried in foreign vessels entering the Treaty Ports.

There were other grievances of the Chinese side. The protection of the British flag was quite legally given to vessels belonging to Chinese lessees of Crown land in Hong Kong. Although they were few in number, the Chinese customs also lost revenue in this trade. The obligation which confined foreign trade to the Treaty Ports was largely circumvented by the fact that the colony's rapidly increasing coastal trade with China was conducted for the most part by Chinese merchants in Hong Kong who served as distributors of foreign goods which they bought from European import agency houses.

On the other side of the argument was the opinion that since the colony was a free port the suppression of this illicit trade was a matter to be dealt with by the Chinese themselves. The bones of contention were many, but the real question between Hong Kong and Guangzhou was which would win the battle for control of the local distributive trade. The sums involved were large. The loss of opium revenue at Guangzhou, normally collected by the Imperial Maritime Customs, was considerable. The *likin* tax levied at the Treaty Ports was $16 per chest of opium sent inland from there. Then there was the $30 per chest levied by the *hoppo* who controlled the collection of Chinese native customs revenues. It was these two agencies who, from November 1867, began to check all native craft operating to and from Hong Kong.

The first episode came in Macdonnell's time when, in November 1867, an opium-carrying junk was seized by Chinese revenue cruisers operating off the entrance to Hong Kong harbour. Macdonnell wrote in strong terms to Robertson, Consul at Guangzhou, demanding the return of the junk and compensation for the value of its cargo — both of which he received. This dispatch was eventually passed from the Colonial Office to the Foreign Office by the Duke of Buckingham who expressed his disapproval of the language used by the Governor, in which he appeared to query the right of the Chinese government 'to exercise its own jurisdiction over its own subjects in its own waters in a manner which it considers conducive to its own interests'.[3]

In the following year nine marine and land customs stations were set up by the Chinese around Hong Kong, all native vessels being subject to stop and search. Rutherford Alcock, British Minister in Beijing, took the Chinese part, referring to the colony as 'little more than an immense smuggling depot'. Both he and Robertson supported the Chinese purchase of gunboats for the purpose of enforcing the blockade. Macdonnell called them 'a new species of corsairs'. The Governor took a strong line throughout, but he was champion of a somewhat dubious cause. Only some of his points were soundly based. The Treaty of Tianjin did allow for the $30 tax on every chest of opium, but it did not provide for the *likin* tax which was therefore illegal. It was true that the blockade failed to differentiate between Hong Kong Chinese and foreign ships, although only Chinese vessels were affected, while ships bound for non-Chinese ports were also affected — commerce which the Chinese had clearly no right to interfere in.

Robertson defended the measures in that they applied solely to opium — to which the Governor replied in effect 'so far'. He also denied estimates of the amount of opium smuggled. Of the 80,000 chests annually imported to Hong Kong, 63,000 went to the northern Chinese ports, and 3,000 to Chinese in California. His estimate was that about one and a half thousand chests were smuggled from Hong Kong, as against the Chinese estimate of thirty to forty thousand. What happened to the remainder he did not say. The Chinese next requested permission to set up customs stations in the colony, and Alcock in Beijing wanted a Chinese consul there, too. Both were turned down by Macdonnell with the retort that it would be inadvisable 'in the special circumstances of this very peculiar place, its very peculiar inhabitants and most peculiar geographical position'.[4] He complained that Alcock and Robertson had approved of the blockade measures without so much as consulting him on a matter which deeply affected the colony.

But Macdonnell found himself well out on a limb, the home government unsupportive. 'More than one of the claims advanced by you', Lord Granville reprimanded him, 'have been exaggerated and untenable . . . the interests of H. M. Service are injured by the tone in which they are advanced . . . I hold you in no slight degree responsible for the want of co-operation which at present exists.'[5]

Under Kennedy, a man more ready to concede points, a commission of enquiry was set up in 1874. But the unruly merchants called a public meeting in September at which the customs cordon sanitaire was roundly condemned, Jardine's representative calling it an 'organized invasion of the freedom of the port'. The motion passed at the meeting went off to London where Lord Carnarvon at the Colonial Office responded in peremptory manner:

> The action of the Chinese revenue cruisers in the exercise of the right of search in close proximity to Hong Kong for the purpose of defeating the attempts of Chinese subjects to defraud the revenue of their country did not affect the freedom of the port and afforded no valid ground for diplomatic remonstrance.

Both the Minister in Beijing and the Consul in Guangzhou took the part of the Chinese. Kennedy had recourse to his 'panacea for all problems', another committee — this one composed of a small number of British and Chinese officials whose duties were to investigate complaints of illegal seizures from vessels. A convention signed in Beijing between the Chinese and the British in 1876 provided for the appointment of a commission on Anglo-Chinese lines consisting of an officer of the colonial government, a Chinese official, and a British Consul, so as to establish a system 'that shall enable the Chinese government to protect its interests without prejudice to the interests of Hong Kong'. Article 3 of the Convention also provided that opium be kept in bond until sold, whereupon the purchaser would pay in a lump sum the transit dues of the provincial governments involved en route to its destination.

Hennessy having taken over as Governor from Kennedy, it was hardly to be expected that much progress would be made towards settlement. On his arrival in Hong Kong he was confronted with the seizure of an opium junk by the Chinese in colonial waters. Correctly, he demanded full compensation for both junk and cargo. But, receiving this, he refused to turn the money over to the junk's owner because the vessel had illegally set sail from port at night without a clearance. Although he was technically correct, mercantile opinion viewed this as an open invitation to the Chinese to continue the blockade.

Later, in March 1878, Hennessy reported an increase in the junk trade, mentioning that complaints about the blockade had 'mostly ceased'. This was a fiction in which, isolated as he was from the merchant community and others, he may well have believed. The Chinese merchants were worried by the Chinese government's interference with the shipping of cotton piece goods, and other legitimate trade. Hennessy planned to solve the opium problem by collecting all dues on it in Hong Kong and then issuing clearances. In the contraband salt trade he thought that if Chinese government agents were to license the trade the matter would be cleared up. In return for these suggested easements he asked for the ending of the blockade. As ever, in a sense correctly, Hennessy's thought was for the Chinese mercantile community on whom, to his mind, the colony's prosperity greatly depended. He ran into profound opposition from the mercantile community to the setting up of any collecting agency in a free port, and these various plans came to naught. The opium trade was still a very significant earner, the 83,000 chests clearing Hong Kong in 1870 worth $48,742,238.

Few events or processes in history are without their brighter, or at least other, side and the blockade, which was not to yield to reason for some time yet, was no exception. The seemingly timeless, sturdy, adaptable work-horse of the coastal trade, the Chinese junk in all its variety of shapes and sizes suited to this or that condition, now began to give way, as sail was giving way elsewhere, to the blandishments of steam. Steam launches of the Chinese Maritime Customs were proving every day that they could overtake the junk in all weathers. Soon enough Chinese merchants took notice. The potential was recognized. The China Merchants Steam Navigation Company was formed in 1874. It did not at first prosper so splendidly as the logic of its formation had given hope it would, yet its very formation marked the end of the foreigners' monopoly of steam navigation, and the beginning of a decline of the junk in sea transport. Competitors among foreign-owned companies included the China Navigation Company established by Butterfield and Swire in 1872, the Indo-China Steam Navigation Company established in 1881, belonging to Jardine, the Douglas Steamship Company, started in 1883, and the Canton and Macao Steamship Company, formed in 1865. By 1877, Kwok A Cheung, a Hong Kong Chinese, had bought 13 steamers, a large enterprise for that time.

Until 1883, the movement of goods from China to Britain exceeded that in the other direction, and since the material was mostly tea and silks which could be shipped direct from the Treaty Ports, Hong Kong did not become a major collecting centre in this trade. Conversely, almost one-half of British exports to China passed through the colony. The 1880 statistics show that Hong Kong handled 21 per cent in value of China's total export trade and 37 per cent of its import trade.

The best indication of the growth of import and export trade in this period, in the absence of figures for tonnage, is to be found in the numbers of ships entering and clearing the port. The data afford an overview of the expansion of trade and of the types of goods involved.

In 1866, 1,896 ships totalling 949,856 tons entered the harbour, and 3,783 ships totalling 1,891,281 tons entered and cleared; by 1881, 'foreign-going ships' other than junks entering port numbered 3,214 totalling 2,853,279 tons — of which 2,750 totalling 2,599,461 tons were steamers. From 1867 figures for the junk traffic are available; in that year 20,787 junks totalling 1,353,700 tons entered, all engaged in foreign trade, carrying cattle, fruit, vegetables, and firewood. They took on opium, rice, salt, lime, cotton, and local granite. In 1874 the Harbourmaster reported that the junk trade had increased each year from 1867 to early 1872, at which point a fall in numbers began. Thus it would appear that the blockade had at first no serious impact. But by 1879 the junk trade had not yet returned to its former volume, and more foreign-built ships were now under the Chinese flag. Hong Kong Chinese vessels by that time carried 42.36 per cent of the total of the colony's inward trade.

That Hong Kong Chinese were taking a larger slice of trade was reflected in their increasingly monied lifestyle, seen in their new appetite for Western property and their growing use of their own steamers, Kwok A Cheung being one example. They were also the biggest ratepayers. In 1881 there were 18 ratepayers with property rated at over $1,000 per quarter, 17 of whom were Chinese — the remaining one being Jardine, Matheson and Company. Old patterns were changing. Important factors in the changes were the lower freight rates following the opening of the Suez Canal and the evolution of improved marine steam engines. The great breakthrough was the invention, patented in 1884, by the Irish engineer Sir Charles Algernon Parsons, of the steam turbine. In conjunction with the high-speed electro-generator, this revolutionized marine propulsion the world over. Its effects on trading patterns in Hong Kong as elsewhere were one of the dramatic events in the evolution of nineteenth-century commerce.

Hong Kong had long been the centre for Chinese migration overseas. From the privations of life in China, from the ravages of bandits, from the periodic scourges of epidemic and hunger, streams of migrants filtered through to Hong Kong's port and, often unwitting of the terms of contracts they were acquiescing to, were shipped over the Pacific — to California as labourers, to endure the horrors of the voyage to South America and virtual slavery there — to the tin mines of Malaya, and to the gold-rush shanty towns of Australia and New Zealand. The trade in human beings was little better than the African slave trade. Such were the abuses in this traffic that in 1869 coolie emigration on contract was prohibited from Hong Kong. But it went on flourishing in Macau where it was said that there were 800 coolie brokers. Kennedy passed this Chinese complaint to London where the Colonial Office asked if it were true that Hong Kong was supplying Macau with the ships to conduct it. Replying, Kennedy admitted this — almost all coolie ships were fitted out in the colony, there being nothing in law to prevent it. And when the law might be broken by work on 'objectionable fittings', these were simply manufactured in Hong Kong and installed at sea. In the first nine months of 1872, 15 Peruvian, 10 French, nine Spanish, one Austrian and three Dutch ships had been dispatched to Macau for the coolie trade.

In London, Lord Kimberley saw this as 'most unsatisfactory' and wanted new legislation and rigorous searches of all passenger ships. Contract emigration from China had been legal since 1860, the process regulated in 1866 by a convention between China, France, and Britain; and further restricted in 1869 when migrants were not permitted to leave Hong Kong for any destination other than the British colonies. Emigration of Chinese other than by contract, termed 'voluntary emigration', was of course permissible. It brought in trade, and returning Chinese often brought bullion. Figures for 1866 show departures at 5,116 and returns at 9,253. In 1872 almost thirty thousand left and almost twenty-four thousand returned; and in 1881 over seventy thousand left and close to fifty-three thousand came back.

The outcome of queries from London on the subject of the coolie trade was an ordinance of 1873 imposing severe penalties on restraining women and children with a view to shipping them abroad, and also on the fitting out and possession of emigrant ships without a licence. When the ordinance was passed, the migrant ships that were fitting out in the harbour immediately sailed.

Voluntary emigration increased. The first five months of 1874 saw over seven thousand coolies take ship for San Francisco, with another 1,211 awaiting passage — most headed for the gold mines in search of wealth.

One further effect of increased Chinese migration in conjunction with the increased efficiency of steam navigation was the expansion of overseas markets for Chinese goods supplied via Hong Kong. Just as did Western communities in foreign settlements, the Chinese abroad always attempted to construct a little China in alien lands. They needed the rice, the dried goods, and all the diverse ingredients of Chinese food. They wanted familiar textiles and house furnishings, porcelain tableware that only the motherland could supply. Most of these goods were bought from China by shrewd Chinese entrepreneurs in Hong Kong and shipped across the Pacific to California, to Thailand, Malaya, and Singapore, to the Indonesian archipelago, and to Australia. The stream of Chinese grew to a flooding river, until restrictive immigration laws were passed in the British Dominions, and until the 1887 Exclusion Acts in America.

15. *Constitutional Reform, and the Legalization of Opium*

AFTER the departure of Hennessy in the spring of 1882 a whole year elapsed before Sir George Bowen, his successor, arrived. The Acting Governor, W. H. Marsh, administered in the interregnum. Bowen left Hong Kong in December 1885, and another gap without a governor ensued for almost two years before Sir William Des Voeux arrived in October 1887. Marsh again held the reins, and in his own absences Major-General W. G. Cameron and the Colonial Secretary, F. Fleming, took over. After Des Voeux left, Major-General Digby Barker administered until in December 1891 the new Governor, Sir William Robinson, came out.

This repeated change of helmsman within the span of a few years was unfortunate, coming in the wake of the turbulence left by Hennessy. Many pressing issues, new and old, required a firm continuity in leadership and administration, and it says a lot for the qualities of the civil service that a moderate and acceptable course was steered.

Both Bowen and Des Voeux had reached the peak of their careers as they arrived in the colony. An academic by early choice, Bowen had later joined the colonial service. Des Voeux had begun as a graduate of the Canadian Bar and had governed two colonies before Hong Kong. His health, never robust, appeared to require him to spend a considerable part of his term shooting duck on the Yangzi. He left Hong Kong in 1890.

Marsh when he took over had to tackle urgently the muddle bequeathed by Hennessy and also to begin the implementation of the Chadwick report. His first steps were incisive — the building of the new hospital, the Central School, and the junk shelter at Causeway Bay. He then upgraded the Registrar-General's office under a cadet named James Russell.

The Colonial Office asked for the appointment of a Sanitary Inspector and Marsh appointed H. Macallum, the apothecary at the Civil Hospital. The whole question of sanitation and public health and what to do about it, hanging over the administration, could scarcely be ignored for ever. Marsh, as Acting Governor, tentatively appointed a triumvirate of officials to sit on a Sanitary Board — the Surveyor-General, Registrar-General, and Colonial Surgeon. In 1883, when Bowen arrived as Governor, he constituted the Board with three members *ex officio*, and the Surveyor-General as Chairman; and he nominated two other members to represent ratepayers.

The wide powers accorded to the Board in the relevant ordinance — powers to inspect insanitary housing and where deemed necessary to disinfect the premises, and to remove for treatment anyone suspected of being a source of infection — were met with vociferous opposition from the community. The Board remained in being but powerless to act in the face of such popular revulsion; and the ordinance was withdrawn, although Bowen added to the Board a Sanitary Inspector and the Captain Superintendent of Police as extra members.

Bowen quit the scene in 1885 having in effect accomplished nothing meaningful. In 1886, Marsh again acting as head of the administration, the Board was strengthened by the addition of four unofficial members (Dr Patrick Manson, Dr Ho Kai, and two others representing ratepayers) and the old proposals were again considered, the Board producing another draft ordinance in 1886, offering wide-ranging powers to a partially elected Board of Health. The proposals included measures designed to compel owners of dwellings to upgrade their property to give adequate ventilation and a minimum of space for the residents. Human nature not having altered in the meantime, this proposal provoked another serious outcry, especially from the Chinese whose spokesman in the Executive Council, Dr Ho Kai, opined that no one should make 'the mistake of treating Chinese as if they were Europeans' — that is, of enshrining in an ordinance the idea that Chinese required the same *Lebensraum* as the ruling class of Westerners.

The then Acting Governor, Major-General W. G. Cameron, took what he thought was action. He simply omitted all the offending clauses in the proposed ordinance. Five years after Chadwick had condemned the disgusting sanitary conditions and had sagely indicated the minimal remedies, a piffling, toothless ordinance on the subject became law. And the question of what amounted to 'challenging an Englishman [not to mention a Chinese] in his castle [and] also traversing the belief of Chinese that once their taxes were paid, they were guaranteed against . . . interference and were free to live or die, avoid, catch, and spread disease as it pleased them' — seemed to have won the day.

In 1887 the Public Health Ordinance established the constitution of the Sanitary Board as consisting of four officials (the Surveyor-General, the Registrar-General, the Captain Superintendent of Police, and the Colonial Surgeon) with up to six other members (four of whom were to be the Governor's appointees — two of these to be Chinese), and two others elected by ratepayers on the jury list.

In this step we see the decisive move towards local government institutions being entrusted with a measure of responsibility for municipal affairs, and also the first elections in the colony not reserved solely to British nationals.

On his arrival in 1887, Des Voeux immediately encountered a petition signed by 47,000 Chinese damning all the powers of the Sanitary Board. The Chinese simply stated that there had been no plague despite the fact that none of the envisaged measures had been taken — so what was the fuss about? They feared that the intended action would force up rents to an unbearable level, and they utterly condemned any idea that Chinese homes could be entered under any circumstances whatsoever.

The Colonial Office in London, however, accepted the terms of the Public Health Ordinance. And now came a rash of new building in order to beat what was in the wind — the Buildings Ordinance which became law under Des Voeux in 1889 and which he tacked on to the Crown Lands Resumption Ordinance — which in its turn embodied the hated clauses about ventilation and minimal space. However, the sop of compensation for property owners was also envisaged. Thus, after years of opposition the property lobby had its way and was to be paid for the destruction of its vile housing. The Secretary of State in London gave his approval.

The implementation of this ordinance was to take place piecemeal over the ensuing 20 years of resumptions and rebuilding of the Chinese areas. Des Voeux's vacillation must certainly be blamed for the inept handling of Chinese dissent and the emasculation of the content of the Chadwick report; and also for the rash of *new* insanitary construction before he promulgated the Buildings Ordinance. Strong Chinese prejudice, and the near unanimity of owners' self-interest presumably scared him away from speedier intelligent action.

But living conditions were altogether too appalling to be left at that. The Board empanelled a two-man committee of investigation. Their 1890 report revealed the extent of the foul conditions. It described rooms subdivided to form between four and eight cubicles, dividers and furniture estimated to occupy about 29 per cent of the available air space. Many city blocks had a population density of 1,500 per acre, and one even of 3,235. Des Voeux's response was to pass an amending act to deal with overcrowding. As to sanitary conditions, little improvement was achieved.

In contrast to these procrastinations action was taken on the public works elements recommended by Chadwick. The Tai Tam water scheme was boldly set in motion, the estimated cost of $60,000 soon proving inadequate. A new and more hygienic Central Market, and the draining of swampy ground in Causeway Bay, were also begun, as were new main drainage and sewers at Yau Ma Tei, and the provision of dustbins and improved scavenging. More Inspectors of Nuisances were employed and a veterinary surgeon to look after the pig and sheep depot.

The old idea of linking the east and west Prayas by a road to seaward of the central naval and military cantonments was revived, and one of the colony's enterprising business men, Paul (later Sir Paul) Chater unveiled his own scheme for a radically conceived reclamation in Central District, to provide fresh land for commercial development. Dr Patrick Manson of the Sanitary Board, a shrewd Scots business man, inaugurated his Dairy Farm Company in the spring of 1886 with a herd of 80 cows quartered on the breezy slopes of Pok Fu Lam. On the board Manson included some of the best brains and business heads in the colony — Paul Chater among them. The establishment of the Dairy Farm Company led eventually, after vicissitudes including the loss of almost the entire herd from rinderpest, to the provision of a supply of milk free from the health hazards of the milk from the Chinese 'dairies'.

Manson was also responsible for starting a college of medicine, obtaining the patronage of China's elder statesman, Li Hongzhang. The first and brightest student to qualify was Sun Yatsen (Sun Yixian). In later years, Sun was to state that his reforming and democratic ideas which were to crystallize in the Guomindang and eventually lead to civil war and the establishment of a Communist regime in China had been gained during his student days in Hong Kong.

Prior to Des Voeux's term, while Bowen was still Governor, one major task confronted him — the reform of the Executive and Legislative Councils. This was a timely bid to lay a firmer foundation for the colonial legislature. In the four decades since the councils were first set up their membership had

Dr Sun Yatsen.

undergone several changes aimed at increasing their effectiveness. The original councils of 1843 consisted of three members each — the same three, the entire senior civil service at that time. The councils were purely official. In 1844 the Lieutenant-Governor was appointed to an additional seat on each council, while on the arrival of the first Chief Justice and first Attorney-General both were given seats on the Legislative Council and the latter on the Executive Council. After that the membership of both councils altered rather frequently. Bonham created two unofficial seats in 1850. Bowring in 1855 enlarged the Legislative Council, throwing meetings open to the public. Robinson laid down that the proportion between official and unofficial members would be 2:1, excluding the Governor, and he also enforced a rule that official members should vote with and not against the government. Hennessy, typically, upset the balance severely; and the position on Bowen's arrival was that there were six officials and only two unofficials on the Legislative Council.

The new Governor at once objected. He thought it incorrect that the Chief Justice should have a seat on the Legislative Council, on the principle that the judiciary should be independent of the remainder of the adminstration. He supported the inclusion of a Chinese, but a problem arose when Hennessy's appointee, Ng Choy, got into financial straits in property speculation and resigned his seat. Bowen thought the choice of a successor — a Chinese British subject who was 'a native gentleman combining in his own person the proper social position, independent means and education', independent of the government, he presumably meant — a difficult matter.

The Governor disagreed with the exclusion of the General Officer Commanding British Forces from the Legislative Council, and disapproved too of the fact that official members filled two of the four places reserved for unofficials — something which was also disputed by public opinion. He therefore increased the membership of the Council by three officials — the General, the Registrar-General, and the Surveyor-General — and added two additional members, giving a total of eight official members and six unofficials. Among the latter he wanted the Chamber of Commerce to nominate two of the unofficials, and the Magistrates one, with three to be nominated by the Governor (of whom one at least should be Chinese). He wanted members to hold office for six years only, not for life as before. He further suggested the Council hold a fixed annual session in which proposed future legislation could be sketched out and submitted for public discussion.

Bowen thought the Executive Council ought to be increased by adding the Colonial Treasurer and the Registrar-General; and he suggested also that the heads of government departments ought to have seats there.

With only minor amendments Lord Derby accepted these ideas, and the new Legislative Council had its first sitting on 28 February 1884. The Chamber of Commerce had nominated as an unofficial the Chief Manager of the Hongkong and Shanghai Bank, Thomas Jackson. The Chamber itself was racially a rather broadly based body with 34 members: 20 British, one American, six Europeans, two Chinese, three Jews, one Parsee, and one Armenian. The 79 Justices of the Peace were all of British nationality, 62 being purely British, seven Chinese, three Jewish, and seven Parsees and Armenians. The election held by the Justices was curious in that they decided the British were already sufficiently represented on the Council, so they voted for Frederick Sassoon who came from an Indian Jewish family and had been educated in England.

The Governor nominated as Chinese member a man named Wong Shing who had been educated at the Morrison Society School and later in America. He had served under Li Hongzhang in China and in the Chinese Legation in Washington. He was reputed, by virtue of his background, to be 'fully qualified to look at Chinese affairs with English eyes and at English affairs with Chinese eyes'. When there seemed some doubt whether the Governor had the right constitutionally to appoint the fifth member, Jackson stood down and Wong took his seat.

The new Legislative Council's members had a 'constitutional opportunity of expressing their opinion of the conduct and proposals of the government'. A request from the Chamber of Commerce that the Legislative Council have the same powers as the Shanghai Municipal Council was turned down by London. But the movement for a municipal council elected by ratepayers was not to be so easily waved aside. It strengthened when the rates were raised in 1885 by 1 per cent. Bowen's attitude was matter-of-fact. There were, he reminded the Chamber, only 83 British ratepayers, heavily outnumbered by 647 Chinese and 98 others, most of whom were Portuguese. He suggested that in an election it was highly improbable that any British person would stand a chance. Then, playing on the British distaste of Oriental habits (as they saw them), he reminded his listeners that Chinese attitudes to 'water supply, sanitation, police, harbour regulations . . . differed widely from those in Europe'. It was unthinkable to put a large garrison town with its trading activity in the charge of the Chinese. Bowen thought that the Legislative Council was near enough to being a municipal council.

He did, however, concede a point by placing municipal rating before the Legislative instead of the Executive Council. He also insisted that it should be a constitutional principle that the majority officials 'should not be used to control an absolutely united unofficial minority, especially on financial questions', a considerable item of progress in constitutional development.

Having put the legislative house in order after the disarray of the Hennessy period, Bowen faced an unusual problem — a threatening international situation brewing almost on the doorstep. In the light of Russia's apparent designs on the Far East, imperial defence had to be taken with more than usual seriousness. In Britain the Colonial Defence Committee had been set up, and the colonies were to provide their own committees so that available resources there could be assessed, integrated, and if required tapped for the common good. Given the geographical spread of the colonies, and the slowness of communication, the process could not but take time.

Apart from Russian intentions, in Hong Kong's near neighbourhood the war between France and China over Vietnam had ended in the Li–Fournier Convention of 1884, but border disputes continued, leading to general tension in the area.

Reacting to these disturbances the colony began defensive works at either end of the island, and a Hong Kong Regiment was formed, mostly from Indians, the officers being British and Indian personnel. Bowen was full of complaints about the defenceless state of Hong Kong, and Russian action in Korea and their 1885 occupation of Port Hamilton prompted a request for torpedo boats from London. The Colonial Office assured him the Admiralty were 'thoroughly aware of what is necessary for the defence of the colony'.

In January 1885 the legislature voted $56,000 for up-to-date weaponry, and further large sums were committed later. More troops were required, and a doubled military contribution from the colony was demanded before the troops arrived. And when they did come, they turned out to be a Madras regiment and not the 'infantry of the line' as promised. The situation was handled by London with consummate insensitivity.

In the interim Hong Kong had suffered the spin-off from the Franco-Chinese conflict. Throughout it Britain had maintained strict neutrality, and Bowen had entertained both French and Chinese officials while protecting British rights. But Chinese opinion in Guangzhou and in Hong Kong was naturally anti-French, and when Chinese newspapers published edicts of the Viceroy of Guangdong urging Chinese to attack French ships and personnel, Marsh (Bowen was in Japan at the time) took four Chinese editors to court. The prosecutions failed. By September 1884 the boatmen handling cargo stopped working French ships, and French owners took 14 of them to court, securing convictions and fines of $5 on each. Whereupon all the boatmen went on strike and the harbour was brought to a standstill. In October a tense situation flared up and rioting erupted. The police were called out and troops paraded the streets. Imprisonment of the rioters served merely to sharpen the antagonism and, when mediation by the Tung Wah Committee failed, a Peace Preservation Ordinance was pushed through the Legislative Council in one sitting. This allowed detention and banishment of persons who, though not convicted, were 'dangerous to the peace and good order of the colony'. In a week or two things had returned to normal. Marsh had made 38 banishment orders but only eight were carried out since the remaining men could not be found.

Another response to threats of war was the reviving of Hennessy's Hong Kong Volunteers, first flung together in 1878 following the Russian war scare. There had always been a touch of patriotism about the Volunteers, mingled with a boys-will-be-boys atmosphere on weekend get-togethers in the style of the as yet unthought-of Boy Scout movement. Under the slightly disapproving eye of the Colonial Office Bowen equipped the corps with guns and rifles. And the Volunteers rapidly took new heart, becoming an accepted part of the colonial social fabric. In 1885 Bowen went further and created the Hong Kong Auxiliary Water Police, with yachtsmen under the command of the assistant Harbourmaster. Four years later a machine-gun corps was formed, partly mounted, armed with Maxim guns paid for by the leading members of the colonial community.

Under Des Voeux the bold scheme for reclamation along the northern shore of the island was advanced by Chater. In essence what he wanted was the creation of a strip of land over three thousand metres long and over seventy wide in front of the existing shoreline, the reclamation to be paid for by holders of the marine lots but under government control. Owners of existing lots were to get the new land at $200 per quarter acre. Des Voeux, studying the scheme which had been approved by Major-General Cameron before his arrival, thought that the government ought to have a larger slice of the financial cake. Meanwhile Paul Chater had been in London pressing his suit with the Colonial Office, and it was he who won the day. The original scheme was approved with only minor amendments: and a grand opportun-

Various modes of conveyance on the old Praya around 1880.

The Praya before reclamation. Markers in the harbour show the extent of the new land to be formed. Wardley House, the Hongkong and Shanghai Bank's second building, is the domed structure just left of centre with the City Hall on its left.

ity for a reclamation that would have benefited the public as a whole was lost. The new Praya, extending seaward from the old one, was to be renamed (with considerable injustice) Des Voeux Road. An enlarged reclamation suggested by the consultant engineer Sir John Goode was turned down by the Governor and by the lot holders involved, and the Praya Reclamation Ordinance was passed. Work began in 1890 and went on to completion in 1904.

Chater's interest in the scheme was considerable. On 2 March 1889 he had joined forces with James Keswick, Jardine's senior representative in Hong Kong, to form a new company called The Hongkong Land Investment and Agency Company Limited, of which he was 'the directing genius from its inception.[1] Working capital was initially $1.25 million, a sum rather more than the total revenue of the Hong Kong government only a few years previously. Two years after the company's formation government revenue reached slightly over $2 million per annum.

The town planning tragedy of the era was the refusal of the Admiralty to move the naval docks to Kowloon, a decision backed by Des Voeux on the spurious grounds that the Kowloon area was growing in value and that the expense of moving would be excessive. Des Voeux also believed that for defensive reasons the Navy ought to be island-based. On these superficial and indefensible grounds the chance to remove once and for all the 'constriction at the waist' was lost.

The 'blockade' at last came to an end during Des Voeux's time as Governor, though not as a result of any specific act by him. One of the obstacles

The new headquarters of the Hongkong and Shanghai Bank, built in 1886.

in the way of ending it had always been the hostility between the colonial authorities and the Foreign Office. This now eased, resulting in a more commonsense view of the Chinese side of the dispute. In 1885 Britain and China had signed a new agreement on opium after two years of negotiation. In this the duty and also the *likin* tax on it were raised to 110 taels per chest, the immediate result being seen in increased smuggling to avoid payment of the taxes. Bowen had sympathized with the Chinese in this. He suggested a compromise, and in 1886 the commission reached agreement. All opium entering the harbour was to be reported to the Harbourmaster; none was to be landed, moved, transhipped, stored, or exported without his express permission and notice being given to the opium farmer, the concessionaire who had paid the fee exacted by the government for the right to import opium; all movement of opium was to be reported and accounted for; night clearance of junks was prohibited; raw opium was to be imported only by the opium farmer, and no import or export of amounts of less than one chest was to be permitted. A branch of the Chinese Maritime Customs, whose head was British and whose revenues were collected by the British and remitted to China, was to be set up in China to sell opium duty certificates at 100 taels per chest. The terms of this agreement were to be set forth in an ordinance and the whole agreement was subject to a similar one being arrived at with Macau — in default of which the Hong Kong controls would merely drive smugglers to the Portuguese territory to operate.

Hong Kong passed this ordinance, and another under which Chinese were forbidden to carry arms (thus pre-empting the depredations of armed gangs engaged in smuggling). The Colonial Office insisted the word 'Chinese' be altered to 'persons'.

The Opium Ordinance when introduced in March 1887 was regarded as offensive by the small traders and owners of junks, and both Des Voeux and Cameron reported that officials in the Chinese provinces would not work under the restrictions. In Hong Kong control and communication with the Chinese was assigned to the new Imports and Excise Department, and in 1888 the opium monopoly was once more sold to the highest bidder. Owing to the complexity of the agreement and the practical problems encountered in carrying out its terms in relation to a very lucrative trade, trouble continued and clashes at the Chinese border with Kowloon were frequent. Few were surprised when a smart Hong Kong opium concessionaire was discovered calmly and at great profit smuggling opium to China instead of confining his operations to Hong Kong. He had perceived a loophole in the law whereby opium which belonged to him was not subject to the provisions of the ordinance.

Added to the hazard of crooked opium concessionaires was the triad menace with its protection rackets and its blackmailed witnesses, among whom many a policeman and other government employee were numbered. Strong action against the triads seemed for a time to reduce the problem but, as successive administrations down to the present day were to find, the triad societies, almost as old in Hong Kong as the colony itself, were virtually ineradicable. Stemming from patriotic institutions far back in Chinese history, these organizations had become an integral part of Chinese society. To disentangle them from the web of social interactions never was easy and constitutes a problem in contemporary Hong Kong where the degenerate descendants of these ancient groupings still compete in organized crime — from the sale of sex to the sale of drugs.

Setting aside those darker aspects of life which emerge from the story of events in the Bowen and Des Voeux periods, the picture of the era varies very much from writer to writer. It also varies with whether the recorder was Western or Chinese. As to the latter, we have rather little evidence. But an article by a Rhenish missionary, J. Nacken, which appeared in the *China Review* of 1873, describes Chinese conditions in the colony which did not alter for many a decade afterward. Nacken, in his stilted, somewhat arch English, succeeds in bringing that life alive in his *Chinese Street Cries of Hong Kong*.[2] The following description is probably unique in its content in written material on the subject.

> The Chinese generally are early risers. Most of them will get up with the sun; then they dress, after which, rich as well as poor look out for their warm water to wash in and have some tea. But the Congee hawker has been up an hour or two before sunrise . . . he sallies forth, two boxes hanging from his shoulder-pole, each containing a large cooking pot and a small wood fire . . . Every Hawker cooks his own brand of Congee . . . Here comes the first crying *Maï chü hüt chuck* [Buy pig's blood congee]; the next *Mai chü shang chuck* [Buy fish congee]. And you can buy mulberry-root flavoured congee, or barley, or kidney, or pork, or a variety of others . . .

Then come the vendors of crabs, shrimps, fresh and dried oysters, shark's fin, and 'others who go about with baskets of live fowl'. In Guangzhou other hawkers employ what the writer terms a 'Western mirror', probably meaning a peep-show:

> but perhaps the Police do not allow them [in Hong Kong] as the . . . pictures are . . . of a licentious character.
>
> At noon tables are set . . . shaded by a large umbrella. A bench for guests stands in front, whilst the . . . cook attends behind . . . Those Chinese who can afford it sit down to *shik an chau* [eat the evening meal] . . .
>
> Here is [a coolie] panting under his load of earthenware; there is another who cries out his bamboo wares . . . baskets, brooms, mats, benches, ginger-grinders . . . Hawkers of fans, pipes, feather dusters, china, firewood, tobacco, salt, oil, cloth, lanterns . . .

Reading these and other lists of Nacken's there emerges the feeling of a man who loves the ambience, and while still considering the Chinese

Auguste Borget made this watercolour of cooked food stalls just before Hong Kong was annexed, but little had changed in this respect by the end of the century and even for many years after.

heathens, cannot but be delighted in his bones at their activities and their ordinariness within the surrounding exotica.

Des Voeux, who was not a great mixer, gives a less animated picture of ordinary life, and a dispirited one of his own. He spent the summers at Mountain Lodge perched on the edge of a precipice on the Peak, rebuilt after the former residence was carried away over the heads of the Kennedy family in the 1874 typhoon. For him the house was a mixed blessing. Talking of mist and cloud, he wrote:

> In our second season, this miserable experience lasted for the greater part of the summer. On one occasion for several weeks together the fog was as dense as the worst that afflicts London in November ... The damp inside the house was such that water ran down the walls in streams and collected in pools on the polished floors ... At such times one seemed entirely cut off from the world, the existence of which was revealed only at rare intervals by the arrival of a government messenger with papers.

Mountain Lodge survived the summer laments of damp governors until the Japanese occupation in World War II, when it was destroyed. No governor since then has been tempted to exercise the privilege of living on the Peak.

Queen Victoria celebrated her Golden Jubilee in 1887, the event marked in the colony by processions, the inauguration of the Chinese Chamber of Commerce, and by municipal resolve to commission a statue of Victoria the Queen suited to the dignity of Victoria the city. Two days after the celebrations, a newspaper carried a letter from an indignant citizen of Victoria who wrote:

> Sir: Yesterday I got into a street chair and told the bearers to take me to *Tai-lai-pai-t'ong*, the Cathedral [that is, the Large Worship Hall]. When one of them caught the right idea he said to his fellow 'It is the *Hung-mo-miu* (Red-hair Temple)' [or temple of the red-haired foreigners — barbarians]. I felt a little disconcerted on that glorious Jubilee morning to hear a nick-name applied to the British people as represented by the august assembly gathering in the Cathedral ...

More than a century later a civil servant recalls seeing a memo in circulation in the Secretariat in Hong Kong, to the effect that clerks should be forbidden from writing on papers destined for Government House the words *Ping Tau* meaning Military Boss, a common term for the governor. Similarly, the Botanical Gardens adjacent to Government House are still often referred to as *Ping Tau Fa Yuen* — the Military Boss's Garden.

Hong Kong was changing quite perceptibly as the century ebbed. Not far from the Governor's residence, on 2 May 1888, the Peak Tramway opened for business. This spectacular piece of nineteenth-century transport engineering, whereby counterbalanced cars ascended and descended what must at the time have been a record gradient from the level of the Cathedral to the Peak, was the instigator of a social revolution. What had been Hong Kong's most desirable area of residence for Westerners — Mid-levels — began almost at once to give way to the airy and frequently mist-wrapped heights of the Peak. There had been a few intrepid and wealthy Peak-dwellers before the tram, but now the slopes began to sprout luxurious mansions. The days when relays of chair-coolies sweated slowly upward from town with what the Chinese might well have called the Yellow Man's Burdens (human and material) gradually disappeared. The tram, swiftly, noiselessly, elevated the privileged to the cool Elysium above the sweating throng of Victoria in a matter of minutes. In those days, at the height of Empire, in the flush and glow of the Age of Steam (by which the Peak Tram was operated), the convenience of it seemed evidence of that splendidly Victorian thing — the march of progress carried forward by the grand superiority of the Empire-builders, brought like some life-saving draught to the subject races. The *Hong Kong Telegraph* wrote with enthusiasm of 'the first car leaving St John's Place — the lower terminal — punctually at 8 o'clock and the succeeding cars being dispatched according to the Company's time table'. That document reveals the information that the 'down' cars departing between 8 a.m. and 10 a.m. were reserved for first-class passengers only — for at that hour it may be presumed that the majority were likely to be gentlemen descending for business. On reaching the lower terminus they found their chairs, each borne by four liveried coolies, and off they went at a jog-trot to the office with a flourish of shouted warnings to straying pedestrians. Until the early 1930s, business men and others were still using the same two linked modes of conveyance.

Some of the numerous late-Victorian travellers add word-pictures, or just a comment or two, which plump out the bare historical facts. Miss Isabella Bird, a writer of many books of travel, was only minimally impressed by Hong Kong. 'The colony', she remarked, 'is moored to England by the electric cable',[3] a view shared by several governors inhibited by quick responses from the Colonial Office. It was also lit by electric light by this time. The first vestigial street lighting had been by means of lamps fuelled by peanut oil. Those were replaced on 1 January 1865 by gas lamps, and by 1888 there were about six hundred of them illuminating the main streets, amid frequent cries that it was the less reputable districts which required lighting to deter criminal activities. By 1890 electricity had superseded gas, although after their successful inauguration the lamps were dowsed by a shower of rain on the following day; but these teething troubles were soon cured. Four of the antique gas lamps still burn at a flight of steps leading from Ice House Street down to Duddell Street — the sole surviving link with that element of Hong Kong's past.

Another visitor, Lord Ronald Gower, found himself, he wrote:

transported two thousand years back in ancient Rome or glorious Carthage. This illusion is helped no doubt by the coloured dresses and fanciful drapery of the Chinese, and by the ... classical style of the white houses ... porticoes and colonades ... sparkling under the intensely brilliant sunshine, outlined sharply against the almost purple sky.[4]

The apparently whimsical attribution of purple to the Hong Kong sky may just have a basis in fact. For in the years after the colossal eruption of the Indonesian island of Krakatoa in August 1883, sunsets around the world were much more colourful than normal.

Another comment on the times comes from a French writer, Jean Chailley-Bert:

The life rolls by, varied, swift, happy, useful. After three or four years one goes to recuperate in old England. After fifteen or twenty years one retires there. One is looked up to by reason of this hard-earned wealth, and thereafter ... one follows and encourages the efforts of those who, in their turn, strive and strain to conduct on so high a plane, with such faith and indomitable energy, the destinies of the Anglo-Saxon race.[5]

An Anglo-Saxon writer, the Hon. George Nathaniel Curzon, later 1st Marquis Curzon of Kedleston and Viceroy of India, gives a more factual account:

it is evident that business competition is much keener now than it ever was before. Large fortunes are made with difficulty; the merchant princes and magnificent hongs of an earlier day have disappeared; Messrs. Jardine, Matheson and Co. ... remain almost alone among the great houses whose establishments almost a generation ago were the talk of the East. Men do not now expect fortunes; they are content with competencies ... The traveller finds the British merchants banded together in a powerful confederacy ....[6]

The truth lay, probably, somewhere among these various assessments.

In 1891 Hong Kong celebrated its first half century as a colony, the Queen sending a congratulatory telegram to the Governor. Anniversaries provoke reflection. Bowen, as he left Hong Kong, had reflected that

in the brief period of forty-three years which has elapsed since this island, then barren and desolate, was erected into a British colony, it has risen, by the blessings of Providence and the enterprise and energy of our race, to the proud position of the third greatest mart of shipping in the British Empire, ranking next after London and Liverpool.

Bowen had made his contribution in the revamping of the legislature, a real constitutional advance. To him must also be ascribed the achieving of the waterworks scheme whereby water ran from Tai Tam through the hills by tunnel and conduit to the filter beds along Bowen Road, augmenting the supply to Victoria. He had also been responsible for the resumption of life, after Hennessy's procrastinations, of the Central School building programme. Completed in 1889 and named Victoria College, it offered education to no fewer than 1,000 boys.

Des Voeux, who had been out of the colony on sick leave, returned to serve a few more months. Probably when he departed on that leave at the end of 1889 he did not think he would be returning at all, for he took the opportunity then to deliver a survey of progress, entitled Report on the Conditions and Prospects of the Colony, dated 31 October 1889. It contains a summing up which, while similar to that of Bowen, enters into more precise reasons for that progress.

> Hong Kong has indeed changed its aspect; and when it is remembered that all this has been effected in Her Majesty's reign and indeed during a space of less than fifty years and on ground in immediate contact with the most populous empire in the world, by a comparatively infinitesimal number of an entirely alien race separated from their homes by nearly the whole earth, and, unlike their countrymen in Australia and Canada, living in an enervating and trying climate; and when it is further remembered that the Chinese, whose labour and enterprise under British auspices have largely assisted in this development, have been under no compulsion, but have come here as free men, attracted by our liberal institutions, equitable treatment, and the justice of our rule; when all this is taken into account, it may be doubted whether the evidence of material and moral achievement, presented as it were in focus, make anywhere a more forcible appeal to eye and imagination, and whether any other spot on the earth is thus more likely to excite, or much more fully justifies, pride in the name of Englishman.

This resounding, splendid, architectural sentence, ringing with the very essence of Victorian trust and delight in the burdens and responsibilities of Empire, must serve as an ironic memorial to the legalization of the opium trade, as it does to a Governor whose main claim on posterity's attention is that he contributed virtually nothing to the colony he ruled.

16. Plague, and the New Territories Acquired

THE age of steam which had revolutionized the Far East maritime trade was the forerunner of the age of electricity. Without the steam-driven turbine to generate electricity, oil lamp, candle, and gas remained the only forms of light when dark fell. Heating was the job of coal, and cooling meant the traditional fan and the punkah, imported from India, powered by a servant activating, by means of a rope, a hanging textile strip to move the humid air.

At Pok Fu Lam, Douglas Lapraik, the watchmaker who became a shipping magnate, built Douglas Castle with its machicolated turrets. A sedan chair and its occupant are being conveyed along the road in this Chinese rendering of the scene.

The concept of architecture, commercial or domestic, suited to Western use in the tropics was based on the need for a current of air flowing through the interiors, themselves shaded from the sun by deep verandahs. The grace of the resulting buildings — and Hong Kong until some time after World War II had preserved its share of them — blending, often enough, Gothic Revival with classical and Romanesque elements, and Mogul and other oriental styles, gave the cities of empire (British, French, and German) in the East a certain charm and lightness. The solid sobriety of much nineteenth-century architecture in Britain was happily almost absent from Hong Kong where it gave place to a structural lightness and brightness of surface quite foreign to Northern Europe, more reminiscent of Italy.

In the 1880s Fung Wah-chuen, the comprador of Russell and Company, set up a small electric power-station in Guangzhou and, a mere 16 years after the opening of the world's first commercial power company in London, that ancient Chinese city received its first hesitant supply. Fung was a product of Queen's College, graduating with the prize for the best spoken English. Under the name Fung Shui, he became an assistant teacher there. The school magazine records him as a Chinese assistant and, later, comprador of Shewan Tomes and Company, the earlier name of Russell and Company. Jury lists of 1882–8 show him as assistant to Yan Wo Opium Firm, and in the 1883 Opium Commission he is described as comprador, National Bank, which he seems to have had a hand in floating. He was also involved in the Wai Sing lottery at Guangzhou in which bets could be placed on the candidates in the Imperial Examinations. Fung was a director of the Tung Wah Hospital in 1892, and in 1894 and 1899 was director and then Chairman of the Po Leung Kuk. The fiftieth anniversary issue of *The Chimes*, the magazine of St Stephen's College at Stanley, names him as one of its founders who, in March 1901, petitioned the Governor for a school in which Chinese children would be taught English and Chinese. St Stephen's opened on 23 February 1903 with seven pupils, one of whom, Fung Man-siu, was probably a son of Fung Wah-chuen.

Fung went on to a brilliant career in Hong Kong — Chairman of the Chinese Chamber of Commerce in 1900, and then in China as deputy of Foreign Affairs to the Viceroy of Guangdong in 1909. And in that year he negotiated the sale of the electric company to new owners in that city. While the Hong Kong Electric Company began production on Hong Kong island in 1890, it was the vision of Robert Shewan (of Shewan Tomes) and Paul Chater, on the example of Fung Wah-chuen, which saw Kowloon as a potential city and which led to the construction of the first power-station there. This company became in time The China Light and Power Company, without whose forward thinking the eventual development of Hong Kong as an industrial giant of the latter half of the twentieth century could not have been so smoothly accomplished.[1]

It was into this setting of the early age of electricity, of still leisured manners, and commerce conducted in buildings cooled by natural breezes and the swinging punkah, that the new Governor, Sir William Robinson, disembarked in December 1891 — the colony's fiftieth year. It was in this year, as Sayer succinctly phrases it, 'that Hong Kong's non-Chinese population rose to over 10,000, her Chinese population to 20,000, her revenue to $2,000,000, and her shipping to 10,000,000 tons'.

Amid the general jollifications, a number of carping voices were raised at the choice of 1891 to celebrate Hong Kong's jubilee. Hong Kong, they said, did not legally become a colony until the signing of the Nanjing Treaty in 1842; and there were even pedants who preferred 1843 when the treaty was ratified, and when Pottinger remarked that it was now 'a bona fide possession of the Crown'.

In 1891 it was apparently a prosperous place, its expansion phenomenal, equalling that of mushrooming Shanghai up the coast, demonstrating the unbeatable qualities brought forth by the combined efforts of the Chinese and British. Lord Curzon described this in admiring terms.

The national love for neatness and decorum [of the British] appears in the private grounds, the *bunds*, the public gardens of the cities where the English are in the ascendant; and, were every other mark of British influence erased tomorrow, it would always remain a marvel how from a scorching rock have been evolved the Elysian graces of Hong Kong.[2]

Sayers takes Curzon up on this: 'It was', he wrote, 'of course the "scorching rock" itself that made an essential contribution to this transformation scene. At the magic touch of British capital and Chinese labour Hong Kong's unprofitable hills had yielded up their hidden treasure and a town of native granite had emerged.'[3]

The new Governor was very much a Colonial Office man from the time when at the age of 18 he began there as a clerk. Twenty years later he was Governor of the Bahamas. In Hong Kong he took over the administration from Major-General Digby Barker. Almost at once the shining face of prosperous Hong Kong darkened. To a degree Robinson was responsible. In his first speech to the Legislative Council he announced a change in the system of accounting by which all accounts for any one year, some previously not settled until January of the next, would be put into the balance of the relevant year. On the books this meant an additional expenditure of $170,000 in 1892. A loan committee put forward two methods of dealing with this problem — securing local bank overdrafts at low interest, and the sale of land (even at depressed prices). A loan of $200,000 in stock was agreed. But retrenchment was to be the order of the day. Less urgent public works were to be postponed and economies were to be made by

Sir William Robinson, Governor from December 1891 to January 1898, photographed with the members of the Legislative Council. On his left is Sir Paul Chater, and the second figure from him on his right is Sir James Stewart Lockhart. Robinson had an almost uncanny resemblance to King Edward VII.

amalgamating certain government offices. A retrenchment committee set up in 1894 suggested staff cuts in some government departments, but it would not countenance any reduction in spending on public works.

With a basically resilient economy much of the cutting back proved temporary. But the situation was impaired by the doubling of the defence contribution in 1890 and the falling price of silver which made sterling payments heavier and pushed up the cost of living, requiring upward adjustments in salaries. At this time, coincidentally, Britain was in the throes of one of its periodic attacks of conscience over opium. In October 1891 the Secretary of State ordered the colonial government to take direct control of opium sales with a view to confining its consumption, in close co-operation with the Opium Commission which sat in Calcutta. This, even at the cost of lost revenue.

Another move was to pay government officials' salaries half at the old rate and half at current rates. But with the announcement of the 1894 revenue figures — $2,207,203, which topped the estimate by almost three hundred thousand dollars, an increase over the previous year of more than two hundred thousand dollars — the economy appeared buoyant enough.

In all this Robinson proceeded in a thoroughly text-book manner. In 1895 he raised stamp duties and almost succeeded in balancing his budget, even under the stress of the military contribution and the continuing public works programme. The deficit was a mere $12,000.

The momentum of certain public works projects continued. At Tai Tam the Water Extension Scheme envisaged a reservoir capacity increased by 400 million gallons to satisfy demand at Shau Kei Wan and Aberdeen. The population of Kowloon was also outdrinking the water supply, but proposals for sinking wells and pumping the water to storage tanks were not approved. The Colonial Office kept insisting on a new gaol, the old one being manifestly inadequate; but here an unforeseen obstacle arose. The unofficials of the legislature, abetted by Dr Ho Kai, argued that separate cells were unsuited to the Chinese. Robinson compromised, proposing a new police station and magistracy which would give room for the extension of the existing gaol on the same site.

On the Governor's innocent head fell blows consequent on his predecessors' lapses of judgement. By omitting fully to implement the recommendations of the Chadwick report, they had paved the way for the 'irresistible logic' of the great bubonic plague of 1894 which then overtook the colony. The beginnings were discovered by chance. No law called for the notification of Chinese deaths, and there was consequently no hint of an unusually large number in any particular area. Plague was endemic up and down the China coast and, after the bitterly cold January of 1893 (the Peak down to 450 feet above sea level was ice-bound for three days),[4] when the weather warmed up, several cases came to notice — the first to be recorded in the city. By May 150 cases were reported, most proving fatal. In the next 10 to 12 days the death toll was 450, and increasing. Thus began the most dramatic episode of Robinson's time, and perhaps the most traumatic in Hong Kong's history to that date.

In great haste a special committee of the Sanitary Board was convened to suggest the necessary action — by-laws permitting radical cleansing and disinfection in the plague areas, compulsory removal of infected persons, provision of extra hospital beds, and the institution of house-to-house visits by an augmented sanitary staff. Other laws, passed later, allowed for the scouring of all buildings thought to pose a danger to health, with the forcible ejection of the occupants. Three hundred troops were impressed to help out, but when five contracted plague (whose cause was unknown at this time) their numbers were reduced. Hong Kong was declared an infected port.

Chinese prejudice against Western medical procedures was almost universal and deeprooted. Chinese dislike of Western intrusion into their private lives and houses was strong, as would Chinese intrusion into the lives of Europeans of the time have been resented (the reciprocity of such feelings was not considered by the foreigners). Such was Chinese dislike of the military house-to-house visits that the Tung Wah strongly urged the Governor to let it take over the treatment of all plague victims. But Robinson, doubtless feeling his authority challenged, unwisely refused.

At this point placards began to appear in Guangzhou warning Cantonese women to refrain from visiting Hong Kong, and accusing Western doctors of gouging out the eyes of children for use in the treatment of plague. Schools in the colony emptied overnight, thousands of Chinese fled in panic to China. Anti-foreign feeling in Guangzhou ran high. A Chinese charitable organization in the city sent junks to Hong Kong to take plague victims away, and also to remove all the dead, an offer which Robinson at first refused. Later he allowed 170 cases to be taken to Guangzhou. One further problem arose — the Chinese custom of keeping the dead for burial on an auspicious day. This, added to the fear of evil influences emanating from the dead which meant that corpses were often deserted, led to situations which aggravated an already dire threat to the whole community. In June, on one single day, 109 corpses had to be collected.

Large areas of Taipingshan were roped off and sealed. About three hundred and fifty houses were condemned and 7,000 Chinese were evicted from

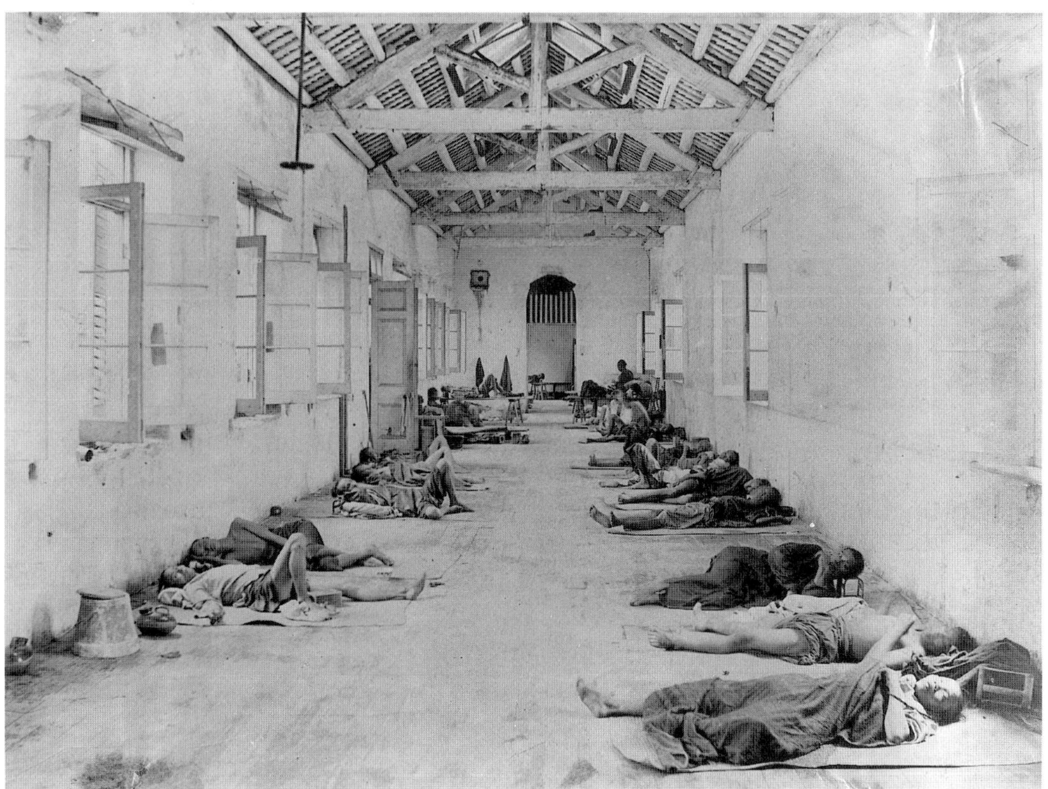

A newly built glassworks was turned into a makeshift 'hospital' for victims of the plague of 1894.

their homes — what happened to them went unrecorded. Room had to be found to set up temporary hospitals. The hospital ship *Hygeia*, a recently built but as yet unoccupied pig depot, and the Kennedy Town glassworks which had likewise not been occupied, were quickly filled with victims.

Robinson was of the opinion that the only remedy was wholesale destruction of buildings in the affected areas, and it seemed, since at least half of the cases recorded came from the Taipingshan region, that this might well be effective. As cooler weather came the epidemic died down, but not before over two and a half thousand persons had succumbed: the figure for those who fled was officially put at 80,000.

The strike among coolies in the following year, 1895, in protest against the provisions of an ordinance giving power to inspect their lodging houses, demonstrated the need for extreme caution in using such powers. An officer of the Chinese Maritime Customs at Guangzhou during the strike, L. C. Arlington, wrote:

> The treatment ... accorded to the Chinese inhabitants caused thousands to flee to Macau and the *Hinterland*. The specific reasons for this exodus were the house-to-house visitations of the 'Whitewash Brigade', the burying of the dead in lime, and the interments higgledy-piggledy at the western point of the island. The 'Whitewash Brigade' used to enter a house and demand a 'squeeze' — otherwise the furniture and other things such as clothing, trunks, etc., were thrown out into the streets and destroyed by fire. The Brigade consisted of foreigners who did the dirty work, and their native helpers and interpreters did the money-making.[5]

Arlington appears to have believed what he wrote — that it was the Chinese in the Brigade who did all the 'squeezing' while the foreigners (who were mostly a raggle-taggle of soldiers whose pay was a pittance) remained ignorant of what was taking place, and were neither tempted to nor took any part in the financial exactions. Or was he merely reciting that nineteenth-century British credo about the incorruptible Englishman? There can be no doubt, as Austin Coates writes of these events, that 'it was the most harrowing situation that had yet arisen between British and Chinese in Hong Kong, on the one side the necessity to cleanse the city of a deadly disease, on the other the people's incomprehension of the need for this ...'.[6] The further provocation of crude blackmail by the instruments of cleansing must have come near to ending in civil strife. Robinson remained firm on the strike, deporting some of the ringleaders and publishing a notice in Chinese explaining the position. And the strike collapsed with no incidents of violence reported.

Trade suffered. Shipping naturally avoided calling at an infected port, but as the plague died down a return to normal did not take long.

Plague, from being a thing that affected China, a remote horror to which a civilized society (in European eyes) was scarcely subject, had now become endemic. Almost every year it was to recur with varying severity as spring came. The Sanitary Board had to bear the brunt of the criticism, only some of it fair. Ayres, in his 1895 report, castigated the Board for its 'long, wordy, windy, desultory, rambling discussions' which led to nothing being done. While the Board had an unofficial majority and an elected element, it relied fundamentally on government favour for its funds. Even its by-laws had to be passed by the Legislative Council, which was also responsible for its policy. The Board existed somewhat tenuously in a legislative and executive limbo, its only real power its power to resign. This its unofficial members unanimously elected to do, in protest against a government decision to appoint a Medical Officer of Health. Thus, by 1895, the Board was to all intents and purposes defunct. Robinson sought permission of London to abolish it, but this was denied, the Colonial Office appearing to perceive in Robinson a degree of panic reaction. Robinson had indeed said at the height of the plague in June 1894: 'I may assert that so far as trade and commerce are concerned the plague has assumed the importance of an unexampled calamity.' In fact its effects were passing. But for Robinson it was 'one of the saddest and most disastrous [years] in the recorded history of Hong Kong'. True. And also, to be just, the Governor had suffered the loss of his wife in the colony. His sorrows were compounded.

In the end Robinson changed his mind, making the Medical Officer of Health a member of the Sanitary Board in place of a lay administrator. But the beleaguered Board was not yet out of the woods. Its every act, it seemed, was destined to provoke public criticism, so that in 1896 Robinson was forced to respond by holding a plebiscite among the British community to decide whether the Board should have an official or an unofficial majority. The result was 331 votes in favour of the latter, with 31 against. This procedure roused the Colonial Secretary in London to remark that 'it is inconsistent with Crown colony government to seek the guidance of a plebiscite'.

Plague, very light in 1895, returned in all severity in 1896. By August of that year, 1,193 cases were reported, of which 1,088 proved fatal. The next year only 17 cases were reported, but in 1898 the epidemic was more serious. Few non-Chinese had so far died, but in that year two European nurses succumbed. The cause of plague, a disease of rats conveyed by fleas deserting the bodies of dying creatures and infecting by their bites the human being on whom they settle for sustenance, was still unknown. Europeans and Chinese alike thought the miasma arising from the advent of hot weather and the season's rains to be the cause. Malaria (from Italian *mal' aria* — bad air) had also been attributed to the same cause before the discovery — by Sir Reginald Ross in 1897 — of the transference of the parasite by the bite of the female anopheles mosquito. Sir Patrick Manson was near to the discovery at about the same time in Hong Kong. The pandemic plague of South China and Hong

Kong would appear to have found its way — doubtless via ships' rats and sailors — round the world in succeeding years, and it remained endemic in the colony until the mid-1920s.

During its ravages not only Chinese but also large numbers of Portuguese left Hong Kong, fleeing to Macau and abandoning residential areas around Caine Road. Ironically, it was in 1894–5 that a group of Japanese researchers under Shibasaburo Kitasato managed to isolate the plague bacillus and recognized the connection between its habitat in rats and other rodents, and the infection of human beings. Yet, some considerable time after this, a government medical official is on record as denying the connection between rats and plague! Aside from the pitiable ignorance of the Medical Department staff, there must have been few enough occasions for laughter during the recurring blight. One was occasioned by the instructions issued to Chinese householders to catch their domestic rats and, unless they wished to be visited by the Whitewash Brigade, to place them in 'rat-boxes' hung on lamp posts. This 'gave rise to a charming Cantonese expression used solely in Hong Kong when, if there is any marked disparity in height between husband and wife, and the husband is slim, the couple ... find themselves affectionately called "the lamp-post and the rat-box"'![7]

By the end of 1895 the government had resumed the Taipingshan area and by the end of 1898 it had been razed and rebuilt.

One other result of the plague was mentioned by Robinson in November 1895. 'It is extraordinary — not to say discreditable — that after fifty-five years of British rule, the vast majority of Chinese in Hong Kong should remain so little Anglicized.' This led to various measures such as the demand for the teaching of more English. Less cogent responses were criticism of the Tung Wah Hospital in the treatment of plague. In fact neither Western nor traditional Chinese medical procedures had any effective treatment for the disease. Government medical men then recklessly demanded the abolition of the Tung Wah. A committee of enquiry of 1896 recognized the organization's valuable work for Chinese poor and sick, but suggested that the Medical Department should act in a supervisory capacity, and that Western medical treatment should be introduced on a voluntary basis under the supervision of a Chinese trained in Western medicine. The Tung Wah agreed to Dr Chung's appointment — he had qualified at the Hong Kong Medical College and was resident House Surgeon at the Alice Memorial Hospital. They insisted that he be paid by the government.

Oddly enough, contrary to general opinion among the British, Chinese patients proved not to be as prejudiced as expected. In the scheme's first month 17 of them elected to have Western treatment. In fact almost the sole superiority of Western medical 'science' at the time lay in vaccination techniques and in a more highly developed system of nursing care.

Before he left Hong Kong, Robinson had one more obstacle to address, the reiterated and now increasingly insistent cry for a Municipal Council. After Bowen's reforms affecting the legislature, its members had tasted a modicum of power in that they voted all taxation and held debates on the appropriations suggested by the Finance Committee. Unofficials were not a majority, but were influential and exerted pressure on a system of government by discussion if not always consensus. By 1894 a petition from ratepayers led by T. H. Whitehead of the Chartered Bank, Paul Chater, Jackson of the Hongkong and Shanghai Bank, and Dr Ho Kai was sent to the Secretary of State in London. Its message, briefly, was that Hong Kong's annual trade was worth $40,000,000; that this prosperous state in the colony had come about largely through the exertions of British merchants and ship owners; yet their reward was only the flimsiest share in decisions affecting the colony. They pointed out that other Crown colonies had been accorded representative institutions, and they wanted the 'common right of Englishmen to manage their local affairs and control the expenditure of the colony where imperial considerations were not involved'. What they suggested was 'free election of British nationality in the Legislative Council', and that the British should constitute a majority.

Robinson, forwarding the petition, thought that the best course might be to add slightly to the unofficial element in both Councils. Lord Ripon in London treated the matter with the utmost gravity, penning a dispatch in which he passed in review the whole history of constitutional reform in Hong Kong. His conclusion was that 'it had prospered because it has been a British

The Marquis of Ripon, Secretary of State for the Colonies from August 1892 to June 1895.

colony', having few lifelong residents of either British or Chinese nationality. He wanted to know if the voters could be of any nationality, if the British were to be from the British Isles, or to be subjects by race only; and, concluding, he had no difficulty in demonstrating the ill-thought nature of the petition, and its tendency towards setting up what would in effect be a little oligarchy. He thought that the addition of more unofficials to the Legislative Council would best be balanced by adding more officials and perhaps by adding a second Chinese; and that as to the Executive Council, unofficial members should be appointed, who might be any subject of the Queen, not necessarily a European. On a Municipal Council, Lord Ripon wrote: 'I frankly say that I should like to see one established', and (prophetically) he thought that the Sanitary Board might in time develop into such a body. But, in view of the continuing Sino-Japanese war, there should be no immediate change.

Lord Ripon was not alone in discerning the defects of the petition. In Hong Kong the Registrar-General, James Stewart Lockhart, soon to be the colony's Colonial Secretary, dissected its contents in a memorandum to the Governor.

> Most of the taxes fall almost entirely on the Chinese. The only tax to which the British and other residents as a whole are subject in the same manner as the Chinese is the tax of 13 per cent levied on the rateable value of house property in Victoria ... This tax yields annually about $470,000, of which over $350,000 are contributed by the Chinese and the balance by all the other nationalities combined. The petitioners, who are not in some instances British, and who do not in many cases contribute directly to taxes, claim [the already quoted 'common right of Englishmen', and so on]. They have, however, carefully omitted to point out that the local affairs include Chinese affairs of which ... they are generally ignorant and which the Chinese have shown no desire that the British merchants and other residents should manage, and to indicate that to the expenditure of the Colony of which they desire the control they contribute a very small portion. Petitioners surely do not wish to maintain that Britishers have an inherent right to control all expenditure ...[8]

After further lobbying the Marquis of Ripon recommended that two unofficials might be nominated to the Executive Council (one of whom was to be Chinese). One official should be added to the Legislative Council (he suggested Major-General W. Black), with two unofficials representing 'retail traders or skilled labour'. These changes were made in July 1896. J. J. Bell-Irving of Jardine, Matheson and Company and Paul Chater became the first unofficials on the Executive Council; Wei Yuk, an astute business man, became the additional unofficial member, and the General became an additional official member, on the Legislative Council in December 1896. With this little sop, the petitioners had to be content; and the clamour for reform temporarily died down.

A vital step had been taken in 1892 towards the goal of honest administration when it was ruled that no government official might own land or property in the colony except his own dwelling, or engage in commerce, or buy shares in local companies. The rule had been laid down once and for all that holding government office was incompatible with commercial interests, which might conflict with absolute integrity in the administration.

The uneasy situation of the colony on the border of a China under attack by Japan emphasized the need to consider its defences. The Hong Kong Volunteer Corps had been revived in 1893, and 1897 saw a new commander installed in the person of the Chief Justice, Sir J. W. Carrington. The 159-member Corps was to come in handy at the take-over of the New Territories in 1899 — the cession of which was negotiated in Robinson's term. The requirement was for strict neutrality on the part of Hong Kong, and in relation to this the case of Dr Sun Yatsen was pertinent. He had been banished, accused of conspiracy against the Guangzhou authorities, and had left for Japan. His dignified letter to the Governor with its threat to appeal to the British public, explaining that he was attempting merely 'to emancipate my miserable country from the Tartar yoke' could hardly have been music to Robinson's ears. And as he left in March 1898 after more than six years (the longest-serving Governor to that date) the colony was on the brink of one

"HOLD ON, JOHN!"

The so-called 'scramble for concessions' of territory from the Chinese around the turn of the century was graphically illustrated in *Punch*. Britain, France, Germany, and Russia are seen tearing at the helpless body of China — Britain with the strongest position, arms encircling the mandarin's chest.

of the most extraordinary events by which it acquired 365.5 square miles of territory — more than twelve times the area of Hong Kong island. The history of how this came about need not detain us long. Broadly, the reasons were the impossibility of defending the colony against attack from the mainland. By acquiring the land whose shores flanked the harbour its defence would be a more feasible proposition. In what was to be called the 'scramble for concessions' Britain negotiated cession of the needed territory in 1898 on a 99-year lease from China. The documents, signed on 9 June, ceded the waters of the two bays east and west of the Kowloon peninsula, and all the waters and islands north of 22°9′ latitude and between 113°52′ and 114°30′ longitude. Civil administration over Kowloon City, unwisely as it turned out, was reserved to Chinese officials. Equally unwisely, the exact frontier was not defined in detail in the treaty, nor were

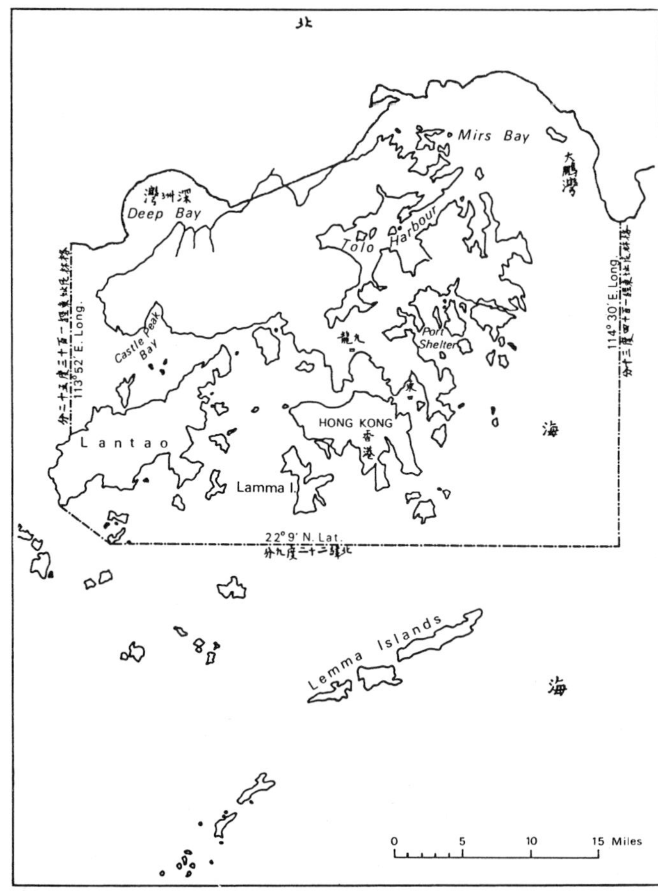

6. The map attached to the Convention between Great Britain and China signed at Beijing on 9 June 1898, demarcating the area leased to Britain. (*Source*: Wesley-Smith, *Unequal Treaty, 1898–1997*, p. 193. Redrawn from MacMurray (comp. and ed.), *Treaties and Agreements With and Concerning China, 1894–1919*, p. 131.)

the positioning and operation of the Chinese customs posts. There was no firm plan for the administration of the territory.

Adding to the prevailing nervousness, the American fleet was anchored in Mirs Bay, intent on taking Manila; and tension was increased by the lack of co-operation between the Foreign and Colonial Offices in London. The confusion was compounded by the fact that the Viceroy of Guangdong was under the impression that China's authority was still paramount in the newly ceded territory.

Stewart Lockhart, in England at the time, was immediately dispatched to Hong Kong to survey the ceded territory. His report prompted the new Governor, Sir Henry Blake, who arrived in November 1898, to suggest a separate administration for it. This was vetoed by Chamberlain in London since it had already been declared an integral part of Hong Kong. After talks between the two sides the boundary was fixed to run from the head of Mirs Bay to the head of Deep Bay, following the Sham Chun river most of the way; the line, with blythe inconsequentiality, running down the middle of the main street (Chung-ying — China-Britain Street) of the village of Sha Tau Kok, where it remains to this day. Initial delight at the cession of the New Territories was soon tempered by doubts of various kinds. The inclusion of Kowloon City with Chinese exercising jurisdiction in it, and the absence of any but the sketchiest knowledge of the terrain and its inhabitants, were but

New Territories villagers using a rotary winnowing machine — an ancient Chinese invention.

two of them. The government was not in any way prepared for the take-over. Lockhart's report offered the opinion that a welcome was by no means assured, and Blake, who had been in Hong Kong only a few months, decided the best way was to proceed with the occupation and not await settlements in all the disputes. He planned to raise the flag over the New Territories on 17 April 1899.

Three days prior to that date, numbers of outraged inhabitants (the total population was estimated at about one hundred thousand) who had not been consulted on their conversion from Chinese to British citizens, rose up in what they must have seen as properly righteous anger to prevent that action. The matshed structures, which had been put up at Tai Po Hui to serve as temporary headquarters for the British administration, were discovered by a party of the colonial police on 14 April to have been burned to the ground; and a threatening band of about one hundred and fifty Chinese was gathered on the hills. The police, under Captain F. H. May (later to be Governor of Hong Kong), decided that the better part of British valour was to retire to the safety of Hong Kong overnight. The next day, 15 April, augmented by a detachment of the Hong Kong Regiment under Captain Berger, the police were sent back by the Governor, who had no expectation of an attack. Reaching Tai Po Hui they were, however, met by considerable numbers of what appeared to be regular Chinese troops entrenched in positions on high ground with artillery. The Chinese took the offensive, many armed with gingalls (muskets fired from stands) and furiously waving banners. But faced with a small, disciplined British force, the Chinese melted away over the hills.

On the following day, 16 April, a larger body of troops under Major-General Gascoigne was sent to the site, and Stewart Lockhart who accompanied them succeeded in raising the British flag.

This did not mark the end of Chinese resistance. That very evening the Volunteers were called out, and on 17 April several thousand armed Chinese were routed by British forces near Kam Tin. After they had retreated to nearby hills and regrouped, another battle took place, resulting in a Chinese defeat which apparently scotched any further thoughts of resistance.

Blake, blaming Tan, the Viceroy of Guangdong, who had undertaken to supervise the transition of power, sent the Volunteers into Kowloon City, and simultaneously seized Shen Zhen as an earnest of his intentions should the Viceroy fail again. The Colonial Office endorsed this action. A Colonial Office minute records the passing of an Order in Council stating that the city of Kowloon should not be under Chinese jurisdiction, 'and the matter is at an end'. Chinese official presence there was not thenceforward permitted. The question of Chinese jurisdiction in Kowloon was discussed between Blake and Li Hongzhang, the new Viceroy of Guangdong, when the latter passed through Hong Kong on his return from a visit to the West in June 1900, but

Sir Henry Blake arrived to take up his post as Governor a few months after the New Territories lease had been signed and had come into effect on 1 July 1898. He sits here with the Viceroy of Guangdong.

no changes were made. Shen Zhen was occupied for several months and the customs officials removed from their stations, the latter being re-established at Lingding, Tai Shan, and Sam Mun.

The occupation was completed, the flag unfurled, the proclamation duly read; the new lords of the Kowloon peninsula took up their duties. Their main problem was not military but administrative. It was decided that, with certain omissions, the laws of Hong Kong were to prevail in the newly acquired lands. A local Communities Ordinance created district and sub-district courts with limited civil and criminal jurisdiction, but there was no power to prevent what immediately occurred — the wholesale buying up of land at rock-bottom prices by at least one syndicate of Chinese among whom, it was suspected, was the Legislative Councillor, Dr Ho Kai. The syndicate appears to have achieved its aims on the pretext that the British, as rumours

Guards at a New Territories Customs Post in 1900. The Englishman is accompanied on his tour of inspection by his wife. Hong Kong people were intensely curious about conditions beyond the familiar hills that formed the backdrop to the Kowloon Peninsula and were keen to travel there once it became possible to do so.

predicted, were about to confiscate the land. Hearing of this, Blake wanted to return the land to the rightful owners, but the legal problems involved were so formidable that the matter was dropped.

The Governor toured the New Territories in August 1899, inspecting the eight districts and 48 sub-districts. He promised to respect Chinese customs, warned that punishments would be according to the laws of Hong Kong, and informed his audience that landowners must register their holdings and that all land rent was payable to the government. In return he promised protection from banditry.

The Governor's subsequent report painted a grim picture of the New Territories, of a population misgoverned by former masters and 'squeezed' by corrupt officials. Disputes had frequently been settled only by clan feuding. It was a land, he reported, where malaria was rife, a land of murders in Shen Zhen, of robbery and piracy round the coasts. He asked for more money to police the area, estimating the sum needed at almost one hundred and fifty thousand dollars for the year.

Much of the early work of organization and the setting up of a workable administration in the New Territories fell to Lockhart who continued, until he left Hong Kong a sick man in March 1901, to interest himself in its problems and their solution, although latterly he was not directly responsible. In his last report, in 1901, he wrote: '... in bidding farewell, I do so with

An ancestral hall in the New Territories, Door Gods painted on its tall portals.

much regret, mingled with pleasant reminiscences of . . . work . . . in the midst of its charming and beautiful scenery, and lessened by the recollection that I have been and still am a strong believer in its future'. The day-to-day work of administration was assigned to three cadets — E. R. Hallifax, C. M. Messer, and J. H. Kemp. Much discussion went on about how to effect improvements in the economic and other conditions, with Charles Ford of the Botanical Gardens Department being asked for advice on vine and camphor culture, and for improvements in sugar-cane and mulberry cropping. Jardine, Matheson, ever active, wanted the coal concession for the whole area.

But conditions remained highly unsettled, the Chinese rebellious. Village elders, requested to attend meetings on land tenure, refused to do so, and in January 1900 an ordinance gave power to summon Chinese to the Registrar-General's office for questioning. This provoked an outcry. A land court was set up to settle disputed claims, and instructed by London not to be too rigorous, the aim being to confirm occupation and to encourage improvement of the terrain. But the facts as they came to light revealed a tangled mass of disputed claim and counter-claim, often complicated by the absence of adequate, or indeed any, documentation. The bemused court discovered that one in 20 claims was disputed, and yet further problems arose in having lands accurately marked on the map. Corps of surveyors were imported from India to deal with this. All unclaimed land was to be held for disposal by the Crown.

To no one's surprise, the land court took until 1904 to complete over 354,000 cases and to determine the real owners of lots, an exercise that cost $143,615. Over subsequent years the New Territories was to prove a costly acquisition. By the end of June 1901 its revenue stood at only $14,140: expenditure amounted to $736,571. Lockhart's optimism seemed unwarranted.

Blake's opinion about administration in the leased area was that 'existing village organizations should be maintained and utilized'. But such organizations had in many cases become invalid, the village elders powerless in a situation where appeal could be made over their heads to British officials. The main problems for the government were law and order and the slippery terrain of land revenue. A workable method of administration was only slowly evolved in the light of long and painful experience.

The New Territories was eventually divided into two geographical and administrative parts: that part between the China border and the Kowloon range of hills became New Territories North; while New Territories South consisted of the tip of the peninsula from the range southward, and all the islands. By 1907 the two chief officers of the northern district, then the Assistant Superintendent of Police and the Assistant Land Officer, became District Officer and Assistant District Officer respectively (the latter office was later abolished). And in September 1910 the Assistant Land Officer (South) was given the title of Assistant District Officer. These civil servants, as well as being in charge of the police and general administration, were also police magistrates, and in 1908 were given power to try petty debt cases up to $200. Education both in traditional village schools and in due course in schools set up by the government was encouraged, and health matters were supervised by the resident Medical Officer — the first holder of that office being a graduate of the College of Medicine, Hong Kong. These arrangements remained in place until 1913.

The acquisition of the New Territories took place against a backdrop of ominous events in China as that country entered its last decade of dynastic rule, and as the Western powers increased their stranglehold on its economy by both military and commercial means. The year 1901 proved to be inauspicious. The old Queen in England died at last as Hong Kong celebrated its diamond jubilee. The military contribution from Hong Kong towards the cost of the British garrison rose from the figure fixed in the 1890s, 17½ per cent of the colonial revenue, to 20 per cent, and plague returned in the worst outbreak since 1894 — so serious that the community petitioned the Secretary of State, alleging the government's failure to implement the Chadwick report's recommendations.

Once again, as Sayer recounts it, 'the *deus ex machina*' in the person of

Water shortage in 1901. A line of people wait to fill their containers from the tanks brought from Tsuen Wan to the Praya.

Chadwick himself returned to the colony, 20 years after his first visit. He must surely have reflected on the irony of the situation, for had his original report been heeded his return would not have been called for. Chadwick brought with him Professor Simpson, a plague specialist. In the following years they produced another report dealing once more with the deficiencies in housing and the appalling shortcomings in public hygiene.

The year 1901 was also the year of a serious drought in which the colony experienced the 'practical value of the newly acquired territory'. Supplies of water were brought from Tsuen Wan by boat to Hong Kong and emptied into tanks set up on the Praya. During the spring and summer it was from these tanks, laboriously, that the population got much of its supply. Drought, hitherto a less serious problem, now made its début (and continued a serious threat sporadically until the 1970s). Steps were taken in 1902 to provide the Kowloon peninsula with an adequate water supply, the old wells at Ho Man Tin being supplemented by a new scheme in which a reservoir was built in the hills near Ma Tsz Keng (Smugglers' Ridge) and a tunnel cut, through which water gravitated down to Kowloon.

It was the contents of the new Chadwick–Simpson report which inspired Ordinance No. 1 of 1903 (the Public Health and Buildings Ordinance). At last it appeared the government was taking the position seriously. Plague deaths in 1898 were 1,175, rising to 1,428 in 1899. In 1900 a total of 1,434 died, and in the following year the epidemic was so severe that numbers of Europeans died and Chinese began to leave the colony. It is open to suspicion that the numbers of Westerners appearing for the first time in the casualty lists may not have had a negative effect on the counsels of the administration. Despite the medical officer's pronouncement that it was more probable that rats caught plague from man than man from rats, it was generally accepted that fleas transmitted the plague from rats to man. Blake had started a great campaign against rats and an offer of two cents for each rat tail produced by members of the public was a stupendous success; 43,000 tails were handed in during 1900, but suspicion grew that the numbers were swollen by imports from the New Territories — even from China — and were not from infected animals.

The Governor had done much to improve general sanitary conditions by strengthening the Sanitary Board and by appointing extra Inspectors of Nuisances and introducing drain inspectors. In 1899 he had pushed through the Insanitary Properties Ordinance to deal with cocklofts, and to restrict the partitioning of rooms into tiny cubicles — all matters recommended in the original Chadwick Report.

Embodied in the Chadwick–Simpson report were meticulous directions for the examination of rats, the rat-proofing of all houses, and the need for more

In 1902, Sir Henry Blake and his family moved into the newly rebuilt Mountain Lodge, the Governor's official summer residence on the Peak.

water. The report also counselled the government that there was no substitute for the resumption and demolition of unsuitable structures, and rebuilding on sanitary principles. In Central District in 1902 there was still an average of 502 persons per acre, in 1904 no fewer than 608.

In the last year of Blake's tenure important public works were begun. The new red brick Post Office and Government Offices started to rise at the foot of Pedder Street; the Supreme Court, designed by Sir Aston Webb, the architect of Buckingham Palace's new façade and of Admiralty Arch in London, was begun on a site next to the Hong Kong Club which, with the statue of Queen Victoria, had been completed in 1898. The memorials to the old Queen — the Victoria Hospital on Barker Road, and Jubilee Street connecting Connaught Road with Queen's Road Central, were both completed. But the enthusiasm of town planners for that civic dream, the long-awaited waterfront road to connect Central District with Wan Chai, was again to be dashed when the Admiralty's 1903 plan to build a dock on the naval site in Central was finally approved. The decision, ill-advised and hasty, was made in response to international tensions and the presumed need for a strong naval base in Hong Kong.

The unveiling of the statue of Queen Victoria, commissioned to commemorate her Golden Jubilee. It was enshrined in the domed construction on the left. Beyond, the new Hong Kong Club building is nearly finished.

Partly in the wake of public realization that British rule had so singularly failed to change the outlook of the Chinese in the colony, the subject of education again raised questions in Blake's time; but another reason was to be found in the dilemma which had been faced many times over in other colonies, particularly in India — the relative value and the position of the local language and English in education. In Hong Kong this problem, not to be solved either soon or easily, was complicated by the demands of British parents for separate schools for their children, and for the introduction of the Cambridge, and later Oxford, Local Examinations, whose standards compelled some schools to raise their own in order to prepare candidates who might want to sit them, and who were mostly English.

There was a growing recognition that Chinese private schools were more sought after by parents than the free government institutions offering similar education. Eitel, Inspector of Schools, retired on a pension in 1897 and was replaced by E. A. Irving in 1901. The new Inspector hailed from Perak and was an advocate of vernacular education. The year saw a petition from the European community on the subject of Europeans-only schools, and the allegation was made that in mixed European and Chinese schools the races held each other back. On the Chinese side, eight leading figures petitioned for schools where children of the 'better classes' would not have to sit with those of the lower classes.

The topic was a thorny one haunted by ill-defined questions of racial as well as educational content, and to deal with it Blake wisely set up a committee of enquiry whose recommendations, given in May 1902, turned out to be of a highly controversial nature. It proposed separate schools for European British subjects, and 'English' schools for non-British children whose parents wanted them to be educated with English as the medium of teaching. Grants to four Portuguese-language schools were to be withdrawn. The report criticized Chinese education, reasoning that it was better to educate a few Chinese well than to attempt the task with the multitude. The low standard of English where it was taught in Anglo-Chinese schools was deplored and it was proposed that the higher forms in these schools be taught by British teachers. Vernacular schools were to be attached to Anglo-Chinese schools under one headmaster.

A well-known Eurasian philanthropist, Sir Robert Hotung, had presented a school in Kowloon to the government, open to all and having English as the medium of instruction. The government now high-handedly proposed to take it as the British school, excluding other races. Belilios had given Hong Kong a reformatory school, and this too was commandeered by the government for use as a British school on the island.

Joseph Chamberlain, Secretary of State, was deeply critical of the report and strongly condemned the racist attitudes which countenanced the setting up of schools exclusively for the British; and was appalled at the misuse of the

Hotung and Belilios generosity in donating schools which were now taken over for British schoolchildren. The report, he thought, was inconsistent since, while advocating an educational system on racial lines, it also wished to do away with the Portuguese schools. 'The first duty was to maintain the vernacular schools', he suggested. And he was against restricting to any one race the entry to Queen's College and the Belilios Girls' School. The purely Chinese classes at the former were to be restored. Since parents had demanded a British school in Kowloon, he sanctioned this. In short, Chamberlain rejected the report as a basis for reform.

Joseph Chamberlain, Secretary of State for the Colonies from June 1895 to December 1905. The artist is John Singer Sargent, one of the fashionable portraitists of the period.

Thus the process of change continued, gradual, unsatisfactory, piecemeal, in the British democratic tradition. The system by which grants were made was amended. Under the next two Governors, Nathan and Lugard, technical education received a boost with the setting up in 1907 of the Hong Kong Technical Institute which also offered teacher training; and later, in 1911, by the formation of the Board of Chinese Vernacular Primary Education — after which the principle of this form of teaching was not again seriously challenged. But the government's reluctance to formulate a realistic education policy closely resembled the foot-dragging of successive administrations in the matters of water supply and sanitary legislation. As in the field of public works, so in education, vested interest as opposed to public interest, the monied Westerners and wealthy Chinese could be seen making sure that their own received the best education. The efforts they made for those in less privileged positions were, if not merely cosmetic, then less than enthusiastic.

Hong Kong entered the twentieth century with a vastly enlarged territory, with an administration groping its way towards a satisfactory means of dealing with 100,000 newly acquired and dubiously loyal citizens — and in an atmosphere filled with the gun smoke in which the Western and Japanese powers had engulfed the Orient. Few people in Hong Kong or indeed elsewhere could then have envisaged that this process, begun by Western mercantile rapacity in China, would result under half a century later in an entirely new, sharply different Orient, one in which their influence (apart from that of Japan) would no longer be paramount.

17. *The First Two Decades of the New Century*

Sir Henry Blake left in November 1903. It was nine months before his successor arrived, the interim filled by F. H. May who had replaced Stewart Lockhart as Colonial Secretary. Sir Matthew Nathan, a bachelor of 39 on his arrival in July 1904, was the colony's only unmarried governor. Although by career a Royal Engineer, he was, as Sayer puts it, 'a natural financier'. He was to put both capabilities to good use.

Sir Matthew Nathan tackled the financial side first, taking measures to stem the constant loss to the treasury incurred as the subsidiary coinage diminished in value in relation to the dollar. He set that department the goal of restoring its proper value. In 1904 and 1905, there was no less than $44 million worth of silver coins in circulation, an oversupply greatly exceeding the needs of the populace. Nathan stopped the issue of further supplies and demonetized all the small silver received until the sag in value was taken up.

Nathan's civil engineering background was the probable spark that fired his interest in the project for a railway to connect the colony with Guangzhou, and from there north to Hangkou, which was already linked by rail with Beijing. The Russian Trans-Siberian line to Europe had already opened in 1903. Nathan's was the inspiration, and later the dogged patience, in the convoluted negotiations behind the construction by British interests of the sector from Guangzhou southwards, while the line from Kowloon to the border was being laid. That section was completed in 1910. By 1912 it was possible to reach Guangzhou by train from Hong Kong. By raising £1,100,000 from the Crown Agents and lending the sum to the Viceroy of Hubei-Hunan at 4½ per cent interest (the principal repayable at £110,000 per annum), the Hong Kong government enabled the Chinese to start the construction of the Guangzhou–Hangkou track. It was at the time 'an act of faith', for 'the line existed on paper only ... and thirty years were to pass before [it] was through'.[1]

In anticipation of further concessions by China following the suppression of the Boxer troubles, the British and Chinese Corporation had been formed by the Hongkong and Shanghai Banking Corporation and Jardine's in 1898. The company built the Kowloon–Guangzhou railway line and later participated in that from Guangzhou northwards.

Meanwhile the reclamation which Chater had initiated, running from Pedder Street to Western Market, was completed in 1905 and two years later had been 'practically built over; there were only one or two lots still vacant'.[2] And the first section of a tramway line along the road from Kennedy Town in the west all the way to Shau Kei Wan had been opened in 1904, the inaugural run made in a tram driven by Mrs Jones, wife of the Director of Public Works — her son 'operating the bell continuously'.[3] The early trams were open, elegant vehicles designed for summer's heat but less convenient in the torrential rains that accompany it. In 1909 Governor Lugard was to show civic pride in this enterprise by taking his guest, the Viceroy of Guangdong, for a ride in a procession of two decorated cars to Quarry Bay to inspect the new Taikoo Docks built there.

John Samuel Swire, founder of Butterfield and Swire, now John Swire and Sons.

By the end of the nineteenth century Hong Kong had become a major port in world trade. One factor which had contributed to this development was, importantly, the undeveloped state of land transport within China, which necessitated the efficient linking of its coastal with its inland water communications, and those with the outside world. By 1900, some 41 per cent of China's foreign trade passed through the colony — forming 33 per cent of Hong Kong's total foreign trade. In the 15 years prior to 1900 the tonnage of shipping clearing the port had reached 14 million, and most of that was accounted for by British shipping (65 per cent) — which also had the lion's share of tonnage clearing China's open ports (58 per cent).

In this all but incredible dominance of China's trade the bulk of the coastal movement was handled by the Hong Kong company Butterfield and Swire Limited, whose China Navigation Company vied with the shipping line owned by Jardine's, the Indo-China Steam Navigation Company. Other lines were smaller — the Douglas Steamship Company (originally owned by Lapraik), and the Macao Steamship Company. Even the inter-ocean scene was dominated by British interests — the Peninsular and Oriental, the Glen Line, the Blue Funnel Line. By the turn of the century sailing ships had largely given way to steamers whose ability to keep to fairly tight schedules was a significant factor in import and export profits. But cost-free wind power, as opposed to the expense of coal, permitted sailing ships to linger on, if only in a minor role. Even in 1920, a total of 26 British and nine American square-riggers cleared Hong Kong harbour.

Another component in Hong Kong's growth was the question of the Chinese language. Written and spoken Chinese having proved an insurmountable obstacle to doing business in other countries, Hong Kong had been quick to offer the conduct of import and export transactions on their behalf.

A third important element in expansion after 1900 related to the changing pattern of things in China where railway development went on apace, and where, after the Treaty of Shimonoseki of 1895, foreigners could operate factories in the Treaty Ports. The railways facilitated the opening up of areas from which local produce could be readily extracted and exported. There was a gradual increase in China's exports and a corresponding increase in her imports of such materials as coal and kerosene, dyes and metals.

But while the Sino-Japanese war allowed foreign expansion in China, it also resulted in a diminution in the export trade through Hong Kong (and also through Shanghai) as Japan extended her sphere of influence over north China. By 1913 the all but 50 per cent of British exports to China which had passed through the colony in the late 1880s had fallen to about 22 per cent. At the same time, however, Hong Kong's trade with other countries was on the increase, and this to some extent offset the decline and began to alter the overall picture of the colony's commerce.

Accompanying this trade expansion and diversification was the need for docking and ship-repairing facilities. The new Taikoo Docks was thought to be one of the most sophisticated shipbuilding and ship-repairing yards in the East. Designed in 1900, the dry dock was capable of taking the largest ship then afloat, the *Oceanic*, a giant 685 feet long with a beam of 68 feet. The docks had been constructed on 52 acres of reclaimed land, the attraction of the site being its close proximity to the harbour's eastern entrance, Lei Yue Mun Strait. With this development and the almost simultaneous naval dockyard extension, Hong Kong harbour reached the peak of its docking facilities — although numerous smaller shipyards sprouted later under Chinese management at such sites as Tai Kok Tsui, Cheung Sha Wan, and the north-eastern part of Kowloon Bay. Together with the Hong Kong and Whampoa Dock Company which owned five docks and had been in business since 1866, the Taikoo Docks sufficed for the colony's needs. These docking companies were the leaders in heavy industry, employing an average of 12,000 workers. A demand for deep-water berthing was satisfied by Butterfield and Swire's wharves and back-up facilities at Kowloon Point (Tsim Sha Tsui), collectively known as Holt's Wharf, and extended in 1915 by dredging to permit ocean-going steamers to berth. By 1925 there were 18 deep-draught berths, and Hong Kong had, tardily, in response as usual to events outside its borders, developed into that 'mart of trade' prematurely predicted over sixty years before.

The Taikoo Docks in use.

Nathan's enquiry into the Sanitary Board in 1907, under pressure for its conversion to a Municipal Council, had served a wider purpose than the exposing of irregularities. It had directed attention to the whole question of corrupt practices in Hong Kong. The large number of Chinese in Hong Kong who had been born and brought up in China saw what was termed corruption in the colony as a normal part of living. It was regarded as neither good nor evil, social behaviour institutionalized and related at root to the miserable salaries paid to Chinese government servants, which they supplemented by levying surtaxes and receiving gifts — what were euphemistically called *kuei-fei*, customary gifts. But the British born and educated cadet officer in the colony was quite another matter. Raised in a climate of values and with a code of behaviour inculcated by public school education, he was not normally tempted into corruption — his salary was generally adequate. Few, however, of the middle and lower level officers of the government came from that background. The Sanitary Board's inspectors and overseers were locally recruited, often former servicemen paid off in the colony; others were beachcombers.

In departments such as the Surveyor-General's (renamed Public Works in 1891), the Registrar-General's (called Secretariat for Chinese Affairs after 1913), and the Police, there were obvious opportunities for corruption. The average Chinese could not reach the officer heading the division or even his Western subordinates. He saw some junior Chinese clerk in the outer office. To obtain the correct form or licence, to voice a complaint, a little money had to change hands in the age-old Chinese manner.

The Hong Kong Gazette of 1898 revealed the extent of police corruption. In the previous year one well-known gambling establishment was raided by the Captain-Superintendent of Police who impounded various receipt books. These revealed that the establishment, headquarters of a Chinese gambling syndicate, had been paying protection money to numerous police constables, and to European inspectors and members of the Registrar-General's department. The outcome, in a self-righteous flurry of public outcry about immoral practices (which everyone knew existed), was that a European police inspector received a six-month prison sentence, three others and a sergeant were dismissed, and two sergeants were asked to resign. Nineteen Indian and 18 Chinese constables were dismissed, and a further 44 Chinese constables resigned — a procedure which left the force at approximately half strength.

Britain and Japan signed the Anglo-Japanese Alliance in January 1902, a pact aimed at isolating Russia. Japan declared war on Russia in 1904 and sank its fleet, emerging as the dominant power in the Far East. China, obliquely, lay under Japanese threat. Into a generally threatening international situation the great typhoon of 18 September 1906 injected a note of terror as it struck Hong Kong with what seemed unparalleled violence and with little warning, leaving in its wake a harbour littered with wrecks, an

The aftermath of the typhoon of 18 September 1906 which, the *Hong Kong Telegraph* reported, 'laid the great part of the city in ruins, annihilated the fleet of shipping'.

estimated 10,000 dead, and a waterfront reduced to rubble and matchwood. During the onslaught, one of many tragedies caught the public interest — the drowning of the Anglican Bishop, Dr. C. J. Hoare, who was on board a mission vessel with his trainees and who lost his life trying to save one of them from the sea.

Nathan departed after scarcely three years in office in April 1907, two months after receiving the Duke of Connaught who came to see for himself the completed Chater reclamation whose beginning he had marked 17 years previously in laying the foundation stone. Once again F. H. May took over the government until the arrival in July of the new Governor, Sir Frederick Lugard, who came from a highly successful career in Africa — to which he returned after his stint in Hong Kong.

He was greeted by both good and bad news. The good news was that May had just opened the first section of the Tai Tam Tuk waterworks which, with its capacity of 200 million gallons, made a recurrence of the 1902 water shortage seem unlikely in the near future. Yet, in the drought of 1910, the cry for water was heard once again as more Chinese poured into the colony from the unsettled conditions on the mainland.

The bad news was the report of Nathan's Sanitary Commission. Lugard's remedy for the situation and its problems was to substitute, for the President

Sir Frederick Lugard poses on the steps of Government House with the Viceroy of Guangdong and his party. Sir Paul Chater and other members of the Legislative Council are in the background.

of the Sanitary Board who was a medical practitioner, a layman from the cadet service, with the Medical Officer of Health as professional adviser. He saw this as replacing curative policies with preventative ones.

As ever, events outside Hong Kong were followed in the colony by perceptible movement in its commercial barometer, and by the reactions of a Colonial Office accustomed to trouble in its most troublesome charge. In an edict of 1906 Guangxu emperor (who reigned in name at least from 1875 to 1908) required all his subjects to cease smoking opium, and set a term of 10 years from 1 January 1907 in which the habit was to be broken. In Hong Kong the legitimate trade in the drug was still considerable. In a memorandum for the Legislative Council, Lugard put the figure at over £5 million in 1906. There was a big local demand over and above the opium sent out of the colony. The home market was supplied by the opium concessionaire who prepared the drug for the licensed divans, significant revenue deriving from this source. In 1901 the concession had been let for $750,000 per annum, rising in 1904 to $2,040,000. In 1907, the Chinese and British governments concluded an agreement to run for a three-year trial period from January 1908, in which India undertook to reduce her export of opium to China by one-tenth of the current annual total (51,000 chests). This meant that by 1917 the trade should have ceased altogether. On 6 May 1908 the Secretary of State announced that steps must be taken to close the divans in Hong Kong, the Chinese government having closed those in China.

On the first of March 1909, 26 divans were closed. Licences were not to be renewed after 28 February 1910. To compensate for the loss of revenue a duty was imposed on imported liquor, tobacco, perfumed spirit, and light hydro-carbon oil, and an *ad valorem* licence fee was instituted on the first registration of an imported motor vehicle. The British government granted compensation — £9,000 in 1910 and £12,000 in the following year. In 1914 the opium concession was taken over by the government and a policy for the extinction of the trade was pursued, no appreciable disturbance to the colony's trade and financial stability being felt.

Thus ended officially, and to a large extent in practice, that miserable commerce by which the British and others had made vast fortunes from the process of slowly poisoning the Chinese, and on the profits from which the very existence of Hong Kong had been based. Opium use in the colony was not fully prohibited until World War II.

A bare five months after he arrived in Hong Kong Lugard delivered a speech in which he strongly advocated the foundation of a university. The 'high water mark of educational facilities' was Queen's College, and of course the College of Medicine turned out degree students, but Lugard had in mind an institution on a broader educational basis. And there was, too, an idea in certain circles that such a facility offered the chance of introducing Chinese youth to both philosophical and scientific areas of Western thought. The example of the College of Medicine was there for all to see. In the Alice Memorial Hospital — built in 1887 as a memorial to his wife by Dr Ho Kai — the college had successfully weathered the death or retiral of the founders, Drs Patrick Manson, W. S. Young, J. Cantlie and the Revd Dr Chalmers. With the aid of the London Missionary Society, and a $50,000 grant from a Chinese business man named Ng Li Hing for a new building, the College was the colony's most advanced educational establishment, by 1901 having 12 licentiates and 23 students in training. Most graduates had found jobs in Malaya and Singapore, and one, as we noted, in the New Territories administration. Others worked in the free dispensaries for Chinese that were being set up about this time. There was every hope, therefore, that a university might spread its graduates far and wide — even to China itself — to further the Western dream.

At the St Stephen's College speech day in 1907 Lugard threw out his suggestion for a university. His other thought was that Western learning might, through the graduates, eventually be spread in China unattached to Christian teaching, as a thing worthy of respect in itself. One of Lugard's admirers, H. N. Mody, offered $150,000 for the building and an endowment of $30,000. But, typically in Hong Kong, the men with most money, the merchants, were less than enthusiastic about it, and the Chinese were still hesitant about endowing a seat of Western scholarship. Mody, the director of so many companies that he was known as 'the Napoleon of the Rialto', retained his enthusiasm and was eventually knighted for his generosity. J. H. Scott, a former *taipan* of Butterfield and Swire, persuaded the company to endow a chair of engineering for $40,000, and in 1921 a further $100,000 was donated towards engineering equipment. By the time the foundation stone was laid in March 1910, over one and a quarter million dollars had been promised, and in 1916, Sir Robert Hotung endowed a chair of surgery.

Lugard thought the university should have two parts — one to incorporate the College of Medicine and the Technical Institute, with an Arts faculty to be added later. The Colonial Office reaction was cool. They dubbed the scheme 'Lugard's pet lamb'. But personal appeals from Lady Lugard brought in more cash, and the university opened in September 1913, with the then Governor, Sir F. H. May, as chancellor and with 72 students (31 engineering, 21 in medicine, and 20 in arts), drawn not only from Hong Kong but from the Straits Settlements, Guangzhou, and the Treaty Ports. The British government, less cool when it saw the institution was more or less self-financing, provided a few scholarships, and Sir Charles Eliot, 'scholar and Orientalist', agreed to be its first Vice-Chancellor. Despite appearances, however, the university was insufficiently funded.

With the turn of the century, the death of the old Queen, and the accession of Edward VII in 1901, the peak of empire had been reached. The worlds of Europe and of the Orient were fast changing in political, commercial, and industrial aspects, and the clouds of a European war that was to be the first world war were crowding the horizons — horizons by now no longer discrete but strung together by telegraphic communication and fast ships. Action in one hemisphere now brought, swifter than ever before, its reaction in another. In the East, Japan had risen to the status of a considerable power and was to demonstrate — first of all the oriental nations — that she was capable of trouncing the might of a Western power, Russia. Japan went on to demonstrate with great aplomb and diplomatic finesse that in terms of remorseless greed she was not to be left behind in the 'scramble for concessions' in which the Western powers were indulging at the expense of a supine China.

Lugard and his successors up to the time of World War I were governors acting against a background of world tension unparalleled in history because

Sir Henry May during his time as Colonial Secretary, with his wife, a Chinese official, and others on the track of the Kowloon–Canton Railway, somewhere in the New Territories, 1910.

nations had never before been so conscious of what others were doing at any given time. Hong Kong, that tropical plant, reacted to each breath of cold, disturbed, hostile air that swept in from any point of the compass, its commercial pulse ever on the edge of missing a beat. But the colony continued, by and large, to prosper.

Lugard's time is not distinguished by much in the way of public works but several important schemes were on the way to completion and several more were finished. The typhoon shelter at Mong Kok progressed, the Kowloon waterworks was completed, as was the British section of the Kowloon–Guangzhou railway. In 1911 the new Post Office, which also housed government offices, was opened in all its splendour of red brick and turrets, and the domed Supreme Court on Statue Square was ready for occupation, stolid alongside the rather feminine charms of the Hong Kong Club. Chater's Jubilee celebration in the form of the Victoria Hospital for Women and Children eventually came into being. Edward VII's accession was marked by the intended conversion of a military area in Kowloon into a public park. But the military obstinately refused to grant the facility and a miserable little recreation ground was all that could be managed.

One reaction to the new knowledge that malaria was disseminated by the anopheles mosquito was yet another demand for separate residential areas for Westerners and Chinese. Western opinion averred that the Chinese could not be trusted to obey the rules for the prevention of mosquito breeding — the draining of stagnant water and the spraying of breeding grounds. The recommendation of a sub-committee of the Sanitary Board was to reserve 20,000 acres between Tsim Sha Tsui and Kowloon City for Western use, on

The new Post Office on Pedder Street was completed in Lugard's time, a handsome building in local granite and red brick. This drawing was made more than a century later, just before its demolition.

the grounds of malaria control and because wealthy Chinese were forcing up rents. The New Territories Land Court also agreed to resume 119 acres previously claimed in that area. Chamberlain in London agreed that a reservation was needed 'where people of clean habits will be safe from malaria'. But he objected to the exclusion of Chinese of good standing so that Europeans could enjoy low rentals. He wanted the reservation open to all persons approved by the Governor. The Peak area came to be reserved on similar conditions under the Hill District Reservation Ordinance of 1904.

Far away to the north, in Beijing, the Old Buddha — the Empress Dowager — died on 15 November 1908, the announcement accompanied by another which gave news of the death of her prisoner, the Emperor Guangxu. The coincidence left much to the imagination since the Emperor was reported normally to enjoy good health. Before she died the Old Buddha had decreed that her three-year-old grandson, the hapless Puyi, should inherit. His father the Regent, with other ignorant and arrogant Manchu princes, did all they could to turn back the now remorselessly ticking clock and halt reform. With the revolution of 1911 there came an end to two thousand years of dynastic authoritarian rule in China and the demise of the Confucian ethic as sanction and underpinning of the state's authority. Entering the scene was the concept of a republic with its innate democratic ideas, inserted into the minds of a nation which had never in all its long history evinced a vestige of democracy or any tendency to democratic thought.

For Hong Kong the most obvious and immediate result was yet another flood of refugees seeking its comparative stability.

In the spring of 1911, Sir Henry May was promoted from his post as Hong Kong's Acting Governor and left to govern Fiji. His replacement was Warren Barnes who died on the polo ground shortly after assuming his duties, and he in turn was succeeded by Claude Severn, a civil servant from Malaya. The Governor, Lugard, left in March 1912, announcing as he did so the impending return of May who had been appointed Governor. The appointment broke new ground — it was the first time that a local cadet officer had risen to be Governor. May had been appointed a cadet in 1881, a decade later becoming private secretary to Major-General Digby Barker, whose daughter he married. From 1893 to 1902 he was Captain-Superintendent of Police, rendering conspicuous service in the 1894 plague and, along with Stewart Lockhart, in the take-over of the New Territories in 1899. His vigorous purge of corruption in the police force was also favourably remembered. As Colonial Secretary he had twice administered the government — at the departures of Blake in 1903 and Nathan in 1907 — for which he had been knighted.

The most visible alteration in Hong Kong between the time when May left for Fiji and the time of his return is neatly defined by Sayer: 'Whereas in the spring of 1911 a Chinese discarded his queue at the risk of losing his head, in the spring of 1912 he risked his head who kept his queue. With this abrupt change of fashion Western clothes and effects were now much in demand ...'. The old order had gone — or, if not exactly gone, had yielded place to disorder, 'and while young China in its foreign cap saw no inconsistency in vociferously denouncing the foreign treaties, old China, in the person of the scholar and official, crept silently away and the immemorial pirate and brigand ventured from his hiding place again'.[4]

Sir Henry and his wife stepped ashore at Blake Pier and were borne away in their sedan chairs by eight scarlet-clad bearers. No sooner had his chair approached the Pedder Street flank of the new Post Office than a shot rang out and an assassin's bullet whizzed past him to lodge in the chair occupied by his wife Helena. The *Hong Kong Telegraph* carried the story the following day, 5 July 1912.

> All records of crime in this colony were eclipsed yesterday when a daring attempt, miraculously unsuccessful, was made ... to assassinate His Excellency Sir Henry May ... The red-coated coolies bearing the Governor's chair had just got into their stride when a man was seen to pass rapidly between the soldiers in front of the Post Office ... He fired point blank, about 3 feet range ...

The would-be assassin was at once seized and almost throttled, and beaten by witnesses. 'Sir Henry preserved a composure which, in the circumstances, was truly remarkable ... The bullet whizzed under the cover of the chair ... splintering the bamboo frame of Lady May's chair.' Sir Henry jumped out at

Sir Henry May replaced Lugard as Governor, arriving in July 1912. Disembarked and in his chair of state, he had just passed the statue of the Duke of Connaught near Blake Pier and was passing the new Post Office when a would-be assassin fired. The scene was captured by a photographer in Union Building opposite as the assailant was wrestled to the ground.

once and 'brushed down his coat . . . On sitting down again he turned a half-contemptuous, half-sympathetic glance at his assailant.' And the procession continued to the City Hall and the address of welcome. The gunman, Li Hong Hung, turned out to be a man harbouring a grudge against May from his days in the police.

There was no connection between the incident and the growing turmoil on the other side of the border, which had prompted the setting up of a line of military posts there. May was to re-lay the foundations of the system of deportation under wide emergency powers.

The perennial problem of silver coinage surfaced again — devaluation caused by the flood of these coins from the Chinese Mint at Guangzhou. Things came to a head when several public utility companies complained they were losing money by being forced to accept the coins. The tramway company refused to take them, and a public outcry ensued since passengers were forced to use other legal tender and were in effect paying more. The Chinese felt their country was being insulted by the boycott of Chinese coins — even if they did bear the name of the now deposed emperor. Such was the new spirit of nationalism. They boycotted the trams. The company appealed to the Governor, and May treated the situation as an attack on his government. In one district of Victoria where the trouble appeared to have started he imposed the provisions of a boycott bill, inflicting a punitive rate on property there. This un-British imposition of collective responsibility for an offence — a traditional Chinese measure — worked like magic. Within days of the bill's publication the Chinese members of the Legislative Council boarded a tram *en bloc*, demonstrating to the little world of Chinese Hong Kong 'that tram-riding was fashionable again'.[5] The tramway company received a cash handout of $45,000 in compensation. The following year saw the passing without protest of an ordinance forbidding the circulation of foreign coins and notes; and the Guangzhou 20-cent piece and the familiar Banco Marino of Macau one dollar note vanished. By 1919, $26 million in small coins had been withdrawn and demonetized.

Lugard had had the satisfaction of having added, as it were, the *piano nobile* to the mansion of Hong Kong education with his university: May was confronted with chaos on the ground floor and basement. The Board of Vernacular Chinese Education set up by Lugard had failed to function, perhaps because its tasks were novel, its guidelines vague. Conservative ideas on vernacular schooling now came face to face with ideas from over the border generated by the revolution. A feeling was growing in Hong Kong civil service circles that this might be an appropriate moment to secure control of the hundreds (the number was not precisely known) of vernacular schools, and decide what they should teach and how they might teach it. May condemned the Board as an 'absolute failure', and the situation was chaotic. His prescription for the malady was clear cut. 'Perhaps in the dim bye and bye', he told the Legislative Council as he introduced the Education Bill of 1913, 'Government may listen to those who wish for an Education Board ... but [government] considers that it can best deal with this matter with its own strong hand.'[6] Every school was now required to register with the Director of Education, to conform with the regulations laid down, and to submit to official inspection. Whatever thoughts of revolutionary radicalism may have simmered in Chinese scholastic minds, the tight new regulations must have nipped them in the bud.

Hong Kong was in the process not so much of change — that was the disorder of the day in China — but of its own kind of consolidation. The words of Sun Yatsen, spoken in reminiscence, come to mind: 'Afterwards I saw the outside world [outside China] and I began to wonder how it was that ... Englishmen could do such things as they had done, for example with the barren rock of Hong Kong ... within 70 or 80 years, while China, in 4,000 years, had no place like Hong Kong.'[7]

The first motor car in the colony is said to have been imported by the successful American dentist Dr J. W. Noble, but he may have been forestalled by a Chinese whose name has not survived in this connection. Others soon followed despite the fact that there were only a few miles of motorable road. The syndrome is still apparent today, when thousands of cars capable of speeds of 150 m.p.h. are imported to be driven on roads not one of which is safe for travelling at that speed. By the time of May's return as Governor, streets that had previously known only horse-drawn carriages (long vanished anyway), chairs borne by teams of panting coolies, the bicycle, the rickshaw, and latterly the tram, now had to withstand the more demanding wheels of the internal combustion-engined chariot. A circular road for the island was planned to link the existing stretches, and another was to follow the rickshaw path to Tai Po in the New Territories. On the island, the western road which already reached the Dairy Farm site in Pok Fu Lam continued on to Aberdeen and was to reach Deep Water Bay in 1915 and Repulse Bay two years later; that between the new reservoir at Tai Tam and Tai Tam Gap was finished in 1918. On the peninsula the corniche from Kowloon to Castle Peak was begun in 1917.

Just as in the Western world, the horizons opened up by such developments in Hong Kong were numerous, although they along with their social and infrastructural implications were at the time scarcely considered. It became increasingly practicable for families whose bread-winner worked in town to live in the suburbs. Places of recreation such as beaches and countryside formerly accessible only by boat offered opportunities for leisure and residence. The Repulse Bay Hotel opened on the first of January 1920, its purpose to exploit the fine sandy beach at its feet. The beach at North Point — far enough away from town — was readily accessible by tram (special trams were laid on in summer, and even military band concerts by moonlight on that long-vanished beach were advertised). The intrepid golfers of the colony had established a course at Fanling in 1889, reached until the advent of the railway to Guangzhou by a bizarre variety of means — boat, two-man rickshaw, walking, pony, and chair. The Deep Water Bay course was accessible only by boat until the coming of the road in 1915, or more adventurously by foot from Aberdeen, or over the gap from Happy Valley — together with a retinue of coolies carrying tiffin.

One old Hong Kong landmark fell victim to the motorized age — the clock tower at Pedder Street and Queen's Road. It had stood there since

1863. As early as 1884 a member of the Hong Kong Club, then diagonally opposite, was urging the removal of the structure, suggesting alternative sites for what he saw as a traffic hazard. A year later the same petitioner, M. J. D. Stephens, tried again, remarking that apart from the obstruction to traffic, because of new buildings the clock was barely visible. Ten years later still the persevering Stephens 'ventured' to write to the Director of Public Works about the now acute traffic congestion, suggesting that as the donor of the clock, Douglas Lapraik, now had a stained glass window in the cathedral his memory was adequately perpetuated without the offending clock tower. 'When the time arrives ... the wonder will be how it was not removed before.' Presumably Stephens then gave up in disgust (or perhaps died in the attempt), and the clock tower lasted another 29 years before it fell to the breaker's hammer. Mr Stephens has no memorial.

Governor May, a keen sportsman, in his former capacity as Colonial Secretary had stocked the colony's reservoirs with fish in order 'to keep his hand in with the rod'. As Governor he took up golf and encouraged the development of the Fanling course. He went to the Christmas and New Year race meetings and attended the annual cricket match against the Shanghai Cricket Club, fostering Chinese interest in sport. But race meetings at Happy Valley were more to Chinese taste than cricket, and the sport there was

The disastrous fire at the racecourse in February 1918.

gambling. Racing started in the 1840s, quickly becoming popular. In the February 1918 meeting May and his party were witnesses to a disaster there. From the matsheds, some several stories high, in which the wealthier Chinese installed themselves and where the midday meal was cooked, panic-stricken Chinese were seen rushing out as the afternoon racing was about to commence. Then followed an explosion and collapse of the matsheds as fire broke out. In under half an hour about six hundred persons met their death, trapped, burned alive, trampled underfoot. The disaster wiped out approximately 0.1 per cent of the population, which stood at the time at something over 561,000.

Since the end of the nineteenth century revenue had gone up, from the 1898 total of $3.62 million to $8.6 million in 1913, and — a huge leap — to over $18.6 million in 1918 — despite a decline in revenue from the opium concession. As well as the public works already noted, the Mong Kok typhoon shelter was finished by 1915 and had already proved its usefulness in a typhoon. The second half of the Tai Tam Tuk waterworks scheme was begun, including a dam designed to hold more than one and a half million gallons of water. It took five years to build and was opened by Sir Henry on 2 February 1918. The Governor remarked in his speech:

> When one sees so much fresh water around, one cannot help reflecting what a pity it is that the residents of this Colony ... do not adopt water as a beverage instead of something stronger. It would surprise some of you people to learn the terrible casualties ... inflicted upon the civil servants by too free use of alcoholic beverages ... Out of every two men who arrive here, whether as policemen, overseers on works like this [reservoir], as Sanitary Inspectors, or as Revenue Officers, not more than one lives and remains in the service to earn a pension. ... I do not include the upper ranks [of civil servants] for I have no figures to go on.[8]

The reservoir and other major works (with the exception of the railway to Guangzhou) were financed from public revenue. Conversely, it was left to a group of Chinese to form the Kaitak Land Investment Company Limited to reclaim land in Kowloon Bay, the name Kaitak formed from the names of the directors, Sir Kai Ho Kai and Mr Au Tack, land upon which some time later the first airstrip was built, and which is still the site of the colony's airport.

A facility of a different kind was offered to Hong Kong in 1914 by Mr (later Sir) Ellis Kadoorie. He had heard of the Governor's wife's interest in the welfare of working non-Chinese women, for whom little suitable accommodation existed. Kadoorie offered $15,000 'for the purpose of erecting a Women's Institute or Hostel ... provided that within two years ... an equal sum of money be realized'. He eventually donated much more, and the Helena May Institute for Women rose on a fine site on Garden Road a little way up and across the road from the Cathedral. Other generous contributors (oddly enough for an institute for Western women, and benignly) were Mr Ho Kom-tong, Mr Chan Kai-ming, and Mr Lau Chu-pak.[9]

Sir Henry's administration was bisected by World War I. In Hong Kong most European nationalities were represented by groups employed there, and with the outbreak of that war, overnight, German business associates and friends became the enemy; and Europeans, formerly classed together by the Chinese, were now seen by them to be divided among themselves. Watched by the Chinese, British merchants and the Volunteers marched their former colleagues and friends to internment. There were similar emotions among the British as they saw German neighbours from the Anglo-French concession at Guangzhou leave to defend the German port, Qingdao (on the Shandong Peninsula), against the Japanese who were allied to Britain in the war.

Japan, anxious to gain further rights in China, presented what came to be termed the Twenty-one Demands to the Chinese government in January 1915 with the request that the contents be kept secret and only published when agreed. Of the five sections, the last was aimed at turning China into a kind of Japanese protectorate. Yuan Shikai, president of the Republic, had no option but to publish the document in the hope of gaining foreign support. But, sadly, China had no real allies. In the end she had to agree to a watered-down version of the demands with the exception of those in the fifth part which was, euphemistically, 'postponed'. The British, allied to Japan and with a fleet thinly stretched in the Far East, could scarcely afford to protest, and most British in Hong Kong appear to have brushed the matter aside. So long as the Japanese did not interfere in the British sphere of interest in China — the whole Yangzi Valley — they were not about to stretch themselves on China's behalf.

Hong Kong followed with avid interest the daring exploits of the German cruiser *Emden*, whose movements read like some adventure story as she disguised herself as a Russian cruiser, and contrived in view of the Penang Club to sink a Russian ship in Penang Harbour. The *Emden* had taken a considerable toll of British shipping including the cruiser *Monmouth*. There was great relief when the news of the sinking of the cruisers *Scharnhorst* and *Gneisenau* in the Battle of the Falklands was received in November 1914. With the destruction of the German Pacific fleet, including the *Emden*, Hong Kong slept more comfortably.

Hong Kong people contributed generously to war charities, raising $5 million as a gift to the British government. In 1917 the Hong Kong Defence Corps was formed from the Volunteers and military service became compulsory. British shipping up and down the China coast was taken over by the British government and normal commercial activity virtually ceased until peace returned. Imported goods became progressively dearer but as if in compensation the value of silver rose in relation to gold, trebling or quadrupling the assets of many a local entrepreneur. But with the war dragging on and British reverses in battle coming one after the other, with the lengthening casualty list, the gloom of Britain settled on the colony. China eventually declared war on Germany on 14 August 1917, her main contribution to the Allied cause being the 200,000 Chinese labourers sent to work behind the lines in France at the expense of the Chinese government.

Sentiment in the colony turned very strongly against the Germans as the situation worsened in Europe. In 1917 the British Chamber of Commerce voted that Germans be excluded for a decade from the colony. It was a melodramatic if understandable gesture with not the faintest hope of gaining official support, and the motion was later reversed without acrimony. The spring of 1918 brought no relief from the carnage in France, and the mood of the colony grew darker. In January a gang of youths were trapped as they robbed a tenement in Gresson Street, Wan Chai. Cornered, the armed robbers decided to shoot it out, taking heavy toll of the police. In the following month came a huge conflagration in the Cheung Sha Wan shipyard, and soon after that the racecourse matshed fire shocked the colony. As if to crown a chapter of horrors, an epidemic of cerebro-spinal meningitis ran through the Chinese tenements like those of Gresson Street with the speed and finality of fire. Meanwhile the daily press published the latest casualty figures from France.

In September 1918 the Governor, who had served a continuous term of six years in the colony, left on a brief vacation. He retired the following January, and a joint meeting of the Executive and Legislative Councils was held to pay tribute to him. (This was the second joint meeting in three months, the previous one having been held to celebrate the end of the War.) The occasion was a memorable one with two principal spokesmen, Mr Lau Chu Pak and Sir Paul Chater, voicing what were certainly the sentiments of the majority of people in Hong Kong. It was a highly charged moment, and speeches tended to be emotional: but the character of Sir Henry May was summed up with fair accuracy. 'Sparing of speech and sparing of smiles', said Mr Lau, 'but he never spared himself in the execution of his duty to the colony.' Chater had the final word: 'As Governor he made a mark which will be indelible from the colony's history.' He had certainly devoted the greater part of his working life to Hong Kong.

With the ending of the war there ended not only an epoch in world history, but a term in the political, social and commercial history of the colony; and it began to be clear that another and sharply different age was dawning, in East and West alike.

18. Inter-war Years — the Twenties

Sir Reginald Stubbs took up office as Governor in Hong Kong in September 1919. He had visited the colony nine years previously to arrange details of a scheme to pay civil servants in sterling instead of dollars. He was therefore slightly familiar with it. But by now, imperceptibly at first, various emphases in Hong Kong life had begun to alter in the light of changing attitudes in Britain in its post-war mood, and partly in response to events over the border in China; and also consequent on the terms of the Treaty of Versailles and the later Washington Treaties of 1922.

The motor car began to be a more visible element in Hong Kong in the 1920s. Looking west in Chater Road in the early 1920s, the tram, the rickshaw, and the handcart are the sole vehicles, with the exception of the one parked car.

Britain's financial and commercial position in the world had suffered drastically from the pressures of four years of total warfare. Long accepted presuppositions about her place in the world were severely shaken. The war had eliminated Germany's colonial and commercial clout in the Far East, and for a time Russian influence there was weakened by the Communist revolution of 1917 and its aftermath. But Japan was a rising sun, Britain's chief rival — something that could have been predicted in the wake of the Twenty-one Demands of 1915 which sought to make China a Japanese dependency.

The Washington Naval Limitation Treaty of February 1922, signed by the United States, Britain, Japan, France, and Italy stipulated that battleships and first-class cruisers held by America, Britain, and Japan were to be respectively in the ratio of 5:5:3. Those of France and Italy were to conform to a ratio of 1.75:1.75. This meant that while Japan had her fleet concentrated in the Pacific, the larger fleets of America and Britain were much more thinly spread around the world. Japan was thus the strongest naval power in the Pacific. The treaty was to remain in force until 1936.

For China, the Nine-Power Treaty in the Washington Agreements perpetuated the Open Door policy with its equality of opportunity for foreigners to trade in China, while preserving her integrity as a state. Such provisions were not accompanied with the means to enforce them. The upshot of what was for China a sad and tangled story of international intrigue and big-power rivalry was that she emerged in much the same state of bondage to the treaty powers as she had been before the war.

The re-emergence of Sun Yatsen's Guomindang at its First National Congress in Guangzhou, in alliance with Soviet Russia in 1924, came at a time of endless warlord rivalry and combat. Faced with country-wide warlord depredations and internecine warfare, Marxist ideology seemed to offer hope, its attractions highlighted by the success of the October Revolution in Russia. Marxism was seen to be more attractive than Western democracry, in part because like Confucianism it was not religion-based. And the Chinese saw themselves, like Russia, defeated by Japan. Moreover, the same imperial powers who had forced on China the Unequal Treaties were seen now by the Chinese to be attacking the revolution in Russia. When Western intervention in Russia was defeated, the Chinese were naturally enthusiastic.

Yuan Shikai's aspiration to be emperor at the head of a new dynastic regime ruling from Beijing came to nothing, and no formula was found there for a workable form of democratic government. Sun Yatsen in the south had the capability of inspiring his followers, but his idealism was not matched by a corresponding strength of political leadership. He called for advice from Russia, and received among other advisers Michael Borodin, who was to train party political cadres. Sun hoped, by linking the nationalism of the

Guomindang to socialist ideas, to make it into a truly revolutionary organization. Under his tutelage efforts were made to harass the Western powers.

In Hong Kong the effects of these events were felt soon enough. Europeans were not totally unaware of the implications. They sensed, if dimly, the new Chinese pride in being a nation and not just (as formerly) a race.

Confronted in early 1919 with a full-blown strike in Hong Kong, Westerners were slow to understand its cause. In fact the strike was about the price of rice which had risen dramatically, in a city where rice and not bread was the staff of life, in response to scarcity caused by the shortage of shipping and the shortfall in the wheat and potato crops in the West. Westerners had turned to rice. Price rises in other commodities in Hong Kong during the war had not been matched by wage increases; and the threat even to the rice supply was seen by the Chinese as insupportable.

Westerners, seldom great rice eaters, scarcely realized the gravity of the situation for their Chinese employees. The large numbers of engineers and fitters employed by various businesses, faced with rising rents, food costs, and now a shortage of rice, politely asked for a 40 per cent wage increase. Their realization of the potential power they wielded was still embryonic; they requested rather than demanded.

Taikoo Docks, one of the largest employers of skilled and semi-skilled labour in the engineer and fitter categories, had also to face the Hoi Yuen or Seamen's Union which was developing under the eye of the more extreme elements in the political context of the Guomindang. The man behind the action taken by the engineers was Hon Man-wai, an educated man with a command of English and a forceful personality. He had begun his career as a teacher in the engineering faculty of the university. By 1916 he had left and set up his own machine shop, a successful business which he ran for the next four decades. His personality was one considerable asset in potential leadership. Another was the fact of his being self-employed. He was not subject to the threat of dismissal. As head of the Chinese Engineering Institute in 1920, his right-hand man was chief of the meter installation department in the Hongkong Electric Company, Li Cheng, who also had some English.

These two well-balanced activists were a phenomenon startlingly new in Hong Kong. Both were capable, responsible men, sharing views on the need for improvement in working environments, not least those of apprentices who toiled in conditions resembling those in the factories of the early Industrial Revolution in Britain. Hongkong Electric was, however, one of the better employers, and Li Cheng spent his entire 50-year working life in their employ.

At first the employers did not take the request for a 40 per cent wage rise seriously. But soon they were forced to face the fact that it was backed by an organized work-force. At a meeting held to discuss what they could do the employers decided to increase the rice allowance. In the hope that trouble would go away, they had not seized the core of the problem — the general rise in the cost of living. In a letter from their lawyer, Lo Man-kam (later an Executive Council member, and knighted for his services), the Chinese Engineering Institute rejected this offer. When the employers ignored the letter deadlock was reached. Employers simply could not credit the fact that they were no longer in a position to control their work-force at will, far less to dictate to the Engineering Institute. It was a shock.

The Secretary for Chinese Affairs, E. R. Hallifax, insisted on a second meeting of employers. At this it was decided to ask the Secretary to negotiate a settlement on their behalf, with the engineers' and fitters' representatives from all dockyards, binding on all other employers of engineers and fitters. Mr Hallifax's prime mistake lay in not realizing that it was with the Institute he ought to negotiate. Austin Coates writes in his book on the history of Hongkong Electric:

> What the Europeans had overlooked was that the following day ... was Ching Ming, the annual festival of remembrance of the ancestors ... At five o'clock closing time, and at various shift changing times, 40 per cent of all fitters in the dockyards, and 25 per cent of the fitters at Hong Kong Electric, politely informed their immediate bosses that they were leaving for their villages to give respect to their ancestors ... Off they all went by night train to Canton.[1]

Several days later, after the festival was over and no one had returned to work, many more fitters in other businesses began to leave also. The major supplier of soft drinks, A. S. Watson, stopped production and hotels lost their engineering staff in charge of boilers and mechanical devices. The docks were silent. Only the telephone and gas services continued operating, although their employees too were asking for a 40 per cent rise.

At this point Ho Man-wai did two highly responsible things. He put out a notice explaining the workers' point of view; and he sent to Guangzhou to persuade the workers to return. The success of his organization — the Institute — had perhaps surprised even him. The workers were not keen to come back. Wages were higher in Guangzhou and the cost of living lower. The *Canton Times* cautioned: 'If the strike goes on, many will find permanent employment in Canton, and Hong Kong will be the loser of a class of men which have [sic] taken so long to qualify for their avocations, and whose places will have to be filled by untrained and inexperienced men — to the detriment of their employers.' And in Hong Kong itself the editorial opinion of the *Hong Kong Morning Herald* was: 'The Chinese cannot put up with living in this way any longer, and are compelled to strike for higher wages.'

Chinese employers offered to concede the 40 per cent, but the Europeans would not budge. An affiliate of the Hong Kong Institute — the Fitters' and

Turners' Guild of Guangzhou — then offered to reduce their workers' claim to 37 per cent, and Hallifax urged the European employers to accept this — but they declined, the Jardine representative being the most obdurate in refusing to agree. Finally the employers offered 32 per cent, which was promptly rejected. It was now a question of face. The engineers had started the conciliatory process by their offer of 37 per cent, and now it was the turn of the employers to do likewise and raise their own offer. The employers, with ill grace, offered 32½ per cent and settlement was immediately made on 19 April. In a matter of hours the workers were returning from Guangzhou by train.

So ended the first major strike in the colony. Its importance in the history of labour relations in Hong Kong cannot be exaggerated. For the first time Europeans were forced to recognize the needs of the labour force. For the first time they realized that they could not any longer rely on a supply of unquestioning cheap Chinese labour — a point of view taken by much of the local press in an attitude unusually at variance with the temper of Western employers. The modern age of labour relations had, belatedly, arrived in the colony.

From the European point of view, worse was to come. In 1922 the Chinese Seamen's Union, the Hoi Yuen, influenced by revolutionary nationalism and the newly established Communist Party of China's Labour Secretariat (whose job it was to organize industrial trade unions), came out on strike, joined by 12 other trade unions. At this point Hong Kong experienced its first general strike, the life of the colony being at once paralysed. The Hoi Yuen took its place as the leader of 70 unions in the Hong Kong Federation of Labour, an organization which listed the struggle against imperialism and capitalism among its objectives.

With a general strike on his hands, Governor Stubbs must have felt his appointment was far from a sinecure; and when the thorny legal problem of *mui tsai* once more raised its head, it must have seemed obvious that a new and abrasive era in human relations in the colony had dawned. This time the question came up with the formation of a Society for the Protection of *Mui Tsai*, and with the combination of the Anti-*Mui Tsai* Society and a decision of the left-leaning trade union leaders in favour of its abolition. Winston Churchill, at the time Secretary of State for the Colonies, telegraphed the Governor on 22 February 1922 demanding that he issue a

> proclamation immediately, making it quite clear to employers and employed that the status of *mui-tsai*, as understood in China ... will not in future be recognized in Hong Kong and ... that no compulsion of any kind to prevent girls over age from freely leaving ... their adopted parents or other employers will be allowed.

In the teeth of the united opposition of the Legislative and Executive Councils an ordinance was passed (No. 1, 1923)[2] to accord with Churchill's wishes. But it was to remain a dead letter until in the latter part of the decade interest quickened in 'child slavery'. The Nationalist government in Guangzhou later (in 1927) issued a proclamation emancipating all slaves and *mui tsai*, and in Hong Kong in 1929 the Governor was instructed to register all *mui tsai*.

The problem, however, proved obdurate. A commission sent out to Hong Kong in 1936, and numerous other measures taken, failed to eradicate the practice. There were still over one thousand *mui tsai* registered in the colony, and probably many more unregistered. Even in the 1970s, cases were still coming to light.[3]

Stubbs' six long years in Hong Kong were among the most socially and politically vexatious in its history to that date. The engineers' and the seamen's strikes were followed by a larger and much longer strike and boycott in 1925–6. In essentials this stemmed from a popular political movement against the privileged status of foreigners in China. The trouble began in Shanghai in May 1925 when an anti-Japanese demonstration developed into a general anti-foreign one; this in turn changed into an anti-British demonstration because of the great preponderance of British commercial interests in China, particularly in Shanghai. The police of the International Settlement, who happened to be British, opened fire on a crowd which they felt was threatening to get out of hand. The incident was exploited by the Chinese. At this time the Guomindang were co-operating with the Communists in fomenting labour unrest in foreign-held settlements, and Hong Kong came in for its share. In the colony the trade unions had developed as a kind of co-operative in such a manner that they were partly trade union, partly under the influence of the Communists, and partly an extension of the traditional Chinese secret societies, their general complexion being nationalist and anti-foreign. The strike and boycott were in large measure politically inspired and concerned the antagonism between the government of Guangzhou and that of Hong Kong. The fact that when a more conservative element gained the upper hand in Guangzhou the two sides were prompt to negotiate a settlement (on 10 October 1926), almost sixteen months after the strike began, makes that point clear.

In the meantime, until the boycott was lifted in October 1926, the position of the colony was grave indeed. A total boycott of British goods was accompanied from 30 June 1925 by the withdrawal of all Chinese workers. The essential services were maintained by volunteers, the armed forces, and by the Hong Kong Volunteer Corps. While the actual strike gradually collapsed, the boycott of British shipping and goods continued.

One noteworthy incident in the strike was the initiative of a well-known Chinese, Dr Co Sinwan (Ts'o Seen-wan) who more or less commandeered an office in the City Hall and publicly called for Chinese volunteers to assist in running services. The response to Dr Co's call was immediate. In three days he had 500 volunteers, and in the next 20 days about three thousand — more than were required. The astonishment of the 'old China hands' was intense.

When the strike was at its peak, the Governor made a speech to the Legislative Council in which he declared (without referring to the Russian influence in Chinese politics of the time): 'This is not a strike but a deliberate attempt to destroy, in the interests of anarchy, the prospects and the very existence of the community.'[4] He was wrong about anarchy — never a Communist policy. Hallifax referred to the strike when it ended as 'the failure of the Moscow-Canton attack',[5] which was nearer the mark. The general effect on Hong Kong was a new feeling of solidarity, which was precisely the opposite of the instigators' intentions. There are no available figures to show the effect of the boycott on trade, but shipping returns reveal something of the picture (see Appendix 5).

Sir Reginald E. Stubbs (front row, far right) with the members of the Legislative Council and others on the steps of Government House. In the centre of the front row is Sir Claude Severn, Colonial Secretary. Sir Paul Chater stands in the second row to the left (white moustache). Albert and Reuben Sassoon are in the second row to the right of Severn, and the well-known dentist and early motor car owner, J. W. Noble, is in the second row to the left of Severn.

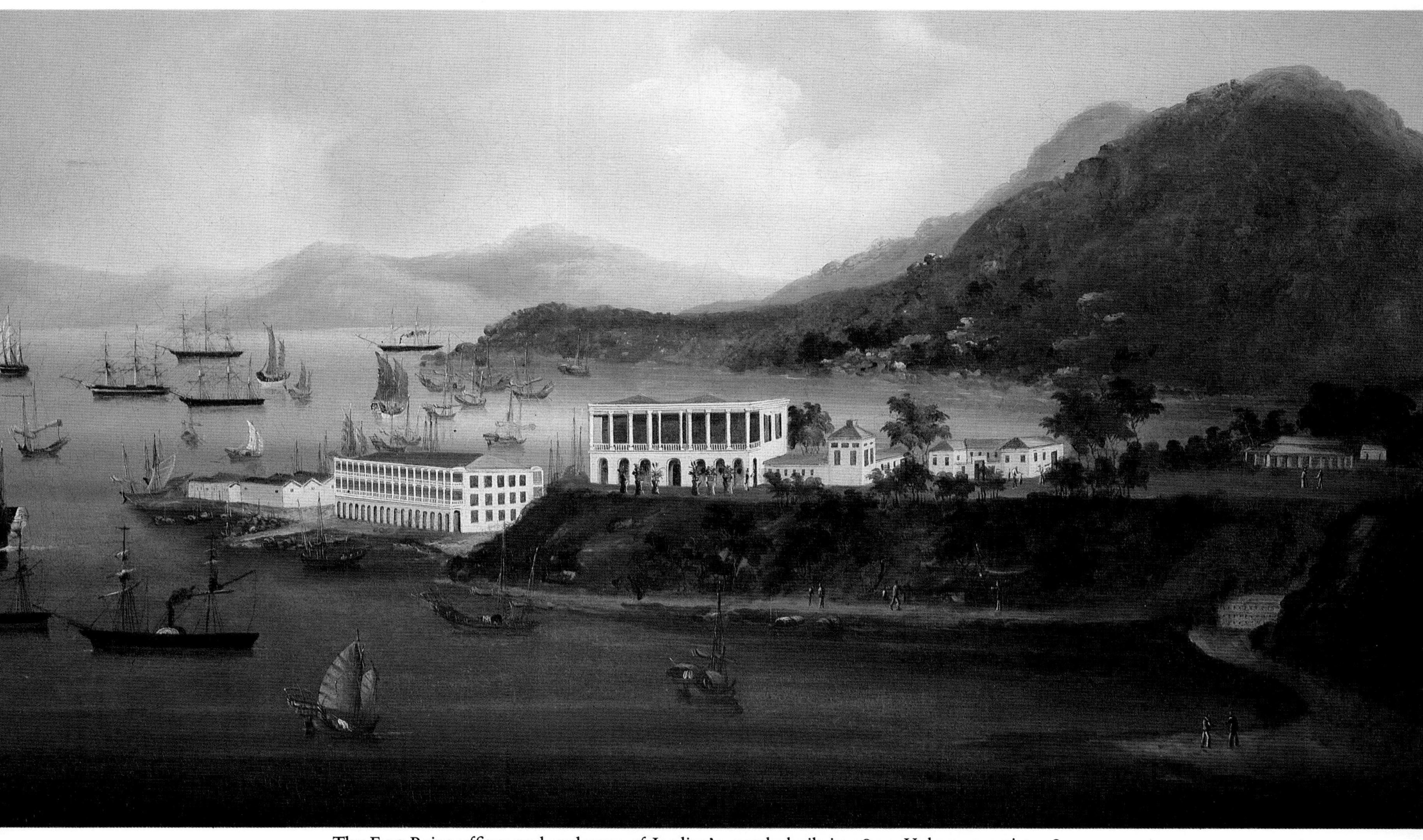

The East Point offices and godowns of Jardine's, newly built in 1844. Unknown artist, 1844.

The residence of the Lieutenant-Governor, Major-General D'Aguilar. Murdoch Bruce, 1840s.

Chinese nursemaids with their charges on the Parade Ground. Charles Wirgman, 1856.

Happy Valley racecourse and the colonial cemetery. Chinese school, late 1840s.

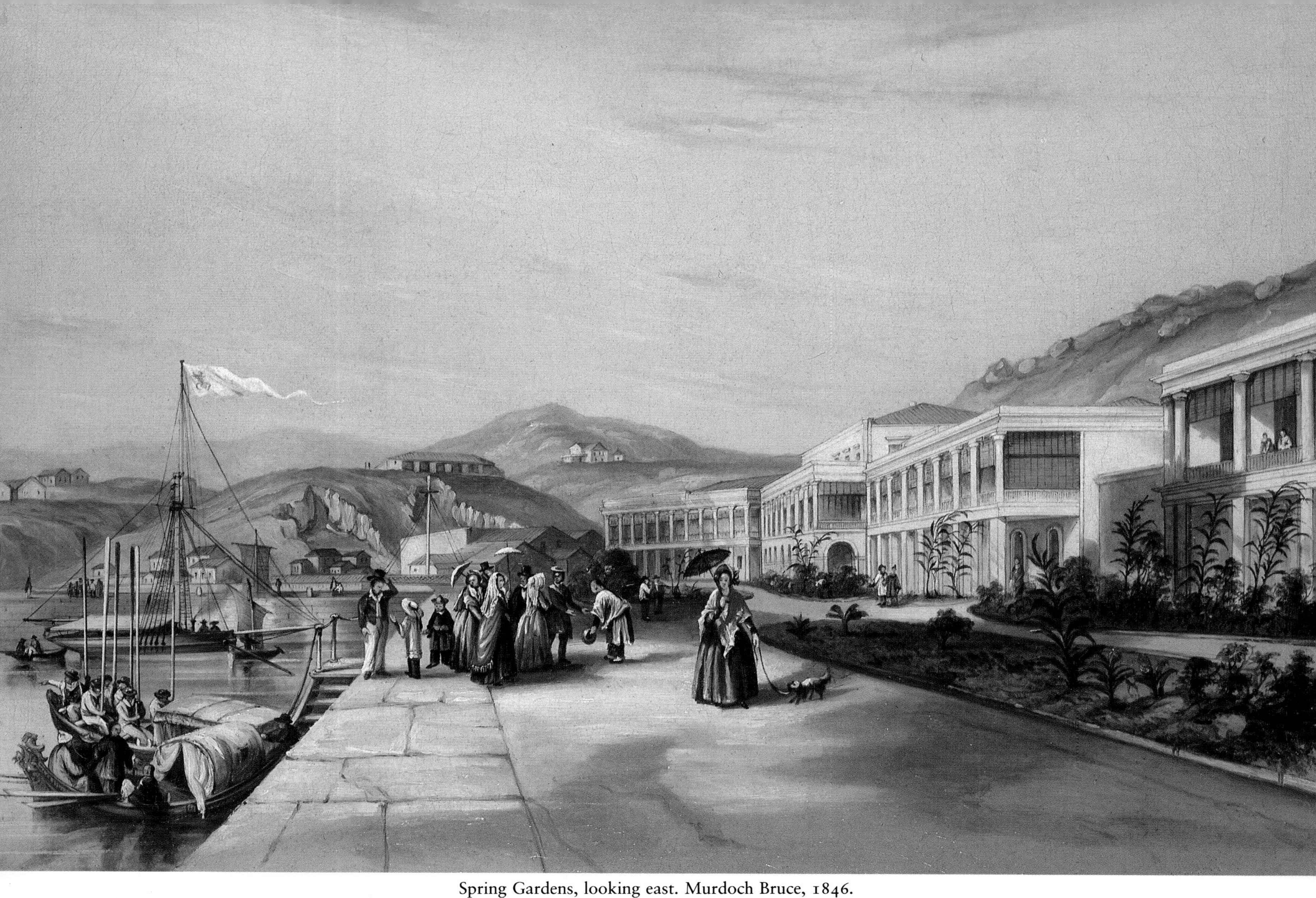

Spring Gardens, looking east. Murdoch Bruce, 1846.

Sir Boshan Wei Yuk, a wealthy business man. Unknown Chinese artist, early twentieth century.

A crowd on the way to the races. Charles Wirgman, 1858.

A street stall and its patrons, still a common sight throughout south China. William Prinsep, 1839.

Hong Kong coolies in the rain, wearing straw coats. Unknown artist, mid-nineteenth century.

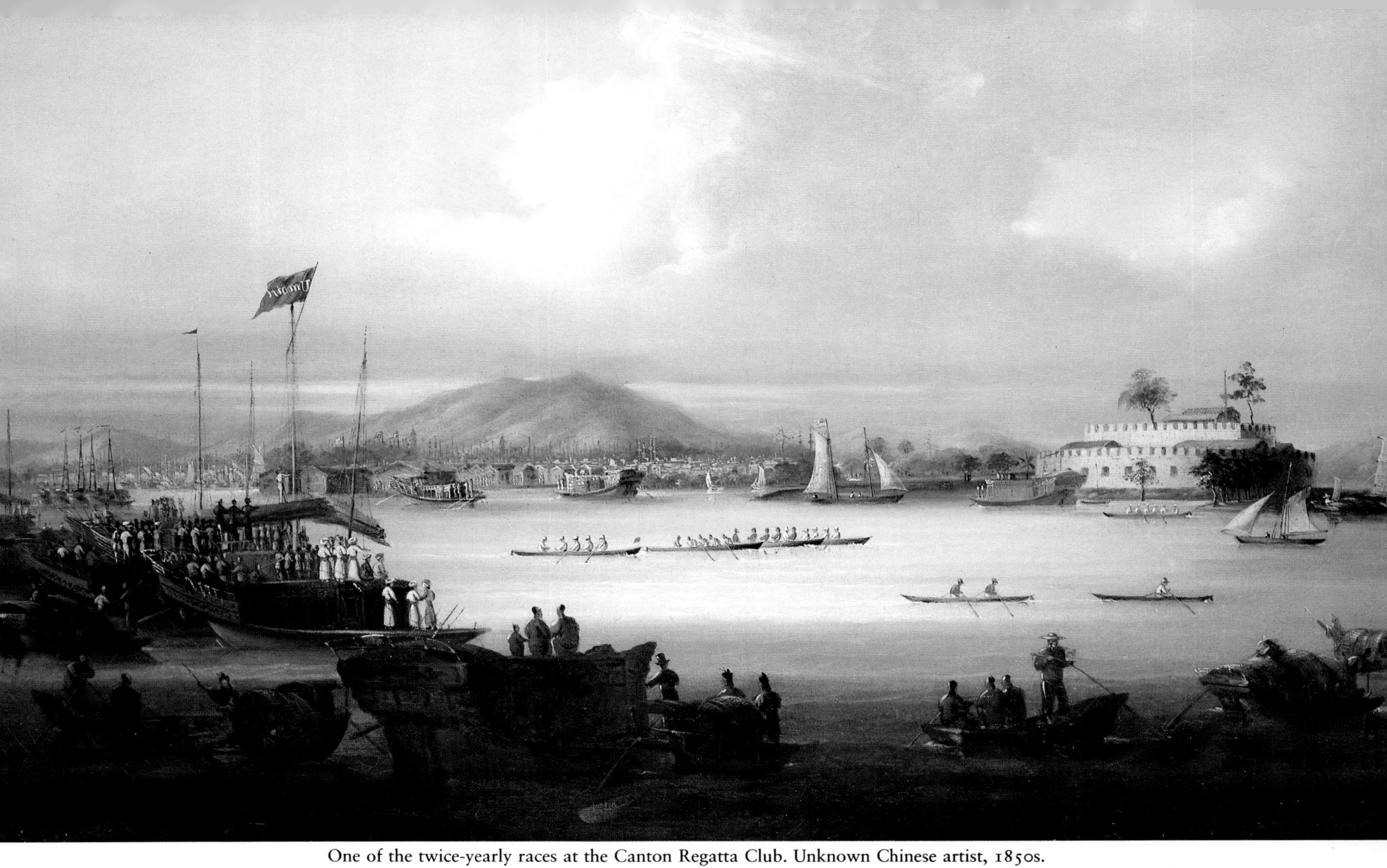

One of the twice-yearly races at the Canton Regatta Club. Unknown Chinese artist, 1850s.

A view of the north shore of Hong Kong island. To the left are the naval docks and in the centre are the business district and, behind this, Mid-Levels. Serried ranks of tall buildings stretch on to West Point, far right. Frank Fischbeck, 1989.

Almost all arriving and departing cargo in 1924 was still handled by lighters and crew, and by gangs of coolies, most of them still wearing traditional clothing.

The pre-boycott number of British steamers entering Guangzhou harbour in the months of August and Setember 1924 varied between 240 and 160: in the same period of 1925 the number varied between 27 and only 2. Hong Kong's share of the China trade fell to just over 10 per cent and continued below 20 per cent until the Sino-Japanese War.

The colony made a slow recovery. Political upheavals within China reduced purchasing power there, but imports from China still ran high. The pattern of the colony's trade altered considerably in the years immediately after the War and until the commencement of World War II in Europe. The old entrepôt trade with China was diminishing in relation to the growing importance of the total colonial trade. And trade with the western Pacific and with South-east Asian countries was on the increase. The trade figures have to be viewed in conjunction with the changing value of the dollar. In 1919 the Hong Kong silver dollar varied between 5s.2d. and 3s.¾d. In 1920 the fluctuation was even wider, and after 1921 the value never exceeded 3s.0d. The 1931 trade recession caused it to drop below one shilling.

The need for currency reform brought, eventually, a commission appointed in London. It recommended that Hong Kong should adhere to the silver standard as long as China did, that banknotes should be convertible into silver bullion, and that note issue be in the hands of a Hong Kong Currency Board, as should the silver bullion reserves. The Chamber of Commerce agreed with this assessment which seemed to consider that the colony was still very closely linked with China in trade, and that it would be advantageous to retain China's silver standard rather than take advantage of a currency based on gold. The Chamber of Commerce, however, argued that since about two-thirds of the Hong Kong note issue was held in Guangzhou, Government control of currency was not desirable.

The impossibility of Hong Kong as an entity — colonial, administrative, or even social — pursuing a course wholly its own has been encountered previously. Hong Kong was, and today remains, very much a reflector of world currents — of the needs of other places in material goods, of the trends in their politics, and even of their social emphasis. At the end of the 1914–18 war, Britain, the 'land fit for heroes', was in the grip of disillusion and social change. Doctrines such as socialism were hotly espoused and equally vehemently denied and vilified. From the human sacrifice that had been exacted by the most terrible of wars there emerged a bitterness as society did not accord those heroes what was said to be their due. And if the age of nineteenth-century *laissez-faire* capitalism had not vanished, it had cooled in the face of left-wing home truths. Hong Kong, the early Victorian child of just such untrammelled private enterprise that put personal and corporate aggrandizement first, had become the prime Asian example of its success, reflecting in the twenties both the British past and also its post-war complexion. Like Britain, it had trouble adapting to the new mood: unlike in Britain that mood came upon Hong Kong society from above and not from the grass-roots, all-classes trauma of human sacrifice in war. It was as artificial in the colony as the fragile British bravado of the 1920s attempts at female emancipation.

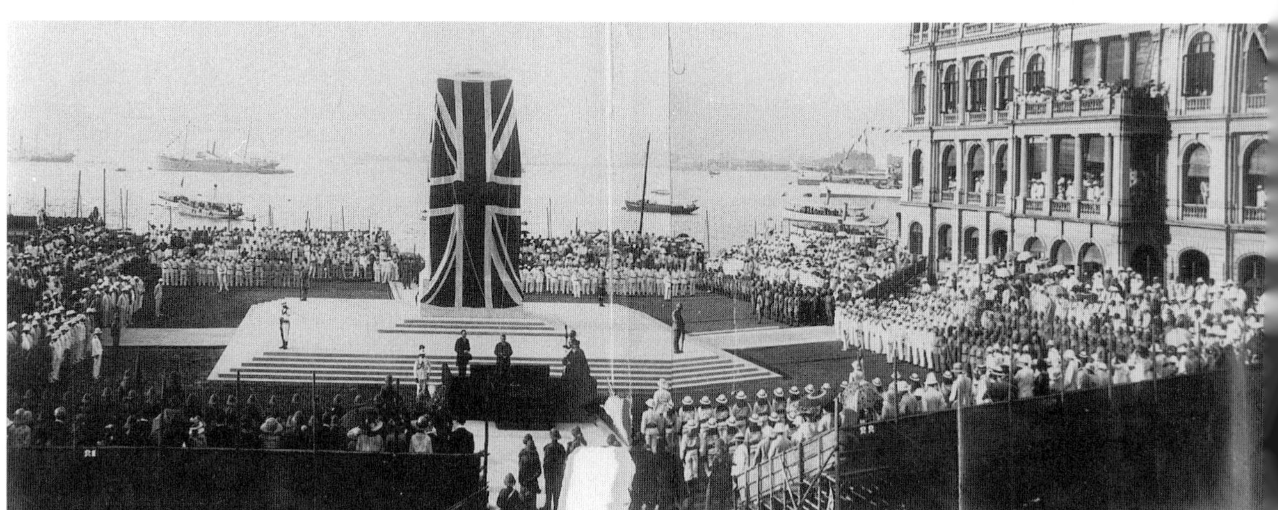

The unveiling of the memorial to the Hong Kong dead of World War I, 24 May 1923.

In 1920, Bernard Shaw and his wife, on a visit to China, passed through Hong Kong where they were entertained by Sir Robert Hotung. From left to right: Mrs Shaw, Ho Shai Lai (Sir Robert's son), Sir Robert, Mrs Simpson, Shaw, Professor R. K. Simpson of Hong Kong University, Lady Hotung.

The formerly self-assured British view in Hong Kong of the Chinese became a little less arrogant with increasing doubts about Britain's role in the post-war world. The growing financial dominance of the United States and the upsurge of Japan's commercial and naval power were but two of the new factors in world change, in which the colony was the merest pawn.

Stubbs was doubtless relieved when his term of office ended. The boycott was not yet over and he had had a hard time as Governor, politically rather out of his depth when it came to dealing with the complexities and crises induced by the metamorphosis in China. He was succeeded by a man who had every qualification to be called the colony's most intelligent Governor, Sir Cecil Clementi. He had been chosen by the Colonial Office in one of its more rational, even inspired, moments as the man most likely to match the subtly, yet in some ways radically, altered circumstances in Hong Kong. Sir Cecil had begun his diplomatic career as one of that select group of cadet officers from whom much that was worthy in Hong Kong's administrations had come. Arrived in the East, the cadets were expected to gain a mastery of the Chinese language at Guangzhou during their first couple of years. Their task was to

Sir Cecil Clementi, KCMG, LL D.

convert themselves in language — spoken and written — into Western versions of traditional Chinese gentlemen. Clementi succeeded better than the others in those tasks and was acclaimed by the Chinese for the excellence of his calligraphy. Both he and Lady Clementi were persons of charm and culture, Sir Cecil described by the Bengal poet and savant Rabindranath Tagore after a lunch at Government House in 1928 as 'one of the most cultivated Europeans I have ever met in the Orient'.[6] Others were to react in much the same fashion.

An administrator of more than usual skills, Sir Cecil was also (what Stubbs was not) a diplomat of some brilliance. It was through his patient efforts in establishing friendly contacts in Guangzhou at the highest level (thanks to his fluency in Chinese) that normalization of Sino-British relations was achieved in the area. During a visit to Guangzhou, Clementi announced British recognition of the Guomindang as the National Government of China; and this was far from his only diplomatic success. In the decade which followed Clementi's term as Governor, practically every important advance in the progress of Hong Kong may be traced in its initiation to him. To Clementi was due the clearance of the slums — those insanitary, inhuman terraces whose sole windows opened on the front and which were built back to back, enclosing a series of airless, windowless cubicles, worse even than the slums of Guangzhou. To Clementi was due the building of Queen Mary Hospital at Pok Fu Lam, opened in 1937, overlooking the Dairy Farm's herds on the airy slopes above the sea. The Shing Mun reservoir, the first major water storage facility in the New Territories, was begun under Clementi.

The Governor was a man before his time — like Hennessy, but infinitely more diplomatic and cautious — on the subject of race relations. His acquaintance with Hong Kong, he wrote in 1926, and with things Chinese, extended over a quarter of a century. One of his major worries was that the Chinese and European communities in the colony, in daily contact as they were, moved in different worlds and had no comprehension of each other's way of life and thought. This, he thought, retarded social, moral, intellectual, and even commercial progress. There were few enough people in his or any other time in Hong Kong who thought in this way. And Clementi was too early in the century to be able to effect a *rapprochement* in any but business relations. It was to require future dire events in the Orient to nudge the process along.

In 1929, on Clementi's initiative, the Hong Kong Flying Club was formed. The year before had seen the arrival of four flying boats from Singapore, but it was to be another six years before Kai Tak was in regular use for commercial planes. By March 1936 the Hong Kong–Penang flight was inaugurated, linking with flights from Britain which terminated there. A year or so later the *South China Morning Post* was carrying advertisements for Imperial Airways: 'Fly to England for the Coronation ... Hong Kong to London in 10 days. Twice weekly.' In the same year, 1937, Pan American linked Hong Kong to Manila, and it was then possible to fly from the colony to San Francisco in six-and-a-half days. In 1938 Kai Tak airport handled almost ten thousand passengers. The journey to Britain by rail through China, and via the Trans-Siberian Railway through Russia, took 18 days; and by steamer five weeks; but the cost of air travel was still prohibitive. In 1939 the single fare to London was £160, compared to the *return* steamship fare of £105 first class; and a one-way ticket on the Trans-Siberian was a mere £57.

Among other memorable events of the Clementi years was the death of Sir Paul Chater, so long a leading figure in business and in philanthropy, at his baroque residence Marble Hall on Conduit Road. It is open to doubt whether Sir Paul ever realized the mocking connotation which attached to that name as a synonym for the worst in bourgeois pretension, and surely he was ignorant of the next line of that early Victorian music-hall ditty, 'I dreamt that I dwelt in Marble Halls', from which it came — 'With vassals and serfs at my side'.[7] Instructions in his will decreed that his death was to be followed by burial within 12 hours. It was presumed that his wish was to avoid public expense, eulogies, and the like. But the stipulation on timing caused near chaos. No radio service was available to inform the numerous persons who should know, and Chater's death at 5 a.m. missed the morning papers. But somehow the Dean of the cathedral got together a service at 11 a.m., attended by a large congregation. Flags flew at half-mast, the Stock Exchange opened only to close immediately. And by 5 p.m. Sir Paul's wish was granted, and he was interred.

Chater's home, Marble Hall, No. 1 Conduit Road.

With the passing of Chater the last but one of the grand barons of nineteenth-century capitalism in the colony had gone. His was the style of business on a grand scale which combined the pursuit of personal gain with public service and, latterly, with philanthropy in a thoroughly British nineteenth-century manner. His fortune accrued from many an enterprise which added to Hong Kong's ambience and facilities — as did that of his friend and partner Hormusjee Mody who was to die before the next war broke out.

19. *Inter-war Years — the Thirties*

THE month of May 1930 brought the next Governor of the inter-war period, Sir William Peel, who was to serve for exactly five years. It was to prove a time of financial difficulties in a rapidly changing world.

In 1931 Britain had to abandon the gold standard and the policy of free trade, and in 1932 came the introduction of imperial preferences for manufactured goods using a minimum of 50 per cent of material of Empire origin or labour. The system had to be modified in order to be applied to Hong Kong, which was a free port and had almost no raw materials. The colony itself imposed an import licence fee on cars not of Empire make. However, its free port status was not seriously compromised, and it stayed outside the sterling area until 1941.

In 1934, in the face of the sharply rising value of silver caused by heavy United States buying of the metal, China was forced to abandon the silver standard and Hong Kong followed suit, with the result that all silver specie was called in and the export of silver was stopped as a preliminary to an overall reorganization of the currency. The Currency Ordinance of December 1935 spelled out the principle of a managed currency linked to sterling, the note issue backed by gold bullion, and by foreign exchange and sterling securities. The dollar levelled out at 1s.3d. Cupro-nickel coinage replaced silver, and three issuing banks were to furnish notes of $10 and upwards, the government issuing those of smaller denominations.

This was the first time the colony's currency was not linked to that of China. The new situation soon proved advantageous. For the first time its trading ties were stronger with other countries than with China. In 1928 China had at last managed to recover tariff autonomy, severing a long tradition by which the revenue from its customs had been paid into three Hong Kong banks, latterly into the Hongkong and Shanghai Bank only, with the Customs Service itself always headed by a British commissioner.

Housed in its stately pillared halls, domed, with the solid grace of a sturdy Victorian taste, the Hongkong and Shanghai Bank continued until 1934 in

In 1935 when China went off the silver standard, shipments of silver arrived by boat in Hong Kong in straw bags which often broke. The silver — coins or even ornaments, since it was valued by weight — had then to be boxed and manhandled ashore.

the old building, functioning as it had from the inception as one of the greatest promoters of Hong Kong trade and industry. Its comprador during this period was Ho Sai-wing, an adopted son of Sir Robert Hotung. A Eurasian like his adoptive father, his natural father had replaced Robert Hotung as Jardine comprador; and Ho Sai-wing's brothers were compradors of the Mercantile Bank, E. D. Sassoon and Company, and Jardine and Arnold Company.

In Ho Sai-wing's time the Hongkong and Shanghai Bank worked still on old-fashioned lines, the ledger entries being made in Chinese brush instead of pen and ink, the abacus still clicking. The Chief Manager, the grandly named Sir Vandeleur Grayburn, however, in the early 1930s urged the need to build new premises, and 1935 saw the new headquarters opened.

Designed, as had been its forerunner, by the local architectural firm Palmer and Turner, this building conveyed an overall effect of up-to-the-minute modernity inspired by examples in the Paris *Exposition des Arts Decoratifs et*

The seventy-strong comprador's staff of the Hongkong and Shanghai Bank in 1928.

Laying the foundation stone of the new Hongkong and Shanghai Bank which was to open in 1935, the third building to house the Bank.

Sir Vandeleur Grayburn, Chairman of the Hongkong and Shanghai Banking Corporation.

Industriels Modernes of 1925, and by rising skyscrapers in New York. The interior was in art deco style, with what at the time was the largest contemporary mosaic, consisting of 4 million glass tesserae, and made in Venice to a design by a Russian emigré named Podgoursky. His creation, 'a pastiche of classical, modern industrial and commercial, Oriental, and Western themes', was intended to reflect the spirit of the thirties. The poet W. H. Auden, in one of his less memorable verses, writing about the colony, refers to the bank:

Here in the East the bankers have erected
A worthy temple to the Comic Muse.

Sir Vandeleur, accused of wasting the shareholders' money, hesitated before finally agreeing to install the then ultra-modern air-conditioning. 'My own impression', he wrote, 'is that air-conditioning . . . tends to diminish disease and certainly renders the staff very much more comfortable and more able to do work efficiently.' Little did he know it then, but within a few years he was to suffer imprisonment without a vestige of air-conditioning in the dire conditions of Stanley internment camp under the Japanese; and, weakened by ill-treatment, to die of meningitis. Ho Sai-wing, his chief comprador, also died of the effects of maltreatment by the Japanese in 1946. The 1935 building was to serve the Bank until 1982, when it was demolished in favour of one which the forward-looking Sir Vandeleur would surely have approved of for its use of today's up-to-the-minute architectural style,

The view of Statue Square from the Bank's new headquarters, the statue of Queen Victoria in its domed shrine in the very heart of the colonial city. The three parked cars date the picture to before World War II.

as interpreted by Sir Norman Foster. The new bank building was opened in 1986.

During the whole inter-war period, while most colonies raised revenue by means of indirect taxation in the form of a customs tariff, among other means, Hong Kong, a free port, was unable to do so. Yet colonial expenditure rose in a fairly steady curve. Until the very end of this period it was thought undesirable to introduce direct taxation, partly because to have done so would have stirred the proverbial hornet's nest in the form of fierce opposition from the merchants and every other element of the business community. Revenue was to a very large extent derived from rates, land rents, land sales, licences, postage stamps and estate duties, and taxes on betting.

Colonial revenue showed a quite steady increase, year by year, except during the 1931 slump. The figure for 1921 was $17,728,000, rising to $33,549,000 10 years later, and to $41,478,000 in 1939. War taxation imposed in 1940 boosted the receipts to $70,175,000. Expenditure in these years also increased: in 1921 it was $15,739,000 and by 1939 it had more than doubled to $37,949,000. Military expenditure over the period also rose, from $2,318,654 to over six million dollars; at the same time police costs doubled. The cost of the social services rose steeply from something not much over half a million to almost two and a half million dollars. Spending on sanitary services doubled to $1,148,000.

The heaviest item of spending was that for defence, amounting to 20 per cent of the total revenue. In a typical year (1939) claims on the revenue after defence were: 9½ per cent for police, over 10 per cent for public works, 5½ per cent for education, and nearly 10 per cent for sanitation and medical facilities. The remainder — something over 40 per cent — went on administration, pensions, and sundry small items. The total revenue in 1939 was $41.5 million and expenditure ran to $38 million — figures almost ten times those of 1901.

The evolution of the educational system in Hong Kong has been characterized as continuing with 'typically British flexibility'.[1] The facts would appear to support the interpretation 'muddled pragmatism'. After the appointment of a Director of Education in 1909, little was done until the setting up in 1921 of an advisory body of officials from the Education Department and representatives of the community. At the end of 1921 the system of grants for voluntary (missionary) schools was terminated except for five schools with specially recruited foreign staff under European management. This type of school later increased in number to 12. Monthly subsidies were paid to other schools needing help, provided they had good reports from the Inspectors. Missionary and secular institutions were treated alike.

Only about 10 per cent of the colony's peasant population could read or write. The majority lived in the New Territories and compulsory registration of schools was extended there in 1921. Medical inspection of schoolchildren had begun in the following year, and a school medical officer was appointed in 1926. The breakdown of schools by type showed in 1923 a total of 471 urban schools with an enrolment of 24,000 pupils. Of these, 164 establishments with 9,397 pupils received subsidies. Rural schools amounted to 192 with 4,665 pupils, one half of them subsidized. European children over nine years attended the Central British School, later to be renamed King George V School, in Kowloon — still in being today. The general pattern thus established continued with gradual improvements until the outbreak of World War II.

Teacher training was carried out at the Technical Institute, and for teachers who would work in vernacular schools, at the Man Mo Temple and the Belilios Public School. New Territories teacher training began at Tai Po in 1925 and on Hong Kong island the Northcote Training College started up in 1939, training teachers for both the Anglo-Chinese and the vernacular schools. On Hong Kong island Chinese boys of well-to-do families went to Queen's College where the demand for places became so heavy that King's College was opened in 1926. A Superintendent of Physical Education was appointed in 1927.

The university, started with such high hopes, was insufficiently funded — a common Hong Kong predicament in places of learning and art. A commission recommended government assistance, and this was approved in 1920. A grant of $1 million enabled the university to pay its debts. The university's share in the Boxer Indemnity (money exacted from China following the siege of the Beijing legations) was £265,000, to which the Rockefeller Foundation added half a million dollars in 1922 for the endowment of three chairs, of medicine, obstetrics, and surgery. One further significant gift was the Fung Ping Shan Chinese Library, built and endowed by a Chinese banker of that name, which was later changed to a museum of Chinese antiquities. Female students were enrolled in 1921; and in 1939, tardily, a science faculty was added. But the only honours degree courses were in the engineering faculty which for many years continued to be, as Lugard had wanted, the largest of the faculties. By 1938 the university had 536 students, of whom, commendably, 118 were women. Just prior to the Japanese occupation a new science building opened, while the technical college and the evening institute offered elementary engineering courses and courses on commercial subjects.

The waving of an administrative magic wand over the Sanitary Board, in 1936, converted the former locus of dispute and disrepute into the Urban Council: but since the wand had failed to confer on it any new powers, the exercise was initially more cosmetic than significant. The new council had five official and eight unofficial members, of whom two were periodically elected on a franchise based on the jury lists, and six (three of whom were Chinese) were nominated by the Governor. The council was to remain for the time being almost toothless in a civic situation requiring considerable mastication. Its officials were salaried government servants, its deliberations resulting in by-laws which were subject to the approval of the Legislative Council which retained the real power in questions of public health. The urban areas were divided into 28 districts, each in the charge of a sanitary officer. For all the urgency of past cries, when even this degree of municipal government became a reality, only one candidate was nominated at the first election in 1936. The first contested election was another four years away in 1940, when two opponents from the Portuguese community stood. Electoral enthusiasm was scarcely striking.

In the 1920s there were three types of hospital in Hong Kong: government hospitals sadly inadequate in services and number of beds; mission hospitals; and the Tung Wah hospitals. Government hospitals came under the Medical Department headed by the Director of Medical Services from 1928 onwards. The incidence of plague had fallen by the early 1920s, but from causes unknown there was a rise in 1922 when over one thousand cases were recorded. But from then on the incidence dwindled rapidly, so that by 1925 plague had all but disappeared from the colony. There were small outbreaks of cholera, while malaria, which had killed off thousands in earlier times, was prevalent only in parts of the New Territories.

A new post of Labour Officer was created in November 1938. Attached to the Secretariat of Chinese Affairs, his duties were to investigate labour conditions in factories and to enquire into trade union activities. In trade disputes he would act as arbiter of wages in relation to the cost of living. He was also charged with applying the Workman's Compensation Act. For reasons unknown, the designation 'protector of labour', held by the Secretary for Chinese Affairs, was transferred not to the Labour Officer but to the Chairman of the Urban Council, under whom the Factory Inspectorate also worked, thus compounding an already muddled chain of responsibility.

British policy towards devolution of power was, and continued to be in the pre-war years, one of reluctance and caution. A Constitutional Reform Association had been launched in 1917, its aim to promote greater representation of the public in the Executive and Legislative Councils, and to press the home government to give Hong Kong a voice in deliberating post-war trade policies. The Association did little until after the war, when it proposed changes in the Legislative Council including allowing more Chinese into the Council. All its suggestions were dismissed by the Secretary of State.

No change was made in the principle that official majorities should control both councils. But the tempo of Chinese nationalism over the border, and the increasing disparity between the numbers of Chinese and of British residents slowly brought about a feeling for minor changes. The mid-1920s strikes pushed the process on. In July 1926 the first Chinese member of the Executive Council, Sir Shouson Chow, was appointed by Clementi, following the death of Chater. This brought the number of unofficials to three, with six official members, of whom four were ex officio. Until the Pacific War no further changes were made. The 1931 slump and economic depression in Europe seriously affected Hong Kong, bringing contracting trade and diminishing revenues for two years. No sooner had trade begun to recover in 1933 than open hostilities began in China as the Japanese attacked.

The Legislative Council was augmented in 1929 by the addition of two unofficial members to a total of eight, and also by two official members, to make 10. Of the unofficials two were elected by the Justices of the Peace and two by the Chamber of Commerce; three were Chinese, and the Portuguese community had one representative. The term of service of an unofficial in the Legislative Council had been reduced in 1922 to four years and in the Executive Council to five.

In concert with the variously expressed community desire for fuller representation in the affairs of Hong Kong, there was an increasing demand for more local people to be appointed to senior government posts. In part this was abetted by the need for retrenchment, and a committee of 1932 came out in support of the idea, suggesting that opportunities for the employment of Asians existed in the Medical and Sanitary Departments, which might be filled by graduates from the university. The employment of trained Chinese nurses was suggested. The policy was ardently championed in the Legislative Council by Sir Man Kam Lo, and was accepted by the then Governor, Sir Andrew Caldecott, in 1935. 'Government', said the Colonial Secretary in the budget debate, 'has fully and frankly accepted the policy of replacing wherever possible European by Asiatic employees.' But it was not until well after the then approaching war that large numbers of Chinese came to occupy senior posts.

Other aspects of the administration were modified, often because of growth, in the inter-war period. The Colonial Secretariat affords an example. By the end of the 1930s the Colonial Secretary was assisted by four cadets in place of the one or two formerly required; sometimes there had been none. The right of direct approach to the Governor was shared by the Colonial Secretary and two others — the Financial Secretary and the Secretary for Chinese Affairs, all three holding ex-officio seats on the Legislative and Executive Councils. The Treasury remained under the Financial Secretary's control. It was administered, however, by heads of three sub-departments — those of the Accountant General, the Assessor (for the assessment and collection of rates), and the Superintendent of Inland Revenue, who administered revenue ordinances such as stamp and estate duties, entertainment tax and betting tax. In the latter part of 1938 the accounts and stores section of the Public Works Department was made into a separate department under the Financial Secretary.

The Supreme Court consisted of two judges — the Chief Justice and the Puisne Judge, with the occasional appointment of a third. Cases were committed to the court by Magistrates, two in Hong Kong and two in the New Territories, the District Officers acting in the New Territories as Magistrates in their divisions.

During those inter-war years the Police Force was made up of Europeans, Chinese, and Indians. The title Inspector General (formerly Captain-Superintendent) was changed in 1935 to Commissioner of Police. He had under him 12 superintendents, one police cadet, 270 European, 843 Cantonese, and 296 Weihai constables, numerous Indian constables and a special force (including some Russians) of anti-piracy guards. The security system also included numbers of Chinese and Indian watchmen, selected by the police but paid and controlled by private individuals or companies, who also employed private registered watchmen. There was also the useful District Watch Force, working in Chinese areas in some degree of co-operation with the police. The Commissioner of Police was usually head of the prisons and fire services as well. The much-needed new gaol was built at Stanley on the southern coast, but from its inception it was too small.

The remaining major departments of the government were the Audit

Department (paid locally but reporting to the Auditor-General in London), the Harbourmaster's Department, the Civil Aviation Department, and the Botanical and Afforestation Department. The Postmaster General had charge of broadcasting and telecommunications other than the local telephone service, which was run by private enterprise. On the outbreak of war in Europe in September 1939 temporary war departments were set up — the Controller of Enemy Property, Controller of Trade, Controller of Food, and Censor and Detaining Officer. In the previous year an Air Raids Precautions Officer had been sent out from London.[2]

Sir Andrew Caldecott governed briefly from December 1935 until April 1937, encountering renewed demand for the appointment of more local men to more senior posts in government. But the pace of implementation remained slow. Outside the Medical and Health Department little was done until after the war. Caldecott was succeeded by Sir Geoffry Northcote who figures among other 'grotesquely famous newspaper-characters — the British Ambassador, the Governor, Sir Victor Sassoon', in Auden and Isherwood's book, *Journey to a War*, revealing how superficial was the judgement of the two young writers. Northcote arrived in November 1937. A year later, with the Japanese just over the border, the first emergency regulations were issued (on 28 September, the day on which, at Neville Chamberlain's urging, the

The Fanling Hunt flourished in the inter-war years, the hounds following the scent laid by trailing a bag of aniseed along the ground prior to the event. Major H. C. Harland, Royal Scots, was a member of the Hunt, which continued to meet until a few days before the Japanese occupation.

Czechoslovak President Eduard Beneš virtually offered to sacrifice his country to Hitler to ensure peace). The regulations were designed to secure the colony's neutrality in the Sino-Japanese war. Repair and victualling of Japanese and Chinese ships engaged in that war was forbidden. Powers to ban meetings and processions suspected to be seditious, and to impose censorship on Chinese newspapers, were taken. The government assumed powers to control food prices, and later to intern Chinese and Japanese combatants should they take refuge in the colony. Another ordinance of March 1939 required the registration of all European males of 18 to 55, and this was followed by conscription in July 1940. In August 1940 came the Hong Kong Defence regulations, and in September the Defence (Finance) regulations. The first Compulsory Service Tribunal sat on 28 August 1939, hearing 250 cases, but conscientious objectors were few. With the first black-out exercises the colony began to feel the effects of the war, yet such was the prevailing nonchalance that as late as spring 1941 air observers noted that Hong Kong was 'a mass of lights'.

Over all the preparations for the unpredictable future, Sir Geoffry presided. Three months before his retirement, in February 1940, he opened the China Light and Power Company's new power-station at Hok Un (Ho Yuen — the Garden of Cranes) in the Hung Hom district of Kowloon. The company had shown itself over the years prepared to invest against higher future demand for electricity, and was now installing new plant with a capacity of 60 MW (the demand in 1940 proved to be only 13.8 MW). Sir Geoffry ended his speech at the opening ceremony with a question which he then, with all the resonance of prophecy, answered: 'What is it that the vision [of the company] foresees? ... Obviously it is to a great manufacturing future for this town of Kowloon that the China Light and Power Company is looking, and I readily take my stand beside them in that confidence.'[3] Events of a catastrophic nature were to overtake the prediction — but the vision of Kowloon as a great manufacturing centre, then a pipe dream, was to come true.

The enterprise of the power company was its response to the tentative industrial growth then just becoming visible. The beginnings of industry went back many years but it had scarcely been a significant factor in Hong Kong's traditional entrepôt economy. In the late 1930s, however, the start of wool-knitting and piece-goods manufacture could be discerned, along with the making of rattan furniture. As goods became harder to find after the beginning of World War II in the West, local entrepreneurs set up factories to supply confectionery, biscuits, cigarettes, and perfumes. Other new manufactures were leather and rubber-soled footwear, hats, vacuum flasks, torches, and batteries. An economic commission in 1934 had reported a total of 166 factories on the island and 253 in Kowloon, all of them small, the total capital just over fifty-one million dollars. This Commission, unlike the

Governor when he opened the new power-station a few years later, was pessimistic about the future. The depressed state of world trade at the time and uncertainties within China led it to the conclusion that the industry of Hong Kong could not develop much beyond its present stage except inasmuch as it might form an economic part of the whole industrial development of South China and even to some extent of North China.

Against the odds enumerated by the Commission, industry *did* grow, in large part due to the dogged persistence of Chinese business men, as the world depression lifted in the mid-1930s. Exports grew modestly, and established lines — knitwear, footwear, rope, cement, preserved ginger and soya products, and electric torches (these last in an Asia for the most part still without electric lighting) — all built quite strong markets. New industries arose — the manufacture of paints, and the umbrellas essential in tropical rain.

Not all those enterprises were well founded — 1935 saw the closure of 53 registered factories, but also the registration of 60 new ones. A fundamental change in the pattern came at the outbreak of Sino-Japanese hostilities in 1937, when there began a slow shift of mainland Chinese companies out of China. They started to move away from threatened areas to the stability of Hong Kong whose markets, in a period when Japan was increasingly tending to supply its own military needs, and when China's goods were less in evidence, expanded into the South-east Asian area. These new industries included steel-rolling, enamel wares, needle-making and allied small metal manufactures. The war in the West provided scope for others — steel helmets, gas masks, water-bottles, field telephone equipment, entrenching and other tools, army radio transmitters. The list soon branched out into bicycles, nails, medicine in tablet form, toothbrushes, and buttons.

The 1938 figure for factory workers stood at 55,000 — a total which included only those in registered factories. There were many unregistered. Three years later in 1941 the count was 90,000.

Prior to the war in the Pacific, however, Hong Kong remained what it always had been, a trading centre. Only about 10 per cent of exported goods were of local manufacture. This general picture, one of piecemeal light industrialization, remained unchanged until some time after the end of World War II. There was no government control, no labour relations mechanism for conciliation in industrial disputes or industrial accidents, nor any provision in cases of sickness or old age. Many of the factories were little more than cramped workshops overfilled with outmoded machinery. Working conditions were abysmal and only the small scale and absence of heavy industry made the picture different from that of conditions in the early stages of the Industrial Revolution in Britain.

With the start of the Sino-Japanese war in 1937, what had become over the years a complex pattern of trading routes with a whole gamut of commodities traded along them, was slowly but inexorably eroded. The major sea lanes connecting China and the rest of the world were cut at Shanghai, Tianjin, and Qingdao; only Guangzhou and Hong Kong served as the country's outlets and inlets for sea-borne trade. While the colony's share of trade with that part of China not over-run by the Japanese (an area continually contracting) increased, by October 1938 coastal trade with the mainland was virtually at a standstill; for it was at that point that China prohibited all imports from Japan or areas controlled by it. The embargo was withdrawn, however, in June 1939 when it became urgent for China to obtain essential commodities by almost any means. Such goods were shipped to Hong Kong for re-export to Free China once relabelled. China's seaports, all under Japanese control, were once again open to ships from Hong Kong, and momentarily trade revived. The colony took advantage of trade with both Free China and that sector occupied by the Japanese, but as one part of the country after another fell to the Japanese, the merchants began the laborious process of exploring alternative routes for their shipments. This continued until the end of 1941 and the occupation of Hong Kong.

In May 1940, a few months after opening the power-station, Northcote, now ailing, left for home. Spanning the end of that year and part of 1941 a 'military governor', Lieutenant-General E. F. Norton held the reins, appointed to administer the government and tighten defence. His successor, the hapless Sir Mark Young, arrived in September. The Colonial Secretary, N. L. Smith, also left and was replaced by F. C. Gimson, who arrived in Hong Kong on 7 December — the night before the Japanese attack on the colony. Both he and the Governor were to be made prisoner for the duration of the occupation.

20. *Invasion and Occupation*

HONG KONG on the brink of the abyss was a troubled place. In the two years since the declaration of war with Germany in September 1939 the course of life and business in the colony had altered very considerably. Apart from the disruption of trade and the uncertainties of the international situation — East and West — the British in Hong Kong were not slow to discover that they were effectively sealed off from Europe, from the home shores of Britain, for the duration of a war whose length there was no way of calculating. Britain, with its forces necessarily concentrated in the West, was in a weak position in the East, forced to be polite to Japan while at the same time attempting to defend treaty rights in China which the Japanese were in the process of over-running. Japan was in a position of strength. Whatever she did in and around China could be and was, for the most part, done with impunity. Hong Kong people noted uneasily the bombing of HMS *Ladybird* on the Yangzi in December 1937, and the casual Japanese apology, which contrasted sharply with the payment of an indemnity and the profound admission of guilt over the sinking of the USS *Panay* in the same attack. It was clear that British power was a vanished dream.

Then came the Japanese violations of the Hong Kong frontier, first in October 1938 and again in February 1939 when Lo Wu on the border was bombed. In June the following year the border was briefly closed by the Japanese in a gesture of contempt for Britain's sovereignty. It was a matter of luck that the colony was not taken by the Japanese in the summer of 1940 — that it did not happen was a question of logistics; the supply lines via the Hanoi–Kunming railway and the Burma Road were seen to be more important than that through Hong Kong, and the Japanese turned their attention to them instead of knocking out the colony. Britain had been forced to grovel to the Japanese in signing the Craigie–Arita Agreement in July 1939 in which, after the blockade of the British Settlement at Tianjin, it was agreed that Britain would take no action prejudicial to the Japanese in China. These and other events of a similar nature brought it home to the people of Hong Kong, Chinese as well as Western, that Britain was in eclipse. An editorial in the *South China Morning Post* on 20 August 1940 summed up popular reaction:

'A poll . . . would disclose that the Hong Kong outlook is compounded of reaction, faith, determination, nervous anticipation, evasion and simple fatalism.'

The flood of refugees from China which poured across the border prior to July 1938, in flight from the Japanese occupation of China's southern provinces, numbered a quarter of a million — cause enough in a city of 1,650,000 people for anxiety. The problems of sanitation and public health, always fragile issues, and even the question of how to provide food and the barest shelter for such an influx, were added and, in the short term, insoluble conundrums.

As far back as mid-1938 the government had proposed setting up three camps for refugees. But soon it became evident that such proposals were ludicrously inadequate. Camps were then hastily organized. The Tung Wah group opened reception centres in their hospitals. But, with overcrowding, conditions were as bad in many ways as in the pre-plague years in Taipingshan. An Immigration Department was set up under a cadet officer, but partly through mismanagement and partly through corruption, this body sparked near panic in the Chinese community over the question of certificates of residence. The cadet officer 'retired' and left Hong Kong — one of very few instances when an allegation of corruption was levelled at an otherwise exemplary body of men.

Whitehall had issued guidelines on measures to be taken by the colonies in relation to the war, and these were enlarged by the Emergency Regulations of September 1939, which were spelled out from the Secretariat by the Governor acting alone as representative of the Crown, not as Governor in Council. Censorship, the mining of the harbour, powers to requisition ships and aircraft, the defining of areas to be reserved for defensive purposes, the repossession of buildings, measures to prevent a drain of hard currency, and not least the interning of enemy aliens and the liquidation of their property — all these had to be done quickly. It proved impossible to control the colony's entrepôt trade, but efforts were made to corner the supply of scarce metals from China used in munitions, thus depriving Japan of such supplies. The anomalous situation of the Hong Kong dollar which circulated in large quantities in the southern provinces of China — now under enemy Japanese rule — was brought under control in June 1941 by strict exchange measures linking the dollar for the first time with sterling.

Starting in 1939, Hong Kong was the first colony to introduce conscription. Men between 18 and 41 who were fit for active service were allocated to the Hong Kong Volunteer Defence Corps (HKVDC), or to the Hong Kong Naval Defence Force (HKNDF), while others in reserved occupations were given some training but forbidden to volunteer for the forces without permission.

In this process friendly European nationals volunteered in considerable numbers, and the HKVDC was put under a professional soldier and regular army discipline. Men over 55 with military experience were formed into a defence unit under their commander A. W. Hughes, manager of the Union Insurance Society of Hong Kong, and soon came to be known as the 'Hughesiliers' or, more amusingly, as the 'Methusaliers'. Auxiliary police, nursing, fire, and air raid precautions services were formed, the last expanding rapidly after the decision not to build public shelters for the populace was reversed in June 1941. Numerous Chinese joined the Volunteers and the British regular forces as drivers and orderlies, while Chinese students with some command of English joined the auxiliary defence services. There were proposals to arm the local Chinese, but British policy was against this in order not to offend the Japanese. The Chinese as a whole stood somewhat apart from all the preparations, leaving it to the foreigners, knowing what happens to civilians who assist armed forces when these forces lose the fight.

For the Europeans the threat of a Japanese attack in mid-1940 brought drastic changes, one being the sudden evacuation of women and children — 3,474 of them — to Australia. This move proved highly unpopular and was followed, as usual in Hong Kong, by backbiting and accusations of favouritism, racial discrimination (which could scarcely be contested), and of unfeeling bureaucratic inefficiency. The order for this evacuation had in fact come from London. And, true to form, one of Hong Kong's sporadic eruptions of scandal then came to light in the Air Raid Precautions Department.

The decision after all to provide air-raid shelters for everyone meant that now the work had to be done at break-neck speed, and a virtually new organization created almost instantly. Huge sums were involved and the urgency led to graft, especially in the architectural branch of the ARP Department. A commission of enquiry under a Puisne Judge was set up in August 1941 as the result of the discovery that the Hongkong and Shanghai Banking Corporation had managed to complete the blacking out of its headquarters in Queen's Road for the total sum of $87 and not the $500 which had been allocated. The Bank, suspecting some irregularity, claimed its $500, duly received it, and reported to the government. The ARP Department architect was asked to give evidence. When he failed to attend, it was discovered that he had shot himself. Another British official in charge of the many air-raid tunnels being dug into the hillsides was admitted to hospital suffering from severe poisoning.

The commission met in the period between 14 August and 7 November 1941, attracting a blaze of media attention. But its findings were never published. The Judge presiding, P.E.F. Cressal, carried the draft report into internment in Stanley camp a month later, where he died in 1944. The draft vanished: after the war the enquiry was quietly dropped.

In spite of massive preparations by both old and new departments of government in the period before the Japanese invasion, there must be a strong suspicion that in some ways these operations were hampered by the unusual turnover in the upper echelons of the government just before the fateful attack. A new Commissioner of Police and a new Defence Secretary were appointed in February and April 1941 respectively. The General Officer Commanding the garrison left in August and his successor, Major-General C. M. Maltby, took over. And the Colonial Secretary and the Governor were also new to the colony.

Funds to pay for the swarm of emergency measures were derived from emergency war budgets, the money coming from direct taxation on salaries, business and corporation profits, and from levies on property. In October 1939 two budgets were announced — the normal one and an additional war budget to enable the colony to fulfil its obligations to the home government as part of the Empire. On instructions from London, income tax was to be considered as the best source of additional taxation revenue. The tax, it was stated, softening what for Hong Kong merchants had always been seen melodramatically as a mortal blow, would be light, and a profits tax was envisaged at a later date. Yield from this source was to be an annual $10 million, of which $7 million (after meeting defence expenditure) would be available as a gift to the United Kingdom.

The outcry was immediate and anguished. Both Chambers of Commerce protested, while all the unofficial members of the Legislative Council condemned the measure. The principal arguments advanced against it were: that flight of capital would result (a possibility); that the Chinese would resent such an inquisitorial tax (probably true); and that all Chinese account books would have to be translated into English (easily circumvented by the employment of Chinese auditors).

The government capitulated. A War Revenue Committee was set up and proposed the imposition of four new taxes: a property tax of 5 per cent of the rateable value; a salaries tax, on the first $5,000 of taxable income, of 4 per cent, and 10 per cent thereafter; a corporation profits tax and a business profits tax of 5 per cent on profits from $10,000 to $100,000, and 10 per cent on profits in excess of that. It was estimated that these new measures would yield six million dollars — $2 million to cover the administrative costs of wartime departments, the remaining $4 million to be spent on building ships for Britain. The taxation came into effect on 1 April 1940. In that year the Legislative Council made two gifts of £100,000 each to the British Government. In the Council's budget debate the following year it appeared that the estimated revenue from those new taxes had been correct, but the estimate of expenditure for the war turned out to be $12 million, not the two million dollars anticipated. The rates were then raised from 5 and 10 per cent to 6 and 12 per cent; and while the government continued to threaten full income tax, the Japanese overran Hong Kong before it could be introduced.

Questions of the defence of Hong Kong during the inter-war years were touched with an aura of unreality in the light of the Washington Naval Limitation Treaty of February 1922, which precluded any extension of the colony's installations. The treaty was denounced by Japan in 1934, with effect from 1936; Hong Kong was no longer bound by its provisions. But it was recognized in the colony and in Britain that Hong Kong could never be a strong base so long as the Japanese, established in Taiwan, could neutralize or even knock it out more or less at will. The garrison was in a tactically no-win situation. Churchill's summing up of the situation in a letter of 7 January 1941 to General Ismay, the British Chief of Staff, was: 'If Japan goes to war with us there is not the slightest chance of holding Hong Kong or relieving it.' Meanwhile it was important to deny the use of its harbour to unfriendly ships. The Japanese occupation of Hainan Island and the Spratlys, and its advance into French Indo-China meant in effect that Hong Kong was surrounded. In his history, *The Second World War*, Churchill amplifies the statement in his letter: 'I had no illusions about the fate of Hong Kong under the overwhelming impact of Japanese power. But the finer the British resistance the better for all.' Hong Kong was to be fought for not on strategic grounds but *pour encourager les autres*.

A defence plan had been formulated in 1937 based on holding Hong Kong island and enough of the opposite shore to protect the harbour. Protection from sea-borne attack was to be afforded by artillery on the southern coast. A land offensive was to be confronted by a line of pill-boxes running from Gindrinkers Bay (Tsuen Wan) in the west of the Kowloon peninsula to Tide Cove off Tolo Harbour, and over the hills to Port Shelter. These were to be manned by heavy machine-guns of the Middlesex Regiment so placed to give a connected line of fire. Supplementary light infantry patrols and mobile artillery were to be added. The plan tacitly assumed that the requisite force would be available to man such a line — later known as Gindrinkers Line.

With the landing of Japanese troops at Xiamen and at Bias Bay, a fresh look was taken at this plan in 1938. A new one was drawn up which envisaged a limited availability of forces in the colony should war in Europe break out, and only the island being defended. The New Territories were to be the scene of delaying tactics so that military stores, installations, bridges, and public utilities could be removed or inactivated. This was thought to offer about 48 hours delay before evacuation to Hong Kong island. The Gindrinkers Line idea was dropped.

The colony's pre-war naval strength normally consisted of four destroyers. On the eve of the Japanese invasion one of those was not in Hong Kong waters and two others had left for Singapore, leaving only HMS *Thracian*. There were also four gunboats, eight motor-torpedo boats, and a few smaller harbour vessels.

The garrison consisted of four infantry battalions: 2nd Royal Scots, 1st Middlesex, 2/14 Punjabis, and 5/7 Rajputs. And there were just over four artillery regiments: two Coastal Regiments of the Royal Artillery, one Medium Defence Battery manning coastal guns, one A. A. Regiment, and the 1st Hong Kong Regiment of the Hong Kong and Singapore Royal Artillery. This last was under strength. A small Royal Air Force flight of three obsolete Vildebeeste torpedo-bombers was accompanied by two Walrus amphibians.

The infantry was distributed on the island — the Rajputs in the north-east sector, the Punjabis in the south-east, and the two British battalions spread over the rest. Beaches were equipped with pill-boxes, a boom was stretched across Lei Yue Mun, and the beaches and the harbour were mined. In the event of an attack the Punjabis were supposed to operate for some time on the mainland, and then to withdraw to their designated sector on the island.

These arrangements having been made, the officer commanding the garrison, Major-General A. E. Grassett, relinquished his post and was replaced by Major-General C. M. Maltby. Grassett, a Canadian, travelled to England via Canada, and while in Ottawa suggested that the government send two battalions to help defend Hong Kong, his argument being that this would assist the forces there to hold out much longer. The proposition appealed to Canada, which was desperately unprepared for war in the Pacific. In London the suggestion was agreed, and the two Canadian battalions,

Major General C. M. Maltby (right), Commander-in-Chief during the defence of Hong Kong — seen here in later years on a return visit with the Governor, Sir David Trench.

the Royal Rifles and the Winnipeg Grenadiers, were chosen. Both were unprepared for combat due to a shortage of up-to-date weaponry, and required large drafts of raw recruits to bring them up to strength. Intelligence reports suggested that a Japanese attack would be some time in coming, and this, it was argued, would allow time for training in Hong Kong. The Canadians arrived on 17 November 1941. Their heavy equipment did not.

Maltby received news of the Canadian force in October and revised his defence plans. Three battalions were now to be deployed on the mainland, with another three, as before, garrisoning the island. Maltby now thought that the mainland could hold out for about a week instead of the 48 hours previously envisaged. And this was essential to any return to the pre-1938 plan whose principal element was Gindrinkers Line. The Line, partly furnished in 1938, now required a great deal of work to complete. This went ahead, and officers were briefed on the scheme. No troops were sent to posts on the Line in case the Japanese thought an attack was feared to be imminent.

No one had many illusions about the Line. Its main weakness was that much of it was overlooked from the vantage point of Tai Mo Shan and from Needle Hill. And it was the first and last line of defence, Kowloon being too near for a second on which to fall back. Another detraction was that the Line was too long to be adequately manned, a problem which Maltby attempted to circumvent in October 1941 by suggesting the recruitment of a battalion of Chinese infantry to man machine-guns. Permission to do this came too late. The battalion would have been the first Chinese battalion in the British Army. On the arrival of the Canadians, Maltby moved the garrisons into position — one brigade of three regiments to Gindrinkers Line under Brigadier Wallis, a second under the Canadian Brigadier J. K. Lawson on the island. The total strength of the garrison was now about 12,000 men but other weaknesses were both obvious and inevitable — the lack of air support left the General with no aerial reconnaissance, forcing him to prepare for attack from almost any quarter; no pre-emptive strike could be carried out; and the two anti-aircraft batteries were pathetically inadequate against air attack. The naval force was also inadequate to prevent enemy landings.

Perhaps the saddest element in the defence of Hong Kong was the effective betrayal of the gallant defenders, even as they prepared for action, by the almost totally erroneous British intelligence reports upon which they had to depend. Coupled with the fact that every Japanese officer in the attacking forces had maps of all the British defence positions and details of how they were manned and equipped, this doomed the defenders to a fate which their small numbers doubtless dictated, but which made a nonsense of their sustained bravery in action, and which was in the outcome of very doubtful utility. Among many inspired decisions taken during the course of the war, Winston Churchill's insistence on the last ditch defence of Hong Kong must be seen as a spendthrift, heartless command.

One example of the inadequacy of British intelligence was that on the eve of the Japanese attack Maltby estimated the strength of the forces opposing him at three divisions. In fact there were four. Other intelligence estimates put the fighting quality of the Japanese as low, and probably even lower against Western troops than against Chinese. They were said to be ill-equipped, their air force inaccurate in its bombing, the pilots unused to night manoeuvres. Reports of the British military attachés in Tokyo, and of others with first-hand experience of Japanese fighting in China, were passed over. The men of the Hong Kong garrison, on the flimsiest of grounds (to put it mildly), were mostly convinced that the island was impregnable. In 1941 every senior officer was boosting the morale of his audience by the claim that 'Hong Kong is a fortress'.

Against this cardboard fortress whose weaknesses every Japanese officer knew in detail, the enemy threw an irresistible force. Their 38th division under Lieutenant-General T. Sano comprised the 228th, 229th, and 230th infantry regiments, each having three battalions under Major-General Ito, backed up by 'mountain artillery, anti-tank guns, field artillery, howitzers, mortars, heavy artillery, engineers, landing craft and [not least] overwhelming air support'.[1] This force was protected at its rear from the Chinese, and although it did not outnumber Maltby's force it could call on three more divisions and was outstandingly better equipped. The Japanese were also masters by sea. Almost every detail given by British intelligence about them proved the exact opposite of the truth. Maltby faced an army of well-disciplined men, intelligently led, flexible in tactics — and in conquering form. The Japanese from the first took the initiative and despite minor local setbacks kept it for the 17 to 18 days that it took to force the colony's surrender.

Winter 1941–2 was one of the darkest periods of the war for Britain and the Allies. Japan planned her attacks on the unprepared base of the American fleet in Pearl Harbor, on Hong Kong, and on the Philippines and Malaya, as simultaneous surprise actions whose sheer daring would gain for her an initial strong advantage. The strategy proved correct almost to the last detail. In Hong Kong insistent Chinese reports had told of Japanese troop movements on the other side of the border, and these had been heeded by Maltby. By the evening of 7 December he had moved his troops into positions both in the New Territories and on the island. The Volunteers were mobilized, the harbour defences manned. The recall of service personnel had been demanded on the radio and even on the cinema screens that evening.

Before dawn on 8 December a signal from Singapore brought news of the invasion of Malaya. Maltby and his staff then entered what was called the 'battle-box', an underground headquarters dating from 1940, 50 feet below Victoria Barracks in Central. Dawn brought news of heavy Japanese troop movements just over the Hong Kong border. At 7.30 a.m. the order to blow up the frontier bridges went out and roads were made impassable as the Punjabis retired towards Tai Po covering the demolition squads. At 8 a.m., 12 Japanese bombers with an escort of 36 fighters put all five RAF planes and eight civilian aircraft (which were on the ground, at Kai Tak, having no air cover and no warning of approaching enemy planes) out of action. Simultaneously the Japanese crossed the Sham Chun River on temporary bridges. They advanced eastward towards Tide Cove and a vulnerable section of Gindrinkers Line, their regiments making speedy progress. The summit of Tai Mo Shan was occupied from the west and the Japanese were poised to attack the below-strength Royal Scots at the key point of Shing Mun redoubt. In a brilliant and unorthodox move the Japanese descended on the redoubt from above and tossed grenades down the ventilation shafts. Five hours' fighting later it was theirs. The way to Kowloon was open. The

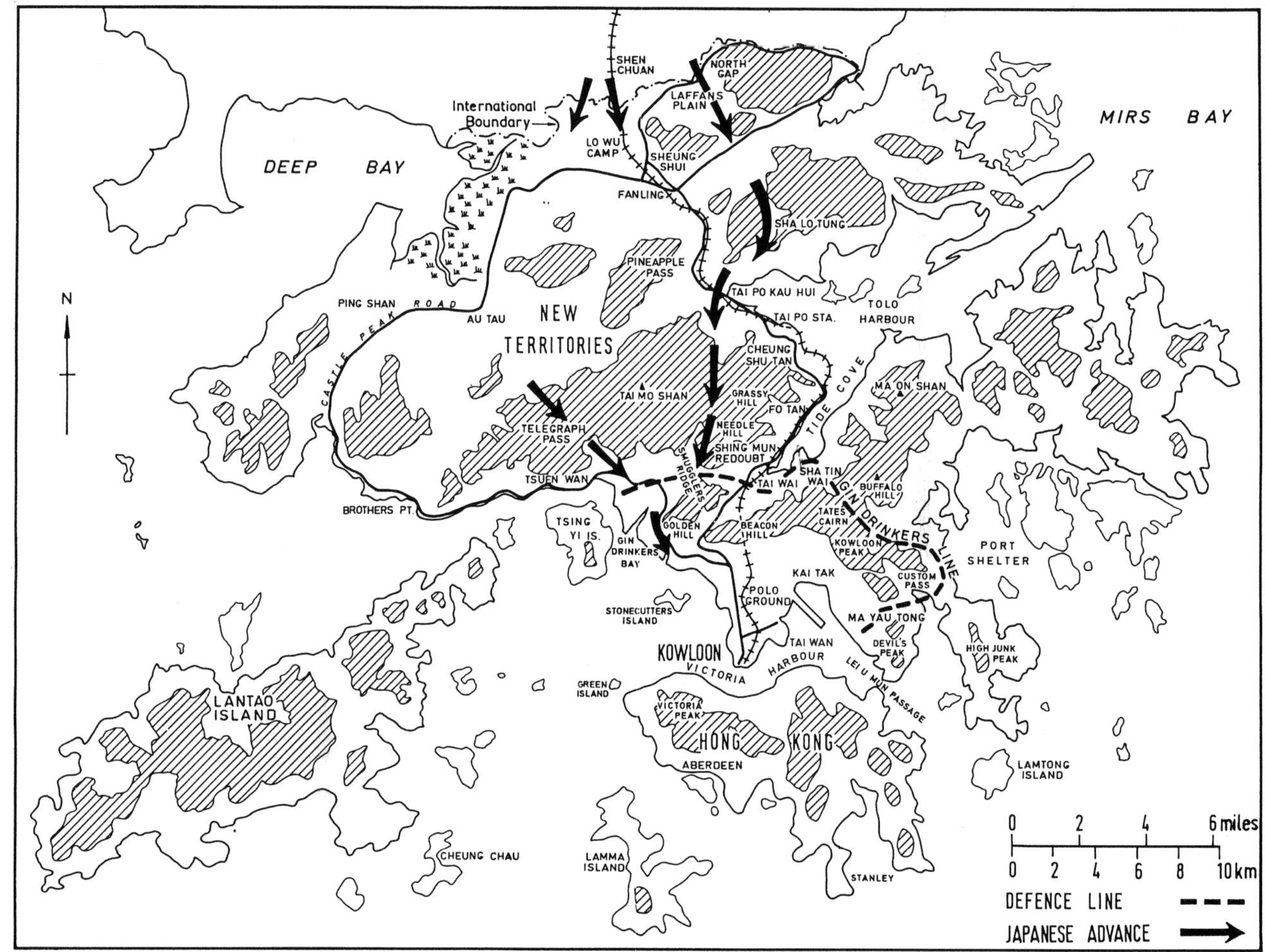

7. The defensive line (Gindrinkers Line) and the routes of the Japanese attack on Hong Kong. (*Source*: Endacott, *Hong Kong Eclipse*, p. 6.)

outcome was never in doubt, but the delaying tactic had to some extent succeeded. By 11 December the order to evacuate was given, and the speed with which this was carried out seemed to bewilder the enemy, little interference being encountered even as the last troops were ferried to the island in broad daylight on 13 December. The mainland forces survived more or less intact, despite the abandonment of 170 mules, stores, ammunition, and other equipment, reaching the island in fair order. The defence of the mainland had lasted just five days.

The plight of the population of Kowloon was unenviable. No official hint of the planned withdrawal to the island had been given, and they had no clear idea of what was afoot, though no doubt most guessed. By 12 December all ferries from Kowloon across the harbour were crowded, the last chances to cross to the island obviously imminent. The police were withdrawn and looting started, terrorizing those who stayed on. That evening a huge load of dynamite being brought on a barge from Green island to Victoria was accidentally blown up by a shot from a patrolman who had not been told of its arrival. The explosion woke the whole city and blew out thousands of windows, adding to the confusion and fear. Among other explosions was that at the power-station in Kowloon as employees disabled the main turbine. Yet others echoed from the docks as installations there were dynamited.

Chaos reigned on the island. The explosion of the ammunition unnerved people crowded in makeshift accommodation, sleeping in public rooms of hotels. A spate of rumours spread by the Japanese fifth column (barbers, waiters, employees of Japanese businesses) which had for years operated in the colony served further to agitate the population.

Thus began five days of suspense before the Japanese assault on Hong Kong island — an island now completely at their mercy. A Japanese staff officer in a boat, with three European women hostages, crossed under a white flag from Kowloon bearing a demand from Lieutenant-General Sakai which read:

> Since our troops have joined battle, I have gained possession of the Kowloon Peninsula despite the good fighting qualities of your men, and my artillery and air force, which are ready to crush all parts of the Island, await my order. Your Excellency can see what will happen to the Island and I cannot keep silent about it. You have all done your duty in defending Hong Kong so far, but the result of the coming battle is plain, and further resistance will lead to the annihilation of a million good citizens and to such sadness as I can hardly bear to see. If your Excellency would accept an offer to start negotiations for the surrender of Hong Kong under certain conditions, it will be honourable. If not, I, 'repressing my tears', am obliged to take action to overpower your forces.[2]

The offer was declined, as was a further one. Then began the systematic shelling of all military targets on the island. At this point, had it not been for

Churchill's order, a responsible Governor would have negotiated the surrender. But Sir Mark Young did not have that option open to him. He replied to the second offer from the Japanese:

> His Excellency summarily rejects the proposal. This colony is not only strong enough to resist all attempts at invasion, but all the resources of the British Empire, the United States, and the Republic of China are behind us and those who have sought peace can rest assured that there will be no surrender ...[3]

Sir Mark Aitchison Young, Governor from September 1941 to May 1947.

It was starkly apparent to all senior officers that the chances of a long resistance were nil and that in the process bloodshed would be severe, among both combatants and the civilian population. Sir Mark, however, obeyed Churchill's orders. The shelling of Hong Kong began on 12 December and continued on the following day. On the evening of the 15th the Japanese attempted a landing at Pak Sha Wan but were easily beaten off. The next day shelling intensified and on 17 December another attempt was made by the Japanese to procure the surrender, and again it was refused. In a severe bombardment, the Japanese tried to reduce the coastal defences of the eastern sector of the island. It was plain that it was in this area that they intended to effect a landing. Then, by bombing and shelling Chinese residential areas and the Central district, by dropping leaflets encouraging the Chinese to turn their backs on the British 'exploiters', the enemy attempted to soften up resistance. On 18 December the bombardment increased all along the shoreline from Causeway Bay to Lei Yue Mun, and that night the Japanese landed at three points, at once surging inland to higher ground. They captured Wong Nai Chung Gap the next day, the defence there cut in two when the enemy advanced downhill to Repulse Bay on the southern shore. The East Brigade was forced back towards Stanley, and despite stubborn and in many a case heroic resistance by pockets of defenders, the courageous, pointless siege of Hong Kong came to a bloody end on Christmas Day 1941 (see Appendix 7).

On that Christmas morning the *South China Morning Post* carried the headline: 'Day of Good Cheer', under which, almost incredibly, the following paragraph appeared.

> Hong Kong is observing the strangest and most sober Christmas in its century-old history. Such modest celebrations as are arranged today will be none the less lighthearted . . . There was a pleasant interlude at the Parisian Grill shortly before it closed last night when a Volunteer pianist, in for a spot of food before going back to his post, played some well-known favourites in which all present joined with gusto . . .[4]

In and around Stanley village and in other places on the cold hillsides, men were lying unattended, bleeding to death from wounds sustained in the defence of the revellers in town.

It was then, on Christmas Day, on the advice of General Maltby (who had in fact advised it 24 hours earlier) that the Governor announced the surrender. With the General, he crossed the harbour, white flag flying, and offered unconditional surrender to Lieutenant-General Sakai. The Japanese newspapers reported that 'the historic meeting between victors and vanquished was conducted in a nice spirit'. And this was later confirmed by General Maltby whom Sakai permitted to stay with his men. Churchill, writing long after in *The Second World War*, concludes:

> Every man who could bear arms . . . took part in a desperate resistance. Their tenacity was matched by the fortitude of the British civilian population [he fails to mention the Chinese]. On Christmas Day the limit of endurance was reached and a capitulation became inevitable. Under their resolute Governor . . . the Colony fought a good fight. They had won indeed the 'lasting honour' which is their due.

And, he might have added, on his orders by their action the war against Japan was carried not one inch forward. Sir Mark was taken prisoner and sent to Wusong in China, and later transferred to Taiwan where he remained until the end of the war. 'I would say generally', he was to write after the war was over, 'that the treatment which I experienced at the hands of the Japanese during my captivity was almost invariably inconsiderate, that it was frequently objectionable, and that it was on occasion positively barbarous.'[5]

It was just a century since the British had taken Hong Kong: now they had lost it. Almost overnight most of that century's achievement vanished. The rule of law, the municipal amenities such as water, gas, electricity, food supply, currency stability, public transport, and the postal service ceased — and with them the *raison d'être* of the colony's existence, trade and commerce. Almost overnight Victoria followed Kowloon into the limbo of occupation's woes: normal life was suspended. With that the population began the long years of makeshift, of near starvation, of ragged existence. But the human spirit is protean in its capacity to fend for the human body. Without gas and electric power to cook the rice, a start was soon made on stripping every vacant building of its combustible material; doors, window frames, even staircases and parquet flooring, were torn out; paper, too, vanished in heat and smoke under the cooking pots, and much of the record of those past hundred years of turbulent administration and equally rumbustious trading disappeared as the rice was cooked. The streets of Wan Chai wore a dilapidated air, the tin helmets of Chinese who had been in the armed or other services lay cast away for fear of Japanese reprisals if they were to be discovered indoors. In the absence of motive power, enterprising former employees of the tramway company hitched a couple of bogies to a wooden platform, and themselves to the makeshift vehicle — hauling passengers for a few cents along the now disused tracks of the fortunately level route through the city.

The weary remnants of Maltby's gallant army, young and old, were rounded up by the Japanese and marched off to one of the most barbaric of prison camps, in Kowloon at Sham Shui Po. All the British civilians — men, women, and children — were sent by truck to Stanley camp on the island's southern peninsula where the existing prison was located, with a school, a small hospital, and the assorted dwellings of the personnel who ran those facilities before the occupation. Conditions were primitive in the extreme, food appalling and inadequate in quantity, discipline harsh and arbitrary, and the death rate as incarceration went on very high. Some military prisoners were transferred to Japan to camps as barbaric as that at Sham Shui Po, others were lost *en route* as the Americans sank the boat conveying them. The Chinese and neutrals not imprisoned subsisted as best they could in conditions as daunting to the body and spirit as may be imagined in a subtropical city shorn of virtually all its amenities. And there, in the decaying urban shambles, in the dastardly camps, all were to remain — those who survived that long ordeal — for three years and eight months until the Japanese defeat and surrender. Until the liberation of Hong Kong.

The half-life of the camps has its literature; but the miseries and endurance of the majority — the mass of Chinese — have no such memorial to life under the Japanese boot. There is not even a casualty list of those killed by Japanese shelling and bombing. Little of substance has been written of the deprivations

February 1942. A group of the colony's bankers being marched to work from the quarters where the Japanese confined them.

European prisoners in Stanley camp, 1945.

of the Chinese people, endured for as long as the foreigners endured those of the camps. Large numbers of Chinese left for China in the slender hope that there they might find means of life better than in Hong Kong — an exodus encouraged by the Japanese whose inept and brutal 'administration' failed to feed the population who had all unwillingly joined the vaunted 'Greater East Asia Co-prosperity Sphere'. There were prominent Chinese who attempted to alleviate the sufferings of their compatriots by intercession with the conquerors, but their efforts came to little. Japanese conquest was aimed solely at Japanese aggrandizement, and amounted to simple rapine — ruthless and cold. The worst aspects of Western colonial expansion pale into insignificance by comparison.

The end was slow in coming for all those who survived in Hong Kong. On 29 August 1945 Rear-Admiral Harcourt sighted the China coast. On the following day his flotilla was in turn sighted by the internees in Stanley camp around 11 a.m. (and doubtless by thousands of Chinese at the same time). A communiqué was issued to the effect that the Admiral had arrived. One of his first duties was to visit Stanley camp where he was greeted with intense jubilation. One of the Royal Marines who was present described the inmates as 'walking skeletons'. He failed to mention the plight of the half-starved Chinese whom he must have seen in quantity on the roads as he passed through the island on his way to Stanley.

30 August 1945. HMS *Swiftsure* passes North Point after entering the harbour following the Japanese surrender. Admiral C. H. Harcourt landed from *Swiftsure* at the naval dockyard in central Victoria.

21. Rehabilitation and Transformation

THE Hong Kong which the liberators found at the end of August 1945 and which the internees rediscovered after almost four years of incarceration was a shambles. The tattered remnant of its population, fallen through hunger-attrition and Japanese emigration policies by about a million from its pre-war 1,600,000, was in rags, creeping about in a drab city mouldering from the years' neglect. The Japanese had capitulated on 14 August.

> Hong Kong people crawled out of the ruins of Japanese occupation dazed, demoralized and destitute, to return to a city that had ground to a halt under alien administration. The population had dwindled to about 600,000 . . . and there was hardly a heartbeat left in the city. Yet as the internees struggled out of Stanley [camp] and the flag went up, first on the Peak on August 18 and then all over, the most obvious thing to do was to set up house again and go back to work. And so within hours of the gates of Stanley being opened, the first small signs of new life appeared. The trams were running [if fitfully] on August 20, followed soon by the ferries. And from then on it never looked back.[1]

In the broadest sense this was true. But there was an infinity of things to be done. As far back as November 1942 it had been recognized in London that the best way to resume the administration of liberated areas when the time came was to set up a military occupation. Each liberated area was to have a Chief Affairs Officer who would take responsibility under the military commander until such time as a civil government could take over once more. A small staff was set up under the Civil Affairs (Military Planning) Unit of the War Office. The move was agreed with the Americans. But in 1944 the Americans put a different construction on the agreement whereby, were any territory to be liberated as a result of a Japanese surrender (and not as the result of an Allied operation) an American force commander would take over. American opinion and that of President Roosevelt ran strongly against the continuance of colonialism and in favour of building up China as a world power. In 1942 the President stated on the subject of Hong Kong: '... let's raise the Chinese Flag there first, and then Chiang Kai-shek can next day make a grand gesture and make it a free port. That's the way to handle it.'[2]

The absence of a realistic appreciation of the situation was perhaps less apparent then than it is now. Chiang was never a man of the grand gesture, most especially when it concerned the idea of a free Chinese port where customs revenues could not be gathered. Both the Americans and the British had signed a treaty with Chiang's nationalist government in January 1943, the British treaty returning to China the International Settlements at Shanghai and Xiamen and concessions at Tianjin and Guangzhou. But on the question of the New Territories, raised by Chiang, Britain made it clear that they formed part of the colony and that she was surrendering 'all existing treaty rights relating to the system of Treaty Ports in China',[3] which did *not* include the New Territories.

Among its problems the Planning Unit needed to recruit personnel with experience of government in the colony. But as most of those were imprisoned, this was hard to achieve. N. L. Smith, a former Colonial Secretary, and D. M. MacDougall, a senior civil servant who had escaped from the colony a few hours after the capitulation, were appointed to the Planning Unit. All members were given army rank. The inner core of eight were all former Hong Kong civil servants.

Thanks to the dropping of the atom bombs on Hiroshima and Nagasaki, victory over Japan came sooner than had been expected, and the Planning Unit was far from prepared on 30 August 1945 for duty in the newly liberated colony. MacDougall, Chief Civil Affairs Officer, and a staff of nine reached Hong Kong on 7 September, the remainder arriving later.

In the colony the Colonial Secretary, F. C. Gimson, who had spent the occupation in Stanley camp, left it immediately on the Japanese surrender. A directive from London of 17 August instructed him to assume responsibility for administration. The guidelines were the immediate restoration of British sovereignty and administration until a force commander arrived to set up the Military Administration. On 27 August Gimson replied that he had already done this. 'I have taken up residence in a building near the Hong Kong Bank ... With me are all members of the Executive Council as well as other senior Government officials ...'.[4] Gimson weathered the storm until the arrival of Rear-Admiral Harcourt with the British flotilla on 30 August. Harcourt then assumed the office of Commander-in-Chief, Hong Kong, and head of the Military Government, temporarily retaining the Gimson administration, and Gimson himself as Lieutenant-Governor. The question then posed itself: in the circumstances, was a military administration necessary? Gimson was against it. But when the advance guard of the interim civil government staff arrived there was less urgency for his presence and that of his colleagues — all of whom sorely needed leave.

F. C. Gimson, Colonial Secretary from 7 December 1941 to 6 September 1945.

The Military Administration was established by proclamation on 1 September 1945. It was to last eight months until the restoration of civil government on 1 May 1946, and during this period most of the problems of getting the colony working again were tackled. Harcourt was to say that the real work of rehabilitation had of course to be done by the Chinese, now given their freedom, food, law and order, and a stable currency. Freedom — yes. Food, in very small quantities — rationing continued into the 1950s. Law and order was easier to ensure, for on the whole the Chinese wanted only to be left alone to build or rebuild their businesses and make much-needed money. The currency was indeed stabilized, by various means.

The term Military Administration was something of a misnomer, for the administration was in the hands of pre-war government officials whose natural leaning was to replicate the way in which the pre-war departments had been run.

After the euphoria of liberation the realities of a city resembling nothing so much as a typhoon-battered junk, dismasted, rudderless, in still doubtful weather, and with a starved crew, began to take mournful shape. Some idea of the magnitude of the tasks ahead appears in the policy directive issued to MacDougall from London. This required the establishment of a police force and military courts, and of camps for the relief of the distressed; the control of the influx of civilians; the provision of medical facilities and sanitary measures; the restitution of essential public services; the establishment of currency, fiscal, and banking arrangements; and the control of prices and wages. Given the state of affairs in Hong Kong, these instructions must have seemed like an order to remove the Peak with pick and shovel. A further brief adjured MacDougall, the Civil Affairs Officer, to be mindful of the long-term objectives, which would involve him in: reorganization of courts, police,

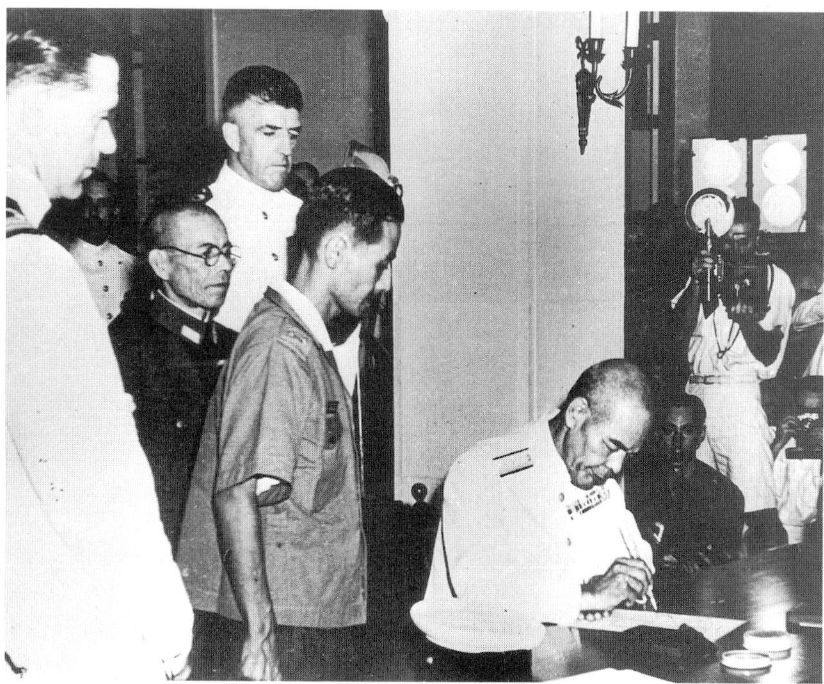

The Japanese Admiral signs the surrender with the Japanese Commissioner for Foreign Affairs (in short sleeves) watching.

and prisons; rehabilitation of commerce and industry, and agriculture and fisheries; reconstruction and redevelopment of public and private utilities including postal and air services; reorganization of the hospitals and the public health and sanitary organs; reorganization of the educational system; and, finally, preparations to transfer the administration to a civil government.

Reading between the lines, it is possible to discern 'the germs of the social welfare policy which was to be a major part of British colonial policy in the post-war years'.[5] A reflection of the Beveridge Report in Britain can be faintly descried, a strange accompaniment to the government's old-fashioned aims of individual responsibility and minimal government interference. MacDougall's instructions included the statement: 'Programmes of departmental activities should form an integral part of a general plan for social welfare, based on the ascertained needs of the community and so constructed as to give proper weight to the requirements of both urban and rural areas.'[6] The fellow-feeling, the humanity induced in the West by the horrors of war, inspired in even the most conservative breast some inclination towards socialist practice, and such measures were to make a brief appearance in diluted form in Hong Kong.

Rear-Admiral Harcourt delegated by proclamation much of his power to MacDougall as Chief Civil Affairs Officer, who was then made responsible to the Colonial Office in London. By mid-November he reported that only 18

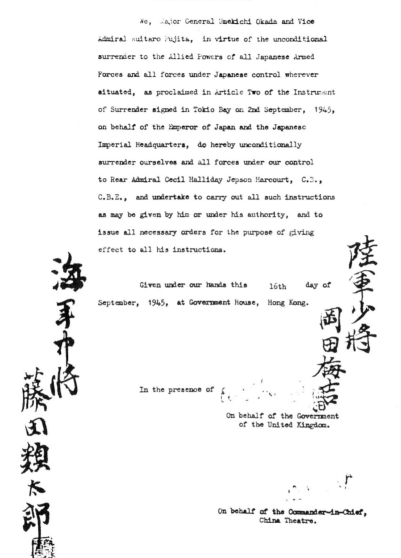

INSTRUMENT OF SURRENDER.

We, Major General Umekichi Okada and Vice Admiral Ruitaro Fujita, in virtue of the unconditional surrender to the Allied Powers of all Japanese Armed Forces and all forces under Japanese control wherever situated, as proclaimed in Article Two of the Instrument of Surrender signed in Tokio Bay on 2nd September, 1945, on behalf of the Emperor of Japan and the Japanese Imperial Headquarters, do hereby unconditionally surrender ourselves and all forces under our control to Rear Admiral Cecil Halliday Jepson Harcourt, C.B., C.B.E., and undertake to carry out all such instructions as may be given by him or under his authority, and to issue all necessary orders for the purpose of giving effect to all his instructions.

Given under our hands this 16th day of September, 1945, at Government House, Hong Kong.

陸軍少將 岡田梅吉

海軍中將 藤田類太郎

In the presence of

On behalf of the Government of the United Kingdom.

On behalf of the Commander-in-Chief, China Theatre.

The instrument of surrender. The Japanese signatures remain legible but the British ones have faded.

per cent of his staff had arrived. The result of this shortfall was the employment of Chinese and Portuguese personnel in positions of considerably more responsibility than those to which they could have aspired in pre-war days. MacDougall paid generous tribute to their performance: 'It can hardly be denied that they thereby established credentials which it would be difficult for any future government to ignore.'[7]

The Union Jack is raised in the gardens of Government House, signalling the return of British rule.

First priorities included the repatriation of prisoners of war and internees, the settling of affairs related to the camps, and the demobilization of Hong Kong's armed forces and Auxiliaries. Medically serious cases among those to be repatriated left on the hospital ship *Oxfordshire* while other groups boarded various liners, a small number going by air. By the end of 1945 a total of 2,557 persons had departed, leaving only 340 remaining temporarily to assist the administration, or occupied with their own affairs. Of all the prisoners from the camps only 120 stayed on in the colony without departing on leave.

During the occupation the Japanese, in an effort to maintain law and order, had given limited police powers to the proprietors of certain gaming houses and their staff. From a force of 321 regular police there were available only 98 officers of the rank of inspector or above, but both Chinese and Indian constables came slowly back to work when it was made clear that their service under the Japanese would not be counted against them. Most were in poor shape, fit for part-time duties only. Students were then recruited and a Police Training School opened; but the degree of malnutrition to which the police, in common with the populace at large, suffered made training slow. So slow that one local wit described the Police Training School as 'a convalescent home'.

Ordinary courts were suspended and a Standing Military Court set up in two separate divisions, dealing mainly with criminal cases, the civil aspect of the law being in effect for the time being in abeyance.

It was obvious that the question of the currency would have to be dealt with at once and effectively, and the authorities were forced to recognize the Japanese yen until a supply of dollars could be obtained. Lord Kadoorie, then Mr Lawrence Kadoorie, recalls how in an effort to get back to Hong Kong after wartime internment in Shanghai, he had reached Kunming in Yunnan Province but could go no further because planes were forbidden to take civilian passengers. By a certain amount of guile and with the help of the American army, he ended up in GI uniform, travelling as freight, on a Hong Kong-bound RAF plane, seated on stacks of banknotes — the desperately needed new currency for Hong Kong.[8] This was on 11 September. Two days later the Japanese yen were withdrawn and notes of the three note-issuing banks (the Hongkong and Shanghai Banking Corporation, the Chartered Bank of India, Australia, and China, and the Mercantile Bank of India) became legal tender.

The fundamental of Hong Kong life and livelihood — its trade — had somehow to be resuscitated. The intention was for the government to handle all trading for six months and then to hand over to private enterprise; but the eagerness of the Chinese community to resume trading overcame government scruples, and on 23 November private trading was again permitted, although under licence — in order to conserve hard currency. The first ocean-going private freighter entered harbour by mid-December. The process of revival was assisted by the closure of the Shanghai International Settlement, many companies based there moving down to Hong Kong.

Another huge problem was food supply. With one hundred thousand Chinese returning to the colony every month, the plight of the populace in terms of food was both severe and threatening. It was estimated that 80 per cent suffered from some degree of malnutrition. Food shortages were aggravated by scarcity of money to buy what was available. The government itself was responsible for feeding members of the Hong Kong Volunteer Defence Corps and their families, and also for approximately twenty-five thousand destitute persons who ate at government rice kitchens. Those destitute also had somehow to be housed. The solution, as envisaged by the Planning Unit in London, had been to set up a large number of camps. In the event only about ten thousand Chinese destitute were so housed and fed, with the help of charitable societies formed for this purpose.

By the end of 1945 the population figure stood at about 1 million — 400,000 more than at the end of the occupation — and the situation looked desperate. The Chinese Nationalist Government remained adamant that it would not accept immigration controls, but eventually an agreement was reached under which food was made available to Hong Kong in return for free entry to the colony. In sober fact, the Hong Kong authorities had no means to control immigration at this time. Rice was rationed and restricted to bona fide Hong Kong residents; so too were sugar and flour.

An acute shortage of accommodation prevailed, with 60 per cent of European and 15 per cent of Chinese housing damaged in varying degrees. A landlord and tenant ordinance was introduced to freeze rents at pre-war levels. Such conditions precluded the return of European women and children, which was forbidden for half a year; only men performing essential services were allowed to return.

The rapid population increase, coupled with malnutrition, and poor public health standards due to neglect in the occupation, had lowered the health of the people. The town was infested with rats, tuberculosis was reaching the proportions of a scourge (and remained so for many a year to come); and neither trained personnel nor supplies of any medical materials were due before the following year. Fortunately the water supply system was in fair order, and by mid-November supplies stood at 25 million gallons daily. A single daily train plied between Kowloon and the Chinese border by early September and the service to Guangzhou was resumed on 14 November; but — a sign of the times — the pre-war fare of one dollar now stood at $15.70.

The scuttling of many ships in the battle of Hong Kong, together with Allied bombing before liberation, had left 30 wrecks in the harbour and one at Holt's Wharf; and there were tugs and lighters sunk beside piers and quays. Only three wharves were in use and there was not a single workable crane. A committee of Far East shipping companies looked after shipping on behalf of the administration. Public utilities were soon operating on a restricted basis, but lack of suitable fuel and damage to plant limited the electricity generating capacity. Gas, telephone, and tramway services resumed in stages, and the Taikoo Dock and Holt's Wharf returned to private ownership in March 1946. The Hong Kong and Yaumati Ferry Company ran all ferries, the Star Ferry Company having lost all its vessels. In February 1946 these were raised from the harbour and repaired. The first private civilian car arrived in February 1946. Hong Kong island boasted six buses and Kowloon another like number — and lorries with bench seats fitted became the familiar means of transport for some time.

All the ills of a place that had survived the torture of enemy occupation were manifest in Hong Kong. The bitter recriminations of one group against another, of individuals against fellow citizens about the thorny question of who 'collaborated' (and what constituted 'collaboration') surfaced as they did in France and elsewhere. The psychological wounds of occupation bulked as large as physical injury and malnutrition. Blackmailers and extortionists appeared like leeches, preying on human frailty under duress during the occupation.

With the cost of living by December 1945 still 500 per cent above that of

1941, labour unrest took over. Wages had not remotely kept pace with soaring prices. In November a permanent Labour Board issued a table of hourly rates for various grades of workers, offered rehabilitation allowances, and set down a cost of living adjustment pegged to the cost of 10 items of food and fuel. The Nationalists exploited this situation, sending delegations to stimulate unrest, until the Guangdong authorities were asked by Hong Kong to appoint an official to control them. The Communist press, however, showed restraint. The situation was hardly ameliorated when in October the Chinese Nationalists wanted to assemble their forces on Hong Kong soil, to depart on American ships for Manchuria as the Japanese evacuated that area. The suspicion was that the objective was perhaps a more permanent stationing of Nationalist troops in the colony.

The Military Administration continued until May 1946 when the Governor, Sir Mark Young, returning to Hong Kong on 30 April 1946 — the first Governor to arrive by air — was sworn in the following day. It was a colourful and moving ceremony at Government House as Admiral Harcourt's flag was lowered. In the main hall the 83-year-old Sir Robert Hotung read an address of welcome in Cantonese. The hall, indeed the whole structure of Government House, was dramatically different from the place that Sir Mark must have recalled from four years previously, the most prominent alteration being the Japanese-style tower added to what was a greatly changed main building. The Japanese Governor, General Rensuke Isogai, had decided neither to live nor to work there. Instead he chose the Hongkong and Shanghai Bank, living in the chairman's flat on the eighth floor. Later on he moved with his family to a European villa on Repulse Bay Road with a view of the sea. Isogai felt, however, that for reasons of prestige something must be done to rehabilitate the crumbling Government House. To this end he brought a man called S. C. Feltham, the designer of Fanling Lodge, out of Stanley camp. But in the end he settled on a relative, Seichi Fujimura, an architect with the South Manchuria Railway Company. Fujimura produced drawings incorporating Isogai's demand for a structure having something of traditional Japanese architecture, and also symbolizing Japan's military presence, suited to the dignity of later Japanese governors.

In the hall Isogai had placed a life-size wooden *samurai* in Tokugawa armour and a tiger which had been shot in Stanley in 1942. The animal had been stuffed by one of the Dairy Farm's butchers taken out of Stanley camp for the purpose. (It was supposed at the time that the animal came from Guangdong Province, but more probably it had been freed by its owner, the keeper of a circus performing in Causeway Bay, just prior to the Japanese invasion.)

Sir Mark Young arrived equipped with what was styled the Colonial Office's 'new angle of vision', defined in 1943 as the British Government's intent to guide the colonial peoples on the path to self-government, providing as far as possible the economic and social conditions favourable to its realization. As a first step in Hong Kong, Young legalized the new civil government by passing three ordinances through all their stages in the Legislative Council on 1 May 1946. This done, the Governor turned to his brief, containing its Utopian profession of liberal principles in the conduct of colonial affairs, outlining its application to the affairs of Hong Kong and looking forward to affording residents a greater share in the management of their affairs — 'the fullest account being taken of the views and wishes of the inhabitants' were his words.

Representative bodies were approached and individuals asked to give their opinions. But — and this remained true of the response to such opportunities to speak out until the mid-1980s — reactions proved lukewarm. There seemed to be an innate reluctance on the part of Hong Kong people of all stations in life to join in political debate. The mass of the people seemed content to be governed as they had been, provided always that the government kept its fingers out of the individual's affairs. Some response was, however, received. On this shaky basis the Governor announced his proposals in August. These became known as the 'Young Plan'.

The plan envisaged a 48-member Municipal Council, one-third to be elected by non-Chinese voters and the remainder elected by Chinese and non-Chinese institutions equally. The Council was to have limited functions in urban areas, while the New Territories would be administered separately. The Legislative Council was to include seven official and eight unofficial members with the Governor having an ex-officio as well as a casting vote — enabling him to hold a balance between the two sides. The new Municipal Council was to nominate two unofficial members, and other institutions four, leaving the existing nominating bodies with one member each as before.

The plan met with a generally favourable reception. In July 1947 it was approved with minor alterations. Sir Mark had by this time left the colony (in May), and it fell to the next Governor to clothe the concept in details, a process which occupied the next two years. In June 1949 three bills embodying the plan made their appearance. It was a sadly belated appearance, doubtless necessitated by the complexity of the details which had to be debated and decided. By that time the concept of what Hong Kong was and might become had begun to alter radically, not from internal pressures but, as so often in the past (and in the future), from the pounding of waves originating outside its shores.

By the middle of 1949 the Guomindang forces had reached the verge of collapse. Hordes of refugees from the mainland were seeking Hong Kong's peaceful little dot of land in ever increasing numbers. And it was in part those refugees, with the business expertise and the manufacturing skills and equipment which some of them brought to the colony, who had begun to change its complexion. On 22 June the Legislative Council debated the issue and a motion was carried delaying the implementation of the Young Plan. The Secretary of State for the Colonies announced in October 1952 that the time for such constitutional changes was not ripe. And there ended the Young Plan, a lone attempt to democratize Hong Kong, relegated to the status of a footnote in the colony's history.

Had the government or the people of the colony at that time possessed the gift of seeing into the future, their excitement would surely have known no bounds. For there, in Hong Kong, in the meeting of those hundreds of thousands of refugees from the horrors of civil war in China, all eager somehow, anyhow, to make for themselves a new life, lay the seeds of the future. In the incubator of the seething territory with its free port, its status as an international entrepôt, with a germinating industrial potential, lay an answer as astonishing as any to the opportunities and hazards of the times.

Out of that chaotic era, out of the concerted human will to survive and prosper, out of accidental factors such as a world hunger for consumer goods, and out of the huge influx of human skills and experience, a new Hong Kong was to emerge as much to the surprise of its inhabitants as to that of the world in general. The metamorphosis was traumatic. It was industrially and socially revolutionary within a capitalist framework. It took place more rapidly than any similar process elsewhere in the world.

The Legislative Council, resuscitated in May 1946, consisted of nine official and seven unofficial members. In 1951 one more unofficial was added and there were then four Chinese and one Portuguese unofficials. By 1953 there were only two European unofficials. Appointments to the Council were made annually from 1951, and three-yearly in 1953. The Executive Council was also revived in 1946, enlarged in May to seven official and four unofficial members. The following year it was revamped and the number of officials and unofficials was made equal with six each, the unofficials being three Chinese, one Portuguese, and two British.

The Urban Council was also revived with five official and six unofficial members, the election of members being indefinitely postponed. This stimulated the birth of the Reform Club in 1949 and the Civic Association in 1955. In another species of reform, localization in the upper ranks of the civil service was brought out again and the dust accumulated since 1932 brushed off. Posts in the Education, Police, Railway, Medical, and Public Works Departments were opened to local men, the action gaining some strength from the recommendation of the 1947 Salaries Commission that no expatriate should be appointed to a government position if a qualified local person was available. The first Chinese cadet was appointed to an administrative-class post in 1946 and a local man attained the position of head of the Medical Department in 1952. By 1951 over 10 per cent of the administrative and senior professional officers were locally recruited. The 1947 Salaries

Commission recommended that a 200 per cent rise in salary be allocated for the lowest grades of civil servant, a 30 per cent increase for those earning $1,000 a month, and a 20 per cent increase to those on salaries above $1,500 a month.

Within the administration several new departments were set up — Labour and Mines, Transport, Information, Statistics and Planning, and Social Welfare. Expansion in the judiciary gave that department a Chief Justice, a Senior Puisne Judge, six Puisne Judges, eight District Judges, and 11 Magistrates. As important at a later date was the comparatively easy victory of the Hong Kong administration in the long struggle to gain financial autonomy, free now, apart from a consultative obligation, to utilize its revenues in whatever ways it deemed most appropriate. This decision, together with freedom for the administration, was announced by Sir Robert Black in the year of his arrival, 1958. Britain's sovereignty remained but as a general rule was to be exercised only in the control of external relations. The localization policies meant that — to jump ahead a little — by 1971, of the 2,874 professional and administrative civil servants, 1,609 were local people — a little under 56 per cent. This trend has continued ever since, although not in an even manner.

The Colonial Office was probably not unpleased to leave Hong Kong to wrestle with its own financial affairs in the immediate post-war period. The colony had a large deficit in London, money spent for war purposes. The estimate of revenue anticipated in the 11 months to July 1947 was thought to be a little over $51 million while the probable expenditure looked like being in the region of $167 million. Tax was raised accordingly on those perennial cash cows, liquor and tobacco, and also on stamp duty, water, meals in restaurants, and on sweepstakes. Government financial pronouncements took on an aura of panic for some time. But, in the face of bankruptcy and to the government's evident surprise, recovery went much faster than anyone could have anticipated. The revenue figure turned out to be higher than had been predicted, at $81 million, while expenditure had shrunk to a manageable $85.5 million. Hong Kong was showing signs of that intense creative vitality which was later to characterize it.

The vociferous anti-income tax lobby, ever active, was side-stepped in 1947 by a technicality. A tax on personal income was not introduced, but in its place four taxes were announced — on property, profits, interest, and salaries. The Chinese community exploded in an uproar and petitioned the Governor, calling on him personally at Government House, and cabling the Colonial Secretary. Three unofficials of the Legislative Council voted against the budget in the vain hope that direct taxation would not become a permanent feature of the fiscal system. The budgeted surplus for 1948–9 was estimated at well over one million dollars — a calculation which turned out to be nothing short of a laughing matter when the actual surplus attained the heady altitude of $35 million. The resurgence of the battered colony could scarcely be described as anything less than exuberant.

On 26 February 1946, as if to mark the end of the painful chapter of defeat, occupation, and disruption of life, the Japanese war memorial which had been erected atop Mount Cameron was blown up, watched by large crowds of delighted people.

Sir Alexander Grantham, who succeeded Young in July 1947, had previously served 13 years in Hong Kong as a cadet officer. He knew the colony better than Young and was now to serve 10 years as Governor — the longest term of any. His concept of what Hong Kong needed in recovering from the war was strong government with a strong emphasis on the *laissez-faire* policies which had been at the heart of its livelihood from the beginning. This was especially pertinent within the general picture of events in surrounding countries. The People's Liberation Army was in control in China, taking the first steps to eradicate the worst evils of the decayed post-dynastic past; a bitter war raged in Korea in which East and West were heavily involved; and a civil war was in process in Indo-China, another in Malaya, and yet another in Indonesia. Instability, rising nationalism, and the gradual dissolution of exhausted colonial regimes characterized much of the Orient. Hong Kong appeared as almost the only place where no upsurge of dire anti-colonial feeling had yet taken place. The administration, accordingly, thought it prudent to encourage the population in getting on with its business with as little interference as possible. By 1948 it was apparent that this formula was working well. The government had in fact little to offer except a rice supply and a stabilizing influence on prices of food and necessities. Wise for the moment, it allowed people to find their own ways out of the slough of post-war problems. While the food situation remained fragile, and rationing was much disliked, they were accepted as necessary evils. Piece by piece the food trade was handed back to private enterprise, the last area being the meat trade which, with the continuing shortage of refrigerated shipping, was delayed until July 1957. The Hong Kong government also operated price and exchange control, the dollar being linked to sterling. No attempt was made to control the free market in other currencies.

By all yardsticks the revival of trade was remarkable. In 1946 the volume (excluding officially sponsored cargoes) was 50 per cent of the pre-war volume, and more than double in terms of value (because of the steep rise in costs since the war), China being the largest importer and exporter; 1947 saw exports reach $1,200 million and imports reach over one and a half million dollars. At this point trade began again with Japan. The total trade figure for 1948 leapt to $3,659 million, and 1949 saw a 30 per cent rise to $5,068 million. This strong upward trend continued apart from a period during the Korean war when the United Nations imposed an embargo on trading with China, which was supplying Communist North Korea. This caused a temporary slump. As industry expanded in the 1950s the increasing emphasis came to lie with domestic exports and less and less with the old entrepôt trade.

Such figures for the expansions of trade and local industry necessarily involved the banks, whose function in the colony had always been intimately linked to trade. At the time of the Japanese occupation the Hongkong and Shanghai Bank had transferred its head office to London, the move being effected by means of an Order in Council of 13 January 1943 in which the transfer was back-dated to 16 December 1941. In 1943 Arthur Morse assumed control of the bank under an order of the Colonial Office. At the end of the occupation another Order in Council (20 June 1946) passed all its stages in the legislature in a single session, and made it possible to call an annual general meeting — something that in the absence of enough directors to form a quorum had not been possible since the war. This permitted the general manager to become a director of the bank, and Morse became its Chairman.

Morse was a remarkable banker. With outstanding courage, he envisaged the role of the bank in the revival of Hong Kong's trade as a crucial one, and acted accordingly. Most traders had lost all their stocks, which in effect meant that each had to start from scratch. What was obviously neeeded at once was plant and the materials for reconstruction: equally obvious was the fact that companies could not acquire these until their internal positions were clarified and the situation of each company regularized and legal again. Morse, however, committed the bank to offering advances by opening confirmed credits which guaranteed payments to shippers while in fact, legally, no one but the bank itself could be called into account for the money; an extremely bold, unorthodox move at a time when there was no solid reason to suppose that trade would revive rapidly. Indeed there was scarcely an assurance that the colony would even remain British when Morse made his move.

After the war Hong Kong did its best to maintain a friendly relationship with China — if only for its own sake — dropping pre-war restrictions on immigration, and giving the Chinese Maritime Customs the right to collecting stations in Hong Kong and to patrol its waters. Significant assistance was offered to China in setting up her Gold Yuan currency, and the colony, which at the time could hardly afford the gesture, in 1948 sent 10,000 tons of rice on loan to Shanghai where food shortage was acute. The Japanese had removed the boundary stones marking the border of China and the New Territories, so British officials met their Chinese counterparts to replace them by mutual agreement.

With China's civil war ending, the Guomindang fleeing to Taiwan, and with Communist armies over the border, Hong Kong residents were understandably nervous. The new ruling force was still an unknown quantity. Britain did the only thing she could in the circumstances to minimize the possible effects on Hong Kong — she recognized the new regime in China in February 1950. This action was not greeted with any particular enthusiasm in Beijing, nor was it followed by many other countries in the near future.

The new situation of the colony of Hong Kong at this juncture, two years into the 10-year term of Grantham's governorship, was evident to all. The turbulent, aggressive events surrounding Hong Kong on all sides took a different and, it seemed at the time, extremely threatening aspect, fired in most cases by the heat of nationalism, a force inimical to the very existence of the colony. But, as if to balance this alarming situation, the first springing of a very energetic industrial growth was plainly visible in Hong Kong; and in the developed world, equally visible, was a hunger for goods of all kinds which the ravages of the war had eliminated or made scarce. Hong Kong had, at least potentially, most of the answers — a vast supply of willing labour, a leavening of skilled, experienced, well-funded Chinese and other industrialists and entrepreneurs ready to equip and re-equip themselves for the production of whatever the world wanted to buy. Hong Kong was a free port, its monetary system was stable, and it held firm to a policy of minimal government interference with business. These characteristics, with the enormous enthusiasm of the millions of displaced Chinese eager to make a new and better life for themselves, were to prove the foundation of the remarkable industrial, commercial, financial, and social changes which were to come. The page turned on the past. A new chapter of a qualitatively different nature was beginning.

22. *Population, Housing, and Education*

It must be unique in the annals of urban growth for a city to add in the space of just over five years 1,760,000 new inhabitants. When Hong Kong was liberated from the Japanese there were no more than 600,000 people left in it; by the end of 1950 it was estimated that the population stood at 2,360,000. The problems posed were of even greater magnitude.

The source of the metamorphosis which was then about to begin, the origins of what was to be the driving force, lay in the struggle for power in the civil war in China. The turmoil there, whose massive first statement, the Taiping Rebellion a century earlier, was eventually suppressed, signalled the inevitable demise of the Qing dynasty. The end came through the depredations of the Western powers, and was hastened by Japanese conquest; and clinched by the establishment of an unconvincing republic and by the civil war in which the Communist armies triumphed.

One effect of these terminal throes, an incidental product, was the endowing of Hong Kong at precisely the right moment with the commodity it required — people. From the millions of harried, displaced, destitute people of China, from its threatened industrial élite, and from their skilled and semi-skilled work-force, the colony began to be populated to an extent never previously envisaged. It was no El Dorado, but for them it represented hope.

As a base for Britain to watch over her Eastern interests Hong Kong had lost relevance — there were no longer any to oversee. The colony now had to be defended for its own sake. Hong Kong, however, was to prove that apart from its defence (its integrity was in the event not at stake) and its foreign affairs, it now had little need of the parent country.

From time immemorial the twin gratifications of making money and achieving success in society have formed the addictive magic of capitalism. Whether it be running a fleet of merchantmen, or selling noodles, money and success are the reward. In this the British and Chinese understood each other very well. Napoleon's comment about the English being a nation of shopkeepers could well have been expanded to include the Chinese. In its broadest sense shopkeeping involves nearly all the processes involved in other businesses. In Hong Kong the government had few peasants to contend with. It was a colony of city-dwellers, and the basis, the motive power which in a couple of decades was to transform the colony into one of the twentieth century's economic miracles, resided in the tacit mutual understanding of those Chinese and British shopkeepers on a commercial level. Their contact was seldom intellectual, as it was often enough in India, nor was it straightforward military occupation as in Gibraltar. The common interest was business, the two races completely understanding each other only in this sphere. And within Hong Kong's British society there never existed the acute class distinctions that divided British society in India into the ruling civil service and army élite, and the 'boxwallahs' — those in business and trade. No such stratification was feasible in Hong Kong since the whole *raison d'être* of life was 'boxwallah' trading, supervised by a civil service which had no loftier ideas than to do just that. Individual governors and other civil servants from time to time affected to despise the merchants. But they were never the best rulers.

The essentials in the making of the new Hong Kong were the sheer numbers of Chinese and their ability to work long hours, for themselves or for others, and generally to apply themselves and their families to the fullest extent in the process of making money.

In the appalling conditions in which most of the newly arrived work-force were obliged to live (and often to work), owing to the lack of appropriate available accommodation, the firm government expectation was that when the course of events in China had settled down the flood of humanity would reverse itself and return to China. This proved totally inaccurate. No such movement showed the slightest sign of taking place. On the contrary, the immigrants showed every sign of settling in the colony and making whatever they could of a new way of life in its comparatively stable conditions.

Britain now found herself saddled with a deeper moral commitment to Hong Kong. In response the Labour government in office in 1949 sent 30,000 troops to the colony to avert the slight possibility that the all-conquering Communist armies might attempt to take Hong Kong back to the bosom of the motherland. Had that happened, the government in London would have come under heavy fire in the then impending general election. The force stationed in Hong Kong could not have stemmed a determined Chinese take-over — there is no certain evidence that such a move was contemplated — and there were difficulties in keeping such a large force in a colony still metaphorically licking the wounds inflicted by the Japanese occupation. This was recognized by the Cabinet Defence Committee in 1952, and in April 1954 it was decided to reduce the garrison. The ships of the Royal Navy left for Singapore. In 1958 the Royal Naval Dockyard closed, and Britain's armed forces in the East shifted to South-east Asia and the defence of Sarawak and Sabah.

Among the major problems facing the Hong Kong government in the late 1950s were, first, housing, and second, education.

The immigrants lived how and where they could. Roof-tops sprouted improvised huts in danger of being blown away in typhoons. Shanty towns grew up on hillsides on the outskirts of the town wherever a trickle of water ran down a ravine, from where it was tapped, collected, and carried to those pitiful shacks for cooking and washing. Ingenious methods of collection were invented, coloured plastic tubes tethered at the source were strung out overhead like some artist's 'happening', to reach individual huts and groups of huts in festoons over the scrub. Sanitation was either absent or primitive, a hazard to public health. But in Hong Kong there was nothing very unusual in that. In town, every stairway in Chinese areas of Victoria and Kowloon had its restless sleepers with their little bundles of possessions clutched to them through the night. Every street where the pavements were wide enough had its clutter of lean-to shelters of cardboard, tar-paper, old corrugated iron, cocooned into some semblance of a dwelling where families were raised, and whose sanitation was the nearest public lavatory — no matter how far away. Not surprisingly the incidence of violent crime rose alarmingly, and by 1950 the government was forced to impose a quota for immigrants.

Shek Kip Mei in December 1953 after the blaze. The homeless return to search in the rubble of their homes.

The first resettlement housing built in Hong Kong was at Shek Kip Mei and housed those made homeless by the 1953 fire. The photograph was taken in 1958.

On Christmas Day 1953 the inevitable happened. The sprawling agglomeration of squatter huts in West Kowloon called Shek Kip Mei caught fire in the evening and, as flames and sparks flew in the cold dry winter air, soon the whole area was a swirling mass of flame — the biggest and most disastrous conflagration in Hong Kong's history. For the people of the ghetto now vanishing in smoke it was a night of terror as 50,000 lost their homes and (most of them) their meagre possessions.

The fire was a disaster which no government could tinker with. There had to be large answers as soon as possible in the shape of housing for the homeless thousands. The remarkable, courageous, and prompt response was the first of the massive rehousing programmes which have continued right up to the present day. The gravity of the situation led rationally to a long hard look at the whole question of housing for the mass of Hong Kong people, a tricky subject only nibbled at in the past. Despite all that had occurred, and all the sanitary and housing ordinances since the black years of plague and fire in the nineteenth-century slum of Taipingshan, house design for the Chinese in the colony had not advanced far. The pre-war population increase between 1937 and 1940 of 500,000 had provoked the construction of some new accommodation, but resulted in more crowding in existing housing and some degree of squatting. But with the massive return of the population after the Japanese defeat and the huge influx as China changed hands, the problem began to take on threatening dimensions. The picture of Hong Kong was by then one of pandemic squatting. Even with new migration virtually arrested in 1950, the city still had to find room for a natural annual increase of something like one hundred and twenty thousand.

Most of this multifarious population (other than squatters) was housed in structures whose design, in essentials, had hardly altered since the turn of the century. In these stews — there can hardly be a kinder description of them — generations of Hong Kong Chinese had been born and lived out their lives, sleeping in tiny cubicles in two- and three-tier bunks. An ordinance in 1955 was aimed principally at altering the basic shape of sites for the construction of tenement buildings, permitting access to living units from a corridor instead of through other people's living space. It also stipulated that housing of 10 or more floors must have lifts. The old walk-up government tenements of anything up to 10 floors now gave way to taller buildings with lifts.

Yet some of the new blocks such as those built at Shek Kip Mei to rehouse those whose homes were lost in the 1953 fire were little better than the old. A government report of 1963 records:

> faced with an initial heavy outlay of key money and with maximum rents, and encouraged by the . . . demand by others for accommodation, the new occupants of premises designed to comply with minimum Buildings Regulations requirements partitioned [them] off into cubicles . . . It was not unknown for 60 to 70 persons to be living in a three-room flat.[1]

Many buildings were constructed to nine storeys so as to avoid the regulation which dictated that a 10-storey structure must have a lift.

This was the general type of building, high blocks with lifts, which the government, via the Housing Authority set up in 1954, built after Shek Kip Mei and the 1955 ordinance. Later developments (growing affluence and new ideas on community housing) resulted in profoundly modified designs as the rehousing programme evolved and became more sophisticated. A new ordinance of 1966 resulted in buildings generally constructed on square sites, entry to each apartment being from a central core containing lifts. The rising expectations accompanying rising incomes forced improvements in style and finish, and such new blocks now offer Western-style apartments in complete and happy contradistinction to the insanitary dormitories of the old tenements.

Hong Kong's record between then and now in housing and rehousing the population is a subject for justifiable pride. If it took a century in coming to pass, at least the results equal or surpass similar schemes elsewhere. The task was, and still is, a colossal one, but the solutions are viable and humane.

In 1961 the government started building another type of housing to cater for low-income families living in overcrowded and sub-standard premises. The Housing Authority then began to produce dwellings for families of moderate means living in unfavourable conditions. These schemes all set a limit on the family income as a means of selecting suitable tenants. An ordinance of 1973 established a new Hong Kong Housing Authority which is responsible for the co-ordination of all aspects of public housing.

In public sector housing by 1984, rented and owned accommodation housed 2.4 million people, representing more than 44 per cent of the population. Another one million were scheduled to be housed before the end of the decade. The Housing Authority programme is constructed so as to produce 215,000 flats over the next few years to 1991, comprising 158,000 public rental flats, 32,000 home ownership flats, and a further 25,000 flats built for sale under arrangements with private developers in the Private Sector Participation Scheme.

The whole appearance of the New Territories, where most of these schemes are located, has radically altered in the post-war years. Until the early 1960s comparatively little change had taken place. Tai Po was still a large village, Yuen Long a smallish one. It was still possible to drive between the villages of the area (those to which a motor road existed) in rural, even rice-paddy terrain, in which in season the *lychee* and the *lungnan* trees were laden with fruit, and where Hakka women in the fields wore their distinctive black-valanced hats. The fashion among young Chinese for making country excursions in groups was still in its infancy, and the country was quiet and seemingly sparsely peopled. The fishing fleet still went out in junks under sail although most had auxiliary engines. Many country people still wore the traditional *sam fu* (smock and baggy trousers) of shiny black cotton. Rice-threshing could still be seen in village squares, and an occasional bride was borne to her wedding across the fields in a red-decorated palanquin, closed except for a small aperture through which her fan-shaded face occasionally peered out, men sounding gongs accompanying the little procession. The two great dams at Plover Cove and High Island were still in the future. The exodus of the younger people from the villages and from isolated islands had already begun, most of them making for Chinese restaurants in England; others to factories in Kowloon. Today there is scarcely a village where the old life continues. Tai Po is a large high-rise town, as are Yuen Long and the formerly charming village of Sha Tin. Others are rising; still more are planned.

In the development of private housing there is a similar story to tell. Several large new high-rise estates have been built on Hong Kong island, including Taikoo Shing estate and later the Kornhill estate on the eastern part of the north shore. Similar developments are sited on the southern shores and slopes where, in the public sector, some of the earlier housing estates were built. The 100-year-old Dairy Farm at Pok Fu Lam, gradually nibbled away in favour of accommodating people rather than cows, finally closed in its centenary year, milk now coming from a larger farm just over the China border. That waterfall so gratefully used by seafarers in the nineteenth century and before

Sha Tin seen from the hills above the Lower Shing Mun Reservoir in 1961 before the new town was begun.

as a source of pure water, is now overlooked by one of the first public sector housing projects — the towers of Wah Fu estate.

Naturally the southern exposure of the island long ago attracted the more affluent, and such bays as Deep Water, Repulse, and Stanley were colonized in the 1920s, their shores dotted with large villas. In 1963, the first high-rise tower was completed in the centre of Repulse Bay, and today the once verdant slopes all around support a solid, uninviting phalanx of luxury blocks, as do other favoured places. Lantau island has its purpose-built colony of luxury houses and there are several others of large extent in the New Territories.

The industrialization which provided the finance by which Hong Kong's public housing achievements were made possible started, as we have seen, in a fairly unsophisticated manner, with family-run small businesses producing goods urgently in demand post-war. But quite soon the types of manufacture which Hong Kong was called on to produce required the use of increasingly sophisticated plant. While to some extent the workers in such factories did not need to be more than semi-skilled, increasingly large numbers of employees did — in industry, in the supporting banking field, in engineering, statistical, insurance, clerical, and other sectors of the overall picture.

An aerial view of part of the new Sha Tin town in 1987, taken from a point similar to that of the opposite plate. Tall residential blocks are the latest design for resettlement housing.

Generally speaking, adequately qualified applicants have been available as these opportunities arose, and in the right kind of numbers, so it would appear that educational opportunities in Hong Kong have been in the main satisfactory, and have been grasped.

While the first post-war educational policies were directed to the rehabilitation of a shattered system, later efforts had to be directed, reflecting the generally liberal post-war climate of the West, to education of all children to the limit of their capacity to learn. At that time it was not foreseen that, starting in the early 1950s, Hong Kong would metamorphose from entrepôt to industrial giant, and vocational training was not then geared to that end. By the end of the Japanese occupation only a few thousand children were attending school, and the standard of what they were being taught and of the teaching was hardly adequate. Numerous school buildings were in ruins, classroom furniture had long vanished to heat the cooking pots, and what textbooks were available were too expensive for all but a tiny minority of parents to afford.

In Chinese tradition the road to success in life had always been through education. The existence of the Imperial Civil Service Examinations throughout centuries of history there — contrasting with their introduction in

Britain only in the nineteenth century — formed the central educational concept in Chinese minds. In Hong Kong the thirst for education manifested itself almost from the beginning of the colony.

By the end of 1946, 52,000 children were attending primary school, but only 1,205 were in secondary schools in urban areas. This compared poorly with the 78,151 and 14,109 respectively at the outbreak of hostilities.

Government spending on education in 1947 was nine million dollars, about half devoted to subsidization of schools. This was woefully short of what was required since something like six thousand children were still without education; 1948 saw the opening of a Technical College (derived from the old Trade School), and the Central British School was renamed King George V School, open to all children with an adequate knowledge of English. While primary education revived rapidly, secondary was slower with, in 1948, only two-thirds of the numbers of the pre-war period. Expenditure on education went up to $13 million in 1948, yet only just over half of the estimated quarter of a million children were attending school. The system, still prevalent today, of one school building serving as two primary schools, accommodated in morning and afternoon sessions, resulted from a shortage of school buildings.

Not until 1971 was the goal of free primary education for all those who wanted it achieved. In that year the total enrolment in all kinds of schools reached 983,495 pupils. A start was made then on enforcing attendance at primary schools. The government began to organize a three-year course of secondary education for all on a fee-paying basis in 1971.

The 1960s and 1970s saw advances in teacher training, and a curriculum development committee got down to work; the Hong Kong Certificate of Education examination was reorganized to permit greater flexibility in the choice of available subjects, and an educational television service was provided for primary schools and extended to secondary institutions at a later date. The 1974 White Paper stated the ultimate objective of a school place for all children who wanted secondary education, and was in effect a blueprint for educational advance in the following decade. The target was nine years of general education for all by 1979, a goal subsequently brought forward by one year. The White Paper of 1978 had as its major target the provision of subsidized senior secondary places for about 60 per cent of the 15-year-old population in 1981, set to rise to over 70 per cent in 1986. The education of teachers was further strengthened, and the curriculum further diversified and enriched.

The seventies saw great emphasis placed on balanced development. To achieve this in practical and technical education five technical institutes were built, offering a wide range of disciplines. The Hong Kong Technical College turned into the nucleus of the Hong Kong Polytechnic which, by the beginning of the eighties, offered places to about 26,000 full-time and part-time students. A continuous link was established in vocational education throughout the secondary school system, leading to a technological outlet in tertiary education.

In late 1981 a Secretary for Education was appointed, thus recognizing the crucial importance of education in the future development of the territory, and in that year a $320 million programme was announced, its aim to improve the standard of the English and Chinese languages in schools and in the community at large.

By 1981 there were over 1.4 million children in school in Hong Kong — 27 per cent of the population. Offsetting this was a generally held opinion that the slow rise in the numbers of students at the two universities might endanger the future of the territory's economic and social prosperity and development. (It may be noted in passing that about this time, and more insistently after 1984, the use of the word 'colony', without any official pronouncement on the matter, came to be replaced by the word 'territory', in genuflexion to the coming absorption of Hong Kong into the Chinese state.)

The general educational situation was investigated by a Panel of Visitors led by a former Director-General of the British Council, Sir John Llewellyn, which carried out a review between April 1981 and November 1982. They probed into all the relevant factors affecting education since the war and up to the present. The eventual report, a sympathetic document bearing the marks of a deep understanding of the special conditions in the territory and its struggle for educational facilities, made the point: 'We try to be practical in our commentary ... We prefer to point to desirable directions [which education might take] rather than to prescribe treatment for immediate ills.' The Panel identified five important areas. It recommended the universal teaching of children in Chinese in the 'formative years accompanied by formal teaching of English as a first foreign language: this would lead progressively to genuine bilingualism in the senior secondary years'. A second recommendation was for improvement in the 'capacity and commitment' of teachers. The criticism was that the language facility of teachers fell short of the recommended bilingual proficiency needed for effective teaching in that context. A third comment stated: 'Examinations dominate the Hong Kong education system, to its detriment.' The Panel pinpointed the need to relieve the strains caused by this and to improve the curriculum by making it 'more relevant to the development needs of the students'. A fourth aspect was the tremendous pressures 'from students, parents, and industry' for variously streamed education, revealing the need for greater diversity of educational opportunities available beyond Form VII, 'so this pressure can be relieved and individuals encouraged to choose from more varied provisions related more closely to their interests, to the requirements of the labour market, and to the community generally'.

The Panel's fifth suggestion was:

> the need to build up a standing capability to conduct research, to analyse and formulate policy options, and to plan developments. This impinges on the community, the professions, the bureaucracy, and statutory policy-making bodies. The governance machinery needs to be thoroughly overhauled.[2]

In due course much of the action recommended by the Panel was included in government policy.

By 1984 there existed four main types of secondary school — Anglo-Chinese grammar schools, Chinese middle schools, technical schools, and pre-vocational schools. The first had an enrolment of 375,673 pupils and offered a five-year course leading to the Hong Kong Certificate of Education examination, the medium of instruction being mainly English. Satisfactory results in this examination allowed pupils to enter a two-year course leading to the Advanced Level Examination for admission to Hong Kong University.

The 63 Chinese middle schools accommodated 36,841 pupils instructed mainly in Chinese, English being a second language.

Secondary technical courses claimed 21,571 students in 22 schools. Qualifying students were then able to continue their studies at the Hong Kong Polytechnic, or the Hong Kong Technical Teachers' College.

Pre-vocational institutions were government-aided secondary schools providing a general education and introducing students to a wide range of technical skills on which future vocational training could be based. In 1984 13 such schools provided 10,039 places.

Three post-secondary colleges were in operation, and various types of special education were available to meet the needs of handicapped children.

On the whole, Hong Kong responded well to the requirements of a population whose numbers were rapidly increasing. The growth of a very large and well-to-do Chinese middle class resulted in a commensurate demand for greater sophistication in education, with all that this entailed. There can be few communities in the world whose government and educational authorities have been faced with such an explosion in numbers, in financial clout, and in expectations for their children, in such a short time. The figures speak for themselves: in 1939 there were over 92,000 children in schools of all kinds. In 1984 the figure had risen to 1,377,432; this, despite the virtual wiping out of the whole educational system in the Japanese occupation.

The University of Hong Kong in the post-war years faced a formidable problem in rehabilitation. Loss of staff and equipment was serious, but by good fortune most of its library survived. The Senate had continued to hold meetings in Stanley camp during the occupation, while some of the students had moved to Lingnan University at Guangzhou where they had continued

The façade of the original buildings of Hong Kong University.

their studies — facts recognized in 1946 when the government voted $20,000 towards its rehabilitation. In Hong Kong the decision to reopen the university was made in July 1946, but no official action was taken until March 1948 when the Secretary of State endorsed the need for a university in Hong Kong. In fact the university was already functioning by then. Financial provision, however, was left, once more, to local generosity. Once again the university was 'condemned to that indigence which had dogged its fortunes'[3] since it was founded in 1912.

Anticipating the Colonial Office's tardy decision, the university had held matriculation examinations and the first classes began in October 1946 with 109 students of whom 31 were female, in arts, science, medicine, and engineering. This act of faith was to be justified when Sir Robert Hotung donated $1 million for the building of a women's hall of residence, and the government granted a capital sum of $4 million, and increased its annual grant to $1,500,000.

Pre-war enrolment had stood at 400 students. By 1970 there were 2,283, and by 1984 that number had risen to 7,000 studying in nine faculties — arts, architecture, dentistry, education, engineering, law, medicine, science, and social sciences. Competition for places at Hong Kong University, mirroring competition for other educational facilities in Hong Kong was, and still is, intense. In 1984, for the 1,618 places available at Hong Kong University there were 15,000 applicants. The arguments in favour of a third university seemed compelling.

The Chinese University was formed in 1963 with three autonomous colleges — New Asia College (founded in 1949), Chung Chi College (founded in 1951), and United College (founded in 1956) — as a self-governing corporation drawing its income chiefly from government grants. The campus occupies a fine site of 110 hectares on a hilltop near Sha Tin. The university has arts, business administration, science, and social science faculties offering bachelor degrees, and a faculty of medicine runs a five-year course of two years pre-clinical studies and three of clinical work. Further courses were inaugurated in 1984–5. Both Hong Kong University and the Chinese University offer extra-mural curricula.

The Hong Kong Baptist College, founded in 1956, runs courses in a similar range of studies. A Vocational Training Council was set up in 1982 to advise on measures to be taken to ensure a comprehensive system of technical education and industrial training suited to the future needs of Hong Kong. By 1984 there were five technical institutes in operation and three more planned, among a growing number of other bodies offering technical education of various kinds. Demand, however, continues mostly to outstrip the facilities for its satisfaction. But the general picture of Hong Kong education is a lively one in almost all spheres, with opportunities for recreational activities being continually upgraded.

23. Growth of an Industrial Giant

WHEN the war in Asia was over two of the basic essentials of Hong Kong's traditional trade — a supply of marketable commodities and adequate shipping to carry them — were both seriously depleted in the Orient and world-wide. Moreover some of the principal items in the entrepôt trade such as foodstuffs and textiles were among those in shortest supply and soon to be subjected to international allocation. Acute shortage of food, raw materials, and machinery for manufacturing was partly assuaged by an immediate post-war reallocation of stocks concentrated by the Japanese in various places in South-east Asia; and it was involvement in this that first brought a demand for the colony's entrepôt facilities, and later brought a rapid growth of business, in 1946. The last available pre-war figures (1939) show imports at $594.2 million and exports at $533.4 million. The 1946 figures reached $935.5 and $756.6 million respectively.[1] But the upsurge was not to be long sustained, and Hong Kong was soon again at the mercy of factors outside her control.

Trade with China, still under the Nationalists, and embroiled in civil war, was conditional on the antiquated process of using armies of coolies to load and unload at her ports (to which she forbade foreign entry). And the position was further complicated by the Chinese trade imbalance of US$412 million in 1945 which made it imperative for her to export more, and to introduce a system of licensing imports. In 1946 this was done, and categories were established; essentials such as raw materials for industry and manufacturing machinery were allowed entry with little formality, while most consumer goods were prohibited. In Hong Kong this had the effect of arresting the boom of the first nine months of 1946.

One important development was China's decision to export most of her textiles through Hong Kong, and it has been suggested that the experience thus gained in the colony may well have helped the growth of Hong Kong's own textile industry in the late 1940s.

As 1946 drew to an end, conditions in China became more disturbed, the civil war expanding with consequent disruption of life. Rampant inflation, restless movements of frenzied people seeking food, security, and a livelihood, together with labour unrest in the main centres, all contributed to the breakup of a bedraggled economy as the Nationalists suffered defeat after defeat and as the influence of the apparently unstoppable Communist armies waxed.

Stringent restrictions on imports meant that cargoes destined for Chinese ports were refused entry, and the colony's warehouses became the dumping ground of goods consigned originally to Shanghai, Tianjin, or other ports. The less securely financed of the colony's merchants failed, one after another, leaving trade largely in the hands of those bigger firms with which it had been for decades before the war. It was into this troubled commercial scene that there erupted a flood of Chinese from over the border: whole businesses and their manufacturing equipment arrived without notice and strove to set up in what seemed to them a blessedly stable environment.

In the last years of the 1940s China's share of Hong Kong trade fell sharply, its place quickly taken by the South-east Asian countries. With the Hong Kong merchants' ability to provide textiles from China in a textile-hungry hemisphere, opportunities opened up for trade in new markets in the Middle East as well, and also with East and South Africa. When the Communists finally became the masters in China in 1949, the flow of exports dried up. The South-east Asian, Middle Eastern, and African markets for textiles virtually fell complete into the hands of the colony's merchants and newly arrived manufacturers.

The Communist revolution in China sealed off that country from virtually any contact — business or other — which the new regime did not wish to entertain. Shanghai port was closed by the stationing of guardships at the estuary of the Yangzi, while the blockade of Taiwan made shipping in that quarter a hazardous venture. All trade, such as it was, with central and north China was routed via Tianjin and Qingdao, and exports from Shanghai came by rail via Guangzhou to Hong Kong. The period was also marked by the illicit export of goods via Macau. High-value goods from south-east China such as bristles and tung oil (used in paint manufacture) were chiefly carried by air, a means increasingly employed in trade at the time. The first train-load of export goods from China after the Revolution arrived in March 1950. But this traffic was suspended at the beginning of the Korean war in June 1950. The confused situation posed a challenge to Hong Kong merchants who continually varied the routes and the methods by which they acquired goods from China for export, but while trade with China dwindled to a trickle it was Hong Kong which monopolized it. The inflated prices of those years give the impression of a much greater volume than was the case, and by the first years of the 1950s a large number of merchant ships lay idle in Hong Kong harbour.

The advent of the Korean war, in which China backed the Communist North Koreans, dramatically altered the picture. Chinese government agencies began buying on a large scale, and to pay for what they were buying the export of produce restarted. Import licences were freely issued by China and, to the relief of Hong Kong's merchant community, the stocks in their godowns were quickly cleared. The goods in demand by the Chinese were those to support the war — petroleum and its by-products, rubber and manufactured rubber goods, vehicles and spare parts, industrial chemicals, machinery, and electrical appliances.

Hong Kong found itself in the position of the Chinese government's chief supplier and warehouse, on which it could draw on demand. In 1950 the tonnage of goods handled in the port leapt by 29.3 per cent, and the total value of trade by 48 per cent to $2,434 million.

But one more drastic change in the pattern of trade was to follow. In December 1950 the United States placed an embargo on the supply of strategic goods to China because of its participation in the Korean war, this to be followed in 1951 by the embargo placed for the same reason by the United Nations. American goods imported by Hong Kong fell by about 50 per cent, as did the colony's exports of Chinese goods to the United States. The Chinese reacted by allowing exports only to the value of imports. The entrepôt business of Hong Kong came effectively to an end.

Such, then, were the principal factors which were to affect Hong Kong during the 1950s and after: the decline in the entrepôt trade; the post-1949 influx of population and manufacturing facilities (labour, capital, and machinery); and the new Chinese government's policy of trading with other Communist countries rather than with its traditional suppliers.

Among that flood of humanity arriving in Hong Kong were men and women, both young and energetic, with an urge to get ahead in life by the use of their intelligence as well as their labour. Others were Chinese already established in life, who brought their considerable capital resources with them — among these the Shanghai textile industrialists whose entrepreneurial skills were now put to use in Hong Kong. At this time, too, there was an influx of capital and business skills from the West and from South-east Asia — the colony being seen as the most politically and economically stable place in the Far East.

Yet other things were working in favour of industrialization. As a British colony the territory enjoyed Commonwealth Preference and membership of the sterling area. While these two factors may not strike the contemporary observer as important (and they have long been abolished), in the aftermath of the war and in the period of doldrums following the embargo on trading with China they had a certain value. Membership of the sterling area made for stability in the Hong Kong dollar; Commonwealth Preference sharpened the competitive edge of products in certain markets.

The clinching element in the rise of industry was the *laissez-faire* capitalism which had been the spring on which Hong Kong had several times in the past rebounded from slump to boom. Government non-interference and the absence of official meddling, economic liberalism and the absence of foreign exchange controls, its status as a free port — all these made Hong Kong an attractive place to set up manufacturing.

It was at this point that there began to form a unique entity which can best be termed an industrial colony. From the start in 1841, Hong Kong had been unique in that it existed as a colony solely because the colonizers needed a secure base from which to expand their illegal trade in opium to China. More or less fortuitously it developed into one of the great entrepôt cities of the world, and so remained until the Japanese war. The war over, there occurred a second birth in different guise. Both manifestations of this strange colony existed without the semblance of material resources. Success came to the first with the opening of China to Western goods, and to the second, a century later, with the virtual cessation of that process due to internal Chinese events — which, incidentally, provided the manpower for its success.

As much as numbers, this manpower had a quality not possessed by the Chinese sojourners — the overseas Chinese — in Malaysia and Singapore, who are from many provinces of the motherland. The Hong Kong Chinese were and are virtually all Cantonese, speaking one version of the Chinese language, the Chiu Chow speakers and others being in such a small minority that they are forced to communicate in Cantonese. The Cantonese of Hong Kong, although not a homogeneous population — there are rich and poor, peasant and urban people — are unique in forming 97 per cent of the total population, more than was ever the case in any other overseas Chinese community in the Orient.

The growth of a manufacturing economy in Hong Kong, for every resident of the colony over the past thirty years, has been a visible, inescapable matter. In the mid-1950s an observer standing on one of the piers in central Victoria (by that time rarely so called in preference to the simple term Central), and looking over the harbour to the north-east, saw the shores of the Kwun Tong area as a virtually empty landscape of green scrub, with one or two small ship-breaking yards. A textile factory and a cotton-spinning mill began operation there at around that time, surrounded by open country. Standing at the same vantage point in 1984, three decades later, one saw that the green hills in the background had been gouged out and presented the raw wound of a vast quarry face, beneath whose ochreous scars there had risen a close-packed industrial area from which every trace of the natural landscape had long disappeared. Intervening between this and the viewer was the long extrusion of the airport runway at Kai Tak, built since the 1950s out into the harbour, serving what has become one of the world's busiest airports.

The industrialization of Hong Kong is an urban epic of perhaps unequalled

Tuen Mun, one of the huge new industrial towns which have sprung up since the 1960s, partly constructed on reclaimed land. What had been villages changed in a matter of a few years into large towns of hundreds of thousands, housing intensive industrial activity.

proportions. In a world still stumbling out of the ruins of the most disastrous war in history, Hong Kong was in the position to supply many of the manufactures that austerity and sheer lack of materials and manpower in that war had made scarce. It was also in the position of a débutante, unfettered by older-generation ideas, willing to equip itself for the exploitation of new processes and the utilization of new materials — and the satisfaction of new appetites.

Plastics were enthusiastically taken up by industry, and as they evolved in sophistication, gradually usurping the place of traditional materials, Hong Kong industry kept abreast of developments and explored the markets. One early product which came to be called in Japan (where the colony discovered a big market) 'Hong Kong flowers' was precisely that. But the fashion passed, as did another which was supplied by Hong Kong, the Western craze for wigs, which for a few years kept some factories running 24 hours a day.

Statistics demonstrate dramatically (in keeping with the actual process) the upsurge in the colony's economic activity in the 20-year period of its transformation into a world industrial and financial centre of mammoth proportions (see Appendix 8).[2]

Looking at some of the figures for 1984, the total gross domestic product had risen to $178,071 million (from $2,489 million in 1949), the total exports to $137,936 million, and imports to $153,955 million; the gross domestic product per capita also rose, to $33,197. The numbers employed in manufacturing in 1984 were 904,709 persons and the number of manufacturing establishments was 48,992. Workers' wages in manufacturing had shot up to $91 per day. In the money and banking sector total deposits in 1984 were $296,103 million and total loans $286,277 million. The revenue of the territory in 1984 reached $36,194 million while public expenditure was $32,338 million.

The activity of the stock exchanges, of which there were four until they were unified in the mid-1980s, by 1980 had almost reached the peak attained in 1973 before the oil crisis (see Appendix 9). By 1984 the figure for total turnover had reached $48,787 million, and the Hang Seng Index ended that year at 1,200.38 (31 July 1964=100).

In terms of the contribution of different economic sectors to the gross domestic product, the manufacturing industry has taken first place for many years, in 1983 contributing 21.9 per cent and in the following year 24.6 per cent.

The vast change in society in Hong Kong is signalled by the figures for money spent on the social services. In 1949–50 their share was 16.7 per cent of revenue; in 1984–5 the total rose to 35 per cent ($13,199 million). The percentages for other government functions in that year were: community services 9 per cent, general services 40 per cent, economic services 3 per cent, and security services 13 per cent.

To deal efficiently with the export of Hong Kong's massive product, and equally to take in its volume of imports, by 1984 the territory had constructed the largest container port in Asia — the third largest in the world, soon to become the largest.

The rise of the banking and financial services sector was equally surprising. In 1984 there were 140 licensed banks in operation, the numbers still rising steadily year by year, their assets in 1984 standing at $903,568 million, a figure which was soon to increase dramatically.

The rapid rise of tourism as a factor in Hong Kong's economy contributed over fourteen billion dollars in 1984 and the numbers of visitors rose to 3,500,000 (up by 12.9 per cent on the previous year). As many new hotels opened and further attractions were added to those already drawing tourists to Hong Kong, the figures looked promising for further increases.

In the past two decades the whole character of Hong Kong has altered radically. The sapling has become a great tree, almost overnight. While a walk around central London or Paris today certainly affords a different feeling from the same stroll two decades ago, the change is largely composed of an accumulation of small details. The place has been smartened up, might be one way of putting the facts. In Hong Kong a stroll through the principal

The waterfront in 1960.

When completed in 1962 the City Hall buildings were soon to be joined by the Mandarin Hotel (under construction, right of centre) and by the Hilton Hotel, under construction on the corner of Garden Road. The cricket ground behind the graceful old Hong Kong Club was still in use.

The panorama of Hong Kong and its harbour in 1988.

thoroughfares in the last year of the eighties reveals scarcely a building which was standing twenty years ago. One or two 'historic' piles remain — the old Supreme Court building, the tower block of the City Hall, new and very modern it seemed in 1962 and now dwarfed by all of its neighbours. Of the major buildings lining the streets of Central *three* decades ago only the Supreme Court and the Bank of China's old building still remain — all else has disappeared and the fabric of the city's centre is in reality a new construction.

The achievement of the early 1970s, a desperately needed amenity, was the completion of the first cross-harbour tunnel for motorized traffic, opened in 1972. By 1984 the tunnel had proved hopelessly inadequate for the rapidly rising number of vehicles using it, and another crossing under the eastern harbour opened in the last year of the eighties. This decade also saw the completion of a highway built above a further reclamation of the coastal waters of the harbour, linking the business district of Central with Chai Wan to the east. About the same time a highway linked the Kowloon peninsula with the China border, and vast improvements were made in the road system of the New Territories, in response to the needs of the new towns with their large populations and growing industry.

In the sixties and seventies a huge effort was made to provide Hong Kong with an adequate water supply. Plover Cove reservoir came first, completed in 1968, the sea drained from the cove after a barrage was built between a narrow peninsula and the village of Tai Mei Tuk along the coast from Tai Po. Later came High Island reservoir, similarly formed and adding another great libation. It has not, however, in the end proved possible to provide adequate water supplies for Hong Kong from within its boundaries. The major supplies come by pipeline from China which sells Hong Kong more than half of the 750,000 million cubic metres consumed annually in the territory.

Water shortages became acute in the early 1960s, and the queues formed as they had done in former days — only the receptacles differing (see p. 199).

More ambitious than any of those investments and developments was the Mass Transit Railway (MTR) which was begun in 1975 and took 14 years to complete at a total cost of over twenty billion dollars. This highly efficient underground railway, air-conditioned, clean, fast, and connecting huge centres of population, transports vast numbers of people daily which it would not be possible to transport on the roads. During its construction the old Kowloon–Canton railway (KCR) was modernized, double-tracked throughout, and electrified. The MTR and the KCR are integrated at Kowloon Tong station, effectively forming one system. The influence of these expanded and new transport facilities has been profound. New patterns of traffic and population movement have emerged. What were to all intents and purposes two separate cities, Hong Kong and Kowloon, have merged in a way which could never have been achieved when their sole connecting links were ferries across the harbour.

The first of the new reservoirs constructed to supply the needs of a rapidly rising population and growing industry was formed at Plover Cove in 1968.

The ferries still run, and the harbour, diminished by extensive reclamations on both sides since the last war, is probably more alive with boats of all types and sizes than at any time in its history. Long gone are the junks, but multiplied as if by spontaneous generation are the ferries linking numerous parts of the territory. Joining conventional vessels are hovercraft that make their swift way up the yellow waters of the Zhu Jiang to Guangzhou and other centres, and the skimming hydrofoils and jetfoils plying every few minutes between Central District and Macau, where that old city has in the past twenty years wakened from its Rip Van Winkle slumbers. Now crowded with new hotels, the mecca of Hong Kong's compulsive gamblers, Macau is experiencing a reawakening, in large part a reflection of Hong Kong's expansion.

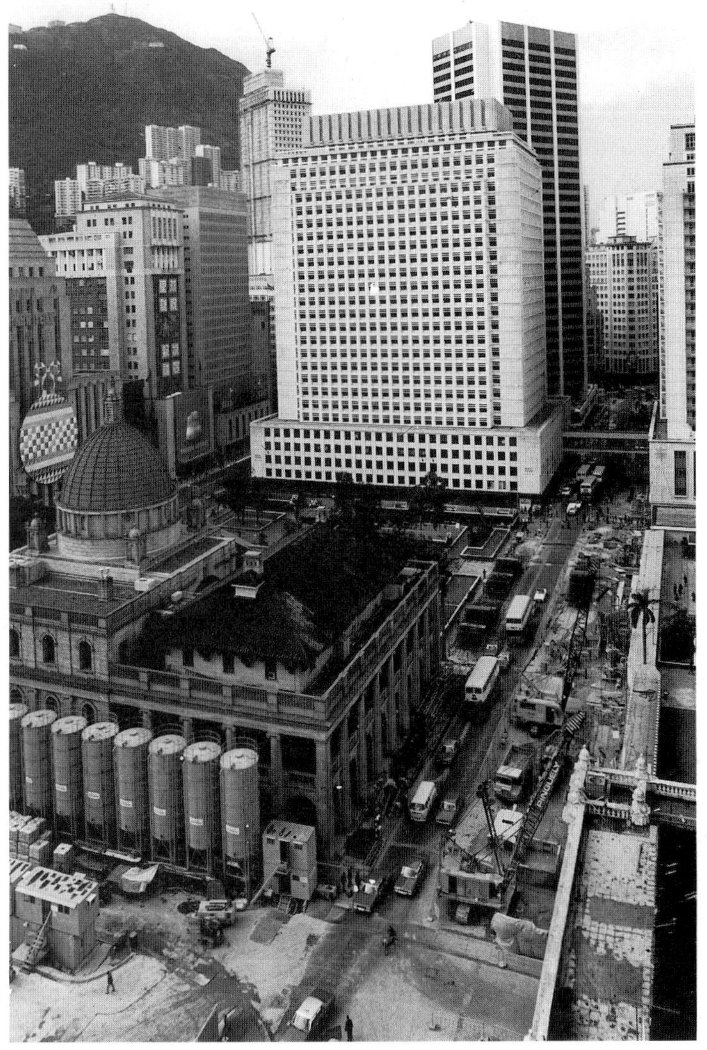

The construction of the Mass Transit Railway, Hong Kong's Underground or Metro, disrupted life for some time.

In Hong Kong also gambling is still a passionate preoccupation with the man in the street. The old racecourse in Happy Valley, during the past few decades equipped with huge grandstands, still functions. The new course at Sha Tin in the New Territories, larger, with even bigger stands and amenities, opened in the mid-1980s and draws crowds whose wagers form the wealth of the Royal Hong Kong Jockey Club. The Club is the largest financial benefactor of Hong Kong, annually donating hundreds of millions to an array of charitable organizations whose needs would otherwise have to be met from the public purse. Hong Kong, it seems, prefers to lose its money by gambling rather than by the surgical incision of income taxation.

In the seventies and eighties Hong Kong has acquired a cultural life, something which it all but lacked before. The occasional visiting theatre companies of the past which entertained the Western population, and the performances of Chinese opera enlivening Chinese festivals, were almost all the art to be discovered in the territory, historically speaking. With post-war internationalization and a rapidly enlarging affluent society came art in its various forms. The visual arts, slow starters because of the long-acting delicious drug of Chinese traditional painting, made an electrifying break-through to the present in the late 1960s when a handful of younger artists developed into painters of stature pioneering new styles. The influence of one man of genius, Lui Shou-kwan (Lui Shoukun), founded a school from which its adherents branched off in their own directions in due course, so that by the first years of the seventies Hong Kong was the leader in contemporary Chinese painting. The catalyst was the impact of Western art and, no less, Western styles of life — as surely as black African rhythms had proved the mainspring in the jazz revolution in America and later the whole world.

The formation of the Hong Kong Philharmonic Orchestra and of various Chinese groups playing old and new Chinese music added a dimension previously lacking in the territory, as did the formation of a resident theatre company playing in Cantonese and English, and a fledgling ballet.

The beginnings, the almost furtive infiltration of appreciation and practice of contemporary arts in Hong Kong, may be traced to the opening in 1962 of the City Hall with its large and smaller auditoriums, affording a home for music and theatre, and for the less commercial aspects of the cinema. Slowly other venues opened, the Arts Centre with theatre and art galleries came in the seventies, the Academy for Performing Arts a decade or so later. In 1972 the *South China Morning Post* began to print regular reviews of art exhibitions and was followed by other publications. Magazines devoted to, or noticing, the arts in major features slowly multiplied as the impact of television was felt. Art exhibitions, once a rarity and mostly of determined parochiality, are now plentiful. Some at least of the work of modern and contemporary artists from the West, from Japan, and elsewhere is shown quite frequently, and large commercial companies have in the past decade begun to patronize the arts in a meaningful way. The phrase 'cultural desert', once heard with depressing frequency (and accuracy), is no longer apt.

Culturally, Hong Kong has, superficially and some depth down, internationalized. But the infusion of Western modes and philosophies in the arts has at best produced a series of variants which bear a singularly Chinese flavour. Culture, if not readily transplantable, is almost infectiously adaptable.

Hong Kong, in the decades of its gigantic explosion in population and productivity, has become a place quite unrecognizable from its pre-war self. Not only is its *raison d'être* basically a different one, but it has become an intensely metropolitan place, a city in which a curious and not unpleasing form of sophisticated Chinese life flourishes. It has a core of diamond hardness as have all great cities, different in quality from the feeling of Chinese Singapore, infinitely more worldly than any city of China itself. The atmosphere is a combination of Chicago, Detroit, and New York, with special intensity lent to it by the dominant Chinese inhabitants, beavering away at their absorbing quests of making money and enjoying themselves. These aspects are combined also with a certain European ambience. Hong Kong exudes success in the manner of a sophisticated magnate, somewhat *nouveau riche*, a little parvenu. But in its boisterousness and in its riches, it is a wonderfully alive and exciting city to live in.

24. *Corruption and the ICAC*

One of Hong Kong's urgent problems in the decades since the war, a problem mirroring to an extent and in a Chinese manner those of cities such as Chicago which showed the same rapid development and access of riches, has been how to moderate the results of the arrival and redistribution of wealth that tumbled like summer rain into the community. The events of the post-war years have been turbulent, in part as ever because of pressures from outside the colony, but as acutely from the rapid social changes taking place within.

Conflict between the British and the Chinese had often centred on their differing concepts of law. The laws of China, customary, unwritten, were intended like those of other nations to establish and maintain harmonious human relations in a society with sufficient means of material survival. Those of Britain, with the same aim were, however, written. The conflict resided as much in the difference between the two civilizations as revealed in their laws as in the laws themselves. The British concept of the absolute right of people to trade reflected a powerful free society: the Chinese concept that trade was a privilege granted by an emperor reflected a largely self-sufficient society which had always lived under authoritarian rule. The responsibility for an unlawful act was to the British that of the person who committed it: to the Chinese the responsibility was the same, but should the culprit not be discovered, then his family, village, or association bore the responsibility and had to pay the penalty.

In Hong Kong, the only urban place where the British had ruled a homogeneous population of Chinese, the two concepts of law came frequently into conflict. It seemed that the differences between the two civilizations were only reconcilable if aspects of one or the other succumbed. This did not happen in any important way until some time after World War II.

At the core the disparity between Chinese customary law and British written law lay to a large extent in the absence in Chinese tradition of the slightest tendency towards a democratic process. Democratic ideas were, after all, quite as foreign to the Chinese as socialist ones (and doubtless

Confucian principles as a foundation for law would be found uncomfortable to live with in a Western country). The fact that Britain had a history of democracy in theory and practice (if rather recent in the latter), and that China had a very long history of Confucian imperial rule in theory and practice, were the constructs of their differing histories and environments. The world's greatest achievements have occurred under democratic, Confucian, and several other types of law. No people or nation has a proprietary right to sole possession of the attributes of civilization.

Chinese society had long been ordered by a Confucian concept termed 'filial piety', meaning respect for persons, especially older males. Hence sons (and all female members of a family) respected and obeyed the father; and the father paid respect to his father and elders; and so on up the pyramid of officialdom to the semi-divine emperor. The emperor bowed only to the gods, and all Chinese were regarded as his spiritual children (we may note the word 'children') — the 'seed of the dragon'. The principal system of advancement was via the civil service examinations from among whose successful candidates there emerged the administrators of the future, with whom under imperial guidance all authority and means of government lay.

In practice, the focus of all real authority was the local magistrate who administered justice, settled disputes on the basis of customary law and Confucian ethics, and had to be petitioned in regard to most requests of a serious nature. The omniscience, the Confucian benevolence supposed to characterize all holders of office, who in turn were answerable to a chain of higher authorities, was often more theoretical than real. Magistrates were pitiably ill paid, and this, with 'human nature', led to what became an institution in itself — the exaction of higher taxes than was permitted, the magistrate creaming off a percentage before remitting the taxes to the imperial treasury.

Hence, as every Chinese knew from childhood, to reach the ear of the magistrate with a request, it was necessary to offer a sweetener to one of his clerks. This was not thought of in the British sense as bribery, nor as gaining an unfair advantage. Life with its problems had to be lived by all and the wheels of authority had to be oiled.

Hong Kong law was British law with certain modifications, and was respected perhaps as much in the breach as in the observance. We have seen numbers of instances of Westerners in breach of the law — venal policemen paid by illegal gambling houses are matched by the equally venal Duddell in his double dealings, and by crooked lawyers. In essence it was the conflict of ideologies and its exploitation by both British and Chinese that led, after scandals had racked the colony, to the setting up in 1974, at the instigation of the then Governor, Sir Murray MacLehose, of the Independent Commission Against Corruption — the ICAC. This Draconian body was at first viewed with dire suspicion, seen by some as a governmental Gestapo or secret police.

But, with its brief to deal without fear or favour with rich and poor, high and low, official and ordinary citizens residing in Hong Kong, it has in the intervening years come to occupy a position of cautious acceptance and some respect.[1]

The post-war upsurge in corruption in Hong Kong on all levels and on a grand scale was in some degree a response to the opportunities offered in a thriving city, with a more or less booming economy, and an absence of official interference in the ordinary affairs of its citizens. Public opinion among the Chinese did not sharply define the subject. The possibility of argument between moralists (corruption is a sin) and fundamentalists or pragmatists (oiling the wheels assists harmonious movement) is a topic of endless debate. Samuel Pepys, Secretary of the Admiralty and president of the Royal Society in the latter part of the seventeenth century in London, was highly thought of in his time as a good civil servant. Everyone knew he lined his pockets, but it was also known that he was not extortionate in so doing. Time and place come into the equation. Hong Kong lacked a Chinese mandarinate in the traditional sense, and it also lacked an élite in the British one; it lacked therefore the sanctions of traditional authority. These considerations are not advanced as an 'excuse' for corruption but as elements in its rise and spread. Sir Hercules Robinson with his cadets had attempted to inject an artificial élite into the civil service, with generally favourable results — few cadets fell by the corrupt wayside. But for the rest of the community — the 'Aristocracy of the Moneybag', to recall Carlyle's damning phrase — Hong Kong society, Western and Chinese, did not lend itself easily to Western rigidity on moral matters. Merchants are by nature pragmatists, as are many Chinese.

April of 1966 saw events which had no precedent in the colony. The first was the appearance of a lone protester garbed in black, who sat in the Star Ferry concourse on the 4th of April from 9 a.m. until the last ferry had departed. On his clothing was written in white: 'Hail Elsie! [Elliot, Urban Councillor] Join hunger strike to block fare increase. Democratic'. This referred to the ferry company's request for a rise in fares of both first and second class accommodation on the cross-harbour run. The government had allowed a 5 cent increase on the first class fare and none on second class. The youth was seen by most people as a crank. On the second day of his 'hunger strike' he was arrested for obstruction. He played no further part in the story.

But what he had achieved (with the incautious assistance of the media) was a focus on the 'youth problem' which was in part a product of the 1960s permissive society phenomenon in the West, and in part a reflection of the so-called Cultural Revolution in China.

There followed three nights of rioting in Kowloon where startled tourists and citizens alike could scarcely believe their eyes as youths rampaged up and down the 'Golden Mile' of Nathan Road. Not one of these rioters was really protesting about a fare increase — few would ever have travelled first class — but it seemed they were motivated, initially at least, by a fear that rising prices were not being properly compensated for by wage rises. There was, too, a certain communal unease at this time, possibly stemming from the failure of the Canton Trust Bank the previous year (1965) in which its 114,000 depositors recovered only 25 per cent of their savings. This had been followed in the February of that same year by the spectacle of the large Hang Seng Bank running into difficulties. The crisis of confidence had been eased by the intervention of the government and the Hongkong and Shanghai Bank which had stepped in and taken over the Hang Seng. Yet another factor in the violent reaction to what was hardly a life-threatening situation may be seen in the Chinese memory of the appalling period when, in its terminal phase, the Nationalist government of China failed to avert the complete collapse of the currency and an untold number of people lost all they had.

The second night of demonstrations saw more rioting in Kowloon and the stoning of police by crowds of youths swelled by others who appeared to join in when they saw the 'fun' becoming more promising. By 8 April the police were in control; 1,400 youths were arrested, one rioter was killed; looting had been severe.

An official enquiry was held, in dramatic circumstances, with the Commissioners led by the Chief Justice, Sir Michael Hogan, seated under the floodlights on the stage of the City Hall Theatre, the audience seated as if attending a play. The tangled, bungled travesty of a procedure which unfolded during the hearings of this ill-conceived Commission need not concern us in detail here. A few facts tell the story. Elsie Elliot, an Urban Councillor, renowned for her support of the 'little man' in his troubles in a new, brash city society, was subjected to harsh and harassing questioning on her alleged part in 'inciting' some of the original demonstrators, which was not proven. She was also brought into the equation by the police who virtually accused her of being a common troublemaker. Certainly she was, on her own admission, a tireless writer of protesting letters to the police on behalf of hundreds of ordinary Chinese, who had no recourse other than to her good offices in their attempt to right wrongs done to them. But the side-effect of her persistence in citing police corruption brought to an acute stage the course of the Enquiry, with the suspicion hovering in the minds of most that the police were 'gunning' for her because she was not only a thorn in their flesh but, more seriously, a potential danger to them.

The Commissioner of Police, Henry Heath, an old-school policeman, was largely distinguished by a fierce loyalty to his force. In them he could see no (or at least hardly any) evil. He was almost comically out of his depth in terms of what constituted the possible bases for the concept of corruption. When Mrs Elliot accused the police of specific cases (on the evidence of a police source which she would not identify because of probable reprisals), the Enquiry reached a climax. She was, as all now acknowledge, merely restating the knowledge of the ordinary person of the colony on the extent of police corruption; but her official audience refused to credit her. Her statements (rightly, as it turned out) were seen by the police as threatening a very lucrative way of life. The time was not ripe for these revelations; it was only later that it all came out.

The Enquiry censured Mrs Elliot, Sir Michael sentencing her (because there was nothing to which he could legally send her for trial) 'to the bar of public opinion where she must meet the censure and repudiation of all those right-minded people who believe in the freedom of the innocent from the taint of unwarranted suspicion and in the principles of frankness and fair dealing in the affairs of men'.

In the history of judgements and in the affairs of Hong Kong men — in the light of what was to be uncovered in the near future — these words must be seen as appalling flummery. The Enquiry proved nothing except that police corruption was to continue.

All unintentionally, the Enquiry had opened a can of worms. The ordinary person, reading its proceedings in the daily press, saw then the obscene wriggling, and smelled the stench which is said to emanate from corruption. The Commissioner of Police had admitted that there was some corruption in the police force 'but not the worst' in relation to that in other departments of government. He also stated that the police needed bribes to pay off their informers!

The Enquiry was obviously baffled about the cause of the riots, stating (in 2,400 pages) that they were not caused by 'political, economic, and social frustrations'. Lethbridge, wittily and appropriately, quotes Auden's lines:

The situation of our time
Surrounds us like a baffling crime.[2]

Once more Hong Kong had excelled itself in a scandal of monumental proportions. Worse was to follow. In due course the whole devious process of the enforcement of law and order came like some carbuncle to a head for all to see. There was an intermission before the crisis and lysis of the last act.

The events of the intermission were largely a reflection of the ongoing Cultural Revolution across the border in China. On 6 May 1967, not long after the conclusion of the Enquiry, a dispute took place between workers and management at the Hong Kong Artificial Flower Works at San Po Kong. In the context of a tense situation the dispute was inflated by the interested parties to absurd proportions. A fever of violence overtook the colony, and for six months clashes occurred between throngs of hysterical demonstrators, egged on by agitators and activists of various persuasions. Large numbers of them were involved, becoming progressively more aggressive under what was

Demonstrators in May 1967 chanting and waving the Little Red Book outside Government House.

evidently a well-organized leadership. Mobs rampaged through the streets in defiance of police orders, causing considerable apprehension amongst the populace. Those who could afford to do so left for safer places, taking with them their valuables.

The climactic pitched battle between a chanting, screaming, Red Book-waving Maoist mob and the police came as the former attempted to move up Garden Road towards Government House, intent on holding an anti-government demonstration there, as they had previously done. They were stopped by police on the corner by the Hilton Hotel. Provoked by the dangerously aggressive crowd, the police launched a classic baton counter-action, arresting numbers of them before they melted away. A game of cat and mouse was then started by the mobs, confronting the police in areas such as Wan Chai where its narrow streets and lanes served as escape routes. The mob would attack, and move away partially or wholly, causing the police to follow, only to reappear on the flank or even at the rear down some other street. The formerly passive police role had necessarily to become an active one involving raids on suspected premises and searches in which incriminating documents were discovered.[3]

In the face of this acute threat to life and limb, and to the government of Hong Kong, police action was generally applauded. Demonstrators who attempt to stab out the eyes of policemen and are caught in the act by cameras are not likely objects of much public sympathy. The police, overnight, turned into heroes. As a force they carried out their duties in exemplary fashion, and numbers of individual officers acquitted themselves with great courage. Criticism of the force, which had been simmering in the wake of the riot Enquiry, died a natural, if temporary, death. Some senior policemen displayed conspicuous gallantry in various episodes during raids on Communist premises. The Chinese police, who were portrayed in the left-wing press as 'running dogs of the Imperialists', also distinguished themselves in episodes requiring a like courage. The police were, for perhaps the first time in their history, popular figures.

When the confrontation was over the death toll was 51: of these, 15, including Chinese children, were killed in a bomb explosion; 10 were police officers. Over two hundred persons were wounded, several severely. Hong Kong business men set up a fund to help the further education of policemen's children; Her Majesty The Queen honoured the Hong Kong Police Force with the prefix Royal; and the Governor, the imperturbable Sir David Trench, went on playing his rounds of golf at Fanling within hail of the border and the gesticulating masses beyond it. Cricket, which had been played on the most valuable piece of sports ground in the world in the heart of Central, under the bemused gaze of Communist workers in the Bank of China adjacent, also went on as usual with the stone-throwing, yelling mobs periodically charging round the perimeter. It was a splendid, late, vintage demonstration of that nineteenth-century heyday-of-the-British-Empire spirit. But the end of the confrontation came not so much as a result of stern British action in the colony, as from the Chinese over the border issuing orders to cool the ardour of their supporters in Hong Kong.

Meanwhile, engaged in crowd control and in making deterrent raids, the police had no time to attend to the more usual forms of law-breaking. Crime flourished as never before. The Triad societies had collaborated with the police during the Maoist uprising — not wishing to see their lucrative territory taken over by leftist puritans. When calm returned they were found to be more deeply entrenched in crime, and more involved as spies and informers with the police than before.

The real nature and extent of what was afoot in the miasma of corruption that hung about the colony was aired initially in an article written in 1970 by an often aggressive custodian of public morality, Leo Goodstadt, in the *Far Eastern Economic Review*. It was headlined: 'Squeeze is a way of life in Hong Kong'. The thought was hardly new. But its accuracy and its public expression were disturbing to the ordinary Westerner and also to the police. The Chinese assumed that government departments were in some degree corrupt; but for the British, whose heads were half-hypocritically, and in some cases actually innocently, buried in the sand of unknowing and reluctance to credit such unsporting practices, the shock administered by the publication was deeply unsettling. Why, they asked, did the government allow such a state of affairs to come about, and how could they have let it continue to such alleged proportions? The Governor, Sir David Trench, on television in the late 1960s, failed to make any reply to the question put to him. His successor, Sir Murray MacLehose, was more frank, in October 1973 agreeing that corruption had been 'on a more extensive scale than I had realised'.

In the ensuing period the various aspects of the problem loosely named corruption began to become evident. Corruption, at base, is essentially a concept that springs from the democratic idea. In corrupt practice you and another — the contact — are conspiring to gain an advantage (whether monetary or other) which is not available legally in that society. In a society where the law or the custom does not prohibit such transactions, at least when they are of a petty nature, then the transaction is not precisely corrupt. Hence in the mind of those brought up in such a society — the society of Pepys's time in England, of China down the dynastic ages, and most assuredly in late Qing times — corruption is a concept which is much more vague, not generally thought of as affecting the ordinary man in the street, but rather an affair of high places. This is not the case in a developed democratic society. In Hong Kong the majority of the populace belonged to a non-democratic tradition, but the tiny minority of Westerners, specifically the British since it was they who ruled, were brought up to regard corruption as reprehensible.

In Hong Kong large numbers of otherwise 'respectable' persons had from the initiation of the colony lived and worked in corrupt dealings of one kind and another — the opium trade being one socially tolerated example. Hence the police force, mostly Chinese, and its higher officers, both Chinese and British, had in theory divided views on the subject. In practice a small number of the British content of the force viewed corruption as anathema, another section as one of the perquisites of office in the Orient where (they would aver) corruption was a way of life. These men had long participated in that alleged way of life.

To eradicate corruption from such a force presented a problem of appalling complexity. It involved Chinese reactions to the possibility of being deprived of a healthy source of extra income regarded as normal 'perks', similar views on the part of the bribe-taking British officers of whatever rank, and the isolation of the few uncorrupt policemen in the force.

The knowledge of widespread corruption was not new — the 1946 Pennefather-Evans investigation[4] had delineated it, and Duncan MacIntosh, the next Commissioner of Police, avowed that 'he had never seen such widespread corruption anywhere else'.[5] This was in 1946. The question can was how to set police to catch police, and the Anti-Corruption Branch established within the CID and given autonomy in 1952 failed to do much about it. In the 1960s, as everyone knew, it was necessary only to have $400 in cash in order to obtain a driving licence — the ability to drive was irrelevant.

The case of Peter Godber in 1973 brought the matter to a scandalous head. Godber had been promoted to second-in-command of the Kowloon District in late 1971. He had been decorated with the Colonial Police Medal for Meritorious Service in 1968, having acted with great courage during the troubles of 1967. In April 1973 the Commissioner of Police, Charles Sutcliffe, was given information privately that Godber was sending considerable sums of money out of Hong Kong. This led to an investigation by the Anti-Corruption Branch which discovered that Godber's resources came to about $4.3 million — six times his salary between 1952 and 1973. It is still not known how much he was really worth — certainly many times that. Godber had asked in the year previously to take early retirement and this had been granted for 20 July 1973. He now asked to be allowed to leave at the end of June, doubtless realizing what was in progress. This was refused. When served with a notice on 4 June, he fainted. He was given a week to 'make representations'. His wife left the colony on 7 June, and in spite of security checks at the airport, Godber himself left for Singapore *en route* to Britain on the following day. He knew that he could not be extradited from Britain for being in possession of resources or property disproportionate to his present or past emoluments, since this was not a crime there.

This saga was widely reported in the colony's newspapers, and also in Britain. The report of the ensuing investigation recommended numerous changes in various aspects of the police force in Hong Kong. On 17 October 1973, the Governor Sir Murray MacLehose, in a speech to the Legislative Council said: 'The escape of Godber was a shocking experience for all of us.' And he went on to argue for an independent anti-corruption unit:

> it is quite wrong, in the special circumstances of Hong Kong, that the police ... should carry the whole responsibility for action in this difficult and elusive field. I think the situation calls for an organization, led by men of high rank and status, which can devote its whole time to the eradication of this evil ...

Sir Murray, then, was the prime mover in the creation of the ICAC. The Governor at this point reached the height of his popularity, his tall presence and entire rectitude exactly what were needed. The ICAC was formally set up on 15 February 1974, its arrival on the scene accompanied by much natural but in fact unwarranted optimism that Hong Kong would soon become a 'clean city'. The depth of *institutionalized* corruption, and its effects on life in the police force as well as in other circles, was hardly appreciated at the time. Those effects were soon to show themselves — with near disastrous consequences.

The Governor, Sir Murray MacLehose, and Lady MacLehose in November 1971.

The ICAC had serious recruitment problems, but under its excellent first head, Mr (later Sir) Jack Cater, it established itself as a permanency. Its prosecution of Godber on an extraditable charge in 1975, and his imprisonment, made a deep impression on the public which was strengthened by the Governor's appointment of Mr (later Sir) John Prendergast, an officer who had worked in Hong Kong previously and was highly respected, as Director of Operations of the ICAC.

In the years that followed, the ICAC concentrated on a series of targets with considerable success. The commissioner in his 1975 review could state that it had been a year of consolidation and 'of preparation for the titanic struggle which lies ahead. For our aim is to break the back of organized, syndicated corruption within the next year or two. 1976 and 1977 are going to be crucial and testing years both for the commission and for the community of Hong Kong.'[6] These were prophetic words.

By 1977, so successful had the ICAC been in prosecuting crooked policemen that those who had already retired had started leaving Hong Kong for safer places, safe from the sudden, before-dawn appearance of its officers at the door and arrest on charges of corruption before retirement. But in the serving force very large fortunes were still being made through syndicated means. In March 1977 the Commission had under investigation no fewer than 23 big corruption syndicates, 18 of them operated by police. By July the Commissioner could report to the Governor that 'no major syndicates were known to exist'. It was this radical cleaning of the nest which proved to be the flashpoint.

With the arrest of 59 sergeants of the Wan Chai Division in 1976, staff had to be transferred to that Division from elsewhere, and a situation had arisen unequalled in its gravity even by the 1897 corruption scandals. The culminating event was the Wan Chai conspiracy trial in which 12 police officers and three civilians were charged with conspiracy to pervert the course of justice and to accept bribes. Police morale plummeted as a result. They felt beleaguered, betrayed by their higher officers. One expatriate Senior Superintendent shot himself after much aggrieved talk about the deleterious effects of the ICAC on police morale. Morale declined in parallel with the decline in police revenue from corruption, a loss of income made graver by the clamp-down on vice establishments from which much illegal money fell into police pockets.

In October 1977, 140 police officers of the three Kowloon divisions were arrested for alleged involvement in syndicated corruption. On 25 October, 34 police including three British superintendents were arrested and detained. This led to the organization of rallies by groups of police to publicize their claims that the ICAC was indulging in harassment. Delegates called on the Senior Superintendent (Administration) of Kowloon and were advised to put their complaints in writing. The next day about three hundred Kowloon police gathered and drafted a letter to the Commissioner of Police. This nine-point document was a curious mixture of special pleading and self-commiseration. Among its complaints were that the ICAC used convicted persons to obtain evidence against policemen on the promise of reduced sentences, which they stigmatized as 'moral corruption' and 'highly prejudicial to the officers involved'. The ICAC was 'perverting the course of justice' by such acts. The hardship caused by early morning arrest and the long period of detention after arrest was felt to be 'particularly burdensome on long-serving officers who have shown their loyalty in many ways, including the 1967 riots'. Senior officers knew of corruption syndicates but took no action, so why were junior ranks penalized? They complained also of the likelihood that criminals would make false allegations against police which would be believed. The document's general conclusion was that all forms of victimization should cease.

The Police Commissioner's response was a statement couched in the level, flat jargon of officialese, and was a model of conciliation:

> I want you to know that there is no lack of concern on my part over the matter of certain aspects of investigations into allegations of corruption in the Force. I realise too the strain that these investigations have placed . . . throughout the Force. I have sought to ensure that members of the Force are treated no differently from others similarly under ICAC enquiry . . .

This cut absolutely no ice. On 28 October at about 9 a.m. some two thousand Hong Kong island police gathered at Edinburgh Place where they were joined by the Kowloon contingent. After a few words from a Chinese superintendent they left, chanting slogans, for Police Headquarters in Wan Chai. In a car park close by the Commissioner's office, they massed. Five rank and file delegates then went in to see Commissioner Slevin (known as the 'Invisible Man'). After an hour they emerged and relayed the message that Slevin had agreed to the formation of a rank and file association, in effect a form of trade union, at least in principle. The large group then disbanded, cheering. But from its midst a small breakaway body marched to Hutchison House where the ICAC headquarters was located. This incensed mob of police officers who had been dismissed, or retired, together with some serving officers, forced its way to the Commissioner of the ICAC's office. Closed glass doors were broken and unlocked and the raiders burst into the premises. They were met by protesting officers of the ICAC and a scuffle took place, the ICAC heavily outnumbered and five of them injured. A police patrol arrived in response to an emergency call, and their police colleagues then left. Each side told a different story of what occurred, the police omitting to mention the cries for the Commissioner's resignation that had been heard, and saying only 40 persons were involved. The ICAC alleged 200 intruders.

In the outcome, an investigation by a team of nine high-powered police led to the prosecution of one person — a retired police sergeant, whom the press were to call, with heavy sarcasm, the Lone Raider. The Attorney-General in the Legislative Council permitted himself the following statement: 'The report submitted to me by the investigating officers contained, save in one case, no evidence at all as to the identity of those who participated in the events and no admissible evidence even as to who were present.' This, despite the photographs of many of those participating which appeared in the press. The decision was political, the government shy of further alienating the police rank and file. But the smouldering fires smouldered on.

Between the Hutchison House break-in and 4 November, large meetings, both private and public, were held by police to plan future tactics. The government hope that the problem would simply go away was unrealistic. The Commissioner of Police's formal reply to the letter of complaint was received on 4 November, and over one thousand policemen met behind closed doors to discuss it. The more extreme views won the day and the reply was found unacceptable. There were demands for industrial action, for a strike, as means to force capitulation on the Police Commissioner's part to the terms outlined in their letter of complaint. It was apparent from the rowdy proceedings that the junior elements were uncontrollable.

There was now quite obviously every prospect that the police would cease to defend law and order and that anarchy might engulf the colony. The situation was taken so seriously by the Governor that he declared a partial amnesty for the police on the following day.

The news was greeted with little short of astonishment in the colony, even with dismay. People could not reconcile the amnesty with the Governor's steadfast assertions and actions in the past on the subject of the absolute need for the ICAC. For now it seemed that Sir Murray was at least indicating some sort of partial retreat from his former stance.

His directive of 5 November addressed to the Commissioner of the ICAC has come to be termed the 'partial amnesty'. Its content was to the effect that in future the ICAC would not normally act on complaints or evidence relating to offences committed before 1 January 1977, other than those relating to persons already under questioning, or persons against whom warrants had been issued, or persons not in the colony on 5 November. The phraseology used — 'not normally act' — excluded from the amnesty such offences considered to be so grave that it would be out of the question not to pursue an investigation. The Governor stressed that such cases would be rarities. The 'partial amnesty' was belatedly given legal teeth in February 1978.

The hotheads, having smelled power, were not to be quelled by this and pressed for a complete amnesty, refusing a compromise. They then planned a march to Government House if no favourable reply was forthcoming on this by 5 p.m. on 8 November.

Sir Murray held meetings on 7 November with his advisers and the Acting Commander British Forces and mobilized support from civilian organs and prominent persons called to a special press conference. At 5 p.m. he called a meeting of the Legislative Council and inside twenty minutes an amendment to the Police Force Ordinance was pushed through. This granted the Commissioner of Police powers of summary dismissal.

The hotheads and the waverers had met their match. Agreement was eventually reached on a pledge of total loyalty to the Commissioner. Roy Henry, Deputy Commissioner, was to replace Slevin the following year.

There was great discussion about what forced the Governor to grant the partial amnesty. The pros and cons were exhaustively weighed. Sir Murray has never commented. The plain fact of the matter was probably that to have failed to grant it would have required the full strength of Hong Kong's British army units and the Gurkhas to step in and act as a police force until such time as the present force (which would necessarily have had to be largely dismissed) could be replaced by another. This alternative was simply not a practicable solution. Sir Murray had virtually no choice of action.

The outcome of the 1977 crisis (as the police prefer to call the events) was a slow conformity by the police in general to the letter of the law, and an immediate and quite prolonged diminution in the powers of the ICAC. Wisdom after the event would have it that the latter pressed too hard and too quickly on the police. That may have been so. It took a long time for these two organizations to get back on speaking terms, far less terms of co-operation. By 1984 this had been in large part achieved.

It would appear from the statistics that corruption in the police force has greatly diminished. To what degree the figures reflect a general lessening in the scope of corruption is an open question. Certainly large-scale syndicated corruption has been vanquished, but just as surely small-scale activities have not.

The ICAC, having lost face and come under the effective control of the Governor at the time of the partial amnesty, came to be regarded for a time with less public confidence. But its later good record in uncovering corruption at all levels and in all areas of Hong Kong society has largely restored it to its former place in public regard.

It would be folly to imagine that corruption has been even 50 per cent eliminated. But perhaps the Hong Kong police nowadays compare favourably with the London metropolitan force — which was certainly not previously the case. The ordinary Chinese still steers clear of contact with the police in everyday affairs, and prefers not to report law-breaking rather than have contact with policemen, who are still seen as liable to take advantage in one way or another of involvement in personal and family affairs.

25. *Final Years*

'WHEN I started negotiations in 1983 [with the Chinese on the question of the future of Hong Kong], there was precious little to be optimistic about', wrote the British Foreign Secretary, Sir Geoffrey Howe, in August 1988. He was replying to a letter published in the *Evening Standard* newspaper in London in which Sir Walter Monckton alleged that the main concern of the Foreign Office was to shed Britain's responsibilities in Hong Kong.

If we, the government, had wanted simply to be rid of Hong Kong, then nothing could have been easier. We had only to let the 19th-century treaties run their course. These required the return to China in 1997 of 92 per cent of the territory of Hong Kong and the remaining 8 per cent would, of course, have been unviable on its own.

Before the negotiations, the Foreign Secretary continued,

the Chinese had made it clear, publicly and privately, that they intended to recover sovereignty over the whole of Hong Kong. They wanted no argument about it. But an argument is just what they got. They got a very hard negotiation.

Britain could and should have argued, writes Monckton, that the people of Hong Kong wished to remain under the government of Britain. If he had read the September 1984 White Paper he would know that that is precisely what we did.

But, to nobody's surprise, we could not persuade the Chinese to abandon their right — even as we see it — under the very same treaty that created Britain's 99-year lease, to the return of Hong Kong in 1997.

What we did achieve by dogged insistence on the need to satisfy the wishes of the people of Hong Kong, was a detailed and legally binding international agreement providing for the continuation for 50 years beyond 1997 of Hong Kong's capitalist economy, its common law system and the rights and freedoms of its people — all built up under British administration.

The agreement contains explicit assurances from the Chinese about how Deng Xiaoping's 'one country, two systems' formula will work, and how Hong Kong will enjoy a high degree of autonomy.

The Sino-British Joint Declaration, to give the Hong Kong agreement its proper name, was signed by the Prime Minister. It was recognized at the time as a great diplomatic achievement ... It was acclaimed by both sides of Parliament. Most importantly, the agreement was well received by the people of Hong Kong and by investors there.

Sir Geoffrey went on to an eloquent defence of the agreement and of Britain's position on Hong Kong. Having sweated blood on achieving such a document 'in tough negotiating sessions in Beijing . . . why should we, of all people, now be trying to give it all away?'

In fact, for almost the whole of the first year of those negotiations Britain had tried to retain some element of British presence in Hong Kong after 1997. But in the end the Chinese would have none of it.

The question of Hong Kong began to agitate the government of the territory and that of the United Kingdom in the latter part of the 1970s. As the span of the lease entered its last 20 years it was forecast that its impending termination, come the early 1980s, would begin to deter investors. It would also inhibit the Hong Kong government from granting new leases on land beyond 1997. By this time the British government had made an examination of the question in consultation with the Governor. He then, in March 1979, paid a visit to Beijing at the invitation of the Chinese Minister of Foreign Trade, and an attempt was made, on British initiative, to solve the problem of land leases. These discussions came to nothing.

In the following two years anxiety on the subject grew in Hong Kong and was expressed in the Executive Council on 1 May 1982. In the previous January the Lord Privy Seal, on a visit to China, was given some indications of the Beijing government's views on the future of Hong Kong. The British government inclined to the view that negotiations should be opened.

With this as background the Prime Minister, Mrs Margaret Thatcher, visited China in September of that year, and during the course of that visit substantive discussions took place. Chairman Deng Xiaoping and the Prime Minister followed their meetings with a statement:

> Today the leaders of both countries held far-reaching talks in a friendly atmosphere on the future of Hong Kong. Both leaders made clear their respective positions on this subject. They agreed to enter talks through diplomatic channels following the visit with the common aim of maintaining the stability and prosperity of Hong Kong.

The first round of talks took place between the British Ambassador to China, Sir Richard Evans, and the Chinese Foreign Ministry, during which the basis on which further talks should be conducted was agreed. On 1 July 1983 it was announced that the second phase of talks would begin on the twelfth of that month. This consisted of formal rounds of talks between the delegations of both sides, led on the British side by the Ambassador, and for the Chinese by a Vice or Assistant Minister of the Chinese Foreign Ministry.

The Governor of Hong Kong, Sir Edward Youde, took part in every one of the rounds of talks as a member of the British delegation.

During these sessions it soon became clear that the Chinese would tolerate no continuing British presence after 1997. The British then cast around to see what could be done in conjunction with the Chinese to maintain stability after 1997, other than by any form of British presence.

The Chinese proposal of creating a Special Administrative Region of the People's Republic in the form of Hong Kong appeared to provide a possible basis for further discussion. By April 1984 it was apparent that the initial discussions had formed an acceptable basis for negotiation, and at this point the Chinese invited the Secretary of State for Foreign Affairs, Sir Geoffrey Howe, to visit Beijing. This visit took place between 15 and 18 April. Further progress was then made, and on his return journey to London Sir Geoffrey made a statement on the talks in Hong Kong. After stating that it was not reasonable to consider a British presence in the territory after 1997, he announced that Her Majesty's Government was examining how to make arrangements for a high degree of autonomy for the territory under Chinese sovereignty, its way of life and present systems being preserved in essentials.

In June a working group was set up to meet full-time in Beijing to consider documents tabled by both sides, and the Foreign Secretary again went to Beijing in July, devoting his time there almost exclusively to the Hong Kong negotiations. On 1 August in Hong Kong he announced that very substantial progress had been made. He also announced the establishment of a Sino-British Joint Liaison Group to come into being when the agreement was signed and to continue until the year 2000, its functions to be liaison, consultation on the implementation of the agreement, and exchange of information. It would have no part to play in Hong Kong's administration which was to continue with the British government until 30 June 1997. After further negotiations both sides approved the English and Chinese versions of the agreement and associated Exchange of Memoranda, and these were submitted to British and Chinese ministers for approval, the texts being initialled by the leaders of both delegations on 26 September 1984.

The negotiations — long as they were — had been conducted on an agreed basis of complete confidentiality. This, it was recognized, would possibly have alarming effects in Hong Kong, but was essential to their success. The members of the Executive Council — the Governor's 'Cabinet' — were kept informed throughout, and advice on the attitude of Hong Kong people was sought all along from the Unofficial Members of the Executive and Legislative Councils (UMELCO). The negotiations were not concluded in haste or without due consultation, and during them UMELCO members and the Governor several times visited London for talks with the Prime Minister and other ministers. Groups and individuals in Hong Kong, and also the Legislative Council, made suggestions for what might be included in the

The signing of the Sino-British Joint Declaration in Beijing in December 1984.

agreement. The government sought to be in close touch with Hong Kong as well as British opinion on the subject in so far as the confidential nature of the talks permitted debate.

The Joint Declaration was signed in Beijing in December 1984 and the instruments of ratification were exchanged in May 1985 (see Appendix 10).

Sir Geoffrey, in his letter already quoted replying to Sir Walter Monckton, which appeared in London on 9 August 1988 and in Hong Kong the day after, continued in defence of the treaty and the British government's concern for the people of Hong Kong as an 'important British interest' which would continue as such 'after 1997'. He pointed to the 'unprecedented strength of investment in the colony since 1984' which, he thought, testified 'to the renewal of confidence there after the bleak years of 1982 and 1983. So too does the astonishing GDP growth of more than 30 per cent in the last three years'. The view, however, could plausibly be advanced and supported that these facts revealed not so much a long-term investor confidence but just the normal inclination for money to be deployed where, for the time being, it is most likely to reap the best profit — to make what killing may be made before it is too late.

He was, moreover, writing before the effects of what was to become a daily topic in the Hong Kong media — the so-called 'brain drain' — became noticeable. The realities of the process whereby many thousands are seeking, and have sought already, refuge in another country from their homes in Hong Kong are hard to assess in the short term; and it is not the intention of this history to comment on events and conditions relating to Hong Kong in the time after the signing of the Joint Declaration. We are much too close to the substance of post-1984 history to have a balanced view. Opinions voiced by all and sundry in the years since the Declaration have varied widely on the probable result for Hong Kong of its implementation after 1997. Few people among the close to six million Hong Kong citizens have actually read the original documents despite the commendable attempts by the government and others to induce them to do so, or at least to take in a digest of their content. Most people have, however, formed some opinion — some notion about the Hong Kong of the future might be a better way of defining it — and most are willing to pronounce on the subject privately. Such opinions range all the way from the fatalistic 'what will be will be', through the doom-laden which predicts Communist oppression accompanied by personal and corporate financial ruin, to various degrees of optimism.

On one aspect perhaps the majority of persons would be in some agreement — scepticism in regard to the continuing interest voiced by Sir Geoffrey and others in London of the home government in the future of Hong Kong people, most especially on the issue of nationality. The British National (Overseas) passport (carrying no right of residence in the United Kingdom) is almost universally derided as a sham. And if the British government is precariously balanced on the knife-edge of political expedience (called realism) between the moral requirement to afford its Hong Kong nationals that right, and the hostility of the British public at large to its granting — that is its own problem (say Hong Kong people) and why should *we* suffer the consequences? The right, were it granted, would be taken up by very few — for Britain is not viewed by the Chinese in Hong Kong with any marked favour as a place to live and work in. But it would in the last resort constitute an escape were conditions in Hong Kong found to be intolerable.

On that last day of June 1997 an event unique in British history will take place. Britain will hand over the sovereignty of a colony not to an indigenous government in that colony, but to the government of a foreign power. There is no important precedent for that action.[1] That the situation is the almost inevitable outcome of the original treaty, extracted under duress from the Chinese, and was arguably foreseeable (given the strength of Communist China), makes the contemplation of the portentous coming event no less equivocal and disturbing for the six million people of Hong Kong.

The vexatious question that posed and still poses itself in the minds of thoughtful citizens, whether Chinese or others who have made a life in the colony, is the degree of autonomy that is likely to remain for even the first of those 50 years after 1997, during which China has promised not to change Hong Kong's systems and life-style. Like China, Hong Kong has not been under democratic rule; but it has been ruled under written laws. The response of the populace has generally been to consent to this. When offered the right to vote, as they were in the District Board elections of 1982, the electorate turned out in very small numbers, demonstrating their reluctance to bother interfering in the slightest way with the due and accustomed state of affairs. Perhaps also the reluctance to vote, the majority of potential voters being Chinese, was also the result of the total absence of a democratic tradition in Chinese history. The concept was perhaps too foreign to be attractive.

Meanwhile changes in the composition of the Legislative Council were under discussion. Until 1964 official members always had a majority over unofficials, but in that year parity was achieved in numbers, with the Governor holding the casting vote. From 1976 it became the practice not to appoint the full complement of official members, allowing the unofficials at first two, later rising in 1983 to 10 votes more than the officials. In 1984, by amendments to the Royal Instructions, the permissible number of unofficials was raised to 32, with officials at 29, in theory ending the possibility that officials could outvote unofficials; the former possibility of appointing extra officials if needed to outvote unofficials also came to an end.

In 1985 the composition of the Council was: officials (inclusive of the President, the Governor) 11; appointed unofficials 22; elected officials 24: total 57. At this point, for the first time in its history, the chamber held 24 out of 57 members who had won their seats in competitive elections, retaining them for three years. Those elections were the result of a Green Paper published by the government in 1984 during the final stages in negotiations with the Chinese on the future of Hong Kong. The publication of the Paper caused some surprise since there had been no special demand for an increase in this aspect of democracy. But, on the principle that a government ruling by consent is wiser to offer more that it is asked for, the move appeared to be a progressive one. Whatever future reforms of the Council or constitutional changes may be made are required to be compatible with the system that China will introduce in 1997. This in large part was spelled out in the finalization of the Basic Law, agreed in early 1990 and approved by China in the spring of that year.

Despite official and unofficial efforts via the media to encourage people to take a more active part in Hong Kong affairs, little general participation followed — until the brutal events of 4 June 1989 in Beijing unfolded on every television screen in Hong Kong and around the world. Only then, with all the affront of a deep sleeper aroused untimely, did the public awaken with cries of mingled bewilderment and horror. If late in registering their opposition to the bulldozing tactics of the Chinese over such matters as the composition of the legislature post-1997, at last they took to the streets, to the air, to the press, and even to lobbying in the House of Commons and in Beijing itself — in loud protest. They saw in the suppression of fledgling attempts at democracy in China the grey shadow of Communist rule approaching with the inevitability of sunset.

The story of Hong Kong as a virtually independent city state thus approaches its end in the form which has evolved over the past century and a half. The future is shrouded in enigma and viewed with enormous and very natural apprehension by the vast majority of its people.[2]

Hong Kong whose achievement, the product of those people, has to be seen as something of peculiar grandeur in the summing up, must meet and accept in July 1997 the imposition of a different authority. City states, nations, empires, it is common knowledge, outlive their usefulness and wither. But it is widely believed, both in Hong Kong and elsewhere (outside China), that Hong Kong will not by then have outlived its usefulness. Will the substance of an agreement between Britain and China to establish in the territory the degree of autonomy envisaged under the 'one country, two systems' notion continue to nurture its evident health and validity? Until the advent of the new administration in 1997 there can be no certainty.

NOTES

NOTES TO THE INTRODUCTION

1. See Appendix 1.

NOTES TO CHAPTER 1

1. An explanation of all unfamiliar terms can be found in the Glossary.
2. Waley, A., *The Opium War Through Chinese Eyes*, p. 29.
3. Wood, H. J., 'Prologue to War: The Anglo-Chinese Conflict 1800–1834', pp. 173–4.
4. Quoted in Chang, H. P., *Commissioner Lin and the Opium War*, p. 49.

NOTES TO CHAPTER 2

1. Hunter, W. C., *The 'Fan-kwae' at Canton Before Treaty Days, 1825–1844.*
2. Foreign Office, General Correspondence, China 17/35.
3. For this and the following quotations I have relied on Waley, A., *The Opium War Through Chinese Eyes*, and Chang, H. P., *Commissioner Lin and the Opium War.*

NOTES TO CHAPTER 3

1. Eitel, E. J., *Europe in China*, p. 60.

NOTES TO CHAPTER 4

1. *Journal of the Royal Asiatic Society*, Vol. 8, 1968, p. 149.
2. Quoted by Crisswell, C. in *The Taipans: Hong Kong's Merchant Princes*, p. 62.
3. Braga, J. M. (ed.), *Hong Kong Business Symposium*, p. 34.
4. Eitel, E. J., *Europe in China*, p. 203.
5. Endacott, G. B., *A Biographical Sketch-book of Early Hong Kong*, p. 62.
6. Eitel, E. J., *Europe in China*, p. 207.
7. Eitel, E. J., *Europe in China*, p. 207.
8. Norton-Kyshe, J. W., *The History of the Laws and Courts of Hong Kong*, Vol. I, p. 188.

NOTES TO CHAPTER 5

1. The correspondence is in the Public Record Office, London, F.O. 682/1977 9 May 1844 to F.O. 682/1981 20 March 1848. A brief summary of its contents is in Wong, J. Y., *Anglo-Chinese Relations 1839–1860*, pp. 109–69.

2. Labouchère, quoted in Endacott, G. B., *A Biographical Sketch-book of Early Hong Kong*, p. 71.

3. Eitel, E. J., *Europe in China*, p. 222.

4. Wong, J. Y., *Anglo-Chinese Relations 1839–1860* , pp. 119ff.

5. A little after this, and probably consequent on the perceived need to tighten up various aspects of the administration, Davis issued on 1 May 1845 the first proclamation on what was legal tender in Hong Kong. Permitted specie were: gold, silver, and copper coins minted in the United Kingdom; the gold *mohur* (Indian) valued at 29s.2d. or at 15 rupees; Spanish, Mexican, and South American silver dollars at 4s.2d.; rupees at 1s.10d.; Chinese silver, and Chinese copper 'cash' at 280 to 1s. This proved totally futile. Gold was not in use to any extent in the Far East, and silver — bullion or coin — regardless of whether it was Chinese, English, or other was in practice valued solely by weight, and not by its sterling value. The silver dollar, duly weighed, continued to be the supreme currency.

6. Endacott, G. B., *A History of Hong Kong*, p. 61.

7. Wong, J. Y., *Anglo-Chinese Relations 1839–1860*, pp. 152–3.

NOTES TO CHAPTER 6

1. Reprinted in *Journal of the Royal Asiatic Society*, Vol. 11, 1971, pp. 171–93.

2. The story of how, eventually, a suitable Government House was built is in Mattock, K., *The Story of Government House.*

3. Smith, C. T., *Chinese Christians: Élites, Middlemen, and the Church in Hong Kong*, p. 22.

4. Smith, C. T., *Chinese Christians: Élites, Middlemen, and the Church in Hong Kong*, p. 22.

5. Endacott, G. B., *A History of Hong Kong*, p. 71.

NOTES TO CHAPTER 7

1. Eitel, E. J., *Europe in China*, p. 287.

2. Endacott, G. B., *A Biographical Sketch-book of Early Hong Kong*, p. 35.

3. Eitel, E. J., *Europe in China*, p. 253.

4. Eitel, E. J., *Europe in China*, p. 282.

5. Eitel, E. J., *Europe in China*, p. 254.

NOTES TO CHAPTER 8

1. The poet Thomas Hood (1799–1845) addressed lines to Bowring, 'a man of many tongues':

All kinds of gab he knows, I wis,
From Latin down to Scottish
As fluent as a parrot is
But far more polly-glottish.

2. Eitel, E. J., *Europe in China*, p. 295.

3. Eitel, E. J., *Europe in China*, p. 297.

4. Smith, A., *To China and Back*, p. 63.

5. Smith, A., *To China and Back*, p. 42.

6. Smith, A., *To China and Back*, p. 33.

7. A résumé of this and the following letters is in Wong, J. Y., *Anglo-Chinese Relations 1839–1860*, pp. 230ff. The letters are also interesting in their revelation of the character of the writers.

8. Eitel, E. J., *Europe in China*, p. 306.

9. Wong, J. Y., *Anglo-Chinese Relations 1839–1860*, pp. 230ff.

10. Bowring's suggestion of a cadet training scheme was accepted by the Colonial Office as a good means of filling posts in the China consular service. The idea was that the cadets should be a body of

men fluent in spoken and written Chinese whose first function was to interpret, especially in the courts. There they were certainly urgently required if Eitel's claim is accepted that in 1859 there was only one interpreter versed in written and spoken [Cantonese] Chinese, and no Chinese whose level of English even began to be adequate. The corps was formed in the time of the next Governor, Sir Hercules Robinson, in 1862.

After basic Chinese language training in London, the cadets came out to Hong Kong and were sent to Guangzhou for a more intensive course under Chinese teachers. The first three cadets were in fact never used as interpreters, such was the demand for administrators with Chinese language skills. Cecil Clementi Smith rocketed into the post of Registrar-General in 1864, W. M. Deane became Superintendent of Police in 1867, and M. S. Tonnochy held the positions of Sheriff, Coroner, and Marshall of the Vice-Admiralty Court in 1865.

Three cadets became Governors — May, Clementi, and Grantham. Two became Chief Justices, and four became Colonial Secretaries.

In 1870 a competitive system was introduced to select them, and it remained in force until 1932. By the 1920s, cadets held every major position in the Colonial Secretariat, and the conduct of government was in their hands. Coming as most did from the British professional class with its educated, stuffy, usually fair-dealing outlook, they formed a body of incorruptible men. In the light of the statement by the director of recruitment for the Colonial Service in the 1930s and 1940s that 'in most colonies the Civil Servant is the Government, and not the servant of Government', their importance in the history of Hong Kong can hardly be exaggerated.

NOTES TO CHAPTER 9

1. Endacott, G. B., *A Biographical Sketch-book of Early Hong Kong*, p. 50.
2. Endacott, G. B., *A Biographical Sketch-book of Early Hong Kong*, p. 50.
3. Endacott, G. B., *A Biographical Sketch-book of Early Hong Kong*, p. 81.

NOTES TO CHAPTER 10

1. Norman, Sir H., *The Peoples and Politics of the Far East*, pp. 25–6.
2. Freedman, M., *Lineage Organization in Southeastern China*, p. 55.
3. Lethbridge, H. J., *Hong Kong: Stability and Change*, p. 61.
4. Quoted in Lethbridge, H. J., *Hong Kong: Stability and Change*, p. 63.
5. Scarth, J., *Twelve Years in China*, p. 256.
6. Mills, L. A., *British Rule in Eastern Asia*, p. 398.
7. Norton-Kyshe, J. W., *The History of the Laws and Courts of Hong Kong*, Vol. II, pp. 445–6.
8. Smith, C. T., *Chinese Christians: Élites, Middlemen, and the Church in Hong Kong*, p. 19.
9. Smith, C. T., *Chinese Christians: Élites, Middlemen, and the Church in Hong Kong*, p. 21.
10. Eitel, E. J., *Europe in China*, p. 247.
11. Eitel, E. J., *Europe in China*, pp. 280–1.
12. Eitel, E. J., *Europe in China*, p. 391.
13. Endacott, G. B., *A History of Hong Kong*, p. 138.

NOTES TO CHAPTER 11

1. Quoted by Endacott, G. B., *A History of Hong Kong*, p. 143.
2. Endacott, G. B., *A Biographical Sketch-book of Early Hong Kong*, p. 83.
3. Eitel, E. J., *Europe in China*, pp. 425–6.

4. Endacott, G. B., *A History of Hong Kong*, p. 158.
5. Endacott, G. B., *A History of Hong Kong*, p. 158.
6. Shakespeare wrote 'When', not 'Whence'.

NOTES TO CHAPTER 12

1. Endacott, G. B., *A History of Hong Kong*, p. 166.
2. Endacott, G. B., *A History of Hong Kong*, p. 167.
3. Eitel, E. J., *Europe in China*, p. 508.

NOTES TO CHAPTER 13

1. Pope-Hennessy, J., *Half-Crown Colony*, p. 79.
2. Endacott, G. B., *A History of Hong Kong*, p. 175.
3. Dyson, A., *From Time Ball to Atomic Clock*, p. 22.
4. Dyson, A., *From Time Ball to Atomic Clock*, p. 22.
5. Endacott, G. B., *A History of Hong Kong*, p. 181.
6. Bird, I., *The Golden Chersonese and the Way Thither*, pp. 31–2.

NOTES TO CHAPTER 14

1. Endacott, G. B., *A History of Hong Kong*, p. 184.
2. Quoted in Lethbridge, H. J., *Hong Kong: Stability and Change*, p. 168.
3. Endacott, G. B., *A History of Hong Kong*, p. 189.
4. Endacott, G. B., *A History of Hong Kong*, p. 190.
5. Endacott, G. B., *A History of Hong Kong*, p. 191.

NOTES TO CHAPTER 15

1. From Chater's obituary in the *Hong Kong Daily Telegraph*, May 1926.
2. Reprinted in *Journal of the Royal Asiatic Society*, Vol. 8, 1968, pp. 128–34.
3. Bird, I., *The Golden Chersonese and the Way Thither*, p. 38.
4. Gower, Lord R., *My Reminiscences*, Vol. II, pp. 214–15.
5. Quoted by Sayer, G. R., *Hong Kong: 1862–1919*, p. 71.
6. Curzon, Hon. G. N., *Problems of the Far East: Japan, Corea, China*, p. 423.

NOTES TO CHAPTER 16

1. Cameron, N., *Power: The Story of China Light*, pp. 18–20.
2. Curzon, Hon. G. N., quoted in Sayer, G. R., *Hong Kong: 1862–1919*, p. 72.
3. Sayer, G. R., *Hong Kong: 1862–1919*, p. 72.
4. Dyson, A., *From Time Ball to Atomic Clock*, p. 52. This excellent work is essential reading on weather in all its Hong Kong aspects.
5. Arlington, L. C., *Through the Dragon's Eyes*, p. 168.
6. Coates, A., *A Mountain of Light: The Story of The Hongkong Electric Company*, p. 41.
7. Coates, A., *A Mountain of Light: The Story of The Hongkong Electric Company*, p. 42.
8. Sessional Papers No. 26, 1896, p. 431.

NOTES TO CHAPTER 17

1. Sayer, G. R., *Hong Kong: 1862–1919*, p. 91.
2. Sayer, G. R., *Hong Kong: 1862–1919*, p. 92.
3. Atkinson, R. L. P., and Williams, A. K., *Hong Kong Tramways*, p. 23.
4. Sayer, G. R., *Hong Kong: 1862–1919*, p. 112.
5. Sayer, G. R., *Hong Kong: 1862–1919*, p. 114.
6. Sayer, G. R., *Hong Kong: 1862–1919*, p. 115.
7. From a speech to the Hong Kong University Congregation in 1925.
8. Report in the *South China Morning Post.*
9. A brief history of the institution is published by The Helena May.

NOTES TO CHAPTER 18

1. Coates, A., *A Mountain of Light: The Story of The Hongkong Electric Company*, pp. 82–3.
2. Lethbridge, H. J., *Hong Kong: Stability and Change*, p. 94.
3. Miners, N., *Hong Kong Under Imperial Rule 1912–1941*, pp. 189–90, appears to accept quite another set of figures.
4. Coates, A., *A Mountain of Light: The Story of The Hongkong Electric Company*, p. 96.
5. Coates, A., *A Mountain of Light: The Story of The Hongkong Electric Company*, p. 97.
6. Coates, A., *A Mountain of Light: The Story of The Hongkong Electric Company*, p. 127.
7. By Alfred Bunn (1796?–1860) from *The Bohemian Girl*, Act II.

NOTES TO CHAPTER 19

1. Endacott, G. B., *A History of Hong Kong*, p. 295.
2. Much of the information in the preceding five paragraphs is succinctly brought together in Collins, Sir C., *Public Administration in Hong Kong*, pp. 150–64.
3. Cameron, N., *Power: The Story of China Light*, p. 134.

NOTES TO CHAPTER 20

1. Endacott, G. B., *Hong Kong Eclipse*, p. 65.
2. Foreign Office 371/27752. Telegraph from the Governor to the Secretary of State, 14 December 1941.
3. Endacott, G. B., *Hong Kong Eclipse*, pp. 80–1.
4. *South China Morning Post*, 25 December 1941. Quoted in Lindsay, O., *The Lasting Honour: The Fall of Hong Kong 1941*, p. 146.
5. Endacott, G. B., *Hong Kong Eclipse*, p. 183.

NOTES TO CHAPTER 21

1. Hutcheon, R., *SCMP: The First Eighty Years*, p. 95.
2. Tuchman, B. W., *Stilwell and the American Experience in China 1911–45*, p. 410.
3. Endacott, G. B., *Hong Kong Eclipse*, p. 259.
4. Endacott, G. B., *Hong Kong Eclipse*, p. 337.
5. Endacott, G. B., *Hong Kong Eclipse*, p. 339.

6. Colonial Office 129 (1945–6) 5432/45 (in the Public Record Office, London).
7. Endacott, G. B., *Hong Kong Eclipse*, p. 264.
8. Cameron, N., *Power: The Story of China Light*, p. 150.

NOTES TO CHAPTER 22

1. The subject is well expounded in Wong, L. S. K. (ed.), *Housing in Hong Kong; A Multidisciplinary Study*, pp. 128–59.
2. Hong Kong Government, *Annual Report*, 1982.
3. Endacott, G. B., *Hong Kong Eclipse*, p. 312.

NOTES TO CHAPTER 23

1. The statistical information in this chapter has been taken principally from government sources. A readily available digest of the material is to be found in the *Annual Reports*.
2. Joseph Y. S. Cheng's compilation *Hong Kong in the 1980s* is a useful overview of the period.

NOTES TO CHAPTER 24

1. Lethbridge, H. J., *Hard Graft in Hong Kong: Scandal, Corruption, the ICAC*. This is the definitive account.
2. Lethbridge, H. J., *Hard Graft in Hong Kong: Scandal, Corruption, the ICAC*, p. 66.
3. Cooper, J., *Colony in Conflict: The Hong Kong Disturbances, May 1967–January 1968*, sets down in detail all the significant facts.
4. Lethbridge, H. J., *Hard Graft in Hong Kong: Scandal, Corruption, the ICAC*, p. 84.
5. Lethbridge, H. J., *Hard Graft in Hong Kong: Scandal, Corruption, the ICAC*, p. 85.
6. *Annual Report of the Activities of the Independent Commission Against Corruption*, 1975.

NOTES TO CHAPTER 25

1. The sole exception is that of the coaling station of Weihaiwei (Weihai) on the Shandong Peninsula which was returned to China in 1930. The action had minimal human or commercial significance.
2. Any attempt to assess the meaning and effect of events in relation to Hong Kong after 1984 must be much more subjective than the analysis of events before current emotions ran high. Except in barest outline this has not been attempted.

APPENDICES

APPENDIX 1

Since archaeological excavation began in 1920, a certain amount of prehistory has come to light. A neolithic culture has left stone artefacts from about 6000 BC, and a later one about 3500 BC produced pottery with designs linked to those on the Shang and Chou bronzes of 1500–221 BC. A number of shoreside sites have yielded evidence of Yueh fishermen building temporary shelters, and it was doubtless they who carved the geometric designs on rocks at Big Wave Bay and elsewhere, discovered in 1970.

There is no hard evidence of Chinese inhabitants until about 200 BC, after which the Chin and Han empires spread from the Yangzi region down to Guangdong. An Eastern Han tomb (AD 25–220) was discovered in Kowloon in 1955 as a site was cleared for housing, and contained pottery and bronze related to the Guangdong culture of that time. But it should not be assumed that the Han were settlers. The earliest written material dates permanent settlement much later, to the Song dynasty in the eleventh century. But Tang dynasty (AD 618–907) garrisons seem to have been set up here and there, one at Tuen Mun (Garrisoned Gate), overlooked by Castle Peak, which was declared by an imperial decree of AD 868 a sacred mountain. Tang lime kilns and others for calcining sea shells continued working well into the twentieth century. The flight of the last princes of the Song ended in the defeat of the Song army and navy east of Hong Kong.

Ming (1368–1644) and Qing (1644–1912) villages and forts and Kowloon City existed, the latter gaining its wall in the first British years. The Portuguese were at Tuen Mun in 1514 and founded Macau just 30 years later.

With the Qing (Manzhu) dynasty in 1644 came suspicions about the local inhabitants' loyalty, and in 1662 the whole population was evacuated 30 miles inland and the seaboard laid waste. The San On (New Peace) district included what was to become Hong Kong, Kowloon, and the New Territories. The official Gazetteer records the hardships of the people driven from their lands, and the year after (1663) the Viceroy was pleading that total clearance be abandoned in view of the misery caused. People were allowed to return in 1669. A contemporary description of this barbaric process gives heart-rending details of suffering, suicide, the selling of children, and starvation. 'The authorities treated the people as no more than ants . . . several hundred thousand . . . died.'

A wave of Hakka people (Hakka means 'stranger' or 'guest') from the neighbouring provinces took over much of the vacated land from the local Punti.

The Gazetteer of San On County first appeared in the late sixteenth century and was published at irregular intervals until 1819. It records, among screeds of gossip, historical facts such as the building of the Tung Lung island fort in the time of the Kangxi emperor (excavated 1979–82), and tells tales of the pirate Chang Bocai, the local Robin Hood, who eventually joined forces with the Qing authorities. Other inhabitants of San On County were two fishing communities — the Hoklo from Fujian Province, and Tanka people said to be descended from aboriginals.

Few current inhabitants of Hong Kong know anything of the Qing villages and the graves, milestones, and fertility-related monoliths scattered over the colony, and only recently has there appeared a guide to such sites.

Source: Bard, S., *In Search of the Past: A Guide to the Antiquities of Hong Kong.*

APPENDIX 2

Hong Kong's long steamy summers appear with great regularity in travellers' and residents' accounts, and the typhoons which occur now and then as climactic points during them have been vividly described. These tropical cyclones are, with earthquakes, nature's most destructive and savage force. The word typhoon derives from the Chinese *tai fung*, 'big wind'.

Forming over the tropical Pacific, the rapidly rotating warm air surrounds a relatively still central 'eye', the whole mass moving towards land where its force soon dissipates.

Until the Royal Observatory opened on 1 January 1884, there were few reliable indicators of the approach or severity of typhoons. When the telegraph linked the colony with the Philippines and other places, at least some warning was available. But not until the deployment of weather satellites did there begin accurate predictions of the severity, speed, direction, and location of such storms.

Records of typhoons affecting Hong Kong are incomplete but severe winds, probably typhoons, are recorded early on. The first came barely six months after annexation in 1841. On 21 July the storm passed to the west, destroying most of the flimsy structures then standing. Others are recorded in September 1848, July 1864, August and October 1867, September 1870, September 1871, and September 1874 — all being severe. There was a merciful interregnum, noted by the *Hong Kong Daily Press*, between autumn 1867 and September 1870. A few years later came the disastrous typhoon of 24 September 1874. On 26 September the same paper chronicled the terror of the events. 'At times even above the fierce howling of the wind could be heard the pitiful cries of thousands vainly battling with the storm. Not a ship in port escaped undamaged and the casualties and loss of life — the latter estimated at 2,000 souls — have exceeded anything . . . before.' Eitel, who was present, recorded: 'The town looks as though it had undergone a terrific bombardment. Thousands of houses were unroofed, hundreds of European and Chinese dwellings were in ruins, large trees had been hurled to a distance, most of the streets were impassable . . . The Praya was covered with wrecked sampans and the debris of junks and ships, whilst in every direction bodies were seen floating or scattered along the ruins of what was once the Praya wall.'

Among subsequent typhoons there was a monstrous one in 1900, and other severe occurrences in 1906 and 1908. More recently, the devastation of typhoon Wanda in September 1962 was a memorable if tragic experience. In 1964 there were five such visitations. Today, as much damage is done by rain as by wind — the yield of typhoons varying between about four hundred and over five hundred millimetres of water. But casualties do not now result from lack of information on the approaching storm.

APPENDIX 3

Population, 1845

	Men	Women	Children	Total
Europeans	455	90	50	595
Indians	346	12	4	362
Chinese in brick buildings	6,000	960	500	7,460
Chinese in boats	600	1,800	1,200	3,600
Labourers	10,000	—	—	10,000
Visitors	—	—	—	300
Chinese in European employment	—	—	—	1,500
Total				23,817

Note: Figures do not include 618 European troops in the garrison.

Source: Endacott, G. B., *A History of Hong Kong*, p. 65.

APPENDIX 4

Figures for 1844 show 538 ships with a gross tonnage totalling 189,257 entered the port. By 1847 the number was 694 with a total tonnage of 229,465. Their countries of origin were Britain with 53 ships, India 114, Australia 33, North America 16, South America, the Pacific Islands, and East Indies 56, the China coast 139, and Guangzhou river vessels 283. Three years later (1850) the totals were 884 ships totalling 229,009 tons.

Source: Endacott, G. B., *A History of Hong Kong*, pp. 74–5.

APPENDIX 5

Volume of Trade, 1924–1927

	Vessels in Foreign Trade		River Trade	
Year	Number	Total Tonnage	Imports	Exports
1924	57,765	38,770,499	493,791	663,802
1925	41,336	32,179,053	201,128	318,502
1926	30,231	28,371,104	117,421	123,322
1927	51,289	36,834,014	No figures available	

Source: Hong Kong Government, *Annual Reports*, 1924–1927.

APPENDIX 6

Hong Kong Trade (per cent)

	Year	Britain	British Dominions	China	Other Countries
Imports	1921	10.24	10.79	19.12	59.77
	1931	9.94	8.88	27.84	53.34
	1939	6.62	7.03	37.95	48.40
Exports	1921	0.91	9.99	64.65	24.45
	1931	0.89	9.09	51.67	38.35
	1939	5.23	13.93	14.83	66.01

Source: Endacott, G. B., *A History of Hong Kong*, p. 291.

APPENDIX 7

The return made by General Maltby listing the casualties in the Battle for Hong Kong makes grim reading. Listed as killed or died of wounds were 74 officers and 971 men of other ranks. There were 2,300 men of all ranks wounded. Of the 1,069 missing 62 were officers and 1,007 men of other ranks. In total Maltby's return shows that there were 4,414 casualties.

It is probably fair to conclude that the total of those listed as missing can be included with killed or died of wounds since death was almost certainly the fate of all but a very few. The heaviest casualties were among the Rajputs who lost every officer and 65 per cent of their men. The Royal Scots and the Royal Rifles of Canada lost over 50 per cent of their men, and the remaining three battalions suffered casualties ranging from 40 to 50 per cent.

Regarding Japanese casualties, on 29 December 1941 a Japanese news agency gave the figures for those killed as 1,996 and wounded 6,000. A broadcast from Tokyo some days later listed as killed 3,000 and wounded 20,000. Maltby's own estimate was killed 3,000 and wounded 9,000.

Source: Lindsay, O., *The Lasting Honour: The Fall of Hong Kong 1941*, pp. 200–1.

APPENDIX 8

Major Indicators of Growth of Economic Activity in Hong Kong (per cent per annum)

Indicators	Nominal Growth Rates			Real Growth Rates			1980 Level
	1960–70	1970–80	1960–80	1960–70	1970–80	1960–80	
Population (mid-year)	—	—	—	2.88	2.44	2.66	5.04 m
GDP (at market prices)							
Total GDP	13.73	18.71	16.32	10.24	9.18	9.68	$106,770m
Per capita	10.94	15.88	13.52	7.54	6.58	7.03	$21,191
International trade							
Total exports	14.49	20.49	17.45	11.93	10.24	11.08	$98,243m
(per capita)	11.28	17.62	14.41	8.79	7.62	8.20	$19,499
Domestic exports	15.72	18.63	17.17	13.13	8.54	10.81	$68,1117m
Re-exports	10.45	26.39	18.15	8.24	15.89	12.00	$30,072m
Imports	11.62	20.29	15.87	9.63	10.53	10.08	$111,651m
Manufacturing							
Employment	—	—	—	9.79	5.15	7.44	907,463
Establishments	—	—	—	13.18	10.56	11.86	45,025
Wages (workers)	8.37	12.31	10.32	5.50	4.96	5.23	$56/day
Money and banking							
Total deposits	18.75	24.26	21.47	15.53	15.49	15.51	$131,206m
Total loans	18.85	34.25	26.32	15.62	24.78	20.11	$183,952m
Money supply, M1	11.32	13.93	12.62	8.30	5.89	7.09	$24,124m
Money supply, M2	17.15	18.88	18.01	13.96	10.50	12.22	$96,862m
Public finance							
Revenue	13.59	21.22	17.34	10.50	12.67	11.58	$21,036m
Expenditure	11.24	22.36	16.67	8.22	13.73	10.94	$18,442m

Source: Cheng, J. Y. S. (ed.), *Hong Kong in the 1980s*, p. 84.

APPENDIX 9

Stock Exchange Index and Turnover, 1970–1980

	Hang Seng Index of Share Prices	Total Value of Stock Exchange Turnover ($m)
1970	212	5,989
1971	341	14,793
1972	843	43,758
1973	434	48,217
1974	171	11,246
1975	350	1,496
1976	448	2,348
1977	404	1,205
1978	496	7,250
1979	879	12,609
1980	1,474	42,174

Source: Cheng, J. Y. S. (ed.), *Hong Kong in the 1980s*, p. 72.

APPENDIX 10

JOINT DECLARATION OF THE GOVERNMENT OF THE UNITED KINGDOM OF GREAT BRITAIN AND NORTHERN IRELAND AND THE GOVERNMENT OF THE PEOPLE'S REPUBLIC OF CHINA ON THE QUESTION OF HONG KONG

The Government of the United Kingdom of Great Britain and Northern Ireland and the Government of the People's Republic of China have reviewed with satisfaction the friendly relations existing between the two Governments and peoples in recent years and agreed that a proper negotiated settlement of the question of Hong Kong, which is left over from the past, is conducive to the maintenance of the prosperity and stability of Hong Kong and to the further strengthening and development of the relations between the two countries on a new basis. To this end, they have, after talks between the delegations of the two Governments, agreed to declare as follows:

1. The Government of the People's Republic of China declares that to recover the Hong Kong area (including Hong Kong Island, Kowloon and the New Territories, hereinafter referred to as Hong Kong) is the common aspiration of the entire Chinese people, and that it has decided to resume the exercise of sovereignty over Hong Kong with effect from 1 July 1997.

2. The Government of the United Kingdom declares that it will restore Hong Kong to the People's Republic of China with effect from 1 July 1997.

3. The Government of the People's Republic of China declares that the basic policies of the People's Republic of China regarding Hong Kong are as follows:

(1) Upholding national unity and territorial integrity and taking account of the history of

Hong Kong and its realities, the People's Republic of China has decided to establish, in accordance with the provisions of Article 31 of the Constitution of the People's Republic of China, a Hong Kong Special Administrative Region upon resuming the exercise of sovereignty over Hong Kong.

(2) The Hong Kong Special Administrative Region will be directly under the authority of the Central People's Government of the People's Republic of China. The Hong Kong Special Administrative Region will enjoy a high degree of autonomy, except in foreign and defence affairs which are the responsibilities of the Central People's Government.

(3) The Hong Kong Special Administrative Region will be vested with executive, legislative and independent judicial power, including that of final adjudication. The laws currently in force in Hong Kong will remain basically unchanged.

(4) The Government of the Hong Kong Special Administrative Region will be composed of local inhabitants. The chief executive will be appointed by the Central People's Government on the basis of the results of elections or consultations to be held locally. Principal officials will be nominated by the chief executive of the Hong Kong Special Administrative Region for appointment by the Central People's Government. Chinese and foreign nationals previously working in the public and police services in the government departments of Hong Kong may remain in employment. British and other foreign nationals may also be employed to serve as advisers or hold certain public posts in government departments of the Hong Kong Special Administrative Region.

(5) The current social and economic systems in Hong Kong will remain unchanged, and so will the life-style. Rights and freedoms, including those of the person, of speech, of the press, of assembly, of association, of travel, of movement, of correspondence, of strike, of choice of occupation, of academic research and of religious belief will be ensured by law in the Hong Kong Special Administrative Region. Private property, ownership of enterprises, legitimate right of inheritance and foreign investment will be protected by law.

(6) The Hong Kong Special Administrative Region will retain the status of a free port and a separate customs territory.

(7) The Hong Kong Special Administrative Region will retain the status of an international financial centre, and its markets for foreign exchange, gold, securities and futures will continue. There will be free flow of capital. The Hong Kong dollar will continue to circulate and remain freely convertible.

(8) The Hong Kong Special Administrative Region will have independent finances. The Central People's Government will not levy taxes on the Hong Kong Special Administrative Region.

(9) The Hong Kong Special Administrative Region may establish mutually beneficial economic relations with the United Kingdom and other countries, whose economic interests in Hong Kong will be given due regard.

(10) Using the name of "Hong Kong, China", the Hong Kong Special Administrative Region may on its own maintain and develop economic and cultural relations and conclude relevant agreements with states, regions and relevant international organisations.

The Government of the Hong Kong Special Administrative Region may on its own issue travel documents for entry into and exit from Hong Kong.

(11) The maintenance of public order in the Hong Kong Special Administrative Region will be the responsibility of the Government of the Hong Kong Special Administrative Region.

(12) The above-stated basic policies of the People's Republic of China regarding Hong Kong and the elaboration of them in Annex I to this Joint Declaration will be stipulated, in a Basic Law of the Hong Kong Special Administrative Region of the People's Republic of China, by the National People's Congress of the People's Republic of China, and they will remain unchanged for 50 years.

4. The Government of the United Kingdom and the Government of the People's Republic of China declare that, during the transitional period between the date of the entry into force of this Joint Declaration and 30 June 1997, the Government of the United Kingdom will be responsible for the administration of Hong Kong with the object of maintaining and preserving its economic prosperity and social stability; and that the Government of the People's Republic of China will give its cooperation in this connection.

5. The Government of the United Kingdom and the Government of the People's Republic of China declare that, in order to ensure a smooth transfer of government in 1997, and with a view to the effective implementation of this Joint Declaration, a Sino-British Joint Liaison Group will be set up when this Joint Declaration enters into force; and that it will be established and will function in accordance with the provisions of Annex II to this Joint Declaration.

6. The Government of the United Kingdom and the Government of the People's Republic of China declare that land leases in Hong Kong and other related matters will be dealt with in accordance with the provisions of Annex III to this Joint Declaration.

7. The Government of the United Kingdom and the Government of the People's Republic of China agree to implement the preceding declarations and the Annexes to this Joint Declaration.

8. This Joint Declaration is subject to ratification and shall enter into force on the date of the exchange of instruments of ratification, which shall take place in Beijing before 30 June 1985. This Joint Declaration and its Annexes shall be equally binding.

Done in duplicate at Beijing on 1984 in the English and Chinese languages, both texts being equally authentic.

For the
Government of the United Kingdom
of Great Britain and Northern Ireland

For the
Government of the
People's Republic of China

* * *

The text of the Joint Declaration is accompanied by three Annexes, an Exchange of Memoranda between the British and Chinese Governments, and a passage of Explanatory Notes. Annex I deals with the setting up of the Hong Kong Special Administrative Region of the People's Republic of China (SAR), and also with the enactment at that time of the Basic Law for the SAR. This Annex, in its detailed points and in its detailed application, contains the crux of the whole matter of Hong Kong's future. It is about the implementation and interpretation of the Annex that discussion has been going on ever since it was announced. Wide-ranging consultations with all parties concerned and the hearing of opinions from everyone concerned who has wished to voice one have been undertaken.

Annex II deals with the setting up of the Sino-British Joint Liaison Group whose deliberations are important in assisting the process of defining meticulously, and to the satisfaction of all concerned, the Basic Law. The Basic Law was finally approved by the Chinese National People's Congress in Beijing in early April 1990.

Annex III deals with land leases, the subject which first brought the 1997 question into public prominence.

The Memoranda outline issues of nationality for Hong Kong citizens after 1997, while the Explanatory Notes further elaborate the whole matter.

APPENDIX II

Governors of Hong Kong

Captain Charles Elliot	(Administrator)	January—August 1841
Sir Henry Pottinger	(Administrator)	August 1841—June 1843
	(First Governor)	June 1843—May 1844
Sir John Davis		May 1844—March 1848
Sir George Bonham		March 1848—April 1854
Sir John Bowring		April 1854—May 1859
Sir Hercules Robinson		September 1859—March 1865
William Mercer	(Administered)	March 1865—March 1866
Sir Richard Macdonnell		March 1866—April 1872
Sir Arthur Kennedy		April 1872—March 1877
Sir John Pope Hennessy		April 1877—March 1882
William Marsh	(Administered)	March 1882—March 1883
Sir George Bowen		March 1883—December 1885
William Marsh	(Administered)	December 1885—April 1887
Major-General W. G. Cameron	(Administered)	April—October 1887
Sir William Des Voeux		October 1887—May 1891
Major-General Digby Barker	(Administered)	May—December 1891
Sir William Robinson		December 1891—January 1898
Major-General W. Black	(Administered)	February—November 1898
Sir Henry Blake		November 1898—November 1903
Henry May	(Administered)	November 1903—July 1904
Sir Matthew Nathan		July 1904—April 1907
Sir Frederick Lugard		July 1907—March 1912
Sir Henry May		July 1912—February 1919
Sir Reginald Stubbs		September 1919—October 1925
Sir Cecil Clementi		November 1925—February 1930
Sir William Peel		May 1930—May 1935
Sir Andrew Caldecott		December 1935—April 1937
Sir Geoffry Northcote		November 1937—May 1940
Lieutenant-General E. Norton	(Administered)	August 1940—March 1941
Sir Mark Young		September 1941—May 1947
Sir Alexander Grantham		July 1947—December 1957
Sir Robert Black		January 1958—March 1964
Sir David Trench		April 1964—October 1971
Sir Murray MacLehose		November 1971—April 1982
Sir Edward Youde		May 1982—December 1986
Sir David Akers-Jones	(Administered)	December 1986—April 1987
Sir David Wilson		April 1987—

BIBLIOGRAPHY

Airlie, S., *Thistle and Bamboo: The Life and Times of Sir James Stewart Lockhart* (Hong Kong, Oxford University Press, 1989).

Allen, L., *The End of the War in Asia* (London, Hart-Davis, McGibbon, 1974).

Annual Report of the Activities of the Independent Commission Against Corruption (Hong Kong, Government Printer, 1975).

Anon., *Hongkong Volunteer Defence Corps in the Battle for Hong Kong, December 1941* (Hong Kong, Printrite, 1953).

Arlington, L. C., *Through the Dragon's Eyes* (London, Constable, 1931).

Atkinson, R. L. P., and Williams, A. K., *Hong Kong Tramways* (London, Light Rail Transport League, 1970).

Bannister, T. R., *A History of the External Trade of China 1834–81* (London, 1932).

Bard, S., *In Search of the Past: A Guide to the Antiquities of Hong Kong* (Hong Kong, Urban Council, 1988).

Barr, P., *Foreign Devils* (London, Penguin, 1970).

Belcher, Capt. E., *Voyage Around the World* (London, Henry Coburn, 1843).

Bird, I. L., *The Golden Chersonese and the Way Thither* (Kuala Lumpur, Oxford University Press reprint, 1967).

Braga, J. M. (ed.), *Hong Kong Business Symposium* (Hong Kong, *South China Morning Post*, 1957).

Brazier, M., and David, S., *Viva Macau* (Hong Kong, Macmillan, 1980).

Briggs, T., and Crisswell, C., *Old Macau* (Hong Kong, *South China Morning Post*, 1984).

Cameron, N., *Hong Kong: The Cultured Pearl* (Hong Kong, Oxford University Press, 1978).

—— *Power: The Story of China Light* (Hong Kong, Oxford University Press, 1982).

—— *The Milky Way: The History of Dairy Farm* (Hong Kong, The Dairy Farm Company Ltd., 1986).

Chang, H. P., *Commissioner Lin and the Opium War* (Harvard, Harvard University Press, 1964).

Cheng, J. Y. S. (ed.), *Hong Kong in the 1980s* (Hong Kong, Summerson Eastern Publishers Ltd., 1982).

Chinese Directory, The, 1872 (Hong Kong, *The China Mail*).

Chiu, T. N., *The Port of Hong Kong; A Survey of its Development* (Hong Kong, Hong Kong University Press, 1973).

Coates, A., *A Mountain of Light: The Story of The Hongkong Electric Company* (Hong Kong, Heinemann, 1977).

Collins, Sir C., *Public Administration in Hong Kong* (London, Royal Institute of International Affairs, 1952).

Collis, M., *Foreign Mud* (London, Faber, 1946).

Colonial Office Records, CO 129 (1945–6) 5432/45. Held in the Public Record Office, London.

Cooper, J., *Colony in Conflict: The Hong Kong Disturbances, May 1967–January 1968* (Hong Kong, Swindon Book Co., 1970).

Cree, E., *The Voyages of Edward H. Cree, R.N. as Related in his Private Journals 1837–56*, ed. Michael Levien (Exeter, Webb and Bower, 1981).

Crisswell, C., *The Taipans: Hong Kong's Merchant Princes* (Hong Kong, Oxford University Press, 1981).

Curzon, Hon. G. N., *Problems of the Far East: Japan, Corea, China* (London, Longmans Green & Co., 1894).

Davis, J. F., *The Chinese: A General Description of China and its Inhabitants* (London, 1836).

Davis, S. G., *Hong Kong in its Geographical Setting* (London, Collins, 1949).

Dyson, A., *From Time Ball to Atomic Clock* (Hong Kong, Government Printer, 1983).

Eitel, E. J., *Europe in China* (Shanghai, Kelly & Walsh, 1895. Revised edition reprinted Hong Kong, Oxford University Press, 1983).

Endacott, G. B., *A Biographical Sketch-book of Early Hong Kong* (Singapore, Eastern Universities Press, 1962).

—— *A History of Hong Kong* (Hong Kong, Oxford University Press, 2nd edition, 1973).

—— *Hong Kong Eclipse*, ed. Alan Birch (Hong Kong, Oxford University Press, 1978).

—— *Government and People in Hong Kong 1841–1962: A Constitutional History* (Hong Kong, Hong Kong University Press, 1964).

Fairbank, J. K., *Trade and Diplomacy on the China Coast* (Harvard, Harvard University Press, 1964).

Freedman, M., *Lineage Organization in Southeastern China* (London, The Athlone Press, 1965).

Gillingham, P., *At the Peak: Hong Kong between the Wars* (Hong Kong, Macmillan, 1983).

Gleason, G., *Hong Kong* (London, Robert Hale, 1963).

Gower, Lord R., *My Reminiscences*, 2 vols. (London, Kegan, Paul, Trench and Trubner, 1883).

Guillen-Nuñez, C., *Macau* (Hong Kong, Oxford University Press, 1984).

Gulick, E., *Peter Parker and the Opening of China* (Harvard, Harvard University Press, 1973).

Harris, P., *Hong Kong: A Study in Bureaucratic Politics* (Hong Kong, Heinemann Asia, 1978).

Hayes, J., *The Hong Kong Region 1850–1911* (Connecticut, Archon Books, 1977).

Hong Kong Government, *Annual Reports* (Hong Kong, Government Printer).

Hong Kong Guide 1893, The (Hong Kong, Oxford University Press, reprint, 1982).

Hunter, W. C., *The 'Fan-Kwae' at Canton Before Treaty Days, 1825–1844* (London, Kegan, Paul, Trench and Trubner, 1882).

Hutcheon, R., *SCMP: The First Eighty Years* (Hong Kong, The South China Morning Post, 1983).

Johnston, A. R., 'Note on the Island of Hong Kong', *Journal of the Royal Geographical Society*, Vol. XIV, 1845, p. 12.

Keswick, M. (ed.), *The Thistle and the Jade* (London, Octopus Books, 1982).

King, D., *St John's Cathedral* (Hong Kong, St John's Cathedral, 1987).

Leeming, F., *Street Studies in Hong Kong: Localities in a Chinese City* (Hong Kong, Oxford University Press, 1977).

Lethbridge, D. (ed.), *The Business Environment of Hong Kong* (Hong Kong, Oxford University Press, 2nd edition, 1984).

Lethbridge, H. J., *Hong Kong: Stability and Change: A Collection of Essays* (Hong Kong, Oxford University Press, 1979).

—— *Hard Graft in Hong Kong: Scandal, Corruption, the ICAC* (Hong Kong, Oxford University Press, 1985).

Lindsay, O., *The Lasting Honour: The Fall of Hong Kong 1941* (London, Hamish Hamilton and Sphere, 1978).

Mattock, K., *The Story of Government House* (Hong Kong, Government Printer, 1978).

McGurn, W. (ed.), *Basic Law, Basic Questions: The Debate Continues* (Hong Kong, Review Publishing Co., 1988).

McLean, R., *The Helena May* (Hong Kong, Council of The Helena May, 1986).

MacMurray, John V. A. (comp. and ed.), *Treaties and Agreements With and Concerning China, 1894–1919*, vol. i, *Manchu Period (1894–1911)* (New York, Oxford University Press, 1921).

Mills, L. A., *British Rule in Eastern Asia* (London, Oxford University Press, 1942).

Miners, N., *The Government and Politics of Hong Kong* (Hong Kong, Oxford University Press, 4th edition, 1986).

—— *Hong Kong Under Imperial Rule 1912–1941* (Hong Kong, Oxford University Press, 1987).

Montalto de Jesus, C. A., *Historic Macao* (Macau, Silesian Printing Press, 2nd edition, 1926, reprinted Hong Kong, Oxford University Press, 1984).

Morales, A. C., *East Meets West: The Modern History of East Asia* (Hong Kong, Macmillan, 1983).

Morris, J., *Hong Kong – Xianggang* (London, Viking, 1988).

Morse, H. B., *The International Relations of the Chinese Empire*, 3 vols. (Hong Kong, Kelly & Walsh, 1918).

Ng, P. Y. L., *New Peace County: A Chinese Gazetteer of the Hong Kong Region* (Hong Kong, Hong Kong University Press, 1983).

Norman, Sir H., *The Peoples and Politics of the Far East* (New York, Scribners, 1903).

Norton-Kyshe, J. W., *The History of the Laws and Courts of Hong Kong*, 2 vols. (London, Fisher Unwin, 1898).

Ochterlony, J., *The Chinese War: An Account of the Operations* (London, Saunders and Otley, 1844).

Pope-Hennessy, J., *Verandah: Episodes in The Crown Colonies, 1867–1889* (London, Allen & Unwin, 1964).

—— *Half-Crown Colony: A Hong Kong Notebook* (London, Cape, 1969).

Royal Asiatic Society, Hong Kong Branch, *Journal*.

Sayer, G. R., *Hong Kong: Birth, Adolescence and Coming of Age* (Hong Kong, Hong Kong University Press, 1937).

—— *Hong Kong: 1862–1919 Years of Discretion* (Hong Kong, Hong Kong University Press, 1975).

Scarth, J., *Twelve Years in China* (Edinburgh, Annan & Sons, 1860).

Smith, A., *To China and Back* (privately printed, 1859, reprinted Hong Kong, Hong Kong University Press, 1974).

Smith, C. A. M., *The British in China and Far Eastern Trade* (London, Constable, 1920).

Smith, C. T., *Chinese Christians: Élites, Middlemen, and the Church in Hong Kong* (Hong Kong, Oxford University Press, 1985).

Thorbecke, E., *Hong Kong* (Shanghai, Kelly & Walsh, no date, but 1930s).

Tuchman, B. W., *Stilwell and the American Experience in China 1911–45* (New York, Macmillan, 1971).

Turner, J. E., *Kwang Tung or Five Years in South China* (Hong Kong, Oxford University Press, reprint, 1982).

Walden, J., *Excellency, Your Gap is Showing: Six Critiques of British Colonial Government in Hong Kong* (Hong Kong, Corporate Communications Ltd., 1988).

Waley, A., *The Opium War Through Chinese Eyes* (London, Allen & Unwin, 1958).
Warner, J., *Hong Kong a Hundred Years Ago* (Hong Kong, Government Printer, 1970).
Wesley-Smith, P., *Unequal Treaty, 1898–1997* (Hong Kong, Oxford University Press, 1980).
Wood, H. J., 'Prologue to War: The Anglo-Chinese Conflict 1800–1834' (Ph.D. Thesis, University of Wisconsin, 1938).
Wong, J. Y., *Anglo-Chinese Relations 1839–1860* (Oxford, Oxford University Press, 1983).
Wong, L. S. K. (ed.), *Housing in Hong Kong; A Multi-disciplinary Study* (Hong Kong, Heinemann Educational Books, 1978).
Young, L. K., *British Policy in China 1859–1902* (Hong Kong, Oxford University Press, 1970).

GLOSSARY

Amah	A female Chinese servant
Bazaar	Area where local people live and trade
Cangue	Portuguese *canga*, a yoke (Chinese *chia*). A square wooden frame fastened on the neck as punishment for minor offences. Prevented lying down or feeding
Cash	From Tamil *kasu*. Small copper coin with central hole
Catty	Malay *kati*. A weight of 1⅓ pounds
Coolie	Hindi *kuli*, one of an aboriginal tribe of Gujarat. A workman
Co-hong	The group of Chinese merchants at Guangzhou with the theoretical monopoly of trade with foreigners
Comprador	Portuguese *comprar*, to buy. A Chinese agent used by Western businesses to buy, sell, and negotiate with Chinese
Cumshaw	Chinese *gan xie*, 'grateful thanks'. A gift of money for services rendered
Factory	A warehouse and place of business
Godown	Malay *gadang*, a warehouse or storehouse
Hong	Chinese *hong*, a row or series. A commercial undertaking, a business
Havildar	Arabic *hawalah*, 'charge' plus the Persian *dar*, 'holding'. Via the Indian army, a sergeant
Hoppo	Chinese *hubu*, meaning Ministry of Revenue. The head of the Maritime Customs in early trading days
Junk	Javanese *jong*. Chinese riverine and coastal sailing vessels, of various types and sizes
Kowtow	The three kneelings and nine knockings of the head on the ground in respect
Laisee	Chinese *li shi*, in Cantonese pronunciation, money offered as a token of goodwill, generally at Lunar New Year
Lorcha	Portuguese. A ship of European design with Chinese rigging
Mandarin	Portuguese *mandar*, to command. A Chinese official. Also the northern pronunciation of the Chinese language
Matshed	Structure of rattan matting on a skeleton of bamboo
Nullah	Hindi *nala*, a brook or ravine. An artificial watercourse
Praya	Portuguese *praia*, a seashore road, an embankment
Ricksha	Abbreviation of Japanese *jinricksha*; *jin*, 'man', rick from *riki*, 'power', *sha*, 'vehicle'. A hooded passenger vehicle pulled by a man
Sampan	Chinese *sam*, 'three', *ban*, 'plank'. A small boat, usually sculled
Shroff	Arabic *saraf*. A clerk receiving or dispensing money
Tael	Probably from Hindi *tola*, a weight, via Portuguese. An ounce (*liang*) of silver. But the weight varied from place to place
Taipan	Chinese *tai*, 'big', *ban*, 'manager' or 'boss'. The head of a business
Typhoon	From the Chinese *tai fung* meaning big wind
Yamen	Official and private residence of a Chinese magistrate in office

ACKNOWLEDGEMENTS

The traditional paragraph or two of author's acknowledgements are the only place where due, and in my case, heartfelt thanks can be offered publicly to those who, in one way and another, bear the responsibility of helping the author achieve the volume in which their names appear. Inherent in those paragraphs there is almost always an inescapable hint of the invidious, for it is never possible to mention every helping hand, and to choose from among them seems almost churlish. I know very well that those who are not mentioned below — a numerous throng — will individually be aware that I am grateful for their help, but that slender reward is regrettably all that I can publicly offer.

It is especially pleasing to acknowledge the large contribution of Martyn Gregory and his wife (formerly Partricia Harland) whose generous loan of so many transparencies and prints of Hong Kong as it has been depicted by a variety of artists both professional and amateur over the decades, and which have passed through their hands at their London gallery, has greatly enriched the illustration of this volume. Their generosity is deeply appreciated. For similar reasons I would like to thank Alice Piccus of Christies Swire (Hong Kong) Limited, Frank Castle of the Asian Collector Ltd., Hong Kong, Margaret Lee, Assistant Archivist, The Hongkong and Shanghai Banking Corporation Ltd. (and the Bank itself), and C.L.A. Haviland, Group Archivist of John Swire & Sons Ltd., London, for their efforts in locating transparencies and prints which have added more visual information to the book. My old friend Freda Wadsworth helped in obtaining reproductions of paintings in the British Government Collection in London, and Patrick Conner assisted uncomplainingly with bibliographical chores. Lam Ka-ping helped with Chinese language.

Last, and very important, I want to thank my editors at Oxford University Press, who for reasons of publishers' protocol cannot be named, for patient, prolonged, intelligent application to the task of editing the manuscript. The results of editorial labours are generally only appreciable by other professionals but they are an integral part of whatever merit the book has.

Naturally, errors and shortcomings are attributable solely to the author himself.

Photographs and illustrations were supplied by, or reproduced by kind permission of the following: The Asian Collector Ltd., Hong Kong 9, 101, 105, 155, 175; Frank Fischbeck 91, 114, 118, 214, 233; Government Information Services, Hong Kong 14, 68, 76, 109, 119, 120, 130, 145, 183, 201, 220, 234, 268, 270, 282, 283, 286, 287, 291, 297, 299 (foot), 300, 301, 302, 315; Martyn Gregory 45, 56, 57, 61, 100, 180; Penelope Harland 246; the Hongkong and Shanghai Banking Corporation Ltd. 99, 102, 137, 210, 224, 232, 238, 239 (top), 239 (foot), 240, 241, 263 (top); *Illustrated London News* 29, 79, 81; Merchant Company Education Board, Edinburgh, Scotland 199; National Portrait Gallery, London 19, 189, 203; Elyse Parkin, *Hong Kong Heritage* (Hong Kong, Oxford University Press, 1979) 215; Public Record Office, London 236; Public Records Office, Hong Kong 133, 185, 217, 231, 299 (top); *Punch* 191; Society for the Propagation of the Gospel, *The Life of Christ by Chinese Artists* (London, 1940) 115; *South China Morning Post* 255, 260, 263 (foot), 264, 267, 269, 311, 323; John Swire & Sons Ltd. 62, 94, 206, 208; United Kingdom Government Art Collection, London 28; Urban Council Hong Kong, Museum of Art 33 (top), 33 (foot), 58, 171, 172; Urban Council Hong Kong, Museum of History 150, 173, 193, 195, 196, 200, 211; R.T. Walker Esq. 230.

Maps: that on p. 6 is reproduced by kind permission of Kelly and Walsh, Hong Kong; that on p. 13 is reprinted by permission of the publishers from Hsin-pao Chang, *Commissioner Lin and the Opium War* (Cambridge, Mass., Harvard University Press, 1964); the lower plan on p. 154 is reproduced by kind permission of Hong Kong University Press; the map on p. 258 is reproduced by permission of Oxford University Press. The endpaper maps are reproduced with the permission of the Director of Buildings and Lands, © Hong Kong Government.

INDEX

Numbers in italics refer to plates.

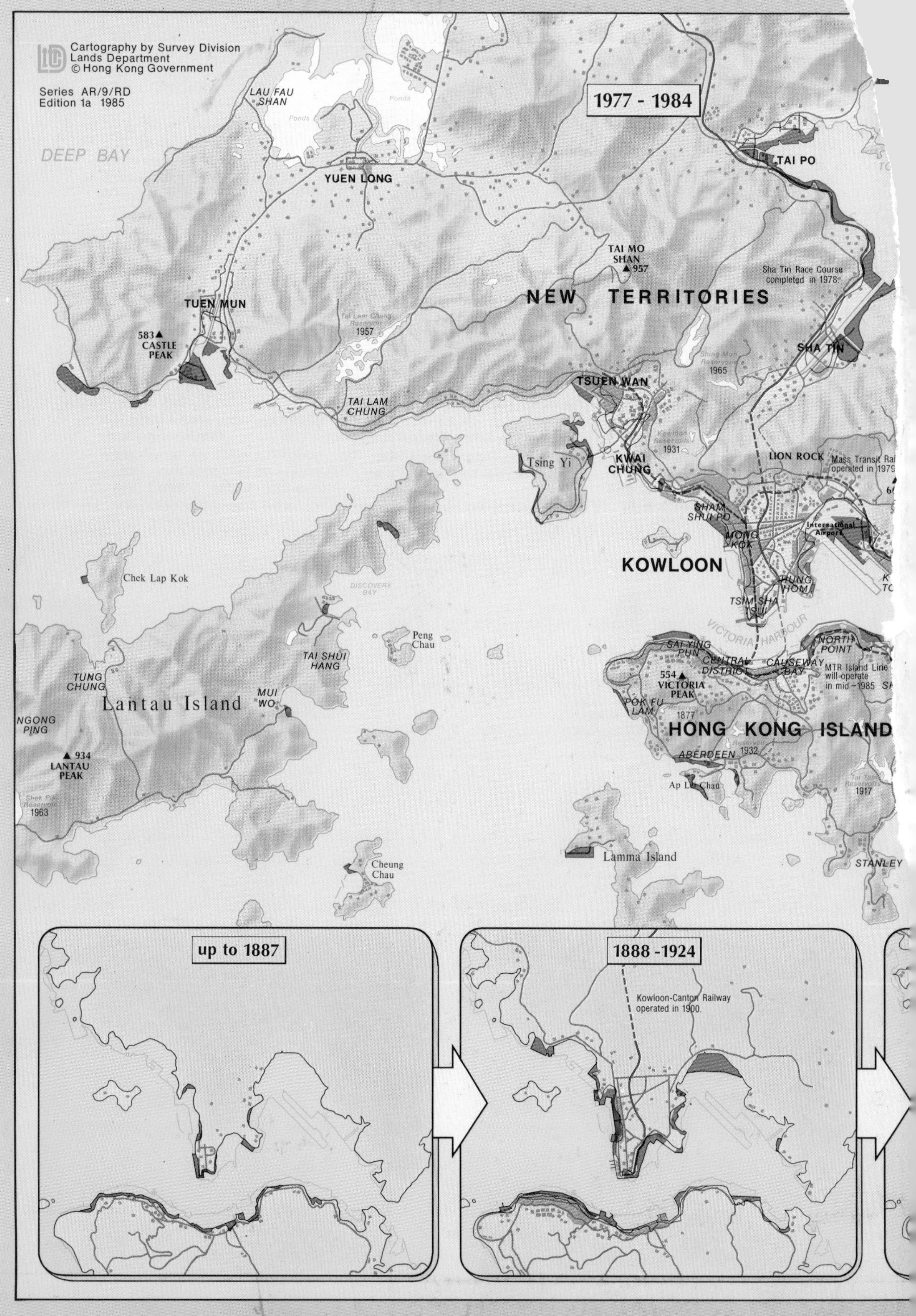

Cartography by Survey Division
Lands Department
© Hong Kong Government
Series AR/9/RD
Edition 1a 1985
1977 - 1984
DEEP BAY
LAU FAU SHAN
YUEN LONG
TAI PO
TAI MO SHAN
957
Sha Tin Race Course completed in 1978.
NEW TERRITORIES
TUEN MUN
583
CASTLE PEAK
Tai Lam Chung Reservoir
1957
SHA TIN
Shing Mun Reservoirs
1965
TSUEN WAN
TAI LAM CHUNG
Kowloon Reservoirs
1931
Tsing Yi
KWAI CHUNG
LION ROCK
SHAM SHUI PO
MONG KOK
International Airport
Chek Lap Kok
KOWLOON
DISCOVERY BAY
HUNG HOM
TSIM SHA TSUI
VICTORIA HARBOUR
Peng Chau
NORTH POINT
TAI SHUI HANG
SAI YING PUN
CENTRAL DISTRICT
CAUSEWAY BAY
MTR Island Line will operate in mid-1985
TUNG CHUNG
554
VICTORIA PEAK
Lantau Island
MUI WO
POK FU LAM
1877
NGONG PING
HONG KONG ISLAND
934
LANTAU PEAK
ABERDEEN
1932
Ap Lei Chau
Shek Pik Reservoir
1963
1917
Cheung Chau
Lamma Island
STANLEY
up to 1887
1888 -1924
Kowloon-Canton Railway operated in 1900.